THE VAMPIRE

The Vampire

Origins of a European Myth

Thomas M. Bohn

Translated from the German by Francis Ipgrave

berghahn
NEW YORK • OXFORD
www.berghahnbooks.com

First published in 2019 by
Berghahn Books
www.berghahnbooks.com

English-language edition
© 2019, 2022 Berghahn Books
First paperback edition published in 2022

German-language edition
© 2016 Böhlau Verlag GmbH & Cie, Köln

Originally published in German as
Der Vampir. Ein europäischer Mythos

All rights reserved. Except for the quotation of short passages for the purposes of criticism and review, no part of this book may be reproduced in any form or by any means, electronic or mechanical, including photocopying, recording, or any information storage and retrieval system now known or to be invented, without written permission of the publisher.

Library of Congress Cataloging-in-Publication Data

Names: Bohn, Thomas M., author. | Ipgrave, Francis translator.
Title: The Vampire: Origins of a European Myth / Thomas M. Bohn; translated from the German by Francis Ipgrave.
Other titles: Der Vampir. English.
Description: English-language edition. | New York: Berghahn Books, 2019. | «Originally published in German as Der Vampir. Ein europäischer Mythos»— T.p. verso. | Includes bibliographical references and index. |
Identifiers: LCCN 2019019138 (print) | LCCN 2019020766 (ebook) | ISBN 9781789202922 (hardback: alk. paper) | ISBN 9781789202939 (ebook)
Subjects: LCSH: Vampires—Europe. | Folklore—Europe.
Classification: LCC GR830.V3 (ebook) | LCC GR830.V3 B6413 2019 (print) | DDC 398.210094—dc23
LC record available at https://lccn.loc.gov/2019019138

British Library Cataloguing in Publication Data

A catalogue record for this book is available from the British Library

ISBN 978-1-78920-292-2 hardback
ISBN 978-1-80073-433-3 paperback
ISBN 978-1-78920-293-9 ebook

If we were to be completely open-hearted in stating our opinion, we would advise against all measures which have the whiff of superstition. It is best that one works towards a genuine reconciliation with the dying person, and forgets all previous adversities since, in this manner, they will fall to sleep with a reconciled heart, and will not lust after anything further in this world. Their fantasies remain dormant and, in the absence of a cause, they can never begin to work upon a living person.

—Michael Ranft, 1732

Contents

List of Illustrations — viii

Prologue. From Original Sin to Eternal Life — x

Introduction. The Vampire as an Imperial Category — 1

Chapter 1
Vampirism in the West — 13

Chapter 2
Vampirism in the East — 55

Chapter 3
Vampirism in the Headlines — 78

Chapter 4
Vampirism in Popular Belief — 125

Chapter 5
Vampirism in the Modern Period — 218

Conclusion. The Vampire as Local Scapegoat — 230

Bibliography — 239

Indexes — 271

Illustrations

Maps

0.1 The Military Frontier and sites of vampirism in Central, Eastern and Southeastern Europe   xvi

0.2 Belief in nachzehrers and vampire conceptions in East Central Europe   xvi

Figures

1.1 Skeletons in a graveyard chase off a knight's assailants   16

1.2 St Catherine of Siena Drinking from the Side Wound of Christ   26

2.1 'The dead struck the people of Polotsk'   57

3.1 Putrid liquid oozing from a swollen corpse   79

3.2 'Visum et Repertum', the Flückinger report   85

3.3 Extract from the Flückinger report with the lettering 'Arnond Paole'   87

3.4 'Arnond Paole' as a pandur?   88

3.5 and 3.6 Vampire treatises from the Enlightenment era   96

3.7 and 3.8 Michael Ranft's *Tractat von dem Kauen und Schmatzen der Todten in Gräbern* (*Treatise on the Chewing and Chomping of the Dead in Graves*) and the motto 'Mortuus non mordet' ('The Dead Do Not Bite')   98

3.9 Carl Ferdinand von Schertz' *Magia posthuma* ('*Post-mortal Sorcery*')   100

3.10 Augustin Calmet's *Traité sur les apparitions des esprits et sur les vampires, ou les revenans de Hongrie, de Moravie, & c.* (*Learned Treatment of Material, on the Appearance of Spirits, and of Vampires in Hungary, Moravia*)   102

3.11 Georg Tallar's *Visum repertum anatomico-chirurgicum* (*Anatomical-Chirurgical Report*)   105

3.12 *Vampyrism by Herrn Baron Gerhard van Swieten*   107

3.13 'Michael Caspareck, who continues to wander following his death in Hungary'   112

4.1 The execution of a vampire in a booklet for enlighteners and non-enlighteners   139

4.2 Festival of Souls in Bosnia   158

4.3 'Vujić discusses vampires with monks from the Monastery of Klisura'   176

Table

3.1 Published works on vampires between 1732 and 1733   94

Prologue
From Original Sin to Eternal Life

For a broad contemporary public, the vampire has become a star, a media sensation from Hollywood. Bestselling authors such as Bram Stoker, Anne Rice and Stephenie Meyer continue to fire the imaginations of young and old alike, and bloodsuckers have achieved immortality through films like *Dracula*, *Interview with a Vampire* and *Twilight*. It is no wonder that, in the teenage bedrooms of our globalized world, vampires even steal the show from Harry Potter. They have long since been assigned individual personalities and treated with sympathy. They may possess superhuman powers, but they are also burdened by their immortality and have to learn to come to terms with their craving for blood. Whereas the Southeast European vampire, discovered in the 1730s, underwent an Americanization and domestication in the media landscape of the twentieth century, the creole zombies that first became known through the cheap novels and horror films of the 1920s still continue to serve as brainless horror figures. Do bloodsuckers really exist and should we really be afraid of the dead? These are the questions that I seek to tackle, following the wishes of my daughter, who was ten when I started this project.

As a professional historian of Eastern Europe, I am also interested in the actual origins of the belief in vampires. Clearly, not every vampire fan is aware that Transylvania is a real place rather than a fictitious location. The Latin term, meaning the 'Land beyond the Forest', refers to the present-day Romanian region of the same name, which lies in the Carpathian range and has been inhabited since the Middle Ages by, among others, German, or 'Saxon', settlers. The impression, created by Bram Stoker, of Transylvania as the homeland of the vampire is also problematic, since vampires actually appeared relatively rarely in this region. Instead, in reading reports from the eighteenth century, one cannot avoid the impression that vampirism was encountered above all in the overlapping contact and border zones of the multinational states and empires of Europe. A sort of 'vampire belt' clearly stretched along the frontiers of Kievan Rus' and the Tsarist Empire, the Polish Lithuanian Union and the Ottoman Empire, as well as the Habsburg Empire and Prussia, all of which meet in the heart of Europe (see Map 0.1). Therefore, in both a literal and a figurative sense, and in both geographical and metaphysical terms, the vampire constituted a border phenomenon.

With regard to vampirism, I identify myself with those writers who, in their works, have already begun to attempt a reconnection of this phenomenon to its historical location, whether this be Elizabeth Kostova in her novel *The Historian*, Markus Heitz in his fantasy novel *Kinder des Judas* (*Children of Judas*) or Fred Vargas (i.e. Frédérique Audoin-Rouzeau) in her crime novel *Un lieu uncertain* (*An Uncertain Place*). If we wish to trace the origins of the vampire, our attention must in fact be directed towards the Ottoman Empire or the Balkan Peninsula in the premodern period. However, we should also not overlook the Sarmatian lands of East Central Europe. Furthermore, I am also of the opinion that the image of the bloodsucker in the Latin West was formed long before the discovery of the vampire in the Danube-Balkan region. Accordingly, in this book, I will seek to rehabilitate the vampire as a European myth.

Seen in historical terms, modern Europe was founded on the processes of state-creation and Christianisation, which reached a high point around the year 1000 AD. A key precondition for the emergence of the belief in vampires was the gradual replacement of the practice of cremation and the funeral pyre with that of entombment or burial in the earth. From this point onwards, the condition of deceased corpses fired the imaginations of the living. This was true both with regard to the role of blood, on the one hand, as the source of life and, on the other hand, to the dualism of the body and the soul. In the New Testament, we read, in a somewhat disturbing manner, that Jesus Christ gave his own flesh and blood to his disciples in the form of bread and wine, as a sign of the new covenant. From the fourth century, the ecumenical creed of both the Roman Catholic and the Greek-Orthodox Churches has, alongside Christ's crucifixion and ascension to heaven, acclaimed the resurrection of the dead. The immortality of the soul and the physical return of the body are therefore preordained in Church doctrine. Common conceptions of death in Europe held that the divine plan for salvation envisaged that the body would fall to dust and that the soul would enter paradise. By contrast, how and why the dead were to spend their time in heaven or hell until the Last Judgment remained largely unclear.

Following the pattern of biblical reports on the resurrection and ascension of Christ, the third day after death and the subsequent time period of forty days was also considered to be precarious for normal mortals. During this time, by holding rituals marking the taking of leave from the dead, those left behind were entrusted with the responsibility of ensuring the transition of the departed's soul into heaven. However, the only information we have about the activities of the dead or 'living corpses' comes from a second or third-hand perspective; hardly a single witness claims to have seen them with their own eyes. As a result, we are only ever dealing with fantasies. What, then, is this book really about? In essence, it is an investigation of disturbances to the peaceful taking of leave from the dead by the living and of the consequences emerging from these. Both have their underlying causes and manifestations in interpersonal conflicts, which have not been resolved by death, or in the outbreak of mysterious diseases, which gave rise to numerous suppositions about a root cause of the epidemic. Regardless of this, there is no need to fear the dead. Here and there, they merely have to serve as scapegoats. What is truly troubling for the living is only ever the guilty conscience arising from moral transgressions or feelings of impotence in the face of a deadly threat. Such forms of stress find their expression in feelings of fear and in nightmare visions.

Apparitions, the spooky and the supernatural have plagued human minds since the beginnings of time. Whereas, in popular belief, 'ghosts' are generally linked to the concrete appearance of persons returning from the dead, 'spirits' represented transcendental phenomena of a very different shade. In terms of superstitious beliefs, their spectrum ranges from natural spirits to spirits of the dead and, in the context of the Bible, from angels to demons. Since popular piety initially ascribed an actual physical presence to those returning from the dead, the Western Church in the Middle Ages sought to replace the belief in 'revenants' with the belief in 'poor souls' who, in purgatory, found a third place between heaven and hell. In opposition to this, the era of the Reformation saw, on the one hand, the strengthening of the belief in a diabolic possession of revenant bodies and, on the other hand, the growing accusation that supposed revenants were nothing more than figments of the imaginations of the living brought about by Satan. By contrast, the horrific visions of the modern period once more viewed the 'undead' as reanimated, albeit soulless, bodies. In the final analysis, ghosts are to be seen as dead spirits who, it is claimed, both bring messages from the afterlife and also, motivated by vengeance, seek to gain retribution for the injustices they experienced during their lifetimes.

Since the Western construct of the figure of the vampire is essentially the product of a literary discourse, this book begins with a discussion of the relevant motifs from Eastern Europe in the Introduction. At the same time, a framework will be constructed from this for the discussions to follow. In the first chapter, taking the conceptions of revenancy in the Latin West, we will then examine the Central European belief in so-called *Nachzehrer* in the sixteenth to eighteenth centuries. This concerns a more harmless and in the meantime largely forgotten variant of the vampire figure in the German-speaking world. Nachzehrers are allegedly active deceased persons who, whilst they remain in their graves and can only be identified through a widely audible chewing on their funeral shrouds, do nevertheless threaten their relatives with serious diseases in a telepathic manner. In this context, in a further step, we also investigate the specific characteristics of the Eastern European belief in vampires. A second chapter will then demonstrate that the so-called *upyr* or *upiór* was already known in the territories of Kievan Rus' and the Polish-Lithuanian Union in c. 1000 AD. Following the conquest of Constantinople by the Ottomans in

1453, the Ecumenical Patriarchate moved towards an unconventional interpretation of the Greek variant of the revenant in order to preserve its authority over the Orthodox population. The so-called *vrykolakas* was now understood to be the nondecomposed corpse of an excommunicated person, whose soul, in a sense, had found exile in its own skin. As the third chapter demonstrates, the figure of the South Slavic *vampire* first became known in the Latin West in 1732 as a result of an investigation into the threat of a plague on the military frontier of the Habsburg Empire to the Ottoman Empire. Both the vrykolakas and the vampire, like their counterparts in Western Europe, were seen as dead persons who were imperishable and who therefore posed a serious threat. Furthermore, in the fourth chapter, I will elaborate further on this, showing that the belief in vampires, in contrast to conceptions of the *nachzehrer*, included the conviction that corpses not only left their graves, but also robbed the living of their life force. Common to all contemporary witnesses is that they all depict bodily apparitions of dead persons whose eternal rest has been disturbed. An overview in a fifth chapter will demonstrate that, alongside the Dracula depictions that dominated the modern media, the traditional belief in vampires still had a place in twentieth-century Eastern Europe. Over the course of time, in thematic terms, the threat of disease has gradually taken a back seat to discussions of sexual behaviour in the oral tradition. The subtext to vampire tales is no longer shaped by collective fears, but rather by moral norms. In this context, finally a conclusion, reflecting on the differing Eastern and Western conceptions of revenancy, comes to an ambivalent result: it was assumed, on the one hand, that the souls of revenants could not find any salvation and, on the other hand, that they inflicted harm upon those they had left behind. It is true that, later, more evidence came to light suggesting that dead persons were not only called upon as intercessors to the other side, but also that their relatives hoped for good deeds from them in this world. However, from the perspective of external observers, whether these were Church or secular authorities, revenancy all too often found its one-sided expression in alleged bloodsucking.

Had it been my intention, in writing this book, to bring a virtual vampire to life, this would have been predestined to failure from the outset since, in the final analysis, we are dealing here with mere fantasies, born out of fear. Instead, I will attempt to unearth something about the beliefs of the peoples of the Danube-Balkan region and Carpatho-Ukraine during the period of Ottoman and Habsburg dominance. This is because it is in the oral traditions and writings from Southeastern Europe and the former Polish-Lithuanian Union that we find the most authentic tales of bloodsucking (although it is always important to distinguish here between the attributions of Western European authors and the beliefs of the Eastern European population themselves). What were these people afraid of and why did their dead not leave them in peace? Why did they need scapegoats and why did they find these in the most defenceless of creatures? In seeking to answer these questions on the basis of the available sources, we emerge, at best, with a history of combatting vampires, and of a constantly repeated canon of exhumations, and the impaling, decapitation and burning of corpses. This only becomes particularly interesting when it allows us, through embedding these occurrences in their historical context, to learn something more about the village communities or urban societies affected. Here, in fact, it was less the alleged bloodsucking that was at the centre of the belief in vampires and much more the phenomenon of the nondecomposed corpse. This has been demonstrated by legends, travel writers and the files of investigative committees. Therefore, it is important to gain a deeper insight into these sources.

Consequently in this book, paraphrasing passages play an important role. Where these relate to reports on concrete cases of revenancy, which fuelled the imaginations of contemporary witnesses, I have used the past tense, in accordance with the historical course of events. As soon as we move on to an abstraction of the vampire motif in ballads and stories, I have adopted the historical present tense, in accordance with the fictional character of the events depicted. In this way, the reader should hopefully be brought a little closer to the proverbial and legendary homeland of the vampire in Eastern Europe. In contrast to other publications on vampirism, I also provide extensive material from the various regions and differing cultural landscapes of Eastern Europe. In order to negotiate a path through the clutter of terms from sometimes exotic languages, Cyrillic words in the text are rendered according to the common English standard for translation, whilst the correct diacritic signs have been preserved for Latin alphabets. Bibliographic references, by contrast, follow the Harvard style of transliteration from the Cyrillic.

Where particular importance has been placed upon the authenticity of a term, this has been rendered in an italicized font (*upir'*). As soon as a term, for which the sources contain various spellings, has become subject to a generalization, the normal (nonitalicized) font has been used (vukodlak). Beyond this, the names of places and persons also play an important role in this book. On the one hand, we must be prepared to depart somewhat from the original spelling in the sources in order to enable the reader to undertake a virtual voyage into the past through the use of atlases and online maps. However, on the other hand, the choice of a particular name also automatically suggests a classification of events within specific national contexts, which were first established by present-day political boundaries. Therefore, in the following, the variant of place names and personal names best fitting the relative historical context will be used, with alternatives or scientifically correct spellings being provided in parenthesis immediately following or at least in the register in any event by way of extension.

Since the Reformation, all vampire reports have been subject to confessional interpretations and, following the age of nationalism, they also clearly reflect ethnic animosities. In light of this, and in relation to the consciousness of peoples from past epochs who have largely not left behind any written witness of their own, we will examine the following questions: why did some human corpses apparently resist natural decomposition? Were these the bodies of the most pious, as had already been suggested in the Old Testament, or were they rather those of excommunicates, as the Greek-Orthodox Church claimed following the dissolution of the Byzantine Empire? How is it possible to balance the veneration of angels and saints on the one hand with the damnation of spirits and demons on the other? Is their ambivalent existence not grounded, simply, in the imagination of a rivalry between God and the Devil in the struggle for Christian souls? And, finally, what role did the alleged bloodsuckers actually play in the premodern societies of Eastern Europe? Did the figure of the vampire simply represent a corruption of Christian martyrology and the Holy Eucharist? The answers I provide to these questions result from a thorough investigation of numerous historical texts that discuss the fates of past generations. In this, my provocative theses may perhaps occasionally be shot through with a touch of exaggerated rhetoric. However, in my academic interpretations, I sincerely hope that I have not provided any deep offence to anyone who has, in a very personal way and in their own social environment, experienced the reality of death.

I would like to thank other authors for their inspiration, many of whom devoted attention in their monographs attention to the ethnologic side of the European vampire, most of all Paul Barber, Tommaso Braccini, Erik Butler, Álvaro García Marín, Klaus Hamberger, David Keyworth, Peter Mario Kreuter, Florian Kührer, Claude Lecouteux, Bruce A. McClelland, Jan L. Perkowski, Erberto Petoia and Thomas Schürmann. Beginning with my time at the Ludwig Maximilian University of Munich, I have had the opportunity to discuss my reflections on vampirism with the participants of several seminars. As a result, my former students Stéphanie Danneberg, Christian Kättlitz, Bernhard Unterholzner, Vlado Vlačić and Jaqueline Winkel already published articles themselves. At the Justus Liebig University – thanks to Kirsten von Hagen – my own research continues in the realm of the Giessen study group on vampirism. I am very grateful to Lidia Gläsmann, Birol Gündogdu, Nazarii Gutsul, Kolja Lichy, Henadz' Sahanovich, Ana Marija Spasojević and Albert Weber for their translation support. The Böhlau publishing house as an arm of the Vandenhoeck & Ruprecht Publishing Company was so kind to support the translation of my book *Der Vampir: Ein europäischer Mythos* (2016). Jaqueline Winkel greatly assisted in the editing of this English edition. In contrast to the German edition we revised and enlarged mainly the endnotes and the bibliography. Afterwards, Jon Lloyd competently proofed the result, and the Berghahn team created a wonderful volume. Last but not least and most of all, I would also like to express my gratitude to Francis Ipgrave, to whom I am deeply indebted for rendering this work accessible to an English-speaking public.

Thomas Bohn
Giessen, All Souls' Day 2019

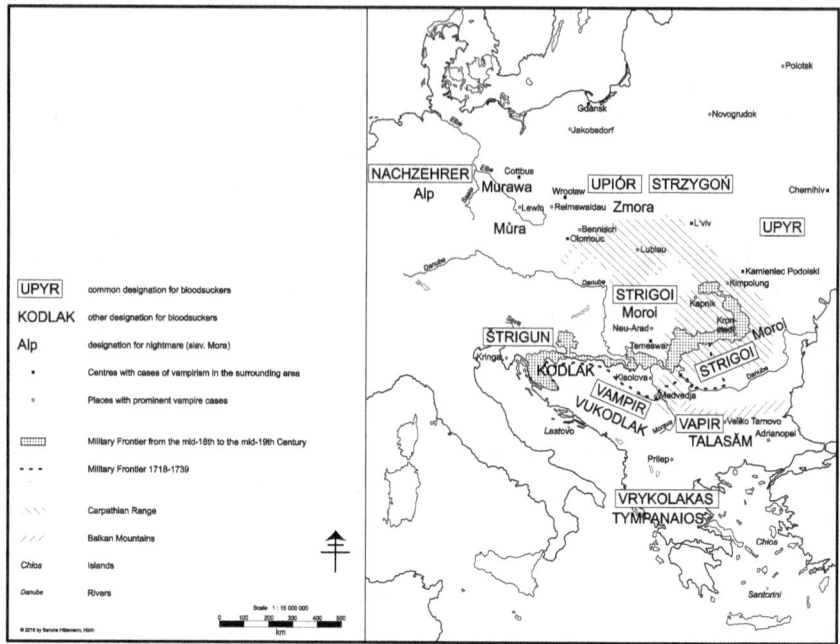

Map 0.1 The Military Frontier and sites of vampirism in Central, Eastern and Southeastern Europe.
© Sandra Karamarinov. Used with permission of Böhlau Verlag GmbH & Cie.

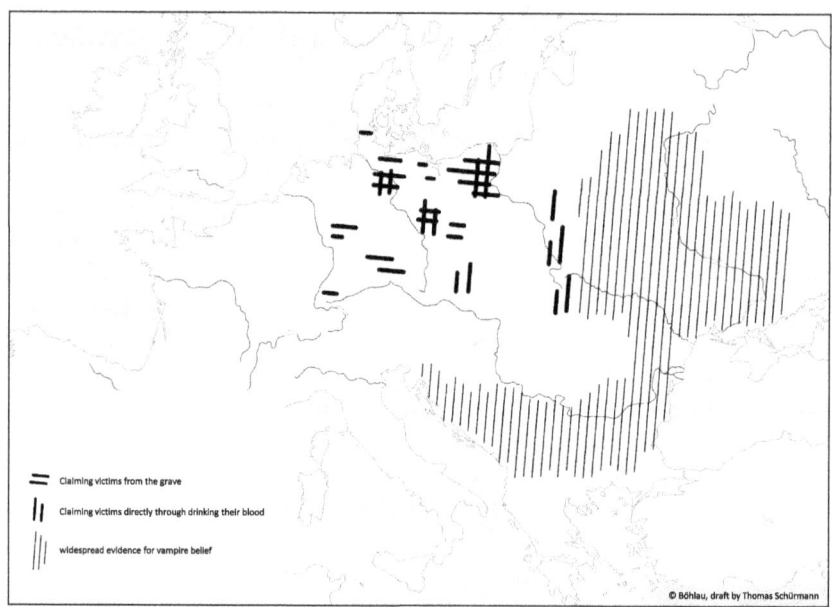

Map 0.2 Belief in nachzehrers and vampire conceptions in East Central Europe.
© Boehlau on the basis of Entwurf von Thomas Schürmann (*Nachzehrerglauben in Mitteleuropa*. Marburg 1990, 123). Used with permission of Böhlau Verlag GmBH & Cie.

Introduction
The Vampire as an Imperial Category

> Here one understands dead human bodies, which walk up out of their graves, suck the blood out of the living and, in so doing, kill them.
> —*Zedlers Universal-Lexicon*, 1745

> This is the name for alleged demons, who draw the blood out of living bodies at night, transferring it to corpses from which it flows visibly from the mouth, nose and ears.
> —*Encyclopédie ou dictionnaire raisonné*, 1765

The definition of vampirism has been shaped, up to the present day, by an intersection of Enlightenment misunderstandings and misinterpretations from the Romantic period. Throughout all of this, negative stereotypes about Eastern Europe have continuously been reproduced. Where does this come from?

On the Balkan Peninsula, the first two decades of the nineteenth century witnessed revolts against Ottoman rule, first by the Serbs and then the Greeks. These developments were followed with interest and sympathy among nationalist and romantic-minded intellectuals elsewhere in Europe. Debates about power political constellations in this period were accompanied by the stereotyping of exotic local characteristics, and this discourse found a symbolic expression in the notion of 'The Eastern Question'. Since, following the failure of the Siege of Vienna in 1683, there could no longer be serious talk of the 'Turkish Threat', the Southeast European periphery came to be seen in Western perceptions as a refuge of backwardness.[1]

In 1827, in keeping with this view, the French author Prosper Mérimée anonymously published an anthology of the fictitious work of the imaginary bard Hyacinth Maglanovich, entitled *La guzla, ou choix de poésies illyriques, recueilles dans la Dalmatie, la Bosnie, la Croatie et l'Herzegowine* (*The Gusle, or a Selection of Illyric Poems Collected in Dalmatia, Bosnia, Croatia and Herzegovina*).

A gusle is a necked-bowl lute, traditionally played in the performance of heroic ballads and that, in Mérimée's interpretation, was not only used to evoke the centuries-long struggle for liberation from the Turks, but also in the performance of ancient rituals seeking to ward off vampires.

Although the French author focused upon the Adriatic seaboard in the northeast of the Balkan Peninsula, making reference to the Illyrians of antiquity, therefore excluding both the Bulgarians and the Serbs as well as the Albanians and the Greeks from his consideration, the German poet Wilhelm Gerhard took over the lion's share of the fabricated material in his 1828 collection *Wila: Serbische Volkslieder und Heldenmärchen* (*Vila: Serbian Folk Songs and Heroic Tales*), which was centred on the Balkan highlands. Rather than the gusle, Gerhard chose to name his work after the *vila*, a female spirit of nature from Slavic folklore.

At the turn of 1832/1833, himself also duped by Mérimée's hoax, the Russian national poet Alexander Pushkin also took on this material (although he did admittedly catch wind of the ruse shortly before the publication of his work in 1835). The geographical attribution in Pushkin's title *Pesni zapadnykh slavian* (*Songs of the Western Slavs*) is somewhat misleading, since the tales are less concerned with the fate of the Poles, who had suffered the partitioning of their territory by the continental Great Powers at the end of the eighteenth century, than with the lot of the Orthodox Christians under the 'yoke' of Ottoman rule.

All in all, whether disseminated deliberately or handed down unconsciously, this Balkan fiction reflected the fact that the examination of vampirism in both Western and Eastern European literature was characterized by misdirected projections. The vampire functioned as an imperial category in the sense of a cultural code that could be applied anywhere. We are dealing here, both in a literal and in a figurative sense, with a border phenomenon, situated on the margins of the multinational empires or in the grey zones of the Western hemisphere. This distorted view of the Balkan periphery in the European cultural capitals of Paris, Leipzig and St Petersburg is particularly evident in the tale of the unexpected guest who visits the family of the Croatian Konstantin Jakubović (or 'Constantin Yakoubovich' for Mérimée, 'Konstantin Jakubowitsch' for Gerhard and 'Marko Yakubovich' for Pushkin) in the Dalmatian highlands.

Out of nowhere, a Serbian soldier, who had been fatally wounded in the struggle against the Turks, arrives at Konstantin Jakubović's house and, immediately upon his arrival, falls dead in his yard. Thanks to his military service, he is buried in a grave in the Catholic cemetery, despite his Orthodox faith. Events then take a sinister turn. Shortly after the burial, Konstantin's son falls gravely ill and begins to wither away. Eventually, a wise hermit discovers a red mark on the boy's throat, which he attributes to the bite of a vampire. Suspicion immediately falls upon the strange foreign soldier. Upon opening his grave – as perhaps should not have been surprising so soon after internment – a seemingly fresh body is revealed, with bloodstained lips. His crimes thus exposed, the alleged vampire faces impalement, but manages to flee from this fate. Nevertheless, the ill boy and all his family members are now able to smear themselves in the soil of the vampire's grave, thus strengthening their bodies' defences. Furthermore, through incense and prayer, the hermit successfully wards off the return of the revenant three times, which he attempts in the form of a giant, a soldier and a dwarf, thus bringing an end to the nightmare.

How, then, did the representatives of Enlightened Europe imagine these South Slavic folk legends? Disregarding the fact that this seemingly authentic story was actually a 'fabrication', the interpreters of this tale did hold views that were symptomatic of the wider reception of vampirism. Therefore, in a footnote answering the question 'What are vampires?', Pushkin, in keeping with his creed of brevity and precision and in a style that is much less excessive than that of his Western counterparts, drew upon two constructed, supposedly South Slavic terms and one Old Russian or Ukrainian term – 'vurdalaki, vudkodlaki, upyri' – and summarized the debates of the Enlightenment: 'Deceased persons who arise from their graves and suck out the blood of the living.'[2] This, in a nutshell, was the European perspective.

While the concept of vampirism connoted a further orientalizing stereotype in the 'mental mapping' of the Enlightenment period, its significance was transformed in the era of Romanticism and Nationalism into a Slavophobe cliché. Furthermore, it should also be mentioned that Prosper Mérimée can also lay claim to the copyright for the vampire's fangs. Through his portrayal, he provided for the cognitive anchoring of the lurid presence and bearing of the vampire, long before Christopher Lee conquered the cinema with his portrayals of the shadowy Count Dracula, winning over viewers with the visualization of the 'kiss of the vampire' on the silver screen. It is striking, after all, that the French Mérimée and the German Gerhard – though not the Russian Pushkin – both arrived at the same explanation for the rising up of the soldier's corpse from the grave, namely the internment of a 'Greek', that is, a follower of the Orthodox Faith, in sacred and consecrated 'Latin' soil. It is also telling that in Pushkin's case, with regard to the Tsarist Empire in the context of the aftermath of Napoleon's Russian campaign of 1812 and the failed Decembrist Uprising, the Russian officers' revolt of 1825, in refusing to acknowledge any shortcoming in the progress of his country, he has fully taken on Catherine II's famous dictum: 'Russia is a European power!' According to Pushkin, therefore, Europe was defined both by military strength and by political enlightenment, but not by confessional distinctiveness. Nevertheless, in Mérimée's and Gerhard's interpretations, it is the Catholic soil that spews out the Orthodox corpse following its burial. The phenomenon of vampirism was thus placed within the broader context of cultural contradiction between East and West. In all this, it is worth remembering that we are referring to works of literature emerging from the pens of supposedly progressive and forward-looking minds, which clearly points towards a 'clash of civilizations'.

From Village Monster to Vampire Count

The definition of the vampire presented by Mérimée and his associates may have had little or nothing to do with the Danube-Balkan region, but, from the final third of the eighteenth century onwards, there has been a return of this concept to its original cultural-historical environment. The 'vampire' began his triumphal march into the learned debates of Western Europe in 1732 as the result of a 'media event' on the Habsburg Military Frontier to the Ottoman Empire and then, initially through Heinrich August Ossenfelder's *Mein liebes Mägdchen glaubet* (*My Dear Young Maiden Clingeth*) of 1748 and John William Polidori's *The Vampyre: A Tale* of 1819, the prototype of the Gothic novel, found his way into the fashionable Western salons as a poetic figure. In his adoption by the West European public, the vampire was robbed of his identity, but nevertheless continued to serve as a contrasting foil. From the perspective of the rulers, seen from this angle, internal political unrest and diffuse social relationships at the imperial peripheries were threatening. As a result, vampirism, as the expression of superstition and popular folk traditions, was an unwelcome phenomenon for the elites of the European Great Powers, that is, Britain, France, Prussia, and the Habsburg and Tsarist Empires.

In this context, a French-language compilation, drawn up in 1840 by the Russian diplomat and author Aleksey Tolstoy, a cousin of Leo Tolstoy, proves to be instructive. In keeping with Prosper Mérimée's example, Tolstoy, in his novel *La famille vourdalak* (*The Family of the Vourdalak*, first published in Russian in 1884 and in the French original in 1950) also drew upon the work of an anonymous chronicler who had allegedly written down the report delivered in a reputable salon by the Marquis d'Urfé, shortly after the Congress of Vienna. In his terminology, Tolstoy remained true to Pushkin's formulation. Here he refers to a fictive incident, which is supposed to have taken place in the following manner in 1759.

On a journey to Moldova undertaken for diplomatic purposes, d'Urfé makes a stop in a Serbian village. He finds shelter in a house whose owner, a man with the artificial name of Gorća (derived from *gorćina* – bitterness), has been away for ten days, taking part in a punitive action against Turkish bandits who have been wreaking havoc in the border region through their criminal deeds. The mood in the village is tense since, before departing for this action, Gorća had predicted to his family that he would only come back alive if he returned within ten days. After this time had elapsed, they should reckon only with his returning in the form of a 'vurdalak' – a word invented by Alexander Pushkin.

According to the narrator, a vurdalak is a type of vampire found among the Slavs who, in contrast to the European species, primarily kills his own kinsfolk and thereby also animates their imperishable bodies to vampirism. This is already an implicit reference to the 'threat from the East' that was to be cultivated, at the latest, by Bram Stoker. In this way, entire communities in southern Hungary and northern Bosnia were condemned to a neverending existence as vurdalaks. As such, Gorća's machinations following his metamorphosis into a vampire have far-reaching implications. 'Vampirism is contagious', a hermit in a nearby monastery pronounces when d'Urfé returns to the scene of the crimes following a sojourn in Moldova. Unexpectedly, Gorća's daughter Zdenka, in whom he believes himself to have fallen deeply in love, attempts to lead him into ruin. Since d'Urfé already appears as the storyteller in the Viennese salon at the start of tale, it is clear from the outset that he manages to escape this ordeal with nothing worse than psychological injuries. He manages to flee from the fate hanging over him by pulling off a risky escape, leaving behind him a seething Balkans, less a powderkeg than a witch's cauldron.

It remains unclear what became of Gorća's family and there is no answer to the question of whether the vampire epidemic spreads beyond the Balkans. In his story, Aleksey Tolstoy ostensibly leaves this problem with the ladies of the Vienna salon, without addressing the broader European public. It is significant that this text was only published posthumously.

As an author, Tolstoy is known only for his tale *Upyr* (*The Vampire*), published under a pseudonym in 1848, which refers back to a concept from East Slavic folklore, but in reality only tackles the quarrels of Russian aristocratic families, without addressing these issues to any extent in their anthropological dimension.

What motives drove Aleksey Tolstoy's literary activities? On the one hand, he was inspired by the subject of the vampire to temporarily quit the diplomatic service in order to pursue his literary ambitions in around 1840. On the other hand, this was precisely the time at which the vigorous debates in Moscow between Westernizers and Slavophiles about the relationship between 'Russia and Europe' were at their peak. Like his fellow writer Ivan Turgenev, who was living abroad from 1855 and who presented a vision of a love-giving and bloodsucking beauty in his 1864 work *Prizraki: Fantasiia* (*Ghosts: A Fantasy*), Tolstoy clearly hoped to underscore the rightful place of Russian literature in European culture. Seeking to surmount the East-West opposition, he integrated the 'Vampire' of Western literature into Russian culture in a curious manner, whilst, at the same time, and in keeping with Pushkin's coinage, stylizing the 'vurdalaks' of Southeast European folklore as a symbol of Otherness. In tethering Orthodox Russia to the Latin West in this manner, he consigned the Ottoman Balkans to the Orient.

Surprisingly, both the Croat Konstantin Jakubović, who resisted vampirism, and the Serb Gorća, who succumbed to it, remained exceptional phenomena in the prose of the nineteenth century. In European literature, following Gottfried August Bürger's poem 'Lenore' (1773) and Johann Wolfgang Goethe's 'Die Braut von Korinth' ('The Bride of Corinth') (1797), the motif of the vampire was strongly bound up with that of the undead bride or the undead bridegroom and, above all, with the interrelationship between Eros and Thanatos, Love and Death. Therefore, the works of authors from the Slavic world, less well known in the West, should not be completely disregarded. In his national patriotic drama of 1823, *Dziady* (*Forefather's Eve*), the Polish national poet Adam Mickiewicz reflected on the spirits of the dead in the popular legends of his Belarusian-Lithuanian homeland (see the section entitled 'Investigations in Eastern Europe' in Chapter 5). Furthermore, in his collections of stories *Vechera na khutore bliz Dikan'ki* (*Evenings on a Farm Near Dikanka*) from 1831/1832 and *Mirgorod* (the euphemistic place name could be rendered in English either as *City of Peace* or *World-City*), the Russian-Ukrainian author Nikolai Gogol drew upon the Ukrainian legends of his childhood, with their devils, witches and nymphs. Particularly worth reading in terms of vampirism is Gogol's story 'Vii', with its flavour of fantasy and nocturnal magic, about the experiences of a student with a demonic witch – a succubus or undead body who conjures up evil spirits. Evidently, the subject of the vampire was not only common in the heart of Southeastern Europe, but also on the margins of East Central Europe.

Whereas the vampire initially entered the poetry of the eighteenth century as an expression of animalistic and blasphemous tendencies, the Gothic novel of the nineteenth century saw the immortal bloodsucker's metamorphosis from a village monster into a decadent dandy. One rare exception to the aristocratic and male-dominated tradition was the figure of Carmilla, a lesbian vampire from Sheridan Le Fanu's 1872 novella of the same name. In this context, it is striking that the 'Father of the Modern Vampire', Bram Stoker, should choose to return the action of his novel *Dracula*, first published in 1897, to the vampire's 'authentic' location, even if Transylvania, Wallachia and the Balkans are depicted as a somewhat hazy geographical region. Whilst the echoes of the historical Dracula in the vampire count are more or less marginal, it is clear that, where the novel speaks of him as an anti-Turkish warrior or a crusader, this is a reference to Vlad the Impaler, the Prince of Wallachia at the time of the Ottoman conquest of Constantinople.

If one bears in mind the 'Eastern Question' and the Congress of Berlin of 1878 as the backdrop to the *Dracula* novel, as well as considering the Russian–British rivalry over the territorial restructuring of the Balkans and control over the shipping routes between the Mediterranean and the Black Sea, it is evident that the decline of the Ottoman Empire and the 'Straits Question' find resonance in Stoker's work. Indeed, following the multiperspectival interpretations of New Historicism, literary scholars began to see the Dracula figure as a 'symbol of Europe'[3] and to consider the leitmotif of 'reverse colonization' as central to understanding the novel.⁴ Thanks to this approach, the key theme is that of the threat posed to the civilized world by primitive forces from the peripheral spheres of influence. The irreconcilability of cultural conscience and geopolitical adventurism leads to an internal conflict in the definition of guiding principles. To some extent, one of the subtexts underlying the *Dracula* novel is that of the interdependency between sin and atonement. The criminal ignorance about the Balkan Christians is punished by the importing of an uncontrollable vampire epidemic. Seen in this way, the slaying of Dracula by representatives of the Western world can be read as a collective action on the part of the Great Powers, undertaken to restore internal order and to cement the territorial status quo. In this view, whether consciously or not, Stoker supported measures that were directed both against Balkanization and against the Russification of Southeastern Europe.

Beyond these geopolitical considerations, which are more evident on a metalevel, an empirical reading of the *Dracula* novel reveals a more or less exhaustive catalogue of vampirism, which draws both upon the clichés that were common at the time and upon Stoker's own notions of horror. Among his sources was a report by Emily Gerard, first published as a newspaper article in 1885 and then in book form in 1888, entitled *The Land beyond the Forest*. From 1883 to 1885, Gerard lived in Transylvania in the Saxon towns of Hermannstadt (today Sibiu) and Kronstadt (today Brașov), where her husband had been stationed as an officer in the Austrian cavalry.⁵ In essence, Stoker borrowed the artificial term 'nosferatu' from Gerard, as a designation for the Romanian variant of the vampire, as well as information she had provided on the defensive measures undertaken by the local population to ward off vampires.

Here, however, Gerard was mistaken. From a terminological perspective, the Romanian designations for revenant corpses is *strigoi* or, alternatively, also *moroi* (see the 'Attributions in Germany' section in Chapter 5), which refers to the unsettled soul of a deceased person; however, Gerard only attributed a secondary importance to these concepts. Her choice of term possibly derives from a misunderstanding of the word *necuratul*, which is still in colloquial use today, which literally means 'the impure' and that is commonly used to refer to the devil. In fact, the purpose of Gerard's book was not by any means to provide ethnological insights into a multicultural region, but rather to cater to the tastes of a broad readership who wanted to learn about the 'hillbillies' of Transylvania, which had been settled by German-speaking colonists since the Middle Ages. The bite of the revenant was contagious and meant eternal damnation, claimed Gerard, in her portrayal of the region as an exotic realm. Only an exorcism could provide relief, either through the impaling of the corpse or the firing of a pistol shot into the coffin. Even more radical measures included decapitation and the filling of the bodily orifices with garlic, or even the removal and burning of the heart. In the Romanian villages, professional mourners were at the ready, who would carry out defensive rites during the burial ceremony, including the placing of the thorny stem of a wild rose upon the coffin.

In the *Dracula* novel, Professor van Helsing defines the vampire count as the personification of evil and the embodiment of stealth. He is indestructible and immortal, and draws superhuman strength from blood, which he sucks out of the living. A whole range of characteristics equip him with a tremendous superiority: he has power both over the dead and the elements; he can also transform his shape, rejuvenate himself and even render himself invisible. In this way, he is able to gain entrance anywhere and everywhere, and, at the same time, to pierce through the darkness with his vision. As a further deterrence, he also allies himself with all manner of vermin and beasts, from rats to wolves. However, humans are not completely defenceless and at his mercy. For all his powers, the vampire can be identified immediately, as soon as he moves among the living, by the fact that he casts no shadow and produces no reflection in a mirror. Furthermore, he has to submit to certain rules that restrict his scope for action. First, his influence depends entirely upon winning over the trust of the living, and he cannot enter a house until he has received an invitation to do so. However, following a first invitation, he can then come and go as he pleases. Second, he is predominantly nocturnal in his activities, since his powers wane away during daylight hours. Moreover, outside his habitat, he can only transform his shape or leave his lair at sunrise, midday and sunset, and he can only cross running water at the incoming and outgoing tide. Finally, he also reacts allergically to garlic and the crucifix. All things considered, therefore, Stoker portrays the vampire count as an 'Übermensch', or as a monster. The prerequisite for his eternal life is stilling his thirst for blood. Reference is admittedly made to the threat of contagion, but, by contrast, the danger posed by a neverending chain of reproduction remains implicit. His living victims experience the vampire above all as a night demon, but they do have the ability to ward him off.[6]

With this canon of characteristics, Dracula was to serve as the dominant prototype of the Western vampire figure for the majority of the twentieth century. However, the gradual emancipation of the undead from the vampire count has led to a gradual decline in the significance of the historical location. Transylvania became downgraded by the public to a more or less fictitious place, just as Dracula was increasingly transformed into a figure of fun.

Metamorphoses of the Vampire in Fiction

The Americanization and domestication of the vampire is most clearly expressed in the bestselling novels of Anne Rice (*Interview with the Vampire* from 1976) and Stephenie Meyer (*Twilight* from 2005). In Rice's book, the frustrated protagonists from mid nineteenth-century New Orleans set off for Europe in order to resolve the mystery of their vampiric identity. In 'Eastern Europe', which is reminiscent in certain respects of Bram Stoker's Transylvania, they are confronted initially with the barbaric customs and rituals that the local villagers follow in their struggle against the vampires. The only European – that is, 'authentic' – vampire whom they encounter reveals himself to be a monster, and they are forced to destroy him on account of his bestial nature, without first having had the chance to pose their existential questions. Nevertheless, they do then encounter a civilized clan of vampires in a Parisian theatre, whose internal conflicts also plunge them into peril. Stephenie Meyer, by contrast, stands for the humanization of the vampire. Her heroes are noble creatures, who follow a certain fundamental asceticism in their interactions with normal mortals.

Other works deliberately referred back to the original settings of vampiric action and were written by authors who were keen to demonstrate their training as professional historians by writing novels located in the grey zone between magic realism and fantasy literature. Whilst *The Historian*, the debut novel of the American author Elizabeth Kostova published to great media fanfare in 2005, allowed the medieval Wallachian ruler Vlad the Impaler to come into his own as the alter ego of the vampire Count Dracula, the German fantasy author Markus Heitz, in his 2007 vampire novel *Kinder des Judas (Children of Judas)*, and the French archaeologist and novelist Frédérique Audoin-Rouzeau in her 2008 crime novel, written under the pseudonym of Fred Vargas, *Un lieu uncertain (An Uncertain Place)*, both incorporated actual events that had taken place on the Habsburg Military Frontier in the eighteenth century into their storylines. Regardless of the fact that there seems to be a trend back towards historical novels in vampire literature, the central themes of bloodsucking and immortality continue to be undisputed.

The Vampire as an Imperial Category

In this light, with reference to Dracula, it seems necessary to raise the stakes again and hold up the mirror to the vampire anew. Not immediately evident on first sight, but discernible at least in its outlines if one drills deeper, is a picture that – so the hypothesis claims – shows the bloodsucker to be a creature of the Latin West. Habsburg military physicians imposed a terminological cloak upon a hazy Southeast European bogeyman, first in an inconspicuous headline of 21 July 1725 and then in a sensational report from 7 January 1732, which rendered the phenomenon of the living dead more tangible in terms of its content. They did so by adopting the colloquial Serbian term *vampir*, for the etymology of which there are all manner of fantastic interpretations, but for which there is no one convincing explanation, particularly since the alternative term of *vukodlak* ('wolf-fur' or 'werewolf') had managed to establish itself in the modern Serbian language being formed in the nineteenth century.[7] In this context, it is remarkable that the Greek *vrykolakas*, who dominated the public discourse up to the end of the seventeenth century, gradually fell by the wayside. Álvaro García Marín therefore offered a convincing answer to the interesting question as to why the literary figure of Dracula should come from Transylvania rather than Greece. Whereas Western Philhellenists denied otherness and orientalism as not applicable to the cradle of Europe, national enlighteners acknowledged the dual identities of an ancient civilized and a modern backward Greece under the premise of self-colonization. The peoples of Southeastern Europe constituted 'haunted communities' in a twofold sense: on the one hand, emancipation from the Ottomans resulted in a process of Westernization, whilst, on the other hand, the educated public believed that the superstition of the common people found its archaic expression in the appearance of the vampire.[8]

The question of why and how the vampire should have enjoyed such a 'triumphal march' into the Western media is directly related to the question of why, and when, Eastern Europe came to be stylized as a 'Refuge of Superstition'.[9] Therefore, we will now turn our attention to the emergence and development of a discourse that took place in the area of tension between Eastern European popular beliefs and Western European clichés.[10] Here it becomes evident that vampirism is a phenomenon located in the border regions between the Latin West and the Byzantine-Orthodox world, an area that the Austrian literary and cultural scholar Clemens Ruthner rather appropriately designated as the 'European vampire belt' (see Map 0.1).[11]

In order to provide the reader with a degree of orientation through the dense thicket of terms, concepts and figures of thought, I will now offer two further guiding theses. These refer to the attempted rehabilitation of the scapegoats of East and Southeast European rural communities, and to the revitalization of a European mythology that, as a central subject, focused on no less a topic than the inexplicable fate of the dead.

The belief in 'living corpses' is a universal phenomenon. Fantasies about revenants who return to wreak havoc and carry out nefarious deeds following their death have been present in all ages and in all cultures. The tales told about them have a great deal in common, and only really seem to differ from each other in terms of certain nuances. Whilst the so-called *nachzehrer* of Central Europe attempts to entice its kinsfolk to follow them into the grave, the family of the Southeast European vampire are condemned to eternal damnation through the sucking out of their blood (see Map 0.2). In contrast to the nachzehrers, who were particularly present during times of plague and who have long since sunken into oblivion, the vampires can thank the Enlightenment for their continued popularity. They became stylized into the personification of a barbaric world, from which civilized Europe could distinguish and demarcate itself. The 'mental maps' of the eighteenth century, with their assessment of backwardness and progressiveness, witnessed a shift in focus from a North–South divide to an antagonism between East and West. In this way, the supposed homeland of the vampire shifted in the educated discourse from Serbia and Hungary, via Moravia and Silesia, to Poland and the Ukraine.

The term 'vampirism' is an imperial categorization. It is particularly applied to the border regions of the multinational empires that faced each other at the heart of Europe. The phenomena of incorruptible corpses and the epidemics of vampiric infections were considered dangerous by the centres of power, since they were accompanied by unrest among the subject population. Accordingly, strategies had to be developed for stabilization and the restoration of domestic peace. Whereas the containment of vampire cases in Southeastern Europe fell under the jurisdiction of the military administration, in East Central Europe it was the responsibility of the Church authorities. One aspect of the diachronic cultural transfer contributed to an intensification of the problem, as Gábor Klaniczay remarked: whereas the witch hunts of the sixteenth and seventeenth centuries gradually spread from the West of the continent to the East, it seemed that, by contrast, the posthumous impalement and burning of suspected vampires in the eighteenth and nineteenth centuries travelled from East to West.[12] From a colonial perspective, therefore, vampirism could be construed as the invasion of primitive forces and became connected with Slavophobe attitudes.

Notes

1. See Maria Todorova, *Imagining the Balkans*, updated edn (New York, 2009).
2. A.S. Pushkin, 'Pesni zapadnykh slavian', in *Sochineniia v trekh tomakch*, vol. I (Moscow, 1958), 371, fn 19.
3. See Vesna Goldsworthy, *Inventing Ruritania: The Imperialism of the Imagination* (New Haven, 1998), 83–84; Eleni Coundouriotis, 'Dracula and the Idea of Europe', *Connotations. A Journal of Critical Debate* 9(2) (1999/2000): 143–60; Jimmie E. Cain Jr., *Bram Stoker and Russophobia. Evidence of the British Fear of Russia in Dracula and the Lady of the Shroud* (Jefferson, NC, 2006); Matthew Gibson, *Dracula and the Eastern Question: British and French Vampire Narratives of the Nineteenth-Century Near East* (Basingstoke, 2006).
4. See Stephen D. Arata, 'The Occidental Tourist: Dracula and the Anxiety of Reverse Colonization', *Victorian Studies* 33 (1990): 627–34, reprinted in Glennis Byron (ed.), *Dracula: Bram Stoker* (New York, 1999), 119–44; William Hughes, 'A Singular Invasion: Revisiting the Postcoloniality of Bram Stoker's Dracula', in Andrew Smith and William Hughes (eds), *Empire and the Gothic. The Politics of Genre* (Basingstoke, 2003), 88–102.
5. See Emily Gerard, 'Transylvanian Superstitions', *The Nineteenth Century* 18(101) (1885), 130–50, at 142; Emily Gerard, *The Land beyond the Forest: Facts, Figures, and Fancies from Transylvania*, 2 vols (Edinburgh, 1888), vol. I, 310–24, at 319–20.
6. See Thomas M. Bohn, 'Der Dracula-Mythos. Osteuropäischer Volksglaube und westeuropäische Klischees', *Historische Anthropologie* 14 (2006): 390–409.

7. See Katharina M. Wilson, 'The History of the Word "Vampire"', *Journal of the History of Ideas* 46 (1985): 577–83, reprinted in Alan Dundes (ed.), *The Vampire: A Casebook* (Madison, WI, 1998), 3–11; Peter Mario Kreuter, 'The Name of the Vampire: Some Reflections on Current Linguistic Theories on the Etymology of the Word Vampire', in Peter Day (ed.), *Vampires. Myths and Metaphors of Enduring* (Amsterdam, 2006), 57–80; Kamil Stachowski and Olaf Stachowski, 'Possibly Oriental Elements in Slavonic Folklore. Upiór ~ Wampir*', in Michał Németh, Barbara Podolak and Mateusz Urban (eds), *Essays in the History of Languages and Linguistics. Dedicated to Marek Stachowski on the Occasion of His 60th Birthday* (Kraków, 2017), 643–93.
8. See Álvaro García Marín, 'Haunted Communities: The Greek Vampire, or Uncanny at the Core of Nation Construction', in Teresa Cutler-Boyes and Marko Teodorski (eds), *Monstrosity from the Inside Out* (Oxford, 2014), 109–42.
9. See Larry Wolff, *Inventing Eastern Europe: The Map of Civilization on the Mind of the Enlightenment* (Stanford, CA., 1994).
10. Cf. Thomas M. Bohn, 'Vampirismus in Österreich und Preußen: Von der Entdeckung einer Seuche zum Narrativ der Gegenkolonisation', *Jahrbücher für Geschichte Osteuropas* 56(2) (2008): 161–77, reprinted in *Kakanien Revisited*, 20 January 2009. Cf. also Andrew Mackenzie, *Dracula Country. Travels and Folk Beliefs in Romania* (London, 1977); Andre Gerrits and Nanci Adler (eds), *Vampires Unstaked: National Images, Stereotypes and Myths in East Central Europe* (Amsterdam, 1995); Tomislav Z. Longinović, *Vampire Nation: Violence as Cultural Imaginary* (Durham, NC, 2011); Duncan Light, *The Dracula Dilemma. Tourism, Identity and the State in Romania* (Farnham, 2012).
11. Clemens Ruthner, *Am Rande: Kanon, Kulturökonomie und die Intertextualität des Marginalen am Beispiel der (österreichischen) Phantastik im 20. Jahrhundert* (Tübingen, 2004), 137; Clemens Ruthner, 'Untote Verzahnungen. Prolegomena zu einer Literaturgeschichte des Vampirismus', in Julia Bertschik and Christa Agnes Tuczay (eds), *Poetische Wiedergänger. Deutschsprachige Vampirismus-Diskurse vom Mittelalter bis zur Gegenwart* (Tübingen, 2005), 11–41, at 20.
12. See Gábor Klaniczay, 'Decline of Witches and Rise of Vampires in 18th Century Habsburg Monarchy', *Ethnologia Europea* 17 (1987): 165–80. See also Karen Lambrecht, 'Wiedergänger und Vampire in Ostmitteleuropa – Postume Verbrennung statt Hexenverfolgung?', *Jahrbuch für deutsche und osteuropäische Volkskunde* 37 (1994): 49–77.

CHAPTER 1

Vampirism in the West

The Revenant of the Middle Ages
The Preformation of the Vampire

In the West, vampirism is the phenomenon where corpses allegedly rise up from their graves in order to wreak havoc upon the living, even drinking their blood. With this in mind, the historical origins of vampirism are to be found neither in Transylvania, the supposed home of Count Dracula, nor in the Balkans, the alleged breeding ground of the bloodthirsty night demons related to him. Rather, in this reading, the roots of vampirism are to be found in twelfth-century England and fourteenth-century Bohemia. A similar prototype, albeit one who survives without drinking blood, is also evident in the Icelandic sagas of the thirteenth century.

However, in the machinations of the Anglo-Saxon monsters and Czech sorcerers, located at the start of vampirism, we are dealing with cases that did not attract as much attention at the time as they were later to do in sensationalist literature. They represented the extremes in medieval attempts to come to terms with the mysteries of death and the transition to the afterlife. Moreover, they stood at the intersection of the parting of the ways of concepts of revenants on the one hand and ghosts on the other. In the course of their demonization, both genres – that of the monster and of the sorcerer, both of which will be explored in greater detail later in this chapter – came to be connected with witchcraft. From an empirical perspective, both also constituted the background from which later interpretations of vampirism were to flow from Roman Catholic quills. The Old Norse revenant (*draugr*), by contrast, personified a pre-Christian tradition.

In order to trace the development of the Church's line of interpretation, it is necessary to bear in mind the answers that Latin Christendom offered to the fundamental questions on the meaning of life and the divine plan for salvation. In the Middle Ages, humanity's attitudes towards death gradually moved from a position of submission to the natural order of things and the endurance of the punishments inflicted by God to a painful experience of concrete cases of bereavement, an experience that was characterized by a recognition of individual destinies and the hope for salvation in the afterlife. On the other hand, an awareness of the inevitability of death and the uncertainty about what comes thereafter can be identified as enduring constants across all the various approaches towards human mortality. The fears arising from these fundamental concerns bring with them both the need for an ordered passing into the afterlife and the concern for peace in death.

Each attempt to make sense of death is based on the basic differentiation between earthly existence and the afterlife, which is tangible at best on a metaphoric level. The solution that the Christian churches offered was to present the summoning of the living and the dead before the Last Judgement as an opportunity for salvation, thus presupposing the continued existence of the soul after the decomposition of the body. This forms the basis both for the hope of admission into paradise and for the fear of expulsion into hell. In death, therefore, people are confronted with the alternative between eternal life and everlasting torment and damnation.

Under these preconditions, death in the Middle Ages underwent a profound ritualization. On the one hand, death was experienced as omnipresent; on the other hand, the act of dying was enacted within the framework of a public ritual, characterized by the taking of leave from the living and intercessions for the departed. The arrival of death was followed by a solemn and ceremonial burial, during which a wide range of rites of passage had to be enacted. The closing of the eyes and mouth was supposed to prevent the return of the soul, and lamentations for the dead, vigils and requiem masses were meant to impose restrictions upon the vitality of the corpse after the burial.[1]

Even though it has received much criticism, Philippe Ariès' *L'homme devant le mort* (*The Hour of Our Death*, 1977), which, through its investigation of the norms of the intelligentsia, rather than a summary of humanity's actual attitudes, describes a longlasting moral decline in relation to the process of dying, remains instructive for an understanding of Western developments in terms of its epochal terminology. Taking four psychological parameters as his starting point – the individual self-consciousness (awareness), the societal struggle for survival, belief in the afterlife and fear of evil – he claimed to be able to identify specific shifts of emphasis in conceptions of death. According to him, in the Middle Ages, 'The Tame Death', which was positioned within the framework of rituals and ceremonies, presented a societal answer to the fears arising from the original sin. Among the elite, 'The Death of the Self' was a characterization and expression of a drama, with the drawing up of a last will and testament in the final hours of death and the covering of the corpse thereafter. Inspired by the ambivalent experience of and relationship between barbarism on the one hand and rationalisation on the other – that is, between plague and famine and enlightenment and science – the early modern period saw the emergence and spread both of the impression of a 'Remote and Imminent Death' and the fear of suspended animation. Furthermore, in the modern period, motivated by concerns for close and loved persons, 'The Death of the Other' moved into the centre of attention. Through the loss of belief in hell and the focus on paradise, the opportunity opened up for overcoming the separation from the deceased other, making possible an emotional confrontation with death. As a result, the advancing secularization of the modern period brought with it 'The Invisible Death'. In the course of medicalization, death underwent an increasing isolation: impotence and aversion created the preconditions for reticence and emotional frigidity.[2]

In the popular culture of the Middle Ages, animist beliefs, which underwent a Christian reshaping, ensured that a life with the dead was experienced on a daily basis. Alongside its demonization of pagan characters, the Church aimed at a Christianization of the dualism of the body and the soul. The omnipresence of the dead inspired instead the fantasies of the living. In the imagination, a dead person remained present until burial and was even invited to partake in mealtimes. The unplanned return of an already-buried person was not seen as particularly unusual and a deceased person could even face criminal prosecution. The phenomenon of a dead person's return was explained as a disturbance in the soul's passing over to the afterlife, or by the necessity of returning to put the affairs of this earthly life into order. A distinction was made here between ghosts in general and revenants in particular. Ghosts, it was believed, arose from the imaginations of the living, regardless of whether they were worthy ancestors, divine angels or evil demons. They stood at the intersection between immanence and transcendence, and symbolized a reversal in the journey of the deceased into the afterlife. Revenants, by contrast, according to medieval conceptions, were 'living corpses'. They appeared in connection to unnatural deaths, or in the context of unresolved questions of guilt. Therefore, reports on them always also reflect the norms and values that structure earthly existence.[3]

From the turn of the eleventh century, not least because of the establishment of the Christian holiday of All Souls, the dead were increasingly granted the function of messengers to the other side. The conception of the doctrine of purgatory in the twelfth century as a 'third place' between heaven and hell led to the banishment of revenants into the realm of nightmarish apparitions. Previously, the inability of a deceased person to find rest was seen as a punishment for violations of the divine laws, but now the fear of an unceasing punishment in the afterlife disappeared, to be replaced with the hope in an eternal life after purgatory. Consequently, in the theological literature of the thirteenth century onwards, ghosts were only conceived of as disembodied dead persons. Accordingly, there now arose in the Latin Church the notion of the departed as ghosts, stewing in purgatory as 'poor souls', dependent upon the intercessions of the

Figure 1.1 Skeletons in a graveyard chase off a knight's assailants.
An illustration in Caspar Neuhauser's book of hours, made by Georg Hölz in 1496 and kept in the Neustift Abbey in South Tyrol, depicts a legend in which a squire, regularly praying for the souls of the departed, is protected by the dead.
Used with permission from Augustiner Chorherrenstift Neustift, Cod. 654, page 33 v.

living. It was not until under the influence of the Reformation that the belief in the physical presence of a dead person was to become virulent, as they became stylized, on the one hand, as vigilantes and, on the other hand, served as examples for the workings of demonic forces.

Overall, reports of ghostly apparitions in the Middle Ages served to fulfil the function of strengthening the fear of God among the Christian community. The living were burdened with the responsibility of shortening the sufferings of the dead in purgatory and of hastening their early entry into paradise. The observance of the funeral rites and burial ceremonies, and the regard for the commemoration of the dead were intended both to ensure a separation of the dead from the living and to render the possibly sinful past of the deceased forgotten. Where homicide, suicide and death in childbirth or the death of an unbaptized child were involved, and the deceased had willingly or unwillingly violated divine law and therefore been denied the promise of salvation, then the community had to reckon with the return of deceased persons, bringing doom and mischief in their wake.[4]

Revenants in Icelandic Sagas

Precursors of the European vampire mythos can be found in the Icelandic sagas of the thirteenth century, which cover several cases of revenancy from the period of the island's Christianization around 1000 AD. In Old Norse tales, the 'living corpse' or 'walking dead' operated under the name of *draugr*. This term, which only rarely appears, designates a deceased person who has left his or her burial mound, inflicted harm on surviving relatives and who can only be stopped through the physical destruction of the corpse. In the context of the overlapping of the world of the living and the world of the dead in the popular imagination, the existence of revenants was not questioned. Their personalities were experienced as real and were described vividly. People who had allowed themselves to be brought into connection with magical elements or evil portents seemed to be particularly predestined for revenancy. However, as a rule, it was largely troublemakers who were reported to have returned, and contemporary stories therefore often reflected social conflicts.[5] In this regard, one particularly striking characteristic of the Icelandic sagas is that the anonymous authors did not seem to be concerned either with chronicling unfolding events or with a canonization of the lives of the saints. Rather, in a literary guise, they were writing a history of the clans living on Iceland.

The *Eyrbyggja saga* (*Saga of the People of Eyri*) outlines the history of the Snæfellsnes peninsula in the west of Iceland from the final third of the ninth century through to the first third of the eleventh century. The beginning of this period saw the colonization of the area by Norwegian Vikings from around 870 AD, a process that culminated in the creation of a free state which rested, from 930, upon the Althing, an annual gathering of the *godar* or clan chiefs and, from 1000, on the legally established acceptance of Christianity. The narrative comes to an end with the death of the Godi Snorri Thorgrimsson in 1031. The background to the writing of the saga was the civil war-like conditions and family feuds of the 'Age of the Sturlungs' from 1180 onwards, which culminated in the godar pledging an oath of allegiance to King Hakon Hakonsson of Norway in 1262/1263.[6]

In the *Eyrbyggja saga* we encounter two types of revenant. First, there is the harmful deceased person, as embodied by Thorolf Baegifot (Halt Foot) from the estate of Hvamm, who was embroiled in several disputes during his lifetime, culminating in murder and manslaughter. He gained his nickname as the result of the loss of one leg. Shortly after his reconciliation with his son Arnkel, he is supposed to have died in 988, near Gram. According to the tale, the events transpired as follows.

Arnkel's preparation of his father's corpse already demonstrated his mistrust. In order to ward off the 'evil eye', a garment was fastened around Thorolf's head and, so as to prevent its returning to the house, his corpse was carried out not over the threshold, but rather through a hole that had been knocked into the back wall. Despite this, the corpse did not rest peacefully in his burial mound for long. After sunset, the people of the neighbourhood could no longer find any rest. In the vicinity of Thorolf's grave, first the cattle perished, and then a shepherd was found dead. Later, the residents of his estate were terrified by a nightly hullaballoo, which created the impression of an infernal horseman galloping across the roof. Finally, Thorolf began to visit his wife, driving her to insanity, so that she, too, gave up her ghost. Here the narrator abstains from any offensive comments, merely stating without comment that the widow was buried alongside her husband. Thereafter Thorolf spared his son Arnkel, and increasingly turned his attentions to the neighbouring estates, whose residents sought their salvation in flight. Furthermore, he began to undertake his nightly escapades in the company of his erstwhile victims, who themselves had also been transformed into revenants. As a result, Arnkel was finally forced to do away with Thorolf. Upon opening his grave, it was discovered not only that his body had not decomposed, but also that it was extraordinarily heavy. It took more than a dozen people to lift the corpse, and two oxen shied away from it violently. Finally, Thorolf was reinterred on a promontory, and sealed off from the living through the erection of a wall. Thereafter, he was not heard of again until Arnkel, in turn, fell victim to an act of revenge. Thorolf's renewed apparition was again accompanied by the death of both men and cattle. Accordingly, his tomb was reopened once again, revealing a black and bloated, but still essentially intact corpse, which was then pulled out on a stake and burned on a pyre.[7] In an epilogue to the story, an infected cow gave birth to a bull named Glaesir, who himself became a threat because of his aggressive nature. However, after he had killed an enemy of Thorolf, he drowned seeking to make his escape across a bog.[8]

According to the saga, just as had been the case during his lifetime, Thorolf was not concerned with seeking peaceful relations with his neighbours. Pagan and Christian ideas seem to mix here. The dead man was regarded as suspicious by his kin because of his wicked lifestyle. In order to prevent its return – as in other cultures – his corpse was not carried out over the threshold. It is therefore clear that, above all else, Icelanders feared apparitions in the house. The narrator only states in passing that Thorolf's wife followed him to the grave, in the truest sense of the term. The period of time for which the posthumous machinations on the estate of Hvamm were tolerated by the neighbours, despite their acute fears, seems unusually long. The conflict is deemed to be a family affair, and it is Thorolf's son Arnkel who is entrusted with finding a resolution. Thorolf is finally only supposedly incapacitated by the relocation of his burial mound into the wilderness, where the radius of his activities seemingly no longer extends as far as the human dwellings. It is only the desire to avenge his son's death that spurs him to return. From a 'vampiristic' point of view, the fact that Thorolf creates a followership of revenants appears almost modern. The most striking evidence of his nocturnal activities is his bloated, nondecomposed corpse. Incidentally, the dead body seems to have been somewhat taboo, and it is only a considerable time after his reinterment that the solution of burning the corpse is finally considered. In contrast to modern vampire stories, the stake is only used here as an instrument for salvaging the corpse. The reincarnation in animal form must be seen as a specific feature of the Icelandic sagas.

The second revenancy case in the *Eyrbyggja saga* concerns Thorgunna, a wealthy and mature woman who had come from the Hebrides to the estate of Froda in around the year 1000 – the year in which Christianity was pronounced to be the state religion of Iceland. According to the tale, the return of Thorgunna's corpse was down to a failure to follow her dying wishes, despite all manner of ominous portents. The inhabitants of the estate believed her revenancy to be the cause both of a plague and of a shipwreck. The saga recounts the story as follows.

The impending disaster announced itself in the shape of a black cloud, which cumulated during the hay harvest, and that started to discharge bloody rain, perhaps enriched with volcanic ash. Unlike the other residents, however, Thorgunna did not tend to the newly harvested grass, and the fact that the moisture clung not only to the grass but also to her sickle was interpreted as a bad omen. She was in fact taken ill shortly after. In wise anticipation, Thorgunna pleaded with the master of the estate, Thorodd, to make preparations for the case of her death. It is no coincidence that the storyteller implied that she requested a Christian burial in Skálaholt (today Skálholt), which was to become the seat of a bishopric in 1056. Thorgunna offered a part of her possessions in return, but also insisted that her bed sheets and bed curtains be incinerated. Following her death, her body was carried into the Church and a coffin was prepared. However, as a result of the greed of Thorodd's wife, the bed sheets were not incinerated as had been promised. Eventually the funeral procession set off, carrying Thorgunna's corpse, which had been wrapped in linens, but not sewn up. En route to Skálaholt, the cortege pleaded for accommodation in a farmstead, which the farmer living there granted them without, however, providing them with food. Then, all of a sudden, a rumbling noise could be heard at night, coming from the storehouse where the corpse was being kept. It turned out that the dead Thorgunna had managed to extricate herself from the shroud and, in a naked state, began to prepare dinner. As she prepared to set the table, the farmer pledged to feed her pallbearers and, at this, Thorgunna disappeared. In order to rid themselves of the apparition entirely, the funeral party made the sign of the cross over the food and sprinkled the farmstead with holy water. Thereafter the journey proceeded smoothly, without any further problems, and Thorgunna was buried at the intended site.[9]

In the meantime, on Froda, the shadow of a strange half-moon was made out on the kitchen wall, seeming to portend further death. With the onset of winter, there were indeed a series of new occurrences, even worse, in fact, than Thorgunna's previous appearance. The first of these was the death of a shepherd, who then returned as a revenant, wreaking havoc on the living and bringing about their deaths through spreading an illness. In this way, like Thorolf Baegifot before him, he gathered his own following of walking dead. A seal's head also emerged from the fireplace that, having wrapped itself in her cursed bedsheets, was taken to be the spirit of Thorgunna, and this could only be forced back into the underworld following a sustained assault. At the same time, Thorodd and his retinue lost their lives at sea, with their bodies never being found. As a result, the fact that the dead then appeared in their sodden state at their own funeral was taken as a good omen. The narrator concedes at this point that the pagan belief in the importance of a personal leave-taking from the dead was still prevalent, despite the recent conversion of the Icelanders to Christianity. On the evening following the departure of the mourners, not only the drenched sailors appeared at the fireplace, but so too did the soil-blemished revenants. Whereas the living now gathered around one fire, the dead congregated around another. Finally, someone, or something, began to devour the stockfish in the storeroom. All that could be made out was a singed oxtail or a bristly seal's tail – taken as further evidence of Thorgunna's involvement. Following a concerted pulling on the tail, the creature did disappear, but by then it had already eaten all the fish. There then followed a further outbreak of disease, with women this time the main victims. From autumn through to winter, 18 out of 30 people died and seven fled. The tale ends with the statement that the Godi Snorri eventually sent a priest at the end of February and also recommended that Thorgunna's bedsheets finally be incinerated, and a heavy weight placed upon the revenant's grave. An excommunication was then pronounced upon all the revenants, forcing them to depart the stage. In this, the priest's blessing lent the whole affair the aura of a divine act.[10]

In contrast to Thorolf Baegifot, Thorgunna is presented less as a dangerous and injurious dead person, and rather as a caring one. When she comes back to life and appears as a cook, providing sustenance for people in a miraculous manner, this is clearly not intended as an allusion to the deeds of Jesus Christ, but rather as a lesson to her less-than-hospitable hosts. The episode with the gluttonous seal that appears in the place of Thorgunna's admonishing spirit, devouring the winter supplies, serves as a transition to the harm that the inhabitants of the estate of Hvamm and the surrounding district suffer in the form of the epidemic. Yuletide – that is, the period before Christmas – therefore offers a perfect backdrop for such spectral stories. In this, the fact that the residents of the estate were forced to pay for their lack of respect towards the dying Thorgunna is only hinted at indirectly. However, the revenants appear in two forms: as corpses rising up from the soil and as the sodden, dripping bodies of the drowned sailors. Although the hearth and the fireplace serve as a meeting place, no actual communication between the living and the dead takes place. The symbiosis between them appears only to be superficial, and the mistrust and fear of infectious disease among the residents of the estate instead ensures that the two groups remain huddled around their respective fireplaces. The powerlessness of the living and their acceptance of their fate here is striking. It is only the Godi's decree and the excommunication, imposed by a secular court of lay judges and sanctioned by the presence of a priest, which finally seem to provide a remedy.

Monsters in Medieval England

The surprisingly early appearance of alleged vampires in England can perhaps be traced back to the influence of the Anglo-Saxons, the Normans and the Vikings. A first case can already be found in the *Life of St Modwen*, written by Geoffrey of Burton in the second quarter of the twelfth century, which was published for the first time in a bilingual Latin-English version in 2002. Furthermore, in his *Historia rerum Anglicarum* (*History of English Affairs*), which was written in the second half of the twelfth century and first printed in its full form in 1610, and that covered the period from the Norman Conquest of 1066 to 1197, the Augustinian monk William of Newburgh, who is regarded by medievalists as a reliable source, discusses four cases of corpses rising from their graves. A further mention of harmful revenants is also made by the Welshman Walter Map, who advanced from the position of lay prebend to become Archdeacon of Oxford. He compiled his collection *De nugis curialium* (*Trifles of Courtiers*, first printed 1850) whilst still canon and chancellor at Lincoln Cathedral.[11]

Geoffrey of Burton became Abbot of Burton upon Trent in Staffordshire in 1114. The veneration of the abbey's founder, St Modwen, began from 1119 onwards. Geoffrey garnished her vita with a series of miraculous stories from the neighbourhood, which he either had become aware of through hearsay or through his own experiences. The tale about the complications arising from the unauthorized relocation of two peasants from the abbey lands to those of Count Roger the Poitevin is particularly remarkable.

The controversy over the harvest that the absconded peasants had left behind escalated into an armed conflict between the abbey and the Count. Whilst the peace-loving monks dedicated themselves to prayer at the shrine of St Modwen, the knights who were allied with them defeated the superior forces of the Count in an unauthorized action. Thereafter, destiny took its course. On the following day, the two absconded peasants fell dead at their dinner. Although they were buried in their home village, they then appeared again in their new village on the following day, carrying their coffins upon their shoulders. Thereafter, the two dead peasants wandered the streets at night, sometimes in the form of coffin-bearers and sometimes in the shape of wild animals, knocking upon doors and calling out the residents to come and join them as soon as possible. After this, the entire village fell victim to a plague. The Count then pleaded to the Abbot for forgiveness and promised to make adequate recompense. The reeve initiated the necessary steps, but then attempted himself to escape the scourge that had befallen the village. In fact, the plague then struck down the last two remaining villagers. Finally, with the approval of the Bishop, the graves of the two original troublemakers were opened up, revealing that the corpses of the two dead men had not begun to decay, and that the burial clothes around their faces were drenched in blood. First they were decapitated, and their severed heads were placed between their legs. Then their hearts were torn out and burned, and a demonic crow was seen to fly up out of the flames. After this, the revenants disappeared, as did the plague. Those who had most recently taken ill made a speedy recovery and then, along with their families, left the village, leaving it abandoned.[12]

As well as the lines of conflict running between both the peasants and the rulers, and between the secular and ecclesiastical authorities, this story also focuses on the relationship between Church dogma and popularly held beliefs. Whether or not human actions are seen as pleasing to God brings with it justice or disaster. The Bishop's sanctioning of the desecration of the graves is therefore not regarded as an act of superstition by Geoffrey of Burton and is not condemned as such, but is rather tolerated as standard practice. The revenants appear as messengers of death and are exposed by the discovery of fresh blood in their graves.

Disregarding the earlier witness of Geoffrey of Burton, William of Newburgh described revenancy as a previously unknown but nevertheless pervasive problem. As he himself confessed, he was only aware of these cases through hearsay. However, in order to bolster the reliability of his information, he also drew upon ecclesiastical informants.

In the clerical interpretation, as we encounter it in the words of William, the apparitions of revenants always follow the same pattern: under satanic influence, the body of an evildoer rises from the grave and terrorises those left behind – sometimes accompanied by the hounds of hell. Since popular belief held the undead to be carriers of 'plague' (*pestis*), the clergy were confronted with demands for the corpses to be burned. The solution to this conflict lies in the interplay of learned advice, episcopal prayer and mob justice. In this, however, William does not speak of 'revenants', but rather of 'monsters' (*monstrum*), although reference is made to at least one 'bloodsucker' (*sanguisuga*).[13]

First case: in Buckinghamshire, according to William, a dead man began to disturb his widow's sleep on the night after his funeral, even threatening to crush her with his weight. When the restless woman asked someone to watch over her on the third night, the dead man began instead to visit first his brother and then his neighbours. Eventually he started to carry out his mischief at daytime. His visitations were only finally brought to an end when his grave was opened and a letter of absolution from the Bishop was placed upon the dead man's breast.[14]

Second case: another dead man was accused of posthumous activities in Berwick-upon-Tweed in northern England. As a result, the man, who had been wealthy during his lifetime, was defamed as a crook. Allegedly, he gave his victims the joking advice that if they wanted to be left in peace, they should burn his corpse. After this was done, a plague then broke out as a sort of belated revenge.[15]

Third case: at Melrose Abbey, also located on the River Tweed, the chaplain of a noblewoman had become renowned for his unethical lifestyle and had been defamed as a 'hundeprest'. Following his death, it seems, he continued to conduct wicked deeds as a revenant. The noblewoman then called upon the assistance of a number of monks, one of whom supposedly succeeded in injuring the nocturnal monster with an axe and, upon his grave being opened, wounds were discovered on the chaplain's corpse. Thereafter, the body was burned.[16]

Fourth case: somewhat more fanciful, and therefore more dramatic, are the incidents at the no-longer-identifiable Anantis Castle. A man who had been on the run following a series of offences, but who had since become reformed, was alleged to be living in this castle. After marrying a local woman, he had become integrated into the local community and his rehabilitation seemed to be complete. However, the problem here was that his new wife was not a faithful woman. When the man began to investigate rumours of her infidelity, he sprung a trap for her, only to fall into it himself. Astonished to catch his wife *in flagranti* with another man, he fell unhappily to the ground, sustaining life-threatening injuries in the process. On the advice of a priest, the last rites were prepared, but the man, in his anger, refused to accept his inevitable fate and declined to accept the final sacraments of a faithful Christian. As a result, a proper Christian burial was not possible – and this, in retrospect, was offered as an explanation for his nightly returning from the dead. The misfortune to which the dead man subjected the living became apparent not only through the mischief that he would carry out during his visitations, but also through the outbreak of plague. Whilst wise men continued to discuss the necessary action to be taken, two youths took matters into their own hands and carried out a posthumous execution. Anticipating the motifs of later *nachzehrer* legends (see the section entitled 'The Nachzehrer of the Early Modern Period' below), the author relates that, upon the opening of the grave, the corpse was revealed to be enormously bloated. When one of the youths stabbed through the swollen body, a gush of blood spurted out, convincing all present that the nocturnal monster they were dealing with was a 'bloodsucker' (*sanguisuga*). Accordingly, first the heart was torn out and then the body was incinerated. Following the destruction of the revenant's corpse, no one else became infected and the plague was contained.[17]

In contrast to William of Newburgh, the Welshman Walter Map outlines his two cases of revenancy from the perspective of a chronicler, thus lending them a certain authenticity. His reports are distinguished by the fact that the influence of the respective bishops is not portrayed in a particularly positive light. It is only the fearless local nobility who are able to provide a satisfactory resolution to the problem. Interestingly, in terms of vampiric motifs, it is here that we first find mention of the angel of death knocking on doors and calling his victims by name.[18]

First case: in the mid twelfth century, the English knight William Laudun turned to Bishop Gilbert Foliot, who was living in Hereford, near the Welsh border, for counsel. A Welshman living in his village, who had led a wanton life, had died in disbelief. Four days after his death, he began to reappear at night and to call upon his neighbours by name. Those whom he had called out were struck down by disease within three days. Therefore, his corpse was exhumed, the head chopped off with a spade and the body sprinkled with holy water. However, these measures did not prove to be successful. When William Laudun himself was summoned by name by the revenant three days later, he attacked him without further ado, following him to the grave and permanently incapacitating him with a knife, thus bringing the visitations to an end.[19]

Second case: in the 1160s, a man who had died in Worcester in an unchristian manner began to wander around at both day and night, clothed in his burial shroud. His neighbours cornered him in an orchard and tortured him for three days. In the meantime, Bishop Roger recommended that a crucifix be placed upon the grave. When the revenant returned, accompanied by the mob, he fled in terror. Consequently, the crucifix was temporarily removed and was only re-erected once the dead man had re-entered his grave. With this, peace returned.[20]

It is remarkable that all the motifs and elements of later vampire stories should appear both in William of Newburgh and, implicitly, in William Map. In the English cases, it seems to be the higher classes of society that are afflicted by the black magic. In all the aforementioned examples, the role of revenant was ascribed to men who were supposed to have committed either secular or religious offences in the context of wider social conflicts. The suspects are defamed as troublemakers and sources of disease, and are demonized in the Christian interpretation. The issue appears to be resolved by the secular and ecclesiastical elites on the one hand, and the rabble and daredevils on the other. In this, Christian and pagan measures seem to stand in competition with each other.

Also striking is the uniqueness of the reports. In later English literature, such incidents only occur on the margins, if at all. This was perhaps a result of the banishing of such 'living' or physically present corpses from theological literature in the twelfth century. Furthermore, it can also reasonably be assumed that earlier tales of bloodsuckers were gradually supplanted in the public consciousness by the legend of ritual murder.

The first death described as ritual murder was that of William of Norwich in 1144. According to the legend, this crime concerned the crucifixion at Eastertide of a Christian boy by members of the Jewish community, who were seeking both to offer up a sacrifice to their God and to mock the fate of Jesus. This legend was popularized by the vita of the Saint, written at the beginning of the 1150s by the Benedictine monk Thomas of Monmouth. Against this backdrop, murderous pogroms were conducted against the Jewish population in several English cities in the years 1189–90, that is, immediately before William of Newburgh's writings. By contrast, it was only after the pronouncement of the doctrine of transubstantiation at the Fourth Lateran Council in 1215 that the notion that Jews were using the blood of Christian boys for their ritual and magical purposes began to gain currency. The literal acceptance of the transformation of the bread and wine into the actual body and blood of Christ during the Eucharist established the preconditions for accusations of desecration of the host. Accordingly, an anti-Semitic polemic emerged, which supplanted the bloodsucking tales of William of Newburgh, causing them to decline into oblivion.[21] Reanimated bodies or walking corpses reappear in *The Chronicle of Lanercost* and in the so-called Byland tales. In the Chronicle of Lanercost Priory, located on the Scottish border, which covers the history of England from 1272 to 1436, mention is made of a case of revenancy, which is said to have taken place in the household of the knight Duncan Delisle in Clydesdale, near Glasgow.

Figure 1.2 St Catherine of Siena Drinking from the Side Wound of Christ.
The mystic Catherine of Siena (1347–80), canonized in 1461, is depicted in this painting from around 1648 by Luigi Primo, or Luigi Gentile (i.e. Louis Cousin; c. 1606–67/68), as a quite literal follower of the doctrine of transubstantiation.
Used with permission from Bridgeman Images.

The body of a recently deceased sinner, who had even been excommunicated, had begun to appear to the priors at night. He then began to visit the house of the aforementioned knight, perhaps in order, at God's bequest, to expose those who had also been involved in his misdeeds. Occasionally, in an indefinable physical form, he also appeared around midday in the habit of a monk. It was not possible to vanquish him with any weapon, since all of these would immediately perish into dust. When the eldest son of the household nevertheless attempted to go up against the 'creature', he met with his death.[22]

In around 1400, an anonymous chronicler at Byland Abbey recorded twelve ghost stories that were said to have taken place in the surrounding area. These incidents follow a common pattern and adhere to the motif of the 'poor soul': a spirit, either a dead person assuming the form of an animal or a reanimated walking corpse, appears to a living person, relating to him the sufferings he is experiencing as a result of his worldly sins, for which he has yet to receive forgiveness. Thereafter, the living person informs a priest, who then pronounces absolution, thus granting the revenant eternal rest.[23]

After 1400, with the exception of references to injurious dead persons in seventeenth-century pamphlets, 'bloodsuckers' largely disappeared from English literature until they were revitalized as a literary motif by Bram Stoker and others in the nineteenth century.

The Shepherd of Blow and the Witch of Levin in Bohemian Chronicles

The somewhat marginal case of the Shepherd of Blow (1336) and the rather more prominent case of the Witch of Levin (1344) are often cited by experts on the 'Magia posthuma' of the eighteenth and nineteenth centuries (see the section entitled 'The Vampire Debate of the Enlightenment' in Chapter 3) as classics and precursors of the vampire. The first reports in this respect originated from Neplach of Opatovice, a former monastery estate on the banks of the Elbe in eastern Bohemia. However, they were to become well known through the writings of Hajek of Libočan, from a town on the River Ohře in Western Bohemia. In the 1360s, as Abbot of the Benedictine Monastery of Opatovice and advisor to King Charles IV of Bohemia, Jan Neplach wrote a *Summula chronicae tam Romanae quam Bohemicae* (*Brief Compendium of the Roman and Czech Chronicle*). In his portrayal of events in the period before 1266, Neplach largely drew upon other chronicles, but his description of developments thereafter and up to 1346 was based on information that he had gathered himself.[24] In the 1530s, Wenceslaus Hajek, administrator of the Vyšehrad Chapter at the Church of SS Peter and Paul in Prague drew up the *Kronika česká* (*Bohemian Chronicle*). This history, which goes up to the year 1526, is full of moments of literary tension, but also includes numerous inaccuracies and embellishments. It was translated into German in 1596 and was avidly consumed by later generations in the early modern period.[25]

Neplach reports the following on the shepherd Myslata (Mislata), who died in 1336 in the village of Blow or Vlow (presumably Flahe or Flahä in the region of Litoměřice), close to the town of Kadaň on the banks of the River Ohře. His apparitions culminated in the choking of a neighbour. When one of his victims attempted to stab the mischief-maker with a stick, Myslata tore this from him, mockingly claiming that he would use it later to chase the dogs away. Thereafter, the villagers decided to exhume the corpse and burn it. They uncovered a hugely swollen corpse, which seemed almost to resemble an ox, even bellowing in a similar manner. This time, however, the dead man could not defend himself, and his body was driven through with a stake. Blood spurted out of the body as if from a full vessel, and the corpse's feet were seen to convulse as if it were still alive. Even the burning of the corpse did not bring the horrid affair to an end, since everyone whom the revenant had called upon on his nightly visits would subsequently die within eight days.[26]

What can we learn from this story? Rumours about Myslata, a named representative of a shepherd profession traditionally seen from a biblical perspective as dishonest, had spread in the rural neighbourhood, accusing him of black magic, and integrating the motifs of the shape-shifter ('Aufhocker') and the incubus. Remarkably – and in contrast to what had been handed down in theological tradition – the dead person could appear in physical form and not only play all manner of mischievous tricks, but also communicate with the living. The two differing varieties of impalement, and their differing consequences, also appear to be interesting. The first action depicts the struggling of a restless undead man, whose invulnerability takes his opponents by surprise. In the second action, by contrast, we encounter less an attempt to bind the monster to his grave and more the desperate endeavour to force the colossal corpse back to a human dimension. The convulsions of the corpse and the noises emanating from it must have been truly horrifying for the novice gravediggers. The representation of the events remains naturalistic. Surprisingly, the shepherd is not portrayed as demonic, nor is a distinction drawn between his body and his soul. According to medieval beliefs, the highest punishment that could be carried out in this respect was to prevent the delinquent's entry into paradise by burning his corpse. What remained seared in the villagers' memory was the calling out of names, held to be responsible for further cases of death. Overall, it seems that Neplach's motivation in tackling this subject was to present his readers with an entertaining fable.

In Hajek's retelling, written 200 years later, the action is moved to 1337 and, furthermore, Neplach's summarized notes are given structure and presented in a more reader-friendly manner. At the same time, thanks to the cohesion of Hajek's representation, little room is left for interpretation. For example, the two defensive measures taken against the unusual transformation of the dead corpse are understood as deliberate attempts to bind the body to the grave, and a stake of oak is recommended as a weapon. Whereas Neplach only recounts the convulsions and noises of a deformed cadaver, Hajek writes of the desperate struggle of an evildoer robbed of his freedom. From a metaphorical perspective, the descriptions he uses veer towards the animalistic. As a logical consequence of the ox-like bellowing, which the corpse is supposed to have made, Hajek describes the stream of blood gushing from the corpse that the executioners delivered to the pyre as being like that of a bull on the slaughtering block. Finally, in drawing an analogy between the death cry of the executed corpse and the bleating of a donkey, Hajek clearly enters the realm of pure cynicism.[27]

A second tale, handed down by both Neplach and Hajek, turns out to be even more complex. Little is known of the anonymous woman who died in 1344 in the non-identified village of Levin, and Neplach only reports that she was discovered to have devoured half of her burial shroud in the grave, and that she was suspected of the same posthumous crimes as the Shepherd of Blow. The impaling of the dead woman's corpse did cause a great deal of blood to gush out, but was not able to curtail her freedom of movement. It was only when, on the advice of an elderly woman, the corpse was burned on a pyre made of rafters from the Church that the impending disaster was averted.

When compared to the events surrounding the Shepherd of Blow, this episode develops rather unspectacularly in Neplach's version. The reference he makes to the devouring of the shroud seems to anticipate the motifs of certain later nachzehrer tales. In Neplach's interpretation, common beliefs are reduced to the rumour mill of old women and reference is made to the amalgamation of pre-Christian rituals with sacred elements.[28]

Hajek places the action in 1345 and, in contrast to Neplach, identifies Bohemia as the scene of the action, referring to Levin, which lies east of Kadaň. In Hajek's free interpretation, the woman concerned is Brodka, the wife of the potter Ducháč – a common family name today, which is derived from the word 'gost' (*duch*).

During her lifetime, Brodka dabbled in black magic and, ignoring the warnings of the clergy, continued to conduct these activities in secret. However, she was not able to escape punishment. In the course of a gathering of spirits, which was not elucidated upon in greater detail, she was more or less inevitably taken by death. As a result of her sinful lifestyle, she was refused internment in the cemetery and was instead buried at a crossroads, the proverbial meeting place of spirits and demons. Subsequently, she arose from her grave and, sometimes in her own reanimated body and sometimes in the form of an animal, scared the herdsmen and cattle of the surrounding area. When she began to visit the inhabitants of the town and surrounding villages, leaving a trail of death and horror in her wake, countermeasures were taken. Upon opening her grave, it was discovered that the veil that had still been wrapped around her head at her burial was now covered in blood and had clearly been devoured by the corpse. When a stake of oak was driven into the breast of the dead corpse, blood spurted out as if from a slaughtered cow. Unexpectedly, however, this did not seem to deter the dead woman, instead spurring her on even further. In a sadistic manner, she even trampled upon her victims with her feet. A second exhumation revealed that she had extracted the stake from her own body and held it in her hands. Subsequently, her corpse was burned and the ashes were poured into the grave. For a long time thereafter, a whirlwind could be heard at the site of the execution.[29]

One sensational aspect of this story is the reference made to the pact with the devil and the witches' sabbath, which were seen as a preliminary stage to revenancy and bloodsucking (see the section entitled 'The Nachzehrer of the Early Modern Period' below). The phenomenon of witchcraft that was becoming virulent at the start of the fifteenth century was associated by contemporaries with levitation, witches' covens, pacts and carnal relations with the devil, black magic and spells. It became particularly prevalent in those regions of Europe in which the major struggles of the Reformation had taken place. The witch hunts that continued from the mid fifteenth century to the mid eighteenth century were in part a reaction to various heresies and in part a reaction to the alleged practice of sorcery (see the section entitled 'The Vampire Debate of the Enlightenment' in Chapter 3).[30] Significantly, neither Neplach nor Hajek write of the authorities' exertion of their influence.

The Shepherd of Blow and the Witch of Levin in the Vampire Tradition

Hajek's literary embellishment of the legends of the Shepherd of Blow and the Witch of Levin was to serve as a model for subsequent writers. It is notable that there was considerable confusion with regard to the geographical location. The Protestant minister Georgius Aelurius (Georg Katschker) adopted the passages on the Witch of Levin in the 1594 *Bohemian Chronicle* in his *Glaciographica, oder Glaetzische Chronica* (*Glaciographica, or Glatz Chronicle*) of 1624.[31] In this he moved the scene of the action from Levin on the Ohře to the village of the same name in the county of Glatz in the Bohemian-Silesian border region. Matthäus Merian also followed this example in his *Topographia Bohemiae, Moraviae et Silesiae* (*Topography of Bohemia, Moravia and Silesia*), published in 1650.[32] Via Carl Ferdinand von Schertz's work *Magia posthuma* (see the section entitled 'The Vampire Debate of the Enlightenment' in Chapter 3), published in Olomouc in 1704, the story of the Shepherd of Blow was drawn upon by Augustin Calmet as the backdrop to another tale of a harmful dead person, whose posthumous activities were reminiscent of those of the Witch of Levin, in his handbook, first published in 1749 in French under the title *Dissertations sur les Apparitions des anges, des Démons et des Esprits et sur les Revenants et Vampires de Hongrie, de Bohême, de Moravie et de Silésie* (*Dissertations on the Apparitions of Angels, of Demons and of Spirits, and on Revenants or Vampires of Hungary, of Bohemia, of Moravia and of Silesia*).[33] The Silesian writer Joseph Kögler took up the case as the first documented reference to the founding legend of the town in his *Historische Beschreibung der Königlichen Stadt Lewin* (*Historical Description of the Royal Town of Lewin*), written in 1793 and printed in 1842. Kögler even reported that, between 1727 and 1730, the Chapel of St John was erected at the crossroads, fifteen minutes from his town of birth, where the 'infamous sorceress' had been burned.[34]

Alongside all the Slavophobic stereotypes connected with vampirism (see the section entitled 'Demonic Figures in East and East Central Europe' in Chapter 4), in the era of nationalism, Czech and German authors argued over where the alleged witch had called home: Levin in northern Bohemia or Levin/

Lewin in Silesia.[35] The difficulty here lay in the fact that in the 1335 Treaty of Trenčín, in order to ward off claims to his own throne, the Polish King Casimir III (the Great) had handed over all of Silesia, including the county of Kladsko, to the Bohemian King John of Luxembourg. Therefore, from the eighteenth century, the two towns of the same name were both under Bohemian rule.

Thus, in Joseph Virgil Grohmann's 1864 anthology *Aberglauben und Gebräuche aus Böhmen und Mähren* (*Superstitions and Customs from Bohemia and Moravia*), the issue was treated less as a geographical one and more as an ethnic one. From his viewpoint, in the form of the bloodsucking *mora* (Czech *můra*), vampirism was more at home among the Bohemians than among the Germans (see the section entitled 'Demonic Figures in East and East Central Europe' in Chapter 4).[36] In the schoolteacher Wilhelm Mader's *Chronik der Stadt Lewin* (*Chronicle of the Town of Lewin*), first published in 1868 and then in a second edition in 1903, the history of the 'Witch of Lewin' was presented as a bizarre example of Silesian superstition.[37] Other collections, by contrast, clearly counted her among the treasure trove of popular German myths and legends, such as Johann Grässe's *Sagenbuch des Preußischen Staats* (*Book of Legends of the Prussian State*) of 1871.[38] The story was even given a sequel in the *Schlesischen Sagen* (*Silesian Sagas*), published by Richard Kühnau in 1910, in the tale of 'Der Grund zur Erbauung der Johanneskapelle bei Lewin' ('The Reasons for the Construction of St John's Chapel in Lewin'). In this story, a witch with red hair and red eyes caused the cattle to perish and the fields to become infertile, and was accordingly sentenced to death by burning. Later, a spirit appeared at the place where the pyre had been, haunting it. Therefore, the local miller erected a chapel at the spot, dedicated to St John of Nepomuk.[39] Thus, the 'Witch of Lewin/Levin' finally entered definitively into the canon of Glatzer/Kladsko legends. Still, in the *Glatzer Heimatblätter* in 1928, Ernst Boehlich made the argument that the north Bohemian locality of Levín in the district of Litoměřice could not come into question as the location for the legend, since it did not receive a priest until 1384, and until the fifteenth century it was called (in German) 'Leben'. Later, however, there was indeed evidence of the tradition of pottery that Hajek had mentioned.[40]

The Nachzehrer of the Early Modern Period

Germans and Slavs

Seen from the perspective of German and Polish historiography, respectively, the terms 'Germania Slavica' or 'Slavia Germanica' describe a historical landscape in East Central Europe. They refer to the zone of German–Polish contact, established by the eastbound settlement of Germans in the Middle Ages.

The colonization of the areas to the East of the Elbe and the Saale between the eighth and the thirteenth centuries was not only accompanied by major legal and administrative changes, but also manifested itself in economic and cultural terms. Against this backdrop, the later Polish-Lithuanian Commonwealth ought to be considered as an area of transition between the Latin and Roman Catholic West and the Cyrillic and Greek-Orthodox East. The emergence of a particular culture of nobility in this multicultural region led to a weakening of the central powers and the decline of the cities in East Central Europe in the early modern period.[41] Inversely, from an imperial perspective, the Kingdom of Prussia and the later German Empire (at least on its Eastern peripheries) can also be seen as multinational empire. Transnational aspects were evident in the fluidity of territorial and confessional borders, for example with relation to the traffic of goods or in the case of the cult of the Virgin Mary (see the section entitled 'Demonic Figures in East and East Central Europe' in Chapter 4).

As far as magic and superstition are concerned, folklorists cannot help but notice a cultural discrepancy between the Germans and the Slavs. However, at the same time, a phenomenon comes back into view that seems to have disappeared from the consciousness of the German public since the 1930s: Germany, too, had its moderate counterpart to the seemingly radical belief in vampires – the concept of the 'Nachzehrer' (see Map 0.2). Whilst the Southeast European vampire was believed to leave his grave and suck the blood of his victims, the Central European *nachzehrer* was characterized only by the devouring of his funeral shrouds and the spreading of diseases.[42]

One of the first reports on nachzehrers dates back to the chronicle of Breslau written by the tutor and deacon Nikolaus Pol at the turn of the seventeenth century and published at the beginning of the nineteenth century. This records the death of 2,000 people in Wrocław (Breslau), which at the time was under the rule of the Bohemian crown.

Since a dead shepherd from Groß Mochbern, the present-day district of Muchobór Wielki in Wrocław was heard to be 'chomping like a sow' in his grave, the impression arose that he was eating his own funeral shroud. This suspicion was confirmed when the grave was opened to reveal bloodstained garments which had to be pulled away from the corpse's mouth. After the head had been severed from the body and placed before the churchyard, the series of deaths in the village came to an end.[43]

The centres of belief in nachzehrers, a belief that reached an initial high point in the period between the 1640s and the 1680s, were Eastern Pomerania, West Prussia, the Hanoverian Wendland and northern Hesse on the one hand and, on the other, the historic eastern Germany and the neighbouring Slavic lands. The reports that have been passed down follow the example outlined above. The noun 'Nachzehrer' first became used retrospectively from the nineteenth century onwards. At the time, contemporaries instead spoke in terms of the 'chomping of corpses in their graves'. Whether because of the central location of the graves in the churchyard or as a result of the less orderly burials that were carried out at times of crisis, it is clear that what was actually being perceived here were the sounds of decomposition.

It is certainly true that reports about nachzehrers were particularly frequent in periods of plague, but such epidemics were not absolutely necessary. Factors that triggered the living to take defensive measures against the posthumous activities of the dead were commonly surviving relatives' fears of an immediate threat to their lives or rumours about the location of the source of a disease. There seems to have been a common consensus in popular belief that such threats could be seen off through the execution of the corpse. If one became convinced that a dead person was tearing at his funeral shrouds or his own body, then he was seen to have evil intentions. There was no unity of opinion among the authorities over how to deal with this problem. Secular and clerical authorities had to reconcile themselves to the fact that the perception of a dead person loudly devouring his own clothing or body appeared more menacing to those concerned than any fear of God's displeasure at the desecration of a grave. Originally, these concerns were shared across all classes, regardless of rank and status. Nevertheless, there was perhaps a fear of the sanctions of the authorities, since actions of vigilante justice increasingly tended to be carried out at night.

Dead women, in particular, were often accused of disturbing the peace in this posthumous manner. According to more recent reports, from the seventeenth century onwards, the nachzehrer's group of victims moved in from the wider neighbourhood or community to focus on their family and close friends.

Since the nineteenth century, as a result of ethnographical field research, it has been possible to identify several different types of nachzehrer according to region. Therefore, vampire-like conceptions can be found in Lusatia, in Eastern Pomerania, in western Prussia and in the Wendland. Whereas vampires tended to be furnished with an individual fate, nachzehrers appeared to act more or less anonymously. According to common beliefs, nachzehrers were soulless beings, who restricted their activities to the grave and who, whilst they could bring about harmful consequences through sympathetic forces, did not in any way come into contact with the living. In contrast to the vampire, the posthumous activities of the nachzehrer were not deemed to be motivated by wicked intentions, but were instead attributed to dark forces; a predestination to become a nachzehrer was merely attributable to physical anomalies or peculiarities. This lack of a definable identity or even an individual biography has meant that, unlike the vampire, the nachzehrer has not undergone any literary dramatization or arrangement.[44]

Reformation and Counter-Reformation

Whereas the term 'Reformation' refers to the period of religious conflict between Martin Luther's alleged posting of his theses to the church door in Wittenberg in 1517 and the Peace of Augsburg of 1555, and the term 'Counter-Reformation' refers to that between the Council of Trent from 1545 to 1563 and the Thirty Years' War from 1618 to 1648, the term 'confessionalization' has focused on the processes of modernization that were connected in part to the development of State Church structures in Protestant lands. In the spiritual sphere, late medieval piety became complemented by an early modern anti-clericalism. Whereas the plague epidemics of the Middle Ages brought with them a keen sensitivity to the ubiquitous nature of death, the fear of what awaited in the hereafter could at least be channelled through indulgences. Broad sections of the population grew increasingly displeased with the secularization of the papacy and widespread simony among representatives of the high clergy. Against this backdrop, the Reformation should be understood as a movement, aiming at renewal of the Church, which led to the division of Western Christendom into numerous confessions.[45] Socioeconomic upheavals, connected with the rise of the cities and the increase in the tax burden imposed by the nobility, culminated in the German Peasants' War of 1524–26. At the same time, the conquest of Hungary by the Ottomans at the Battle of Mohács in 1526 and the ensuing Siege of Vienna in 1529 ensured that the 'Threat of the Turk' also became a proverbial byword in the West.[46]

The Counter-Reformation represented a concerted effort at 're-Catholicization', through the use of force, diplomacy and propaganda. Starting with the Peace of Augsburg of 1555 and then further sanctioned by the Treaty of Westphalia in 1648, the religious orientation of the population of the Holy Roman Empire became tied to the confession of their respective rulers, following the formula of 'cuius regio, eius religio' ('Whose realm, his religion'). At the same time, the intertwining of religious and political aims also resulted in concerted attempts to construct and impose a comprehensive social discipline.

In this ambivalent atmosphere, it was not only the persecution of witches that took on an excessive character. Raging at the same time was the issue of the nachzehrer, particularly in the Protestant territories, where intellectuals argued for a rationalization of religious belief. Whilst Catholics could still call upon the saints as intercessors to God and focus on the probation of purgatory, the Reformation led to a demonization of the ghost in Protestantism to the extent that transcendental apparitions from the afterlife became regarded as reactions to transgressions in this world. Whilst Protestantism saw ghosts in particular as fraudulent conceits, behind which lay the devil, it sought to re-interpret dead spirits as poltergeists or 'rumpelgeists' ('rattle ghosts'), sent to lead the faithful into temptation.

Whereas, from a Protestant perspective, the period up to the mid seventeenth century was thus characterized by a 'confessionalization of the belief in ghosts', the mid to late seventeenth century saw a certain reversal, and the interpretation of ghosts as a 'bulwark against atheists'. In the context of the transition from Lutheran orthodoxy to pietism, the eighteenth century saw a further shift of emphasis in the instrumentalization of the belief in ghosts: the 'spectacle of devilish obsession' – the haunting in the parsonage – gave way to the 'spectacle of divine enthusiasm' – the enactment of spiritually motivated experiences of conversion.[47]

The Chomping Dead in Protestantism

The first Protestant statement on the belief in spirits can be attributed to Luther directly. In one of his *Table Talks* from the 1630s or 1640s, he is said to have responded in a mocking tone to a question from a Wittenberg pastor over to how to deal with the panic in a village caused by supposed revenancy. According to Luther, the spirit was a deception of the devil at most, and the series of deaths were solely attributable to the influence of superstition. He was convinced that it was merely an evil rumour that had spread among the mob. Luther allowed only prayer as a defence against this demonic suggestion and recommended to the misguided believers that they repent in a church service.[48]

The issue was illustrated more vividly by the Protestant pastor Martin Böhm from Lauban in Upper Lusatia. In his 1601 sermons on *Die drey großen Landtplagen Krieg, Teuerung und Pestilenz* (*The Three Great Plagues of the Land, War, Inflation and Pestilence*), he stated: 'in times of pestilence it has been experienced that persons who had died of the plague, particularly womenfolk, carry out a chomping in their graves, like a sow when it eats: and that through such a chomping the plague increaseth dramatically, and people of the community often die, one after the other'. This statement laid down the canon for all further interpretations. The cause for mass deaths across the wider region was held to be the spreading of the plague, but the reason for the transmission of the disease in the locality has been seen as the chomping of the dead in their graves. However, the agent of the plague, so solidly identified in this manner, was not given a name. Nevertheless, as in the aforementioned entry in the Breslau chronicle from 1517, both the comparison with a 'sow' and the attribution of guilt to the female sex appear as central motifs in the tradition.

Since the case had already been clarified in detail by Luther, it was only left to Böhm to discuss the defensive measures that were to be taken, which usually consisted of the opening of the grave and decapitation. A suspicion can generally be regarded as confirmed, according to Böhm, when the dead body gives the impression of devouring its shroud. Should blood then gush out from the corpse following the posthumous execution, the evidence can be deemed to be conclusive. With reference both to the Holy Scriptures and to common sense, Böhm claimed that such behaviour could reasonably be dismissed as superstition. Therefore, he warned his congregation against repeating such offences.[49]

Taking Luther's *Table Talks* and Böhm's sermon as a starting point, the discussion of chomping corpses entered into learned debates. In 1610, Heinrich Kornmann published his *Über die Wunderdinge der Toten – De miraculis mortuorum (On the Miracles of the Dead)*, and in 1670, the town physician of Chemnitz, Christian Friedrich Garmann, who had written his doctorate in Leipzig, published a much-cited book under the same title. In his treatise, written in Latin but dotted with German phrases, Garmann described the nachzehrer simply as 'Schmezzende Tode' (Chomping Dead). He also related the following widely held popular belief: 'They prophecy, that death will come back to take the nearest relatives and friends.'[50] It is from the substantive of the German verb that he uses in this context, 'nachholen' (to collect somebody afterwards or to integrate somebody into a group later), that the new designation was indirectly to arise. The term 'Nachzehrer' arose from a combination of 'Verzehrer des Leichentuchs' ('one who devours his shroud') and 'Nachholer von Angehörigen' ('one who comes back from the grave to claim his relatives'). The issue was later summarized for the first time in scientific terms for an early modern Enlightenment readership by Philip Rohr in his historical-philosophical dissertation *Über das Schmatzen von Toten – De masticatione mortuorum (On the Chomping of the Dead)*.[51] Taking this concept, the deacon Michael Ranft from Nebra in Thuringia would then go on, in the 1730s, to create the bridge to vampirism in his work *Von dem Kauen und Schmatzen der Toten in Gräbern (On the Chewing and Chomping of the Dead in Their Graves)* (see the section entitled 'The Vampire Debate of the Enlightenment' in Chapter 3).

Shape-Shifters and Poltergeists in the Silesian Tradition

Even today, it is not particularly well known that Silesia was considered by German ethnologists in the nineteenth century to be a true El Dorado for vampire researchers. In the era of nationalism, this region, rich in myths and legends, was naturally of particular interest for regional ethnographers because of its ethnic mixture of Germans, Poles and Czechs, and because of its changing political allegiance to the Polish and German crowns and, later, to the Habsburg and Prussian Empires.[52]

Originally situated in the sphere of influence of the Great Moravian Empire, Silesia fell under Polish rule in the High Middle Ages. Following the Mongol invasion, the Piast rulers invited German settlers into the depopulated region. Whereas the Slavs were gradually assimilated or marginalized in Lower Silesia, a multicultural German-Slavic environment emerged in Upper Silesia. With the annexation to the Kingdom of Bohemia in 1348, Silesia then became a part of the Holy Roman Empire in the late Middle Ages and, in 1526, fell under the influence of the Habsburgs. Protestantism established itself in Lower Silesia in the sixteenth century, whereas Catholicism continued to hold the upper hand in Upper Silesia, among both Germans and Slavs. The Counter-Reformation that began to set in from the first quarter of the seventeenth century brought with it the signing of numerous treaties and agreements of tolerance. Following the Silesian Wars, the large majority of the region fell under the control of the Kingdom of Prussia in 1742. The Habsburgs retained only a few areas in the southeast, the so-called Austrian Silesia.[53]

As a result of the multicultural character of the region, nachzehrer and revenant conceptions overlapped in Silesian popular culture, with no real confessional or ethnic distinctions. Retrospectively, reports on 'nightmares' ('Alpdruck') and on 'shape-shifters' ('Aufhocker') or 'Poltergeists' can be seen to include certain vampiristic qualities, although the central motif of blood-sucking is absent. Nevertheless, the subject seems to have become radicalized on the Polish-Lusatian and Bohemian-Moravian borders, that is, in the areas of transition from predominantly German to overwhelmingly Slav-populated regions.

On closer inspection, the impression arises that witchcraft was seen as a precursor to vampiric revenancy (see the section entitled 'The Revenant of the Middle Ages' above). As a sort of rule of thumb, the following observations can be made for the areas of transition between East and West: whereas the witch hunts and burning of scapegoats at the stake spread from East to West in the sixteenth and seventeenth centuries, as a sort of countermovement, the belief in vampires and the burning of seemingly uncorrupted corpses travelled in the opposite direction in the seventeenth and eighteenth centuries (see the section entitled 'The Vampire Debate of the Enlightenment' in Chapter 3). The differing attitudes of the authorities are interesting here: where witches had the official status of a conspiratorial community whom it was necessary to fight, the measures taken by the common people to ward off vampires were decried as a violation of corpses, although, in reality, they were quite helplessly tolerated.[54]

The Posthumous Activities of a Shoemaker and a Mayor

The tales of revenancy documented by the Breslau gymnasium teacher Martin Weinrich are legendary, both in a literal and a figurative sense. They were published by his son Karl in 1612 in the preface to a Strasbourg edition of Giovanni Pico della Mirandola's work *Strix sive de ludificatione daemonum dialogi tres* (*The Strix, or a Pastiche of Demons in Three Dialogues*).[55] As early as 1653, The English philosopher Henry More provided a summary of these cases in his treatise *An Antidote against Atheism*,[56] and a bibliographic mention can also be found in the *Silesiograhica renovata*, a new 1703 edition of the regional history by the historian and lawyer Nicolaus Henel von Hennefeld, originally published in 1613. Here, in reference to the famous case of Johannes Cunze (or Kunze), the Latin concept of *lemur* is used, harking back to the ghosts of the departed in Roman mythology.[57] The tales of the dead shoemaker and the dead mayor were translated into German by the Breslau gymnasium teacher Christian Stieff and, in the *Schlesisches Historisches Labyrinth* (*Silesian Historical Labyrinth*), immediately brought into connection with the contemporary debates over the Serbian vampires on the Austrian military frontier (see the section entitled 'The Discovery of the Vampire' in Chapter 3).[58] Stieff's version was reprinted many times, notably under the titles of *Der gespenstige Schuster zu Breslau* (*The Ghostly Shoemaker of Breslau*) and *Der Poltergeist und Vampyr zu Bendschin* (*The Poltergeist and Vampire of Bendschin*) in Johann Gräss' 1871 *Sagenbuch des Preußischen Staates* (*Book of Legends of the Prussian State*),[59] and in the chapter 'Vampirsagen' ('Vampire Legends') in Richard Kühnau's 1910 anthology *Schlesische Sagen* (*Silesian Legends*) (see the section entitled 'Demonic Figures in East and East Central Europe' in Chapter 4).[60]

Martin Weinrich had the following to say.

In September 1591, a shoemaker in a sizeable Silesian town – identified by later compilers as Breslau – slit his own throat. In order to ensure a Christian burial, his wife attempted to cover up the suicide. Nevertheless, the rumour mill ensured that the truth came to light. Given the lack of clear evidence, the shoemaker's relatives initially sought to resist the demands of the town council for an exhumation of the body. Because an increasing number of residents began to report that a ghost had started to wreak havoc in the town and that his activities had become increasingly destructive – there was talk of people being crushed and strangled in their sleep and waking up with bruises – the anguished citizens were nevertheless able to push through their demands. When the grave was opened in April 1592, the corpse was found to be in a more or less intact state. With reference to a metaphor used by Leo Allatius in his work on Greek vampires (see the section entitled 'The Vrykolakas among the Greeks in the Ottoman Empire' in Chapter 2), it is remarked that the body gave the impression 'of being inflated like a drum' ('inflatum ... tympani modo'). There was no sign of rigour mortis; in contrast, the limbs seemed very supple. The skin of the feet had peeled off in places, only to renew itself. Since popular belief held that sorcerers bore a physical mark, a rose was also identified on the corpse's big toe, without the meaning of this symbol being discussed at further length. Allegedly only the garments that covered the murderous wounds on the throat smelled at all; there was no discernible stench coming from the corpse itself. The body was then displayed publicly for a period of two weeks and a guard was placed upon it. However, the rumours about his nocturnal machinations did not come to an end. Once the corpse had been placed under the gallows, the activities only seemed to increase. Eventually even the shoemaker's widow caved in and permitted a posthumous execution. In the meantime, rumour had it that the corpse had put on considerable weight. Thereafter, on 7 May 1592, the council ordered the executioner to cut off not only the head, but also the hands and feet, and to extract the revenant's heart through the corpse's back. Thus mistreated, the corpse resembled a slaughtered calf. Finally, the body was burned on a pyre, and care was taken to ensure that no one gathered up the ashes and bones in order to conduct further witchcraft, with everything being disposed of in the river. After this, the ghost did not reappear.

The story is instructive in that it anticipates numerous observations that were to cause a sensation in the 1730s in relation to the alleged nondecomposition of several corpses in the Habsburg military frontier region in Northern Serbia. Particularly striking and revealing, with reference to the possible backdrop to the Serbian cases, and something that was not discussed in the sources, are the motivations underlying the behaviour of the civil society in Silesia. The religious sin of suicide not only represents individual misconduct, but also a failure of the community at large. The hallucination or illusion of an incubus, which is said to leave a vivid impression in the wounds it left behind, is further disseminated through rumour. The process for confronting a revenant is also interesting. On the one hand, the leaving of the grave is seen to be self-evident and, on the other hand, the defensive measures taken against the tormentor follow a logic that even the authorities cannot resist. The archaic elements in the posthumous execution also demonstrate the extent to which pre-Christian and magical beliefs were still widespread among the population.

According to Martin Weinrich's commentary, this 'story of a new house-spirit (*lemur*)' was so widespread in Silesia that there was no cause for doubting it, not least because contemporaries could still be found 'who had witnessed these devilish antics (*phantasma*) with their own eyes, and who themselves had been plagued by the poltergeist (*larva*)'.[61] However, even more sensational than the case of the suicidal shoemaker was that of Johannes Kunze, which is said to have taken place in 1592 in 'Pentsch' (the colloquial term that appears in Weinrich) or 'Bendschin' (according to Stieff, the correct name at the beginning of the eighteenth century). 'Bendschin' is also mentioned, alongside the variants 'Bentzen' and 'Benitsch', in the *Topographia Bohemiae Moraviae et Silesiae*, published by the engraver and publisher Matthäus Merian in 1650.[62] This mention refers to the free mining town of Bennisch (today Horní Benešov) in the principality of Jägerndorf.

Jägerndorf (Czech Krnov), which today lies directly on the border with Poland in eastern Moravia, attained the status of a duchy in 1377 before becoming part of the Kingdom of Bohemia in 1411. Its inhabitants included a large number of German colonists. In 1523, the region between Moravia and Silesia was purchased by the Hohenzollerns and was to be a centre of Protestantism in the run-up to the Battle of White Mountain in 1620. Thereafter, the

Habsburgs assumed sovereignty over the region and introduced a programme of re-Catholicization. Following the First Silesian War of 1742, the principality remained a part of Austrian Silesia.

Although Bennisch was granted a mining regulation as a free mining town in 1590 and had both a silver and an iron mine, it did not have a great deal more to offer after the Thirty Years' War. It is possible that a shortage of water in the mines and the debasement of precious metals had already led to the onset of stagnation in the mining industry before this conflict. In addition to economic problems, social conflicts also emerged. This was because the mining regulations had not only granted the miners certain privileges, but had also seen the construction of a new settlement for them at the mine. Since the established farming community was obliged to pay interest and to provide labour, they were keen to keep the privileged miners away from the city government. Due to the economic situation, the number of inhabitants rose from 500 in 1559 to 1,000 in 1610, only to fall back to 548 by 1651. The temporary upturn was also reflected in the adoption of a new school regulation in 1602. In the realm of jurisprudence, on the other hand, certain curtailments of competences were still in effect at Kunze's time. Up until 1584, high justice was still the responsibility of the hereditary reeve and his lay assessors. With the introduction of Roman law, which, among other things, led to tougher sentencing, the Brandenburg district office in Jägerndorf claimed the right to have the final say on all the judgments of the Bennisch Court. The last hereditary reeve took up office in 1589.[63]

Johannes Kunze was born around 1532 in Lichten (today Lichnov) in the principality of Jägerndorf. Following his move to Bennisch, he made his name first as a woodcutter and then as a shingle-maker. He was admitted to the city council and in the years 1573, 1580 and 1592 took up the office of mayor, always for a short period.[64] His good standing was only cast into doubt following his death. Following his posthumous incineration, rumours began to spread that the parents and brother of his second wife had also been accused of revenancy after their deaths. No less a figure than the pastor also allegedly mocked Kunze for having fallen asleep at times during church services. The compiler and translator Stieff claimed to have identified the Protestant pastor Johann Vogt as the author of the report, which is teeming with illusions to magical signs and symbols.[65]

According to Martin Weinrich, the events took place as follows.

Four days before his death, caused by a riding accident, Kunze had publicly pondered, in the context of an upcoming baptism, whether he could become a godfather again. His third wife and his children later concluded from this that he had foreseen his own death. Implicit in this assumption was an accusation that he had made a pact with the devil. Significantly, it was not possible to trace back Kunze's considerable fortune either to an inheritance or to the proceeds of his professional work. Some even suspected that he had sold one of his children to an unknown person.

On 4 February 1592, Kunze's favourite steed kicked out violently, catching him hard. Although there were no discernible wounds, he complained of internal injuries. Some people claimed after his death that this story of his being kicked by his horse had been a deliberate ruse, designed to cover up the fact that the devil had come to claim him. When his youngest son came to his bedside, Kunze desperately expressed his desire, for his sake, to be allowed to remain on earth for a further few years. On the one hand, he pleaded to God for mercy and, on the other hand, he appealed to the boy's godfather, who was present, pressing him to take up his promised duty of care for his son. At the same time he considered it unnecessary to call upon the services of a clergyman. Eventually, Kunze's eldest son, who lived nearby, was called to the bedside and kept vigil until his father's death at three in the morning. Beforehand, however, a black cat sneaked in through an open window, jumped up onto the deathbed and sprang upon Kunze's face.

Despite this dark omen, and in spite of the deceased man's alleged personal misconduct, his son was able to convince the pastor the following morning to provide a proper funeral. As a member of the town council, Kunze was assigned a place of burial to the right of the altar in the church. Subsequently, there was also much talk of a very generous donation. As the corpse was being prepared for burial, a hand allegedly shot out suddenly, laying itself on the spot that had been struck by the horse's hoof. This was not even the final ominous portent since, during the funeral procession, a ferocious storm also broke out suddenly, with thunder, lightning and hailstones.

Three days after the funeral, rumours began to spread around the town that an incubus or an 'infernal spirit' (*ephialtes*) had been appearing in the form of Kunze. On the day immediately after the funeral, the dead man was said to have assaulted a woman, pestering her and pulling her over. Following the burial, he also allegedly visited and threatened a person in their sleep. The night-watchmen reported that, at night, they had heard a banging and a great din coming from the house of Kunze's widow. According to a maid, someone had also ridden around the house on horseback at night, banging on the doors and windows, and fresh hoofprints found in the snow were thought to confirm this. On 24 February, the godfather of Kunze's youngest son told the pastor that the dead man had visited him at night, pleading for him to support his offspring. He was supposedly concerned that his eldest son would embezzle a chest containing 400 guilders. Regardless of his well-intentioned words, the revenant had also clattered around the house, frightening the cattle.

For fear of further nocturnal activities, Kunze's family ordered guards to watch over the house. These guards drank a considerable amount of alcohol, hoping to build up their courage, and began to provoke the ghost. At this,

Kunze vented his anger upon the animals, revenging himself in particular on the horse who had been responsible for his death. The clearly shaken and restless steed had to be put down. Accordingly, some began to call for the demonic creature to be burned at the stake. As soon as the lights faded, his family claimed that they could feel and hear the presence of the ghost. Those whom Kunze had left behind tried to avoid falling sleep since, despite the presence of the guards, they were visited time and again by nightmares and tormented by fainting attacks. Kunze's widow suffered particularly badly, and Kunze even forced her into sexual intercourse. Furthermore, he drank the milk pans empty and also promised gold coins to his recently weaned youngest child if he would only follow him into the grave. One courageous family member was strangled and crushed so severely by Kunze that he was covered in bruises.

Increasingly, the revenant began to extend his activities beyond the house to the wider town and the surrounding countryside. He was said to have torn up huge columns with his superhuman strength and to have wreaked great havoc in the area, riding around on a three-legged horse. Kunze seemed to delight in turning unwritten laws on their head – for example, he allegedly did the laundry of a maid who had failed to wash it herself on a Thursday, as custom dictated. He also caused a drunk man, who had been trying to defend himself against his wife, to injure himself by flailing his arms in the air and striking a wall. His antics even went so far as to suck dry the udders of cows and to bind their tails together. The horror he caused proved to be life-threatening for the weakest members of the community, the elderly and the orphans. The situation was particularly dangerous for women in childbed, since he not only squeezed the milk out of their breasts, but also stole the newborn from their cradles. The only implicit reference to vampirism that can be found here relates to the treatment of calves, whom he robbed of their life force by 'sucking out' the udders of the mother cow. The common people also claimed to have discovered mouseholes in Kunze's grave in the church, as was to be expected for sorcerers and wizards. However, attempts to seal these up proved to be futile. Instead, the altar and the baptismal font were found to have been besmirched with blood. The apparitions and mischievous tricks did not even spare the parsonage, and on 8 July the ghost apparently terrorized the family of the pastor, emanating stinking, infectious fumes.

After Bennisch had fallen thus far into disrepute, the inhabitants began to consider the tried and tested remedy of the execution of the corpse. In order to locate the source of the trouble, and ignoring the warnings of the pastor, following Luther, they opened up a great number of family graves. This suggests that the people were not at all certain at this time which dead person should be held responsible for the malevolent sorcery and that many incidents were first attributed to Kunze retrospectively. Therefore, the solution to the mystery only became clear for the contemporaries through the opening of Kunze's grave on

20 July. In contrast to others who had died both before and after, the mayor's corpse seemed not to have decomposed at all, even though it had been in the grave for a quarter of a year. The blackish discolouration of the skin on the face and the breast were attributed to the fact that these areas had been smeared with hydrated lime before burial. This type of disinfection is applied in order to a preserve a corpse temporarily and was therefore initially intentional. It is possible that the aim had simply been to delay the process of decay because of the body's presence in the church, so as to prevent unpleasant odours. However, instead of the expected mummification, it was now found that the skin had begun to regenerate itself. There was no evidence of rigour mortis and all the limbs still seemed to be fairly supple. The dead man continued to grasp a rod that he had been given firmly in his hand. Once the corpse had been raised, it turned its face from one side to the other overnight. The vitality of the corpse was further emphasized by the fact that it had the appearance of a 'fattened, lardy swine'.

With these findings, the evidence for revenancy was deemed to be conclusive. It was therefore agreed upon that Kunze's body should be thrown on the pyre. However, in order to be certain, it was felt to be necessary to obtain the permission of the prince beforehand. After a delaying response had been received, the townspeople summoned an executioner at short notice from a neighbouring community, who satisfied himself with Kunze's horse as payment. A hole had to be knocked out in the wall of the church in order to take the corpse out and prevent its re-entry. The body proved to be extremely difficult to transport, which was taken as a sign that the dead person was fighting desperately against his fate. His execution was staged as a collective action, in that all the inhabitants participated in the gathering of firewood. Initially, only his head and hands caught fire and, when the corpse was chopped up further as a result, a great deal of blood gushed out. After all the mortal remains had been burned, under observation, the remaining ashes were cast into the river. With this, the horrors came to an end.

Nothing is recorded of the response of the authorities. However, the affair was to have a sequel of a different kind, which proved the continued turning of the rumour mill. When a maid in the Kunze household died, all manner of objects were placed in her grave so as to prevent potential witchcraft. Nevertheless, a poltergeist did appear eight days after her death, wreaking havoc for a month. Thereafter, her body was dealt with in the same manner as Kunze's.

According to the compiler Stieff, the phenomenon of the poltergeist resembled that of the vampire, although 'even more strange circumstances' were identified in the graphic description of events in Bennisch than in the vampire cases on the Austrian military frontier.[66] On the basis of the Latin terminology, the author Weinrich did use the term 'Alp' ('nightmare' – *incubus*), but it is nevertheless striking that Kunze's story, just like that of the suicidal shoemaker, seems to lack any of the motifs that were later attributed to the

Southeast European vampires (see the section entitled 'The Discovery of the Vampire' in Chapter 3). Because of the manner in which they were handed down, and despite the embellishments that emerged from the imaginations of contemporaries, both these stories retain a certain authenticity. This can be seen, for example, in the bloated state of the supposedly harmful corpse in the grave. Furthermore, these reports also reflect both all manner of conflicts of interest within the affected families and certain social problems within the wider communities. They clearly demonstrate that there was already a conception of the vampire before the term itself was to become widely known. Post factum, Kunze is accused of having sold his soul to the devil. What is still lacking is the explicit interpretation of his evildoing as bloodsucking; the reference to the robbing of life force is restricted to the drinking of mother's milk. Sexual violence only finds expression in relation to nightmares, and even there only subliminally: where the tormenting of cattle is discussed openly, the defiling of women only receives superficial treatment. The neglect of children was also a central issue in contemporary discussions. Beyond all the insinuations related to the violation of moral norms, at heart the story of Kunze's revenancy is motivated solely by his concerns over the destiny of his youngest son and by the familial conflict over his inheritance.

In the nineteenth century, this tale of revenancy became furnished with all sorts of further associations, ensuring that it eventually took on the characteristics of legend. In his 1859 book *Mythen und Gebräuche des Volkes in Österreich* (*Myths and Customs of the People of Austria*), Theodor Bernaleken reported that the Mayor Kunz galloped around at night on a three-legged white horse. When wagoners attempt to cross a particularly challenging hill, they seek assistance by calling out: 'If only Herr Kunz would come!'[67] In 1867, in the second volume of his collection *Volksthümliches aus Österreichisch-Schlesien* (*Folklore from Austrian Silesia*), Anton Peter, a gymnasium teacher from Troppau (Opava), recounted a variant of the story that was embellished with even greater artistic licence, entitled the 'Hexenmeister Kunze aus Bennisch' (The Sorcerer of Bennisch). In this version, the 'sorcerer' tempted children from their graves at night and went around the area accompanied by them. When he began to wreak havoc after his death, his corpse was banished to a grave in the wall of the church. As in Bernaleken's version, Kunze has also been invoked by wagoners ever since.[68]

Suspicions Concerning a Dead Magistrate

The last prominent poltergeist in Silesia before the appearance of the vampire is the case, documented by the court clerk Johann Christoph Raab, of the magistrate Georg Eichner, who died on 20 May 1709. This case can be found in the village chronicles of Reimswaldau (Rybnica Leśna), published in 1868 in the *Schlesische Provinzialblätter*.

Immediately after Eichner's funeral on 23 May 1709, rumours began to spread about the appearance of a poltergeist. The relatives of the dead man vehemently defended his integrity and piety, and even proposed an exhumation of his corpse in order to save his honour. Initially, however, this offer was declined. Instead, the Count of Schloss Fürstenstein (Zamek Książ) ordered that guards be placed at Eichner's grave from 5 July onwards to placate the fears of the population. In the meantime, the number of claims from his contemporaries that he had been absolutely fixated on money before his death and that no rigor mortis had set in thereafter continued to increase. The guards also claimed that they had witnessed butterfly-like figures emerging from the grave and one woman even stated that Eichner had come naked to her in her bed in his ice-cold state.

On the basis of these claims, the grave was opened for the first time on 11 July. According to the statements of witnesses who had been present at the opening of the grave, no process of decomposition had set in. Furthermore, the injuries inflicted on the body had led to fresh bleeding. It was therefore ordered that the guarding of the grave be continued and the widow, who had yet to provide the confession which was expected of her, was placed under house arrest.

Since the accusations of revenancy refused to let up, the authorities summoned an experienced gravedigger on 18 July, who recommended that an executioner be called for. Having called upon an archpriest, who concerned himself primarily with the futile interrogation of the widow, an episcopal commission was established on 24 August. Out of respect for the authorities, the widow now finally confessed that her husband had already appeared to her on the first night after his body had been laid out. Therefore, on 24 September, the ecclesiastical authorities handed the dead man over to the secular authorities and, as a poltergeist, he was sentenced to decapitation and burial in an unmarked and unknown location.[69]

Evidently, the rumours about the nocturnal apparitions in Reimswaldau had led to the belief that a poltergeist was on the loose. Interestingly, the problem for the community seems to have been that a speedy resolution was being hindered by the reluctance of the widow to accuse her departed husband. Whilst it is true that the authorities did not shrink from disturbing the bodily repose of the dead man or from removing the body from the world in a figurative sense, the refusal to burn the corpse posthumously nevertheless left open the opportunity for salvation.

Giure Grando as a Slovenian Prototype of the Vampire

The revenants Giure Grando from the Croatian Kringa (1672) and Michael Kasparek from Lubló (Stará Ľubovňa) in Upper Hungary (1718) (see the section entitled 'The Vampire Debate of the Enlightenment' in Chapter 3) have been seen by specialists in 'Magia posthuma' as prototypes for the Serbian vampire. Both were active on the peripheries of Western history. The initial reception of the first reports and the further retelling of their alleged activities were clearly characteristic of public tastes in German-speaking regions. Above all, Giure Grando and Michael Kasparek particularly appealed to sexual fantasies. This is shown, on the one hand, by the archetypical intertwining of Eros (Love) and Thanatos (Death), and, on the other hand, by the trivialization of posthumous activities that is evident in the narratives surrounding them. Typologically, the two figures fall somewhere between ghosts, sorcerers and nachzehrers. It was only the rumours surrounding them and, then, the sensational reporting of these that lent their cases a certain significance. Both characters represent the personification of the vampire, even if Giure Grando seems to have been portrayed by the ghostwriter involved in writing up of his history more as a nachzehrer or a poltergeist of the Western type.

Giure Grando has been rescued from historical obscurity by the *Vampir* novel of 2006 by the Croatian author Boris Perić, and the alleged vampire has even been used in recent years by the Croatian tourist board as a marketing device. However, this case did not constitute much more than an anecdote in the regional history book *Die Ehre des Herzogthums Crain* (*The Glory of the Duchy of Carniola*), published in 1689 by the ambitious Slovenian natural historian, topographer and ethnologist Baron Johann Weichard Valvasor.[70]

The Habsburg Duchy of Carniola was established on the territory of present-day Slovenia in 1364. From the end of the fifteenth century to the middle of the sixteenth century, and in the context of feudal oppression and numerous raids by the Turks, the region experienced an era of continuous peasant unrest and the onset of the Reformation. The Bible was translated into Slovenian, a Slovenian grammar was drawn up and several further Slovenian-language books were also published in Tübingen. The combined forces of the clergy and the nobility were nevertheless able to ensure the violent re-Catholicization of the Duchy, and the region was spared from further unrest over the following three centuries. The second half of the eighteenth century even saw an economic upturn under the rule of Maria Theresa.[71]

A particular feature of Valvasor's monumental work is that it was published with the active participation of Erasmus Francisci, who worked as a lector for the Nuremburg bookseller and printer Johann Andreas Endter and who, as such, sought to defend and represent the economic interests of the printing house. The historian, compiler and hymnwriter Francisci was particularly receptive towards esoteric subjects. Alongside his work on *The Glory of the Duchy of Carniola*, in 1690 he published an extensive treatise on *Der Höllische Proteus oder Tausendkünstige Versteller* (*The Infernal Proteus or the Thousand-Form Masquerader*). Taking an allegory of the devil as his starting point, Francisci first provides a lengthy subsection that, in a circular argument, apparently traced the belief in ghosts back to 'imagination', 'insanity' and 'fallacy'. However, in the introduction to the book, he then effectively provides a counterthesis to this, in which he underlines his interest in true and substantial spirits 'which make themselves visible in certain forms or can make themselves heard invisibly through banging around or through their voice alone'. Finally, seeking to provide empirical evidence for this, he provides a chapter on the 'Chomping Dead', bringing together all the previously reported cases of nachzehrers and revenants.[72]

Whereas Francisci pursued his fascination with miracles and found his inspiration in the debates surrounding demonology and the persecution of witches, Valvasor, in keeping with his scholarly background, sought to provide rational explanations for natural and seemingly miraculous phenomena. The contrast between these two approaches can be found not only in the comprehensive annotations, but also in the text itself, particularly in those sections where the editor has made clear the position of the 'main author'.[73] In this way, Western 'vampire conceptions' were already superimposed on the phenomenon of Southeast European revenancy before the term 'vampire' itself, partly spread in the Balkan region, was to become known in the West.

In the sixth volume of their joint work, both authors write about sorcerers and warlocks who, according to popular belief, 'drank the blood of young children'. In this respect, a witness statement from the first half of the seventeenth century, which was only finally published in 1837, was overlooked. In a description of the region of Istria, the Italian scholar Giacomo Filippo Tommasini had mentioned the phenomenon of the *kresnik* or *krsnik* (rendered here as 'cresnidi') and portrayed them as the counterpart to the *vukodlak* (here 'uncodlachi') (see the section entitled 'Investigations in Eastern Europe' in Chapter 5). In the Slovenian mythology of the nineteenth century, the krsnik was seen to be a sun-hero. In popular culture, by contrast, and as a result of the literal interpretation of the components of his name from 'cross' and 'baptism', a krsnik referred to a person who had been born with their placenta wrapped around their heads and who were thought to be capable of assuming the form of those animals into whom dead persons entered, bringing harm and damage. According to Tommasini, the krsnik and the vukodlak come from the same family and, in the struggle between them, it is always the good that wins out.[74]

In their work, neither Valvasor nor Francisci attributes such properties to the revenants. The designation they use is also different. Thus, according to the German edition of *The Glory of the Duchy of Carniola*, 'bloodsuckers' were referred to in common parlance as 'strigon' or 'vedarez' (although the only term that has been attested is that of *vedomec* for an 'evil spirit'; according to the Croatian linguist Vatroslav Jagić, the term *kodlak* was to be found in coastal regions, whereas štrigun could be heard in the hinterland).[75] In an annotation, the term 'strigon' is traced back to the Latin word 'strix', a bird of ill omen in Roman mythology, who stole the milk from wet-nurses' breasts and thus endangered the lives of newborn infants. However, since the various motifs and themes become somewhat muddled, the message of Valvasor's country description remains unclear. In the main text, the alleged bloodsucking is once again relativized. Thus, after his death, the štrigun goes from house to house, knocking on the doors. From each house he chooses to knock upon, one person has to die. It was said of those who departed this life before their time that a štrigun had 'devoured' them.

In addition to the alleged bloodsucking, the two authors are also interested in one further aspect of the revenancy: farmers are supposed to have reported not only that the štrigun was carrying out black magic, but also that he was acting out his sexuality. For the authors, it was self-evident that this hinted at the disapproval of widows and the problem of adultery.

As a final point, the authors also identified the measures that could be adopted to ward off the štrigun. According to this, the farmers would wait for the štrigun to return to his grave at midnight in order then to pierce him through with a stake fashioned from thorn-wood. The injuries thus brought about caused a heavy flow of blood from the corpse and an impulsive writhing of the body. However, since such desecrations of the grave were contrary to Christian beliefs, they were not tolerated by the authorities.[76]

The unique and therefore sensational story of the 'night-walker' Georg or Giure (Slovenian Jure) Grando from Kringa, in present-day Croatia, from 1672, is mentioned as many as three times in *The Glory of the Duchy of Carniola* (in volumes 6, 8 and 11).[77] The market town of 'Krinck' in Istria, close to Pazin – at the time also known as Mitterburg – was once surrounded by a wall with defensive towers, according to Valvasor, but had in the meantime seen a decline in the number of both houses and inhabitants.[78] Valvasor also vouches explicitly for the authenticity of the revenancy case: 'There is no doubt as to the certainty of these events, since I have myself spoken with people who were there.'[79] What does the 'main author' have to tell us about this case?

The statement, which can be found in the country description of Slovenia, that Giure had died sixteen years before its publication has provided the tourist industry with the opportunity to claim that he carried out his posthumous activities over a lengthy period of time. However, the time distance between the date of 1672, explicitly referred to elsewhere as the date of the case, and its transcription in 1688 is more significant, since it ensured that the events received an anecdotal character from the outset for later readers. The ironic style in which the report is written does at least allow for doubts about its sincerity. The reader is never informed about the supposed black magic, as if this was never a subject of interest. The information provided in this respect is limited to the remark that Giure left his grave after sunset and moved around as a 'night-walker', even though he had received a proper Christian burial.

The first person to encounter Giure after his death was Father Georgio, who had conducted his funeral. Georgio had seen the dead man behind a door as he had partaken in the funeral meal with his widow and friends. This impression seems to be reasonable, within the context of a commemoration of the dead man, and in hindsight at least allows this occurrence to be exaggerated as a clue in the explanation of the succeeding irregularities. The priest emerged unscathed, though terrified, from this incident. However, over the following period of time, people began to die in those houses upon whose doors the dead man had allegedly knocked, thus ensuring that his memory was not forgotten by the living. Thereafter, he began to sexually assault his widow who, in her plight, turned to the *suppan*, i.e. the sheriff, who was subordinated to the local prince.

The focus of the tale now shifts completely from the endangerment of the community, whose internal set-up remained fairly diffuse, to the amateurish and sometimes comical attempts undertaken to ward off the alleged revenant: acting on his own authority, the suppan summoned all the neighbours and encouraged them to drink up some Dutch courage. Nine of the men, thus strengthened in their resolve, then armed themselves with lanterns and crucifixes, and set off for the graveyard. They opened the grave to reveal a fresh, red corpse, openly and cheekily grinning with his mouth open. The ghostbusters immediately fled from the scene out of sheer terror. The suppan then attempted to discipline the deserters, but they were no longer prepared to drive a hawthorn stake into the stomach of the corpse. Therefore, the suppan held a crucifix before the face of the alleged štrigun and began to chant invocations like a clergyman. In a bizarre reaction, the spirit was moved to tears. Finally, a couple of foolhardy men began to try, initially from a safe distance and then, one from an immediate proximity, to hack off the revenant's head with a hook. At this, the dead man not only began to wail and writhe, but also started to bleed like a living person.

When one contrasts the awful situation with the humorous retelling of the events, one cannot escape the impression that the supposed authenticity of the case rests entirely upon the amateurishness of the vampire-fighters. All the same, it is remarkable that it already seemed to be clear what measures should be taken at a stage where the concept of 'vampire' was not yet known. In Giure Grando's case at least, they seem to have been successful. Perhaps the real scandal for the inhabitants of Kringa was less the actions of the deceased Giure Grando, about whose life we learn nothing, and more the behaviour of his widow, who was courted far too vigorously by the suppan.

Notes

1. See Marianne Mischke, *Der Umgang mit dem Tod: Vom Wandel in der abendländischen Geschichte* (Berlin, 1996); Peter Dinzelbacher, *Die letzten Dinge: Himmel, Hölle, Fegefeuer im Mittelalter* (Freiburg im Breisgau, 1999).
2. See Philippe Ariès, *The Hour of Our Death: The Classic History of Western Attitudes toward Death over the Last One Thousand Years*, trans. Helen Weaver (New York, 1981).

Cf. Héctor Wittwer, Daniel Schäfer and Andreas Frewer (eds), *Sterben und Tod: Geschichte – Theorie – Ethik. Ein interdisziplinäres Handbuch* (Stuttgart, 2010).
3. See Hans-Peter Hasenfratz, *Leben mit den Toten: Eine Kultur- und Religionsgeschichte der anderen Art* (Freiburg im Breisgau, 1998); Nancy Mandeville Caciola, *Afterlives: The Return of the Dead in the Middle Ages* (Ithaca, 2016).
4. See Claude Lecouteux, *Witches, Werewolves and Fairies: Shapeshifters and Astral Doubles in the Middle Ages*, trans. Clare Frock (Rochester, VT, 2003); Claude Lecouteux, *The Return of the Dead: Ghosts, Ancestors and the Transparent Veil of the Pagan Mind*, trans. Jon E. Graham. (Rochester, VT, 2009); Jean-Claude Schmitt, *Ghosts in the Middle Ages: The Living and the Dead in Medieval Society*, trans. Teresa Lavender Fagan (Chicago, 1998); Helmut Birkhan, *Magie im Mittelalter* (Munich, 2010).
5. See Hans Joachim Klare, 'Die Toten in der altnordischen Literatur', *Acta Philologica Scandinavica* 8 (1933/1934): 1–56; Ármann Jakobsson, 'The Fearless Vampire Killers: A Note about the Icelandic Draugr and Demonic Contamination in Grettis Saga', *Folklore* 120 (2009): 307–16; Ármann Jakobsson, 'Vampires and Watchmen: Categorizing the Mediaeval Icelandic Undead', *Journal of English and Germanic Philology* 110(3) (2011): 281–300; Matthias Teichert, 'Nosferatus nordische Verwandtschaft: Die Erzählungen von vampirartigen Untoten in den Isländersagas und ihr gesamtgermanisch-europäischer Kontext', *Zeitschrift für deutsches Altertum und deutsche Literatur* 141 (2012): 2–36; Matthias Teichert, '"Draugula": The Draugr in Old Norse-Icelandic Saga Literature and His Relationship to the Post-medieval Vampire Myth', in Barbara Brodman and James O. Doan (eds), *The Universal Vampire: Origins and Evolution of a Legend* (Plymouth, 2013), 3–16.
6. See *Die Saga von den Leuten auf Eyr. Eyrbyggja saga*, ed. and trans. Klaus Böldl (München, 1999).
7. Ibid., Nr. 34, 80–82.
8. Ibid., Nr. 63, 139–44.
9. Ibid., Nr. 51, 116–20.
10. Ibid., Nr. 52–55, 120–26.
11. See Ernst Havekost, 'Die Vampirsage in England', Ph.D. dissertation (Halle/Saale, 1914), 54–58; Robert Bartlett, *England under the Norman and Angevan Kings* (Oxford, 2000), 612–15; Jacqueline Simpson, 'Repentant Soul or Walking Corpse? Debatable Apparitions in Medieval England', *Folklore* 114(3) (2003): 389–402; Eugenio Olivares Merino, 'El Vampiro en la Europa medieval: el caso inglés', *Cuadernos del Cemyr* 14(12) (2006): 205–32.
12. Geoffrey of Burton, *Life and Miracles of St. Modwenna*, ed. and trans. Robert Bartlett (Oxford, 2002), 193–99. Cf. Robert Bartlett, 'The Miracles of Saint Mordwenna of Burton', *Staffordshire Studies* 8 (1996): 24–35.
13. *Chronicles of the Reigns of Stephen, Henry II, and Richard I. Vol II: The Fifth Book of the 'Historia rerum anglicarum' of William of Newburgh*, ed. from manuscripts by Richard Howlett (London, 1885; reprint: Wiesbaden, 1964). Translated as *The History of William of Newburgh*, trans. from the Latin by Joseph Stevenson (London, 1856; reprinted 1996).
14. Ibid., Ed. 1885/1964, cap. XXII, 474/475; Ed. 1856/1996, chap. XXII, 656/657.
15. Ibid., Ed. 1885/1964, cap. XXIII, 476/477; Ed. 1856/1996, chap. XXIII, 657/658.
16. Ibid., Ed. 1885/1964, cap. XXIV, 477–82; Ed. 1856/1996, chap. XXIV, 658–61.
17. Ibid., Ed. 1885/1964, cap. XXV, 482–84; Ed. 1856/1996, chap. XXV, 661–63.

18. Walter Map, *De nugis curialium. Courtiers' trifles*, ed. and trans. M.R. James, revised by C.N.L. Brooke and R.A.B. Mynors (Oxford, 1994).
19. Ibid., chap. 27, 202–5.
20. Ibid., chap. 28, 205.
21. See Friedrich Lotter, 'Innocens virgo et martyr: Thomas von Monmouth und die Verbreitung der Ritualmordlegende im Hochmittelalter', in Reiner Erb (ed.), *Die Legende vom Ritualmord: Zur Geschichte der Blutbeschuldigung gegen Juden* (Berlin, 1993), 25–72; Rainer Erb, 'Die Ritualmordlegende: Von den Anfängen bis ins 20. Jahrhundert', in Susanna Buttaroni and Stanisław Musiał (eds), *Ritualmord. Legenden in der europäischen Geschichte* (Vienna, 2003), 12–20.
22. *The Chronicle of Lanercost. 1272–1346*, trans. with notes by Herbert Maxwell, 2 vols (Glasgow, 1913; reprint: Penbryn Lodge, 2001), 118/119.
23. James, M[ontague] R., 'Twelve Medieval Ghost Stories', *English Historical Review* 37 (1922): 413–22. English translation from the Latin in M.R. James, *A Pleasing Terror: The Complete Supernatural Writings*, ed. Christopher and Barbara Roden (Ashcroft, 2001), 457–68.
24. 'Neplacha, opata Opatovského, krátká kronika římska a česká: K vvdání upravil Josef Emler', in *Fontes rerum Bohemicarum*, vol. III (Prague, 1882; reprint: Hildesheim, 2004). Cf. Kamila Svobodová, 'Dva příklady vampyrismu v Neplachově kronice', in Tomáš Borovský et al. (eds), *Ad vitam et honorem Jaroslao Mezník: Profesoru Jaroslavu Mezníkovi přatelé a zaci k pětasedem desátým narozeninám* (Brno, 2003), 571–77.
25. [Hayek z Liboczan, Waclaw] *Kronyka Czeska* (Prague, 1541); *Václava Hájka z Libočan Kronika česká: Podle Otiginálu z r 1541*, ed. V. Flajšhans. Vol. I. R. 644–904. *Doba Pohanská*. Vol. II. *Zánik Pohanství*. R. 905–1100. Vol. III. *Cechy vévodké*. R. 1101–1253. Vol. IV. *Čechy královské*. R. 1254–1347 (Prague, 1918–33). German version: Wenceslaus Hagecius, *Böhmische Chronica* (Prague, 1596).
26. 'Neplacha, opata Opatovského, krátká kronika římska a česká', 480/481.
27. *Kronyka Czeska*, 306; *Václava Hájka z Libočan Kronika česká*, 353–54; Wenceslaus Hagecius, *Böhmische Chronica*, 168.
28. 'Neplacha, opata Opatovského, krátká kronika římska a česká', 480.
29. *Kronyka Czeska*, 312 verso; *Václava Hájka z Libočan Kronika česká*, 387–89; Hagecius, *Böhmische Chronica*, 419/420.
30. See Wolfgang Behringer, *Hexen. Glaube, Verfolgung, Vermarktung*, 5th edn (Munich, 2009).
31. Georgius Aelurius [Georg Katschker], *Glaciographia, oder Glätzische Chronica. Das ist: Gründliche historische Beschreibung der berümbten und vornemen Stadt, ja gantzen Graffschafft Glatz, auch des Münsterbergischen Fürstenthumbs in Schlesien* (Leipzig, 1625), 236/237.
32. *Topographia Bohemiae, Moraviae et Silesiae, das ist Beschreibung und eigentliche Abbildung der Vornehmsten und bekandtisten Stätte und Plätze in dem Königreich Boheim und einverleibten Ländern Mähren und Schlesien* (Frankfurt, 1650), 44.
33. Augustin Calmet, *Dissertations sur les Apparitions des anges, des Démons et des Esprits et sur les Revenants et Vampires de Hongrie, de Bohême, de Moravie et de Silésie* (Paris, 1746), 273. Revised edn: *Dissertations sur les Apparitions des Esprits, et sur les Vampires et Revenans de Hongrie, de Moravie, etc. Nouvelle Edition, revue et corrigée*, 2 vols (Einsiedeln, 1749), vol. II, 28. English translation: *Dissertations upon the apparitions of angels,*

daemons, and ghosts and concerning the vampires of Hungary, Bohemia, Moravia, and Silesia (London, 1759), 195/196.
34. Joseph Koegler, 'Historische Beschreibung der königlichen Stadt Lewin (geschrieben im Jahre 1793)', in *Chronicken der Grafschaft Glatz von Joseph Koegler* (Glatz, 1841/42) 415–46, at 417, 440/441; reprint: 'Historische Beschreibung der Königlichen Immediatstadt Lewin', in Joseph Kögler, *Die Chronicken der Grafschaft Glatz*, vol. I: *Die Stadt- und Pfarreichroniken von Lewin – Mittelwalde – Wünschelburg – Neurode-Wilhelmstal*, revised edn by Dieter Pohl (Modautal, 1992), 21–74, at 30, 73/74.
35. Cf. Kättlitz, Christian: '". . . Man braucht also nicht nur auf dem Balkan zu suchen." Oder: Wie slawisch darf Dracula sein?', *Bohemia* 50 (2010): 333–50.
36. *Aberglaube und Gebräuche aus Böhmen und Mähren*, collected and edited by Joseph Virgil Grohmann, vol. 1 (Prague, 1864), 24, 191.
37. Wilhelm Mader, *Chronik der Stadt Lewin* (Habelschwerdt, 1868), 2nd suppl. edn (Lewin 1903), 9/10.
38. J[ohann] G[eorg] Th[eodor] Grässe, *Sagenbuch des Preußischen Staats*, 2 vols (Glogau, 1868–71), 198/199.
39. Richard Kühnau, *Schlesische Sagen*, vol I. *Spuk- und Gespenstersagen* (Leipzig, 1910), 196–98 and 198/199.
40. E. Boehlich, 'Die Hexe von Lewin (1345). Ein Beitrag zur Geschichte des Vampirismus', *Glatzer Heimatblätter* 14(1) (1928): 1–16, at 14.
41. See Christian Lübke (ed.), *Struktur und Wandel im Früh- und Hochmittelalter: Eine Bestandsaufnahme aktueller Forschungen zur Germania Slavica* (Stuttgart, 1998).
42. See Thomas Schürmann, *Nachzehrerglauben in Mitteleuropa* (Marburg, 1990).
43. Nikolaus Pol, *Jahrbücher der Stadt Breslau*, ed. Johann Gustav Büsching, 4 vols (Breslau 1813–1824), vol. 3, 1/2.
44. See Schürmann, *Nachzehrerglauben*.
45. See Martin H. Jung, *Reformation und Konfessionelles Zeitalter (1517–1648)* (Göttingen, 2012). See also Edward A. Eckert, *The Structure of Plagues and Pestilences in Early Modern Europe. Central Europe, 1560–1640* (Basel, 1996).
46. See Almut Höfert, *Den Feind beschreiben: 'Türkengefahr' und europäisches Wissen über das Osmanische Reich 1450–1600* (Frankfurt, 2003).
47. See Miriam Rieger, *Der Teufel im Pfarrhaus: Gespenster, Geisterglaube und Besessenheit im Luthertum der Frühen Neuzeit* (Stuttgart, 2011), 16–25.
48. *D. Martin Luthers Werke: Kritische Gesamtausgabe. Tischreden*, vol. 6 (Weimar, 1921), no. 6823, 214.
49. *Die drey grossen Landtplagen Krieg, Teurung, Pestilenz, welche jetzundt vor der Welte Ende in vollem Schwang gehen. Den frommen Kindern Gottes, welchen bey dieser kümmerlichen Zeit herzlich bange ist zu Lehr und Trost: den sichern Weltfindern aber zur warnung und schrecken, in XXIII Predigten erkleret durch Martinum Bohemum Laubanensem, Predigern daselbst* (Wittenberg, 1601), 135–43, at 141.
50. Christian Friedrich Garmann, *De Miraculis Mortuorum: Über die Wunder[dinge] der Toten*, facsimile of the original edition of 1670 with translation and epilogue edited by Silvio Benetello and Bernd Herrmann (Göttingen, 2003), 27.
51. Philippus Rohr, *Dissertatio historico-philosophica de masticatione mortuorum* (Lipsiae, 1679).
52. See Christian d' Elvert, 'Die Vampyre in Mähren', *Schriften der historisch-statistischen Section der k. k. mährisch-schlesischen Gesellschaft des Ackerbaues, der Natur- und Landeskunde* 12 (1859): 410–21; Josef Klapper, 'Die schlesischen Geschichten von den

schädigenden Toten', *Mitteilungen der schlesischen Gesellschaft für Volkskunde* 11 (1909): 58–93. See also Thomas M. Bohn', Schlesien als Eldorado für Vampirjäger', in Thomas M. Bohn and Kirsten von Hagen (eds), *Mythos Vampir – Bissige Lektüren* (Bonn, 2018), 45–56.
53. See Ludwig Petry (ed.), *Geschichte Schlesiens*, vol. 2: *Die Habsburger Zeit 1526–1740*, 3rd unchanged edn (Stuttgart, 2000).
54. See Winfried Irgang, 'Die Stellung des Deutschen Ordens zum Aberglauben am Beispiel der Herrschaften Freudenthal und Eulenburg', in Udo Arnold (ed.), *Von Akkon bis Wien: Studien zur Deutschordensgeschichte vom 13. bis zum 20. Jahrhundert. Festschrift zum 90. Geburtstag von Althochmeister P. Dr. Marian Tumler O. T. am 21. Oktober 1977* (Marburg, 1978), 261–71, in particular 266–70; Karen Lambrecht, 'Wiedergänger und Vampire in Ostmitteleuropa – Postume Verbrennung statt Hexenverfolgung?', *Jahrbuch für deutsche und osteuropäische Volkskunde* 37 (1994): 49–77, at 49/50, 68; Karen Lambrecht, *Obrigkeiten und Hexenverfolgungen. Zaubereiprozesse in den schlesischen Territorie* (Vienna, 1995), 383–401, in particular 383/384, 401.
55. *Joh. Francisci Pici Mirandulae Domini Concordiaeque Comitis Strix Sive De Ludificatione Daemonum Dialogi Tres / Nunc primum in Germania eruti ex bibliotheca M. Martini Weinrichii. Cum eiusdem Praefatione luculenta, continente narrationem duorum operum magicorum & iudicii de iis lati, ut veriβimam, ita cognitione digniβimam, itemque Epistola Ad Cl. Medicum Et Philosophum D. Andream Libavium, de quaestione, Utrum in non maritatis & castis mola possit gigni? Et post mortem eius editi Studio & opera, Caroli Weinrichii, F. Argentorati* (Argentoratum [Straßburg], 1612). Cf. Daniel Wojtucki, '"'Żywe trupy'': wiara w powracających zmarłych w jednym ze śląskich miast w latach 1591–1592', in Filip Wolański and Leszek Ziątkowski (eds), *W kręgu myśli Władysława Czaplińskiego* (Wrocław, 2016), 151–62.
56. Henry More, *An Antidote against Atheism, or, An Appeal to the Naturall Faculties of the Minde of Man, wether there be not a God* (London, 1653); 2nd edn corrected and enlarged (London, 1655), 215–26.
57. Nicolaus Henelius, *Silesiograpia renovata necessariis scholiis: Observationibus et indice aucta* (Breslau/Leipzig, 1704), 26/27.
58. *Schlesisches Historisches Labyrinth oder Kurzgefaste Sammlung von hundert Historien. Allerhand denckwürdiger Nahmen, Werter, Personen, Gebräuche, Solennitäten und Begebenheiten in Schlesien: Aus den weitläufftigen gedruckten Chronicken und vielen geschriebenen Uhrkunden zum Vergnügen allerhand Liebhaber Schlesischer Geschichte, in einem kürtzern und bessern Zusammenhange mit vielfältigen neuen Beyträgen zu der alten und neuen Schlesischen Historie verfertiget* (Breslau/Leipzig, 1737), 330–93, in particular 351–62 ('Von dem Gespenste eines sich selbst ermordenden Schusters' ['The Ghost of a Shoemaker Who Commited Suicide']) and 363–93 ('Johann Cuntzische Gespenster-Historie' ['The Ghost Story of Johann Kunze']).
59. Grässe, *Sagenbuch des Preußischen Staats*, vol. II, Nr. 161, 176–79; Nr. 203, 214–23.
60. Kühnau, *Schlesische Sagen*, Nr. 174, 162–68; Nr. 185, 175–90.
61. *Joh. Francisci Pici Mirandulae Domini Concordiaeque Comitis Strix Sive*, 12/13; *Schlesisches Historisches Labyrinth*, 362.
62. *Topographia Bohemiae, Moraviae et Silesiae*, 124.
63. Rößler, Helmut, *Die freie Bergstadt Bennisch. Ein Rückblick auf Schicksal und Lebensart einer sudetendeutschen Kleinstadt* (Munich, 1962), 34/35, 54, 62/63, 83.
64. Ibid., 74.
65. *Schlesisches Historisches Labyrinth*, 381.

66. Ibid., 389.
67. Theodor Bernaleken, *Mythen und Bräuche des Volkes in Österreich: Als Beitrag zur deutschen Mythologie, Volksdichtung und Sittenkunde* (Vienna, 1859), 50/51.
68. Anton Peter (ed.), *Volksthümliches aus Österreichisch-Schlesien*, vol. I: *Kinder und Kinderspiele, Volkslieder und Volksschauspiele, Sprichwörter*, vol. II: *Sagen und Märchen, Bräuche und Volksglauben*, vol. III: *Leben der Oppaländer in Vergangenheit und Gegenwart* (Troppau, 1865–73), vol. II (1867), 62.
69. 'Exempel, wie man zu verfahren hat, wenn ein Verstorbener im Dorfe spukt: Aus der Reimswaldauer Dorfchronik mitgetheilt von H. Palm', *Rübezahl der Schlesischen Provinzialblätter* 72(7) (1868): 26–28. Cf. Daniel Wojtucki, 'Przypadek Poltergeista z Rybnicy Leśnej z 1709 r. Przyczynek do wierzeń w magia posthuma na Śląsku', in Elżbieta Kościk et al. (eds), *Staropolski ogląd świata: Nulla dies sine linea. Księga jubileuszowa dedykowana Profesorowi Bogdanowi Rokowi w 70. Rocznicę urodzin* (Toruń, 2017), 229–243.
70. Johann Weichard Valvasor, *Die Ehre des Herzogthums Crain. 15 Bücher in 4 Bänden* (Nürnberg, 1689; new edn: Novo Mesto, 1877–79; facsimile: Munich, 1970–74). Cf. Jaqueline Winkel, 'Vampire zum Anfassen: Jure Grando und Michl Gašpareks Metamorphosen von gefürchteten Wiedergängern zu touristischen Stadtlegenden', in Thomas M. Bohn and Kirsten von Hagen (eds), *Mythos Vampir – Bissige Lektüren* (Bonn, 2018), 45–56.
71. See Joachim Hösler, *Slowenien. Von den Anfängen bis zur Gegenwart* (Regensburg, 2006).
72. Erasmus Francisci, *Der Höllische Proteus oder Tausendkünstige Versteller, vermittelst Erzehlung der vielfältigen Bild-Verwechslungen Erscheinender Gespenster, Werffender und polternder Geister, gespenstischer Vorzeichen der Todes-Fälle, Wie auch Andrer abentheurlicher Händel, arglistiger Possen, und seltsamer Aufzüge dieses verdammten Schauspielers, und, Von theils Gelehrten, für den menschlichen Lebens-Geist irrig-angesehenen Betriegers (nebenst vorberichtlichem Grund-Beweis der Gewißheit / daß es würcklich Gespenster gebe)* (Nuremberg, 1690), 10, 253–300.
73. Irmgard Palladino, *Johann Weichard von Valvasor (1641–1693): Protagonist der Wissenschaftsrevolution der Frühen Neuzeit. Leben, Werk und Nachlass* (Vienna, 2008), 96, 99.
74. Giacomoa Filippo Tommasini, 'De Commentari storici-geografici della Provincia dell'Istria', *Archeografo triestino. Raccolta di opusculi e notizie per Trieste e per l'Istria* 4 (1837): 1–554, at 519; *Bajke in pripovedke slovenskega ljudstva: Z mitološkim uvodom uredil Jakob Kelemina* (Ljubljana, 1930), 35–40. Cf. Maja Bošković-Stulli, 'Kresnik – Krsnik, ein Wesen aus der kroatischen und slowenischen Volksüberlieferung', *Fabula. Zeitschrift für Erzählforschung* 3 (1960): 275–98; Zmago Šmitek, 'Kresnik: An Attempt at a Mythological Reconstruction', *Studia Mythologica Slavica* 1 (1998): 93–118.
75. V. Jagić, 'Vukòdlak – Kodlàk vor Gericht', *Archiv für slawische Philologie* 6 (1882): 618–20.
76. Valvasor, *Ehre*, vol. 6, 335/336.
77. Ibid., vol. 6, 335; vol. 8, 758; vol. 11, 317–19.
78. Ibid., vol. 11, 317.
79. Ibid., 319.

CHAPTER 2

Vampirism in the East

The Upyr or Upiór in Kievan Rus' and in Poland-Lithuania
The Roots of Vampirism among the Eastern Slavs

The traces that the belief in vampires have left in the early history of the Russians and Poles can today only be identified in indistinct terms. A few examples of the use of the old Russian term *upir'* (Russian *upyr'*, Ukrainian *upyr*, Belarusian *vupor*) can be found in the eleventh and twelfth centuries. In the course of the ongoing Christianization of the Kievan Rus' from the ninth century and the increasingly anti-Latin writings in the Grand Duchy of Muscovy, which was growing in strength in the fourteenth century, the term gradually disappeared from use. It is also worth bearing in mind that the historically Russian lands that fell under the sovereignty of the Mongol Horde from the thirteenth century to the fifteenth century were cut off from West European developments. The word then first reappeared at the end of the seventeenth century in the old Polish variant of *upir* or *upier* (modern Polish *upiór*).

It is likely that the belief in vampires survived among the Ruthenians living on the territory of the Grand Duchy of Lithuania and the Polish Noble Republic, that is, among the Eastern Slavic and Orthodox sections of the population from which the Ukrainians and Belarusians were to emerge in the fifteenth and sixteenth centuries. In the concept of the 'unclean' (*nechistye*) dead – those who had been murdered, committed suicide or died at a young age – and that of the 'hidden' (*zalozhnye*) dead – buried in the undergrowth – lay the foundations of an Eastern Slavic variant of the 'Magia posthuma'.[1] In any case, the Estonian-American Finno-Ugrist and Slavist Felix J. Oinas argued that the term 'upir' was replaced in the theological literature of the Tsardom of Russia in the sixteenth and seventeenth centuries by the term 'heretic' (*eretik*), which had polemic connotations and referred to 'man-eaters'.[2] Against this backdrop, German scholars of myths in the era of nationalism argued that the vampire had entered into Prussia across the Eastern border, whereas Polish ethnologists continue to argue to the present day, with good reason, that the concept as such had its roots in Russian lands and was first made well-known in Polish popular culture through the ghosts stories of the Romantic period (see the section entitled 'Demonic Figures in East and East Central Europe' in Chapter 4).

Revenants in Premodern Russia

A first reference to conceptions about revenants can be found in the oldest Eastern Slavic chronicle, drawn up during the flowering of Kievan Rus' in the second decade of the twelfth century, the so-called *Primary Chronicle*, in the entries for the years 1015 and 1044. The first reports on the death of St Vladimir the Great, who accepted baptism following his Damascene conversion and brought Christianity to Kievan Rus', adopting the Byzantine Orthodox rite. Despite this, however, his retinue – clearly fearful about the return of his animated corpse – refused to carry him out over the threshold of his house in order to bring him to his laying out in the church. Instead, they broke a hole through the ceiling and lifted out his body, which had been wrapped in a carpet, with the help of a winch. The second entry indicates that Prince Vseslav the Sorcerer of Polotsk was born with a caul. In medieval times the presence of a caul at birth was sometimes described as a sign of good luck; by contrast, in modern folklore it was often seen as a signal of a potential revenant. In the chronicle, it serves as an explanation for the Prince's future bloodletting. Indeed, Vseslav undertook later a couple of military campaigns against the princes of Kiev and in this context again was described by the Kievan chroniclers as the incarnation of a wizard, who was surrounded by all kinds of demonic symbols.[3]

The appearance of evil spirits is also noted elsewhere in the *Primary Chronicle*. However, as is the case with the burial of Vladimir or the caul of Vseslav, the apparitions remain somewhat hazy in the Orthodox versions when compared with the Icelandic sagas (see the section entitled 'The Revenant of the Middle Ages' in Chapter 1). According to the *Primary Chronicle*, the Rus' had not only entered into conflict with the neighbouring steppe peoples, but were also afflicted by a series of droughts and fires. As a result, in 1092, epidemics began to spread, meaning that no less than 7,000 coffins had to be manufactured. Against this backdrop, several unusual apparitions were reported in the city of Polotsk in present-day Belarus.

At night, invisible demons began to carry out their activities in the streets. When someone took it upon themselves to investigate the racket that he could hear coming from the street, he mysteriously became infected with a fatal disease. As a result, the townsfolk began to barricade themselves in their houses. Thereafter, the demons also began to appear at daytime, although their presence could only be discerned through the hoof prints that their horses had left behind.

The explanation of the *Primary Chronicle* is that 'the dead [*navi*] struck the people of Polotsk'.[4] The *navi* (singular *nav'e*) were the invisible souls of deceased persons. Revenancy was therefore not entirely unknown in ancient Rus'.

Figure 2.1 'The dead struck the people of Polotsk'.
This miniature, originally dating from the thirteenth century and preserved in copies of the fifteenth-century *Radziwiłł Chronicle*, depicts the illusory apparitions that caused widespread panic among the inhabitants of the present-day Belarusian town in the plague year of 1092.
Source: *Radzilovskaia letopis*, sheet 124. Used with permission from the Library of the Russian Academy of Sciences in St. Petersburg, signature 34.5.30.

However, one cannot talk of vampirism in the sense of the Western conception of bloodsuckers.

Nevertheless, the Old Russian word for vampire, *upir'*, did appear indirectly in the context of a translation of the Old Testament Book of the Prophets. The epilogue to a 1047 version of this translation was signed by a certain 'Pop Upir' Likhoj'. This name has been handed down in manuscripts from the fifteenth century that were found at the north Russian Kirillo-Belozersky Monastery and at the Trinity Lavra Monastery at Sergiyev Posad, close to Moscow.

The Swedish Slavic scholar Anders Sjöberg traces the peculiar first name of the 'Pop', or priest, back to a rune carver from Uppland called Ofeigr Upir. According to Sjöberg, 'ofeigr' or 'likhyi' means 'not destined for death' or 'going beyond the measure' (however, in modern Russian, both can also mean 'reckless' or 'bringing disaster'). Sjöberg therefore believes that the author of the epilogue was a person whom fate had granted with a long life. Upir, on the other hand, was a name given in Sweden to a loud person. Therefore, it can be assumed that a north Russian Pop of Scandinavian origin called Upir Likhoi had once worked in Uppland as a missionary and made a living by carving runes. In 1100, following the triumph of Catholicism in Scandinavia, his presence there became superfluous. However, the word *upir'* remained connected with his name thereafter and was later used as a designation for vampires.

The concept of the vampire probably became more concrete in the period following the break-up of Kievan Rus' into its constituent subprincipalities in the eleventh to thirteenth centuries, when a translation was made of a fourth-century sermon on heathen ideas by Gregory of Nazianzus, furnished with new 'explanations'. These explanations, which became known as 'word on idols' (*slovo ob idolakh*), have been handed down in manuscripts from the sixteenth and seventeenth centuries. These use the terms *upir'* and *beregina* (river fairy) as expressions of a pre-Christian cult of the dead. It is probable that they refer, on the one hand, to the souls of those who died in a violent manner and, on the other, to the souls of those who had drowned.

When these explanations were discovered in the mid nineteenth century in a collection at the Kirillo-Belosersky Monastery, the experts drew upon contemporary popular traditions in their interpretations of them and referred to the wandering dead in the ancient Rus' culture.[5] It remains unclear whether the polarization between good and evil taken up in one of the 'explanations' was a device designed to enable the message of Jesus Christ to break through or whether it can be seen as evidence of the development of a belief in vampires from the combination of animistic ideas with the practice of burial in the ground. After all, no less a person than Tsar Ivan IV, known in English as 'the Terrible', used the term *upir'* in a 1573 missive to the Kirillo-Belosersky Monastery, including it in a list of other swear words such as 'fool' and 'evil spirit'.[6]

Revenants in Poland-Lithuania

In the territory of Poland-Lithuania, a political entity that was constituted on a Roman Catholic foundation, first as a personal union following the Union of Krewo in 1385 and then as a political union following the 1569 Union of Lublin, and that at one stage stretched from the Baltic to the Black Sea, the issue of vampirism first emerges in the era of confessionalization. The devastating wars between Sweden, Russia and Poland in the 1650s and 1660s became known by contemporaries as 'The Deluge'. The Polish Noble Republic (Rzeczpospolita) was characterized by the powers of a parliament (Sejm), which was founded, from 1505, on the principle of legislative competence (*Nihil novi*) and, from 1652, on the further principle of unanimity (*liberum veto*). Since the central powers were politically very weak, the Catholic Church assumed a particular role as a moral authority and as a force for preserving order.[7] Reports of revenancy, which often arose in the region of Western Ukraine, are therefore less often found in records of court cases than in questions posed by local clergymen to higher clerical authorities, often abroad, and then, in the era of the Enlightenment in particular, in theological treatises on superstitious beliefs. Here, reference was more commonly made to 'sorcerers' (*strzygoń*) than to 'vampires' (*upiór*). The sources seem to reveal that vampirism was predominantly a subject for intellectual discussion.

The first case, which still carries undertones of the belief in *nachzehrers* (see the section entitled 'The Nachzehrer of the Early Modern Period' in Chapter 1), is outlined by the physician Hercules Saxonia, from Padua. In his work *De plica quam Poloni gwoździec, Roxolani kołtunum vocant* (*On the Vistula Braid, Which the Poles Call a Pin, and the Sarmatians a Tuft of Hair*), published in 1600, he referred to an outbreak of plague in the city of Lwów in 1572: the epidemic was soon linked to a woman who had recently been buried in the neighbourhood and who had been accused of practising black magic during her lifetime. When her grave was opened up, not only was she found in a naked state, but the corpse also gave the impression that she had been eating her shroud. Following her decapitation, according to the tried and tested custom, the pestilence came to an end.[8]

It is possible that Pierre des Noyers, the Secretary to the French princess Marie Louise Gonzaga, who married the King of Poland in 1645, was inspired by this case when he wrote to the astronomer Ismael Bouillard on 13 December 1659 about a marvellous 'disease from the Ukraine', which had been attested to by several respectable persons. Apparently, a person who had been born with a full set of teeth had begun, after his death, to devour his burial shroud and his hands. At the same time, his relatives had also started to die. Therefore, as a result of these posthumous activities, his grave was opened up and his head was removed from his body. In contrast to Hercules Saxonia, des Noyers refers in his depiction to the Ruthenian term 'Upior' (Ukrainian *upyr*; Polish *upiór*) and the Polish expression 'Friga' (Polish *strzyga*).[9]

The second case, which already reflects more recognizably vampiric conceptions, is dated 1674. It is to be found on the final page of a 1692 edition of *Summa Angelica de casibus conscientiae* (*The Angelic* [i.e. Angelo Carletti's] *Summary of Cases*, first edn 1486), held by the University of Toruń. This is a handwritten note, entitled 'Casus de Strigis' ('The Case of Witches'). Referring to the colloquial Polish term *strzygoń* (fem. *strzyga*), it reports on a man from the village of Trzeszawa, near the small town of Bodzentyn in the county of Kielce, who allegedly left his grave after his death and strangled and beat his relatives. Upon the opening of his grave, a corpse seemingly full of fresh blood was discovered. The turning over of the body onto its stomach, carried out according to established customs, did not have the desired effect. On the contrary, the dead man apparently visited his son the following night and beat him to death. Thereafter, the corpse was decapitated, even though the priest had his doubts about the legality of this undertaking.[10]

The third case was discussed in France in 1693/1694, possibly in response to a query from a Pole to the renowned theological faculty at the Sorbonne, as Augustin Calmet leads us to believe in his printing of three otherwise nonverifiable documents from the region. In any case, the supposed incident of bloodsucking on the territory of Poland was also reflected in several editions of the Parisian *Mercure galant*.

According to Calmet a young woman in the vicinity of an unidentified place in Poland was being tormented by the spirit of her dead mother. Whereas the body of the daughter increasingly seemed to be wasting away, that of the mother was revealed, upon the opening of her grave, to be remarkably fresh and lifelike. It was still considerably supple, somewhat bloated, and reddish in colour. After a stake was driven through the heart of the dead woman and her head was cut off, the daughter began to recover. All of this took place without the knowledge of the priest. The question was therefore now raised of how a confessor should be expected to act in such a situation.

In their opinion, the Parisian professors concluded that both the desecration of the grave and the robbing of the corpse should be regarded as serious sins, for which absolution could not be granted. Furthermore, they also accused the grave-desecrators indirectly of having entered into a pact with the devil. This was because the mixing of the blood of the harmful corpse with flour in order to bake bread, the consumption of which was believed to offer a defence against dangerous illness, showed that devilish misdeeds were being carried out with godless impunity.[11]

A French Debate on Polish Revenants

More or less independently of this, the *Mercure galant* also initiated a similar debate, which had a somewhat marginal note as its starting point.[12] In an edition from March 1693 and then in a separately published study *A Justification of the Divining Rod* (*La Baguette justifiée*), the theologian and mathematician Claude Comiers offered the thesis that the souls of the murdered could influence a diviner so much as to reveal to him their murderer. However, because of his early death, Comiers was never able to expand upon his planned comparison with the Polish cases. He merely pointed out that the Poles decapitated their dead when these were believed to be devouring their shrouds or, through telepathic forces, drinking the blood of their relatives.[13]

In May 1693, the same Pierre des Noyers who had already commented on the Ukrainian cases thirty years earlier offered his response to the thesis of Comiers. In the meantime, he now placed the scene of the action in Poland and Russia, and in particular in the Ruthenian (i.e. Belarusian and Ukrainian-inhabited) territories of the Noble Republic. In dramatic fashion, he now claimed that the so-called 'striges' (masc. *strzygoń*; fem. *strzyga*), also referred to in common parlance as 'upierz' (masc. *upir*; fem. *upierzyca*), left their graves from midday to midnight in order to drink the blood of both people and cattle. The consumption that this caused among the victims would inevitably lead to death and, since no one was certain of being spared from this fate, it was necessary to open the suspected corpse's grave and to draw out the blood through opening up the heart. This blood would then usually be mixed with bread and given to the living for the purposes of disinfection.[14] These claims were confirmed in a report on the curious Polish cases that appeared in the Parisian *Mercure historique et politique* in June 1693.[15]

Eventually, in January and February 1694, the lawyer Marigner published a two-part treatise in *Mercure galant* under the heading of 'Creatures des elemens' ('Creatures of the Elements') or 'Sur les stryges de Russie' ('On the Striges in Russia'). From the consumption that afflicted the supposed victims of the bloodsuckers and from their recovery after their alleged destruction, Marigner concluded that it was clear that there could be no question of demonic work at play. Rather, he made the assumption that there was an interaction between corporeal and spiritual forces in the relationship between the living and the dead. Within the context of demons and damned souls, the 'Russian' vampirism constituted at best an impression of divine punishment for superstitious or even barbaric behaviour. After death, the souls were simply being prevented from entering heaven and, as such, bloodsucking is not presented as a life-threatening epidemic, but rather as a moral appeal.[16]

A Review of Polish Nachzehrer Conceptions

As a result, two Polish Jesuits, Jerzy Gengell and Gabriel Rzączyński, both took up a stance on the phenomenon. In his work *Eversio Atheismi* (*The Refutation of Atheism*), published in 1716, Gengell commented on reports about the suppleness and mobility of corpses. He called upon eyewitnesses from Poland, Russia and Lithuania, whom he believed to be credible and who claimed to have seen seemingly intact corpses that gave the impression that they were devouring their shrouds and parts of their own body. In this context, he adhered to a radicalized variant of German *nachzehrer* conceptions. He therefore reported that, among other things, a suspicious body would move about and strangle people. In providing a designation for these harm-inflicting dead persons, Gengell drew upon the supposedly Ruthenian terms of *upier* (for males) and *upierzyca* (for females). In etymological terms, these words can be traced back to 'fluff' or 'feather' and can thus be linked to flying night-demons. Accordingly, their posthumous activities were brought about by the possession of the dead body by a demon. So long as the black magic continued, the corpse could not decay and the soul could not escape. In order to set the process of decomposition into motion, the common people turned to decapitation. Gengell saw a certain logic in this, since, through this action, not only would the living be delivered from the plague, but the dead person would be also freed from the demon. However, Gengell also admitted that auditors from the Holy See only accepted medical remedies and exorcism, among others, the donation of sacraments and the invocation of the saints.[17] Although Rzączyński in his 1721 *Historia naturalis curiosa regni Poloniae* (*Natural History of the Curiosities of the Kingdom of Poland*) merely repeated Gengell's characterization of the nachzehrer and revenants in a more concise form, it proved to be his work that was more commonly cited thereafter.[18]

The Ruthenian – that is, the Eastern Slavic – origins of the Polish conceptions of revenancy were once again specified in the article 'Von dem Polnischen Upiertz oder sich selbst fressenden Todten, und der daraus entstandenen Furcht vor Pest und Vieh-Sterben' ('On the Polish Upiertz or Self-Devouring Dead, and the Fear of Plague and Cattle-Deaths Resulting from This'), which appeared in January 1722 in the journal *Sammlung von Natur- und Medicin- Wie auch hierzu gehörigen Kunst- und Literatur-Geschichten* (*Collection of Natural and Medical Tales, Including the Art and Literature on This*). In this article, reports from Podolia – a region in southwestern Ukraine – which had been published in Warsaw newspapers in December 1721 were offered as evidence to expose the nachzehrer conceptions in German lands as a fraud and to explain them away as cases of suspended animation. The occasion for this was a commentary on the subject by the Lutheran pastor and botanist Georg Andreas Helwing from the East Prussian garrison town of Angerburg in Northern Masuria. He reported that, according to letters from the town of Kamieniec Podolski, Podolia was afflicted by a cattle disease, the cause of which was identified as the machinations of a supposed 'upiertz'. According to the newspapers, this was a dead person who was devouring itself posthumously and who had summoned up the plague, for which it had been decapitated. Helwing saw the newspaper reports to be an expression of the superstitions that were rife among Jews and nonbelievers – by which he clearly meant Orthodox Christians. Paradoxically, however, he could not resist pointing out that his own homeland could have served as a model for these supposedly Polish bad habits, since graves had also been opened in Harschen near Angerburg in 1710 in order to ward off a plague. Yet, since the gravediggers had not been able to find any suspects, they had prepared a corpse to meet the superstitious expectations. However, punishment would swiftly follow, since, following the posthumous execution of this corpse, those who had been involved in making it up in this manner also died as a result of infection.[19]

The Vrykolakas among the Greeks in the Ottoman Empire

Medieval Grave Desecrations

Contrary to the common belief that the vampire is a genuine creature of the Balkan Slavs, hardly any sources can be found to support this for the time period before the eighteenth century. In medieval Serbia, only one indirect reference can be found, at best, in the Legal Code of Tsar Stefan Dušan, under whose rule the Serbian Empire was able to extend its dominant position in the Balkans to an impressive extent from 1331 onwards. At his coronation as Tsar in 1346, Stefan also appointed a Serbian Patriarch. In return, the Legal Code of 1349 envisaged a role for the Tsar as defender of the Orthodox Church. However, until the arrival into Europe of the Ottomans from Asia Minor, the only real threat came from the Catholics who, according to Orthodox doctrine, had deviated from the resolutions of the ecumenical councils of the first Christian millennium.

Interestingly, Stefan's Legal Code recognizes the exhumation and burning of the dead as a criminal offence, which demonstrated that such collective actions were being carried with the participation of the local clergy. Village communities that were found guilty of these offences were forced to pay a fine and the priest responsible was to be defrocked.[20] In this context, it remains unclear whether the primary motivation was the combatting of pagan or pre-Christian traditions, in which revenants played a role, or whether this was rather a measure that was directed against the marginalization of scapegoats, who were held to have been responsible for the Black Death, which arrived in the Balkans via Constantinople in 1348.

The case of a female revenant named Priba, which was documented in the Hungarian-ruled Croatian port city of Zadar in June 1403, can be interpreted accordingly. A surviving note from Governor Pavel Pavlović reports on the unusual occurrences on the island of Pašman, just off the coast: since the inhabitants claimed that they were being terrorized by the deceased Priba, they were permitted to open her grave. Upon uncovering a body that had not begun to decompose, a stake was then driven through her heart. Although the original Latin note did not provide any special designation for this harmful dead woman, when this source was published in 1896 in the journal *Zbornik za narodni život i običaje južnih slavena* (*Collection on the Popular Life and Manners of the South Slavic People*) the editor, the Croatian historian Vjekoslav Klaić, claimed that the story represented an early example of a 'vampire' (*vukodlak*).[21]

Excommunication and the Incorruptibility of the Body in the Orthodox Patriarchate

Overall, vampirism seems first to have become relevant in Southeastern Europe following the onset of the Ottoman expansion in the region from 1354 onwards. After the conquest of Constantinople by Mehmed II 1453, the Orthodox Patriarchate there became subordinate to the Ottoman Empire, but the Orthodox Church was able to retain a certain degree of autonomy in relation to the affairs of the community.[22] According to Karen Hartnup's thesis, the Orthodox Patriarchate increasingly drew upon excommunication as a means for social disciplining from the mid fifteenth century, since they claimed to hold the monopoly on decisions concerning the separation of the body and the soul, which represented a precondition for entry into paradise. The twist herein lay in the fact that, according to Orthodox doctrine, the incorruptible body of an excommunicated person entrapped the soul of the deceased permanently. Whereas the people demanded the destruction of allegedly harmful bodies on the pyre, the Church saw this as not only a surrender of the dead person's possibility of salvation and their condemnation to damnation, but also a questioning of their mediatory role between the earthly sphere and the afterlife. On the one hand, therefore, the Church stylized the *vrykolakas* as a devilish illusion, whilst, on the other hand, they retained the sole means for destroying a revenant – that is, through the granting of absolution – for themselves.[23] The numerous tales of revenancy that emerge from the Greek community in the period before the discovery of the vampire therefore need to be interpreted against the backdrop of the conflict between the official doctrine of the Orthodox Church and popular beliefs.

In the seventeenth and eighteenth centuries, a legend based on the relationship between excommunication by the Church and the nondecomposition of corpses did in fact stir up considerable attention among experts on Greece. This tale was published in 1584 by the classicist Martin Crusius from Tübingen in *Turcograeciae*, a collection of texts detailing the situation of the Greeks under Ottoman rule, published in both Greek and Latin. This story, which was dated back to the patriarchy of Manuel Malaxos, apparently convinced no less an authority than Mehmed the Conqueror himself of the legitimacy of the Patriarch's omnipotence in relation to excommunication and absolution.

The background to the legend was a question posed by the Patriarch Maximos III, who was in office from 1476 to 1482, as to whether the nondecomposed bodies of excommunicated persons could decay following the granting of absolution by a Bishop. Maximos recalled the case of the widow of a priest named Clero who, despite the repeated warnings of the Patriarch from 1454 to 1464, Gennadios II Scholarios, had continued to carry out wicked acts.

Clero's widow even went so far as to accuse the Patriarch of violence towards her. Thus defamed, the Patriarch called upon the judgment of God in the Holy Mass. Should the widow have spoken the truth and find mercy from God, her body would decompose after her death, he proclaimed in his sermon. If not, she would be threatened with excommunication from the community of believers and a condition of permanent corporeal incorruptibility. Forty days after the sermon, the woman died and, more than a decade later, Patriarch Maximos ordered her grave to be opened. As expected, an intact and blackened body was revealed, which had the appearance of a swollen kettledrum. In order to prevent any manipulations, the Sultan took the corpse into safekeeping. (This serves to make the manner in which the Patriarch passed the test posed by

Mehmed the Conqueror seem all the more convincing.) Precisely at that moment in the subsequent church service at which the Patriarch granted absolution to the sinful woman, those present heard, as if in a miracle, the sound of disintegrating bones. With the decomposition of her body, therefore, the dead woman had clearly received divine forgiveness. Freed from the torments of hell, her soul was now able to enter paradise.

As the heart of the tale, Malaxos maintains that Mehmed the Conqueror, when told of these occurrences, recognized the primacy of Christianity over Islam.[24]

An early testimony to the widely held beliefs of the population was printed in *Stephan Gerlachs deß Aelteren Tage-Buch* (*The Diary of Stephan Gerlach the Elder*) in 1674. Gerlach was preacher and chaplain at the Embassy of the Holy Roman Empire in Constantinople from 1573 to 1578. In his description of his travels in the region, he mentions a case of a Greek man, from the year 1575, who was burned two years after his death due to suspicions that he was wandering about at night and killing people. In this context, Gerlach also reports that the Greeks were convinced that the bodies of those who had received the last rites from a priest would be preserved from decay for thirty years. On the other hand, in an entry from 1577, Gerlach also included the statement of an interpreter who claimed that the bodies of those who had been sinners in their lifetimes or who had been excommunicated from the Church could not decompose. The devil took possession of their bodies at night and terrorized the living, threatening them with life-endangering illnesses. It was therefore widespread practice for these allegedly harmful corpses to be dug up and burned, often even with the participation of priests.[25]

Harmful Dead in the Ottoman Empire

Indigenous tales on the phenomenon of nondecomposed bodies or the monstrous deeds of revenants are rare in the era before the discovery of the vampire by the European Enlightenment, but a few occasional examples from Greek and Ottoman quills can be found. Two of these are the rules for the behaviour of monks on the scared Mount Athos on the Eastern Greek Chalkidiki peninsula and the legal guidelines for Muslims living in the Ottoman Balkans.[26]

The practice of impaling and burning the nondecomposed corpses of those who had been accused of posthumous activities was explicitly criticized in the *Investigations of Markus of Serres on Revenants*, which has been preserved in a sixteenth-century codex from the Iviron Monastery and that was published in 1904 in the journal *Ellinomnimon* (*Greek Memory*). The subheading, in which the Church claims for itself the prerogative of interpretation, is significant: 'the Holy Church does not accept that they cause plagues and eat the living, as is commonly thought'.[27] It is also striking that, while both black magic and the eating of humans is referred to, there is no mention either of black sabbaths or bloodsucking.

In a missive on the exorcism of demons that, according to a late nineteenth-century catalogue at the Xeropotamou Monastery, which originated from the sixteenth century, but that its translator Charles Stewart dated back to the late seventeenth or early eighteenth century, a section that has unfortunately only been partially preserved writes of the vrykolakas: 'He is not real, but a creation of the devil, and he is a creature of our imagination arising from the imperfection of our faith.' Upon the discovery of a nondecomposed body, a mass and a funeral banquet were to be held. Thereafter, it was necessary to say prayers over the corpse and sprinkle it with holy water. With this statement, the source breaks off.[28] It can therefore only be speculated upon as to whether a degenerate soul can be granted entry into paradise through the lifting of the excommunication or whether it was considered permissible to preserve the living from harm through the destruction of a cursed corpse.

Since the conduct of their Christian subjects not only posed a public nuisance but could also serve to corrupt Muslim citizens, the Ottoman authorities also felt themselves compelled to turn their attention to the issue. As early as the mid sixteenth century, the legal scholar Mehmed Ebussuud Efendi already provided several responses to this issue in his legal opinion (*fatwā*). He considered the reanimation of corpses in the grave as a mystery underlying the laws of God and beyond human comprehension. However, with reference to 'infidels', i.e. non-Muslims, he found that harm-inflicting revenants, inspired by the intrinsic wickedness of their lifetime, were a phenomenon that had to be treated seriously. Since he assumed that deceased Muslims could not be drawn into this suffering, he warned against the desecration of graves, recommending instead that the authorities be consulted. On the other hand, in the Christian revenant who was alleged to have brought about a series of deaths in a village near Selanik, the present-day Thessaloniki, he recognized a danger for other nonbelievers and took traditional defensive measures such as impaling, decapitation and incineration very much into consideration.[29]

Consequently, the poet Mustafa Cinânî also tackled this subject when he included four ghost stories in his anthology of fairy tales from Anatolia, Africa and the Balkans, composed at the request of the Sultan Murad III, *Bedâyiü'l-âsâr (Precious Tales)*. In one of these, he writes of the fortress of Dıraç, the Albanian Durrës, where souls supposedly entered into the bodies of the dying and, speaking in their voices, approach their relatives for intercession. The narrator draws no distinction between Muslims and Christians here. In both cases, either a legal scholar (Ulama) or a priest (Pope) is called upon, who tackles the issue by reciting from the Qu'ran or the Bible. The workings of the Almighty can be discerned behind all of this, and these stories all seem to be concerned with a generally accepted truth.

In another tale, from the Peloponnese, a Muslim maidservant seeks assistance from the scribe Piri Dede. The girl claimed that, three or four months after his burial, her former master had begun to abuse her sexually. Although the scribe is able to ward off the spirit by daylight with an iron stake, the maid follows her master into the grave ten days later.[30]

On the one hand, the Ottomans had to respond to the fears of the population, but, on the other hand, despite their scepticism, they never fundamentally tackled the question of revenancy. Initially, it remained unclear as to whether this was an expression of Ottoman tolerance towards their Orthodox subjects or whether the Muslim community itself had also become infected with this hysteria. At the very least, the vigilantism that was evident in dealing with alleged revenants constituted a challenge to the competences that the Orthodox Patriarchate in Constantinople claimed for itself in this respect.

In 1701, the Judge of Edirne reported to the Grand Vizier about the fears among the population of a village near to a town on the right bank of the Maritsa, the present-day Greek Marásia, that sorcery or magic (*cādū*) was afoot. The dead man concerned was even a Muslim, and evil spirits were said to be carrying out their wicked deeds at his grave. In his report, the judge referred to the legal opinion of Mehmed Ebussuud Efendi, who had seemed to accept the permissibility of the desecration of the corpse, at least with regard to Christian revenants. The Grand Vizier therefore established a commission, which reported a slight change in the position of the dead Muslim's corpse as well as a slight reddish colouring of the body. What happened thereafter is unknown. In the case of a Muslim woman who had also been accused of revenancy, the Grand Vizier ordered the head of the police to set up an examination of the body by four women and to take countermeasures, where necessary, in order to placate the fears of the population. It is remarkable, first, that vampirism seemed to have transferred from Christians to Muslims and also that, in the interests of maintaining the peace, the Ottoman authorities seemed to demonstrate a certain tolerance in their attitudes towards the desecration of graves.[31]

The Vrykolakas from the Perspective of Western Theologians

The issue of Greek revenants and the instrumentalization of excommunication by the Orthodox Patriarchate in Constantinople in this respect increasingly captured the interest of Catholic theologians and Western travellers to the region. The background to this were the ongoing attempts of Rome to work on the idea of a possible union of the Catholic and Orthodox Churches. These found expression in the establishment of the Pontifical Greek College of Saint Athanasius in Rome in 1577 for seminarians from Southeastern Europe and the Middle East, and in the foundation of the Congregation for the Propagation of the Faith in 1622, which sought to provide pastoral care among the Catholic diaspora and to promote dialogue with the other Christian confessions.[32]

A key example of the Catholic interest in Orthodox attitudes towards revenancy is provided by Leo Allatius. This convert to Catholicism, born on the island of Chios in the eastern Aegean, just off the coast of Asia Minor, made a name for himself as a theologian and librarian with his research on the Orthodox tradition in the Ottoman Empire. In this he saw himself as a mediator between the two Christian confessions, which had been going their own way since the final schism of 1054. Since Allatius had already moved permanently to Italy at the age of nine, his knowledge of his Greek homeland was largely academic and did not necessarily derive from his own empirical observations. He studied at the Pontifical Greek College in Rome, where he later also taught. In 1623, because of his wide reading, he was appointed librarian of Cardinal Francesco Barberini and, in 1661, he moved to the Vatican Library. Due to his profession, Allatius was likely well acquainted both with the Catholic literature on revenants and with Protestant teachings on nachzehrers.[33]

In his 1645 book *De templis Graecorum recentioribus* (*Newer Temples of the Greeks*), Allatius referred to Malaxos' tale of the miraculous conversion of Mehmed the Conqueror, thus placing the phenomenon of vampirism on the agenda of Vatican theologians for the first time. In this he uses the Greek terms 'vrukolakas' or 'burcolaca' and traces these back to the expressions 'vurka' or 'burka'. Both refer to the mouldiness of decaying bodies, accompanied by a bestial stench, although Allatius sought to apply these unpleasant properties only to a 'very wicked and criminal person'. In truth, however, he was not at all concerned with making a moral appeal. Rather, he sought to highlight a previously unknown characteristic of the nondecomposed corpses of excommunicate persons, which popular belief held to be true. Since their bloated corpses, covered with leathery skin, could be struck like a kettledrum or timpani, he came up with the designation of *tympaniaios*. He reported a case that he himself had witnesses as a child on Chios. One day, the children of the village chanced upon an opened grave beneath the stairs of the church and had discovered a nondecomposed body, which had the appearance of a timpani. Neither sticks nor stones seemed to have an effect on the corpse. After a few days, the clergy then closed the grave.

In accordance with official Church doctrine, Allatius rejected the popular belief that revenancy was the result of a demon taking possession of the body of a dead person, particularly where it was alleged that the demon spurred on the corpse to leave the grave, preferably at night, and to haunt the living. According to popular belief, the corpse would knock on doors, calling out in a loud voice. Since anyone who answered this call could be expected to die shortly thereafter, the inhabitants did their utmost to ignore it. Nevertheless, it was not only the voice or the touch of the revenant that could prove fatal, but also their glance.

Since the mass deaths took the form of an epidemic, the affected villagers called for all those graves that were under suspicion to be opened up in the presence of a priest. Where a nondecomposed and bloated corpse was revealed, this was driven through with a stake and burned. In order to denounce these customs as superstitions, Allatius cited a nomocanon from a collection of Church teachings, which portrayed the witnesses' supposed impressions to be the work of the devil and that defined the desecration of the grave as a sin.[34]

Finally, Allatius sought to resolve the contradiction between the belief in the nondecomposition of the corpses of excommunicate dead persons in the Greek Church on the one hand and the belief in the incorruptibility of the bodies of the saints, held by the Catholic Church, on the other. In this Allatius presupposed the visibility of the corpse, be this in its laying out before the funeral or during a reburial. He argued in phenotypical terms, claiming that the bodies of the excommunicates were not only bloated like a kettledrum, but also spread fear through their sheer hideousness; the bodies of the pious, by contrast, invited adoration through their beauty and pleasant fragrance.[35]

Also of interest is a thought that Allatius was to explore further in his 1655 work *De utriusque ecclesiae occidentalis atque orientalis perpetua in dogmate de Purgatorio consensione* (*On the Continuing Correspondence between the Churches of the West and the East in their Teachings on Purgatory*). In this he sought to present excommunication and the captivation of the soul in a nondecomposable, drum-like corpse (*tympaniaios*), as a third or 'other place' between heaven and hell, which comes something close to the Catholic doctrine of purgatory.[36]

The term of 'vrukolakas' used by Allatius was taken up by other writers in the seventeenth and eighteenth centuries (however, in keeping with modern spelling, this term will be rendered in the following as 'vrykolakas'). First the Jesuit François Richard took a critical look at the issue in his *Relation de ce qui s'est passé de plus remarquable a Saint-Erini* (*Report on the Remarkable Events on the Island of Santorini*), published in 1657. As a 'missionary' for the Congregation for the Propagation of the Faith, Richard was expected to keep himself out of political discussions, and to integrate and adapt himself culturally, since the Congregation was seeking a potentially productive cooperation with the Orthodox Church on the territory of the Ottoman Empire. Richard's report is therefore characterized by a certain restraint, although it is not entirely able to conceal a certain schoolmasterly tone.

Richard begins by describing the alleged possession of dead bodies by the devil and the supposed inflecting of harm upon the living that accompanied this. Exorcisms took place on Saturdays when, according to popular belief, the dead did not leave their graves. When this did not accelerate the process of decomposition, the heart was then taken out and the corpse burned. Time and again, according to the locals, the dead would come back to participate in the lives of their families, or to settle their worldly affairs. The shoemaker Alexander from the village of Pyrgos, for example, had continued to take care of his family after his death, until the intervention of his neighbours.

Richard also related the case of the usurer Ianettis. At the hour of his death, Ianettis, who had become reformed in the final year of his life, attempted to settle his remaining debts. However, since he was not able to do so, he then haunted the population posthumously, wreaking all kinds of havoc. Richard claimed to have been present at the exhumation himself and stated that he could only make out a very slow process of decay. It proved impossible to restrain the evil spirit through exorcism and it was only when the widow settled his remaining debts that the apparitions finally came to an end. In this context, Richard could not avoid the passing remark that, in terms of meeting his financial obligations, the revenant might serve as an example to French atheists.

Furthermore, Richard also reported on the merchant Patino from the island of Patmos. Patino had died on a journey to Anatolia and, despite having received a Christian burial on his home island, began to inflict harm upon his neighbours, who sought their salvation by sending his corpse back to Anatolia. However, on their journey to the mainland, the sailors stopped at the first uninhabited island and burned his body there. As an explanation for this, Richard points out that suspicious corpses were often banished to uninhabited islands since it was believed that revenants could not traverse seawater.

Finally, Richard mentions a dispute into which he entered with a local clergyman and in which they discussed examples of revenancy in both Orthodox and Muslim communities. Richard claimed that the Latins – that is, the Catholics – were protected from the attentions of the devil by the workings of the holy oil at the extreme unction, through the power of holy water and through the sacredness of their cemeteries. By contrast, the imagined vrykolakas symbolizes the eternal damnation of Orthodox sinners and their exclusion from the divine plan for salvation. In conclusion, and by way of analogy, Richard also moved on to discuss the role of purgatory in the Roman Catholic Church, although without explicitly mentioning Allatius or the tympaniaios. In the final analysis, posthumous activities could be traced back both to magic and to natural phenomena such as the oozing out of superfluous urine.[37]

The Vrykolakas and Western Travel Writers

Furthermore, the issue of nondecomposed bodies was also discussed in the second half of the seventeenth century by numerous travel writers who visited the Greek islands, although they did not contribute anything new to the debate. The first of these was the French linguist and botanist Jean de Thévenot, who undertook a tour of the eastern Mediterranean between 1655 and 1659. In his *Relation d'un voyage fait au Levant* (*Account of a Journey in the Levant*), published in 1664, he recalled what he had discovered about the nondecomposed bodies of excommunicates on Allatius' home island of Chios. The inhabitants of the settlement at St Helena believed that if it did not begin to decay within forty days, a dead corpse would transform into a 'zorzolacas' or 'nomolacas'. An informant had encountered a priest in April 1637, thirty miles from the town, who spoke of a corpse which had not shown any evidence of decomposition, even fifty days after the funeral. The only thing that had happened was that a worm had crawled out of the dead body's eye. The narrator did not relate this disgusting feature merely to spice up the grizzly scene; rather, this detail was interpreted as a trick through which the devil had sought to demonstrate how easy it was to enter a human body. Echoing Allatius' remarks, Thévenot also recounted that an undead spirit had been said to wander through a village inhabited by poor shepherds at night, knocking on doors and calling out the inhabitants by name, in order to then carry all those who answered his call with him into the realm of death within three days.[38]

The next contemporary witness was the English travel writer Paul Ricaut, who served as Secretary to the English Ambassador in Constantinople in the 1660s, and then in the 1670s headed up the Consulate in the predominantly Christian port city of Smyrna in Asia Minor. In 1679, Ricaut published *The Present State of the Greek and Armenian Churches, Anno Christi, 1678*. In this he addressed the issue of the incorruptibility of the corpses of excommunicates at considerable length. By contrast, he only mentioned posthumous activities in passing and revenants in the true sense are never really spoken of, and the typical local designation for the phenomenon is never even mentioned.

According to the Greek tradition, the bodies of excommunicates were possessed by an evil spirit who, on the one hand, prevented the decay of the body and, on the other hand, animated the 'living body' to provide itself with sustenance. In this context, Ricaut used the English verb 'walk' without explicitly describing the leaving of the grave. Nevertheless, he did report from hearsay that the dead bodies under discussion would still have a fresh and reddish complexion forty days after burial. When these corpses were driven through with a stake, a fresh stream of blood would spurt out. Here he pointed to the tale told by the preacher Sofronio from Smyrna.

In the light of some misdemeanour, a certain man from the Peloponnese had fled to the Cycladic island of Milos without, however, being able to escape excommunication. Following his death, the local peasants fell into panic at the onset of 'strange and unusual apparitions'. Upon opening the grave, they uncovered a corpse which was still seemingly fresh. In order to placate the supposed revenant, they filled his grave with fruits and nuts. According to the established tradition, Sofronio's fellow monks recommended that the body be cut up and cooked in wine. In the meantime, out of concern for his salvation, the friends of the dead man had undertaken, out of necessity, to bribe the clergy in order to gain a pardon from the Patriarch in Constantinople. The corpse then decayed precisely at that moment in the Church service when the Patriarch proclaimed absolution.

Ricaut also claims that he himself once had the opportunity to be present at the opening of the grave of a suspected revenant, whose supposed nightly apparitions had spread panic among the local villagers. However, he did not personally experience anything of these alleged activities or of the dead body's supposed consumption of food. Nevertheless, this did not surprise him, since such spectacles were common in Asia Minor six to seven days after death, among both Christians and Muslims.[39]

Finally, in 1717, the French botanist and travel writer Joseph Pitton Tournefort published *Relation d'un voyage du Levant* (*Account of a Voyage to the Levant*). At the bequest of King Louis XIV, he had undertaken a voyage from April 1700 to June 1702 that had taken him from Crete, via numerous Aegean islands, to Constantinople and, from there, further along the Black Sea coast and, by land, into Georgia and Armenia. In his chapter on the state of the Greek Church, Tournefort discussed the subject of the role of death and local burial rituals at greater length. He was particularly taken by the mourning women who, for a suitable fee, would give their all in providing a suitable accompaniment for the deceased person in their passage from this world into the afterlife and, hopefully, into paradise. Tournefort also bore witness to an actual case of supposed revenancy on the Cycladic island of Mykonos, and his encounter with a vrykolakas led him to make the mocking remark that the population, in order to prove the authenticity of posthumous activities, had presented him with the writings of the Jesuit Richard. Beyond this he had the following to report.

Two days after the burial of a peasant who had been killed in the surrounding fields, rumours began to spread in a village that he was moving about at night and wreaking havoc. At first the population found his antics amusing. However, the attempt to bring an end to the apparitions through the saying of a mass proved to be fruitless, although a gathering of local dignitaries nevertheless came to the resolution, at least for the time being, not to take any further measures. Ten days after the funeral, the grave was opened and a bungled attempt was made to extract the heart of the dead man. A disgusting stench clouded the senses of all present at the exhumation, the blood of the dead man was found to be red, and the body itself still felt warm. Following the burning of his heart, the farce surrounding the dead peasant degenerated even further. The corpse then flailed around wildly, visiting the houses in the village and emptying bottles and jars – in order to still his thirst, as Tournefort commented. Nevertheless, the whole situation was taken very seriously by the population and mass hysteria broke out. People deserted their homes and yards in order to sleep in the marketplace. The authorities did post guards, but the short-term arrests had little effect upon the so-called vagabonds. Eventually the corpse was burned on 1 January 1701. The local clergy declined to participate in this, out of fear of sanctions from the bishop. Thereafter, the Turks imposed a financial punishment upon the community.[40]

In his 1709 dissertation *De absolution mortuorum excommunicatorum seu tympanicorum in ecclesia Graeca* (*On the Absolution of Deceased Excommunicates or Tympaniaios in the Greek Church*) and then in his 1711 book *Eigentliche und wahrhafftige Abbildung der alten und neuen Griechischen Kirche* (*A Real and True Depiction of the Old and New Greek Church*), Johann Michael Heineccius, a pastor from Halle, also discussed the 'burcolaccas' depicted by Malaxos and Allatius, and the belief in the incorruptibility of the corpses of excommunicates at greater length.[41] Although Heineccius gathered together important information on the Greek vrykolakas, his arguments would find no place in the debates on the Southern Slavic vampires two decades later.

Excommunication and Vampirization in the Danubian Principalities

The ecumenical Patriarchate of Constantinople's confrontation with vampirism found a vivid echo in the second half of the seventeenth century in the discussions of clerics from the principalities of Moldovia and Wallachia, which were also under Ottoman sovereignty.

In his 1645 work *The Seven Sacraments of the Church* (*Sapte taine ale Bisericii*), for example, Varlaam Moțoc, the Metropolitan of Moldovia, also reported on the desecration of graves and on supposedly saturated 'vrykolakas' (*vârcolac*), drawing upon the Greek terminology.[42] The fact that the issue of revenancy was viewed as a primarily theological one is reflected in the discussions on demonic figures in popular belief that the former Voivode of Moldova, the polymath scholar Dimitrie Cantemir, who was working in St Petersburg from 1714 onwards, presented in his 1714 Latin-language *Descriptio Moldaviae* (*Description of Moldova*). This work, which was published in German in 1771 under the title of *Historisch-geographisch- und politische Beschreibung der Moldau* (*Historical, Geographical and Political Description of Moldova*), refers to figures such as the 'Dracul (Romanian *drac*) im Tal' (Dragon in the valley), i.e. a water spirit, 'Zburatorull' (Romanian *zburător* – drifting/shifting sand), i.e. an invisible spirit that would prey in particular on fiancées in the form of a handsome young man, 'Miaza nopte' (Romanian *miazănoapte* – North), i.e. a midnight ghost who was active at crossroads, particularly in the form of an animal, 'Striga' (Romanian *strigoica* – witch), i.e. an old hag who would kill babies and infants through black magic, and 'Prikolitsch' (Romanian *prikolici* – werewolf), i.e. a man who would transform into a wolf at night (falsely rendered in Cantemir's book as 'Trikolitsch').[43]

After all, the Statute Book of Wallachia, which was drawn up in 1652 on Byzantine foundations by Prince Matei Basarab, reflected upon 'sorcerers and witches' (*strigoi*) who, as a result of 'diabolic illusion' behaved in their graves as 'vrykolakas' (*vârcolac*). With regard to the vrykolakas, the Statute Book referred only to the phenomenon of the bloated corpse, whilst neglecting to address the issue of bloodsucking, which was seen to be a misconception.[44] Furthermore, the belief in vampires was also instrumentalized in interconfessional confrontations, as is demonstrated in the treatise 'On Excommunication' which the Patriarch of Jerusalem, Chrysanthos Notaras, composed at the turn of the seventeenth and eighteenth centuries at the bequest of the Prince of Wallachia, Constantin Brâncoveanu. Referring back to Leo Allatius, Notaras maintained that excommunication led to damnation as a tympaniaios. This was a miracle of the Eastern Church that the Roman Church did not recognize. Nevertheless, it remained God's divine prerogative either to absolve dead excommunicates or to punish people who had not been excommunicated with vampirism.[45]

Notes

1. See Dmitrij Zelenin, *Russische (Ostslavische) Volkskunde* (Berlin, 1927), 319–33, in particular 327–30 and 393/94.
2. See Felix Oinas, 'Heretics as Vampires and Demons in Russia', *Slavic and East European Journal* 22 (1978): 433–41, reprinted in Felix Oinas, *Essays on Russian Folklore and Mythology* (Columbus, OH, 1985), 121–30.
3. *Die Nestorchronik: Der altrussische Text der Nestorchronik in der Redaktion des Abtes Sil'vestr aus dem Jahre 1116 und ihrer Fortsetzung bis zum Jahre 1305 in der Handschrift des Mönches Lavrentij aus dem Jahre 1377 sowie die Fortsetzung der Suzdaler Chronik bis zum Jahre 1419 nach der Akademiehandschrift* (reprint of the 2nd edn, Leningrad, 1926–28) (Munich, 1977), 130 and 191.
4. Ibid., 214/215.
5. 'Slovo sv Grigoriia, izobreteno v toltsekh, o tom kako pervoe pogani sushche iazytsi klanialisia idolom i treby im klali', in N.M. Gal'kovskii, *Bor'ba khristianstva s ostatkami iazychestva v drevnei Rusi*, Parts I–II (Khar'kov, 1913–16), here Part II (1913), 17–35, at 22–25 and 32. See also V.J. Mansikka, *Die Religion der Ostslaven*, vol. I: *Quellen* (Helsinki, 1922), 160–86, at 162, 163, 174. Cf. B.A. Rybakov, *Iazychestvo drevnikh slavian* (Moscow, 1981), 11–25; Stella Rock, *Popular Religion in Russia: 'Double Belief' and the Making of an Academic Myth* (London, 2007), 26–31.
6. Ivan Groznyi, 'Poslanie v Kirillo-Belozerskii monastyr' (1573)', in V.P. Adrianova-Peretts (ed.), *Poslaniia Ivana Groznogo* (Moscow, 1951; reprint: Düsseldorf, 1971), 162–92, 351–69, at 175, 359.
7. See Mathias. Niendorf, *Das Großfürstentum Litauen: Studien zur Nationsbildung in der Frühen Neuzeit (1569–1795)* (Wiesbaden, 2006).
8. Hercules Saxonia, *De plica quam Poloni gwoździec, Roxolani kołtunum vocant* (Padua, 1600), 51/52.
9. *Lettres de Pierre des Noyers pour servir a l'histoire de Pologne et de Suède de 1655 à 1659* (Berlin, 1859), 560–63, at 561.
10. Bonifacy Zielonka, 'Stanowsko wielkokulturowe w Adolfinie w pow. Aleksandrowskim', *Przegląd archeologizny* 13 (1960): 197–204, at 201/202, Note 2; Rudolf Grenz,

'Archäologische Vampirbefunde aus dem westslawischen Siedlungsgebiet', *Zeitschrift für Ostforschung* 16 (1967): 255–65.

11. Augustin Calmet, *Dissertations sur les Apparitions des Esprits, et sur les Vampires et Revenans de Hongrie, de Moravie, etc. Nouvelle Edition, revue et corrigée. Partie I–II* (Einsiedeln, 1749), Oart II, 227–34 (in the original Latin; the entry is missing from the 1746 version); English translation: *Dissertations upon the apparitions of angels, daemons, and ghosts and concerning the vampires of Hungary, Bohemia, Moravia, and Silesia* (London, 1759).
12. See Koen Vermeir, 'Vampirisme, corps mastiquants et force de l'imagination : Analyse de premiers traites sur les vampires (1659–1755)', *Camenae* 8 (2010); reprint: 'Vampires as Creatures of the Imagination: Theories of Body, Soul, and Imagination in Early Modern Vampire Tracts (1659–1755)', in Yasmin Haskell (ed.), *Diseases of the Imagination and Imaginary Disease in the Early Modern Period* (Turnhout, 2011), 341–73.
13. Claude Comiers, 'La baguette justifiée, et ses effets démontrez naturels', *Mercure galant* (March 1693): 105–61, at 115/116. *La baguette justifiée, et ses effets démontrez naturels* (Paris, 1693), 13/14.
14. *Mercure galant* (May 1693): 62–70 (untitled article by Pierre des Noyers).
15. 'Lettre écrite de Pologne sur un sujet sort surprenant', *Mercure historique et politique* 14 (June 1693): 670/671.
16. [Marigner: 'Creatures des elemens,'] *Mercure galant* (January 1694): 58–166; Marigner: 'Sur les stryges de Russie', *Mercure galant* (February 1694): 13–119, in particular 15–22, 112/113.
17. Georgio Gengell, *Eversio atheism, seu pro deo contra atheos libri duo* (Brunsberg, 1716), 122/123.
18. Gabrielis Rzaczynski, *Historia naturalis curiosa regni Poloniae, magniducatus Litvaniae, annexorumq; provincarium, in tractatus XX divisa* (Sandomiriae, 1721), 365.
19. 'Von dem Polnischen Upiertz oder sich selbst fressenden Todten, und der daraus entstandenen Furcht vor Pest- und Vieh-Sterben', in *Sammlung von Natur- und Medicin- Wie auch hierzu gehörigen Kunst- und Literatur-Geschichten. 19. Versuch* (Leipzig, 1722), 82–88.
20. *Zakonik Stefana Dušana Cara Srpskog 1349 i 1354*. Anew edited and described by Stojan Novaković (Beograd, 1898; facsimile, 2004), 158.
21. 'Bilješka o vjerovanju u vukodlake na otoku Pašmanu god. 1403', collected by Vjekoslav Klaić. *Zbornik za narodni život i običaje južnih slavena* 1 (Zagreb, 1896): 223/224.
22. See Steven Runciman, *The Great Church in Captivity: A Study of the Patriarchate of Constantinople from the Eve of the Turkish Conquest to the Greek War of Independence* (Cambridge, 1968).
23. Karen Hartnup, '*On the Belief of the Greeks*': *Leo Allatios and Popular Orthodoxy* (Leiden, 2004), 318. Cf. Álvaro García Marín, '"The Son of the Vampire": Greek Gothic, or Gothic Greece?', in Isabel Ermida (ed.), *Dracula and the Gothic in Literature, Pop Culture and the Arts* (Leiden, 2016), 21–43.
24. Martin Crusius, *Turcograeciae Libri Octo: Quibus Graecorum Status Sub Imperio Turcico, in Politia et Ecclesia, Oeconomia et Scholis, iam inde ab amissa Constantinopoli, ad haec usque tempora, luculenter describitur* (Basel, 1584), 133–36.
25. *Stephan Gerlachs deß Aeltern Tage-Buch der von zween glorwürdigsten römischen Kaysern, Maximiliano und Rudolpho, beyderseits den Andern dieses Nahmens höchstseeligster Gedächtniß, an die ottomannische Pforte zu Constantinopel abgefertigten und durch den Wohlgebornen Herrn Hn. David Ungnad, Freiherrn zu Sonnegk und Preyburg u. Römisch-*

Kayserli. Rath mit würcklicher Erhalt- und Verlängerung des Friedens zwischen dem Ottomannischen und Römischen Kayserthum und demselben angehörigen Landen und Köngreichen glücklichst-vollbrachter Gesandtschafft. Herfür gegeben durch seinen Enckel Samuel Gerlach (Frankfurt, 1674), 94, 375.

26. Rafael Levković, the Croatian Franciscan Archbishop of Ochrid, mentioned in an unpublished biography, which was written in the 1640s, the burning of a revenant in a Macedonian village. Stjepan Antonljak, 'Sultan Jahja' u Makedoniji', Godišen zbornik na Univerzitet vo Skopje 13 (1962): 109–66, at 152/153.

27. See Ioannis Zelepos, 'Vampirglaube und orthodoxe Kirche im osmanischen Südosteuropa: Ein Fallbeispiel für die Ambivalenzen vorsäkularer Rationalisierungsprozesse', in Andreas Helmedach et al. (eds), Das osmanische Europa. Methoden und Perspektiven der Frühneuzeitforschung zu Südosteuropa (Leipzig, 2014), 363–79, at 366/367.

28. Charles Stewart, Demons and the Devil: Moral Imagination in Modern Greek Culture (Princeton, 1991), 255–59, quote on 258.

29. Marinos Sariyannis, 'Of Ottoman Ghosts, Vampires and Sorcerers: An Old Discussion Disinterred', Turkish Historical Review 4 (2013): 83–117, at 99. See also Johannes Benzing, Islamische Rechtsgutachten als volkskundliche Quelle (Wiesbaden, 1977), 23.

30. Sariyannis, Of Ottoman Ghosts, 204/205.

31. See Markus Köhbach, 'Ein Fall von Vampirismus bei den Osmanen', Balkan Studies 20 (1979): 83–90.

32. See Gerhard Podskalsky, Griechische Theologie in der Zeit der Türkenherrschaft (1453–1821): Die Orthodoxie im Spannungsfeld der nachreformatorischen Konfessionen des Westens (Munich, 1988), 33, 52–54.

33. See Hartnup, 'On the Belief of the Greeks'.

34. Leo Allatius, De templis Graecorum recentioribus, Ad Ioannem Morinum; De narthece Ecclesiae veteris, Ad Gasparem de Simeonibus; Necnon De Graecorum hodie quorundam opinationibus, Ad Paullum Zacchiam (Cologne, 1645), 142/143, 148.

35. Ibid., 148.

36. Leo Allatius, De utriusque ecclesiae occidentalis atque orientalis perpetua in dogmate de Purgatorio consensione (Rome, 1655), 41/42.

37. François Richard, Relation de ce qui s'est passé de plus remarquable a Saint-Erini isle de l'Archipel, depuis l'établissement des Peres de la Compagnie de Iesus en icell (Paris, 1657), 208–26, in particular 215/216.

38. Relation d'un voyage fait au Levant dans laquelle i lest curieusemet traite des Estats sujets au Grand Seigneur, des Moeurs, Religions, Forces, Gouuernemens, Politiques, Langues, & coustumes des Habitans de ce grand Empire. Par Monsieur Thevenot (Paris, 1664), 82/83; English translation: The Travels of Monsieur de Thevenot into the Levant (London, 1687), 98.

39. Paul Ricaut, The Present State of the Greek and Armenian Churches, Anno Christi, 1678 (London, 1679), 271–92, in particular 277–83.

40. Joseph Pitton Tournefort, Relation d'un voyage du Levant, fait par ordre du roy, 2 vols (Paris, 1717), vol. I, 158–64; English translation: A Voyage into the Levant perform'd by command of the late French King, 2 vols (London, 1741), vol. I, 101–7.

41. See Io[annes] Michael Heineccius, Dissertatio thoelogica inauguralis de absolutione mortuorum excommunicatorum seu tympanicorum in ecclesia Graeca (Helmstedt, 1709); Io[annes] Michael Heineccius, Eigentliche und wahrhafftige Abbildung der alten und neuen Griechischen Kirche, Nach ihrer Historie, Glaubens-Lehren und Kirchen-Gebräuchen in III. Theilen (Leipzig, 1711), 419–21.

42. See Matei Cazacu, *Dracula. Suivi du Capitaine Vampire. Une nouvelle roumaine par Marie Nizet (1879)* (Paris, 2004), 335/336.
43. *Demetrii Kantemirs historisch- geographisch- und politische Beschreibung der Moldau.* (Frankfurt, 1771), 314–19.
44. See Cazacu, *Dracula*, 337/338.
45. See Zelepos, 'Vampirglaube', 369–72.

CHAPTER 3

Vampirism in the Headlines

The Discovery of the Vampire

The Prelude: Peter Plogojowitz

On 21 July 1725, the Austrian state newspaper *Wienerisches Diarium* (*Vienna Diary*) published a report from a regional administrative authority under the nondescript heading 'Copia eines Schreibens aus dem Gradisker District in Ungarn' ('Copy of a Report from the Gradiska District in Hungary [Gradiška in Northern Bosnia]'). In this, the Cameral Provisor Frombald, who was responsible for the Northern Bosnian sector of the Habsburg Military Frontier, reported on an unknown plague that had broken out in the village of Kisolova three months after the death of a certain 'Peter Plogojoviz'. This name, which was later given in the distorted form of 'Plogojowitz', referred to a South Slavic peasant called Petar Blagojević. The fact that the patronym of Blagojević is given, derived from his father's name of Blago, suggests that we are dealing with a long-established family, for which a fixed family assignment existed among the village community. The location concerned is most likely the village of Kisiljevo near the Danube, close to the Serbian-Romanian border. According to Frombald's report, nine people died in this community within two days. Before their deaths, they all declared that Petar had visited them in their sleep, lying upon them and choking them. The testimony of Petar Blagojević's widow, in which she claimed that her deceased husband had visited her in order to collect his shoes, caused particular excitement. Regardless of the particular meaning that can be attached to this action, it does strengthen the impression of the actual physical presence of the dead man. Behind the indirect hint at plans for a longer journey, implicit sexual insinuations can also be made out.

In order to firmly identify Petar Blagojević as the harmful revenant, so Frombald reported further, the villagers called for his grave to be opened. What they feared to find in such suspicious cases was a nondecomposed corpse, showing transformations to the skin, hair and nails that would suggest a continued natural growth process. Such bodies were referred to by the local population as 'vampyri'. Since the villagers threatened to leave the village, Frombald saw himself as compelled, in the company of the local priest, to attend the exhumation of Petar Blagojević's body. Alongside the 'wild sign' of an erection, Frombald seemed to be particularly fascinated with one further circumstance: fresh blood seemed to be flowing from the mouth of the dead man, which, according to common statements, was the blood that he had drunk from his victims. His

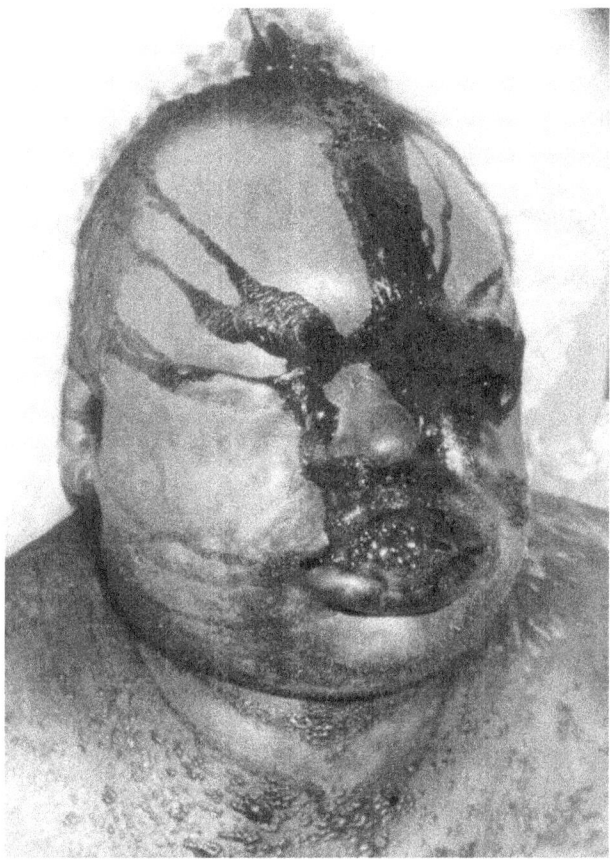

Figure 3.1 Putrid liquid oozing from a swollen corpse.
In this photograph, taken from his professional practice and presented at a conference in Vienna in 2008, the pathologist Christian Reiter documented the presumed appearance of the supposed vampire corpses that the military physicians had identified in 1731/1732.
Source: Christian Reiter, 'Der Vampyr-Aberglaube und die Militärärzte', in Christoph Augustynowicz and Ursula Reber (eds), *Vampirglaube und Magia posthuma im Diskurs der Habsburgermonarchie* (Vienna/Münster, 2011), 125–146, here the appendix on p. 278. Used with permission from LIT Verlag.

misdeeds thus exposed, the accused was executed posthumously. His heart was driven through with a stake and his body was burned on a pyre. Frombald laid the responsibility for the desecration of the grave and the robbing of the body at the feet of the mob and, in light of the general panic, he sought to defend himself in front of his employers against accusations of having acted incorrectly.[1] From today's perspective, Frombald's report is fascinating not only because it brings the glamorous term of 'vampire' into the headlines for the first time, but also because it lends a certain authenticity to the idea of bloodsucking. The case clearly attracted considerable international interest. The Protestant theologian Michael Ranft in far-off Leipzig was motivated by a local newspaper announcement to compose a treatise *Das Kauen und Schmatzen der Toten in Gräbern* (*The Chewing and Chomping of the Dead in their Graves*) (see the section entitled 'The Vampire Debate of the Enlightenment' below). He supposed that 'Peter Plogojowitz' had become embroiled in an argument with his neighbours and had been poisoned by his wife.[2] However, Ranft's investigations were only to find wider relevance in the 1730s, when headlines began to report on the vampire cases in Medveđa.[3] In 1725, the time was not yet ripe for a report on vampirism to catch the imagination of the broader public. The Habsburg military authorities placed the case on file, without attaching any particular significance to the alleged vampire. Why was it, then, that the Austrian Habsburg Military Frontier subsequently came to be seen as the breeding ground for vampirism?

The Military Frontier as a Breeding Ground for Vampirism

The Habsburg Military Frontier was a protective zone against the Ottoman Empire which had developed since the first quarter of the sixteenth century. In legal terms, it encompassed a region that, by the mid eighteenth century, spread from Croatia (1538) to Slavonia (1702), the Banat and Northern Serbia (1742–65), and to Transylvania (1761–64).

The Croatian-Slavonian Military Frontier was largely settled by refugees from the central regions of the Balkans, who pledged themselves to unsalaried military service in return for the granting of personal freedom and the right to own land and property. Since there was neither a nobility nor large-scale land ownership, the border community was characterized by the principle of equality and, since there were neither merchants nor traders, a natural economy dominated.[4] The Banat and Northern Serbia were settled by armed peasants known as 'hajduks' (but commonly grouped together in contemporary language under the collective term of 'vlachs'). These were originally wandering herdsmen who, on the one hand, hired out their services as cattle-drovers and, on the other hand, formed small bandit groups. As pastoral warriors, they entered into the service of both the Habsburg and the Ottoman armies.[5]

Following the failed second Siege of Vienna by the Ottomans in 1683, a number of major territorial changes at the frontier and large-scale movements of migration led to great turbulence. From the late sixteenth century onwards, as a result of the gradual replacement of 'military fiefs' (*timar*) by 'landed estates' (*çiftlik*), the South Slavic peasants in the Ottoman Empire had been subject not only to a gradual curtailment of their rights, but also to an increase in the tax burden. Against this background, thousands of Serbian volunteers signed up to the Habsburg army following the outbreak of the Great Turkish War. When the Ottomans responded with retaliatory measures, some 30,000–35,000 families fled north in 1690, with the Patriarch of Peć at their head. These emigrants were settled in the Banat region of the Military Frontier, following the reconstitution of Hungary, which had been sealed at the Treaty of Karlowitz in 1699. Thereafter, in 1704, the administration of the Military Frontier was transferred from Graz to the Imperial War Council in Vienna, and the military jurisdiction was extended. Among other things, this led to the division of the border region into numerous regiments, the collating together of neighbouring villages into companies and – in the interests of recruiting those people who were not required in the agricultural economy – a ban on family divisions.[6]

Under these conditions, the 'home collective' (*zadruga*) lifestyle common to the Western Balkans was subject to a constantly changing process of disintegration and resurgence. This was a community centred around goods and production, which brought together different generations and was constructed on a patrilineal basis. Since the complex Balkan family was defined as an ancestral grouping, it provided both for the integration of its members and, at the same time, for the exclusion of others.[7]

Overall, the Military Frontier was a region that was not only characterized by economic backwardness and continuous small-scale conflicts, but also by traditional relationships and lifestyles and syncretic ideas. It is significant that the outbreak of the alleged vampire disease first became noted at a time where the affected areas of Northern Bosnia and Northern Serbia had temporarily become part of the Habsburg Empire, that is, in the period between the Treaty of Passarowitz in 1718 and the Treaty of Belgrade in 1739.[8]

In order to guard these newly acquired territories, known as the Neoaquisita, a national militia was established in 1718, formed of hajduks, which was stationed from 1719 to 1733 in Belgrade and was placed under the command of Charles Alexander of Württemberg.[9] The necessity of such a defensive measure was demonstrated by the first inspection conducted by the Habsburg military authorities immediately after the conquest, which revealed there to be a great number of depredations in the region. The level of settlement was also very low. In the peripheral border districts, only 415 inhabited and 342 uninhabited places were registered, with a total population of 2,456 subjects, i.e. families, which equated to an average of only seven households in each inhabited locality. Clearly, many locals were sceptical towards the new rulers and opted to remain on the Ottoman side of the border. By 1721, the situation had only marginally improved, and 446 villages were now counted in fifteen districts, with 6,020 households. The fact that 507 married brothers, 459 unmarried brothers and 383 married sons lived on the estates demonstrated that large families did not constitute the norm in the border regions. Alongside cultivation, cattle-farming was also common. On average, each family had two to three oxen, one or two milking cows, three to four pigs, four to five sheep and five to six goats. Only every second family had a horse of their own. This was therefore a region characterized by subsistence farming.

According to a report from 1724, the taxable subjects were distrustful of their new rulers, and many even preferred the 'Turkish yoke' to the 'Christian rule'. Clearly, they saw Ottoman taxation as cheaper and more differentiated than the Habsburg tax system. A further report from 1727 shows that, by this time, the hajduks had taken the most pleasant villages and the most fertile soil for themselves, thus pushing out the taxpayers. Half of the region was now in their hands and, furthermore, they also had a monopoly on the transport of goods and other sources of income.

In order to avoid a further decline in the number of taxpayers, the authorities issued an order in 1728 stating that only those who came from the neighbouring Turkish regions, and who could therefore be integrated into the village communities as self-sufficient persons, were to be recruited to the national militia. In 1729, this militia was composed of eighteen companies, which should in theory have amounted to a force of 4,500 men, but, in practice, counted only 2,390. Despite the benefits to be had, service in the militia therefore seems not to have been particularly attractive. It was inevitable, in retrospect, that the simultaneous pacification and militarisation of the border region would lead to a whole range of social conflicts, and the nine hajduk villages were eventually cut off from the other villages.[10]

In its attempts to maintain peace and order, the Imperial War Council in Vienna was also shaped by two further factors: the need to ward off the spread of plague on the one hand, and the desire to push through a unification of the Catholic and Orthodox churches in the face of popular opposition on the other. From the sixteenth to the eighteenth centuries, the 'Morbus hungaricus' – which has now been identified as typhus and that claimed the lives of numerous soldiers and colonists in the marshy low-lying areas of Pannonia – particularly animated the minds of scholars in German-speaking countries. The resistance of Hungarians and Turks to this disease was traced back, interestingly, to their attention to hygiene and to their healthy diet – including plenty of garlic.[11]

After plague gradually disappeared from Western and Central Europe in the second half of the seventeenth century, concerns about a renewed outbreak in the eighteenth and nineteenth centuries were focused solely on the eastern and southeastern periphery of the continent, and in particular on the frontier with the Ottoman Empire. Through the plague order of 1728, the Habsburgs therefore attempted to establish the Military Frontier as a 'permanent barrier against the plague', both by restricting the free movement of goods and persons, and through setting up quarantine stations.[12]

At the same time, the colonialist behaviour of the military administration and the curtailing of the prerogatives of the Orthodox Bishop of Marča – to the east of Zagreb, near Ivanić – led to a popular uprising in Lika in 1728, a region stretching along the coast in central Croatia. In 1733, there was then renewed uproar when a group of peasant soldiers were deployed beyond the Military Frontier for the first time, in Italy. Although the Council of War did make certain concessions with regard to salaries and the Church issue, the Uniates were temporarily expelled from Marča by Orthodox monks in 1735.[13] From a Habsburg perspective, the territories won during the Great Turkish War brought with them not only confessional but also social conflicts. Beyond this, the region was also viewed as a horde of backwardness and disease, particularly the North Serbian and North Bosnian areas of the Slavonian sector of the Military Frontier.

The Main Act: Arnond Paole

Against this backdrop, it is understandable that the vampire cases that became known at the start of the 1730s attracted much greater interest than the case from 1725, which seemed to belong more to the tradition of Western *nachzehrer* legends. However, the figure of 'Arnond Paole' or 'Arnold Paul', who was later stylized in West European debates as the prototype of the vampire, did not even appear in the first of the two military physician's reports under discussion here.

In the final two months of 1731, thirteen people died from an unknown disease in the village of Medveđa – written in the sources in the Hungarian style as 'Medvedgya' – on the West Morava river, 200 kilometres from both Kisiljevo and Belgrade. However, when the plague physician Glaser, who was stationed in Paraćin (to the north of Stalać), arrived in the village on 12 December 1731, he was not able to identify any infectious disease, beyond the effects of gluttony that were common in the Advent period of fasting. There was therefore no immediate danger, at least from the perspective of the Habsburg military authorities. However, according to the statements of the villagers, 'vampires [Vambyres] or bloodsuckers [Bluthseiger]' were responsible.

Since the deaths of their relatives could not be traced back simply to fever and aching limbs, a real panic broke out among the villagers. Several families grouped together at night in one house and took it in turns to keep guard, and the peasants also seriously considered the idea of leaving their home village. The only solution seemed to be the destruction of the vampires.

In this context, in his report to the authorities in Vienna, Glaser reported the existence of a risk – albeit only an imagined one but one that, at the same time, was considered to be real – of contamination through the act of '(self-)vampirization'. Placed under such great pressure, the plague physician permitted ten graves to be opened, although without undertaking any autopsies. The main suspects were both refugees from the Ottoman Empire: an old woman named 'Miliza' (Milica), who had supposedly eaten the meat of a sheep that had fallen victim to vampires, and a young woman named 'Stanno' (Stana), who had allegedly smeared herself with the blood of a vampire and had then died in childbirth.

Since Glaser himself considered several corpses to be 'suspect', and bearing in mind the unusual size of the settlement, he advised the military authorities to set up an investigative commission in order to placate the fears of the inhabitants.[14] His hinting at the village's importance provides an indirect insight into the social relationships between its inhabitants. Located directly on the Ottoman border, it had – as the information we have makes clear – a richly mixed population, composed of long-established families, refugees from the Ottoman Empire and representatives of the Habsburg militia. This was therefore an environment that could not have been entirely free of social conflicts.

Furthermore, the plague physician also informed his father, the physician Johann Friedrich Glaser, about the occurrences. He, in turn, then wrote a letter on 13 February 1732 to the Nuremburg editors of the *Commercium litterarium*, which was published on 12 March 1732. In this, Glaser senior wrote that there was a great uncertainty among the frontier people as to whether or how bloodsucking was taking place, since the only evidence there was were the illusions of sleeping people.[15] Therefore, beyond highlighting the impact of nightmares, Glaser junior had nothing more to contribute to an explanation of the vampire phenomenon. He was clearly much less interested in the nondecomposed bodies than in the unknown disease. The commission that Glaser had called for commenced their work in the second week of January 1732, under the direction of the regimental physician Flückinger. The subject of their investigation were the claims that so-called 'vampyrs' had killed people by sucking out their blood. Expanding upon Glaser's visits to the sick and inspection of the corpses, more or less professional autopsies were carried out in the hope of providing further information on the causes of death and the process of decay. According to Flückinger's report, which was given the title 'Visum et Repertum' ('Proofed Report'), ten of the sixteen corpses had not begun to decay and were thus suspected of vampirism. They had all died of a plague within three days and then lain in their graves for six weeks to three months. The weak were particularly affected, that is, the very young and the very old.

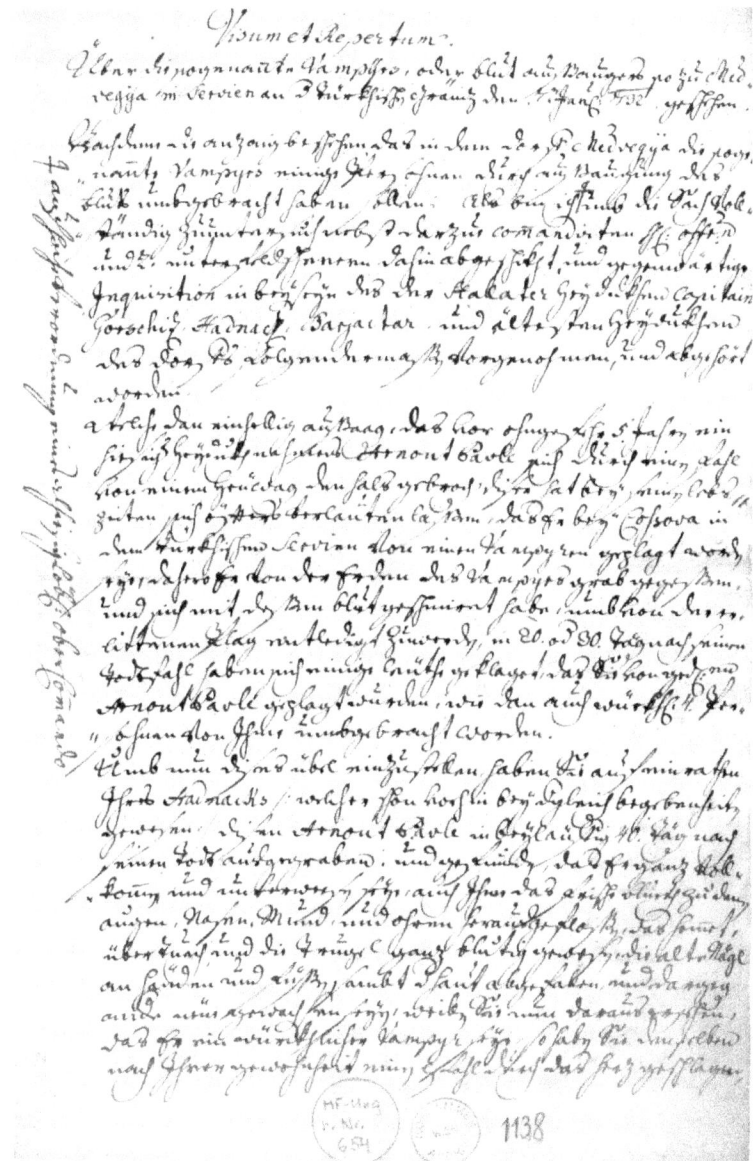

Figure 3.2 'Visum et Repertum', the Flückinger report.
The discovery of the vampire by Enlightenment Europe has been traced back to this report by a regimental physician, entitled 'Proofed Report: On the So-Called Vampire, or Bloodsucker, Such as Has Been Seen in Medvegia in Serbia, on the Turkish Border, on January 7th 1732'.
Used with permission from the Österreichisches Staatsarchiv, Hoffinanz Ungarn, rote Nr. 654, fol. 1138r.

Flückinger also mentioned that the twenty-year-old wife of a hajduk, 'Stanoicka' (Stanojka), claimed to have been visited at night and choked by the son of a hajduk, called 'Miloe' (Miloje), who had died at the age of twenty-five. This suggests that nightmares should also be taken into consideration. In this context, Flückinger did point out that there was a finger-length red patch under the woman's right ear, without, however, drawing a connection with bloodsucking. The Leipzig vampire expert Michael Ranft later concluded that the young man and woman concerned had had 'impermissible interactions'.[16]

In order to restore order to the village, the investigative commission agreed to a posthumous execution of the suspects, who were decapitated and burned. In carrying this out, the local Roma population were called upon as executioners since, as outsiders, they were felt to be less bound by scruples in this respect. Only the deceased relatives of the military leaders of Medveđa were able to escape this fate and were declared not to be suspect.[17]

How is this vampire disease to be understood from a contemporary perspective? On the basis of the surviving autopsy reports and the identifiable climatic data, the Vienna pathologist Christian Reiter recently concluded that the fatal disease in Medveđa was most probably a splenic fever. The virus could survive well in the boggy fields of the region, and the dry summer of 1731 had led to sheep injuring themselves on the hard ground in their search for food. Furthermore, as a legal forensic specialist, he accused his colleagues from the eighteenth century of downright deception, since the complete decomposition of a corpse in a grave cannot be expected before ten years at the earliest. The appearance of a buried corpse after half a year in the grave should be expected closely to resemble that of a body that has only been buried for several days. The swelling of a corpse is a common early stage in the lengthy process of decay, caused by a build-up of gas in the body. The real scandal in the Medveđa investigations was therefore that the military physicians claimed that several bodies had already fully decomposed just a few weeks after their internment. In so doing, they not only appeased the fears of the village elders who were worried about the salvation of their relatives' souls, but also justified their own employment. After all, the physicians were concerned with creating a source of income from the exhumation of corpses. That, with their diagnosis of 'decomposed' or 'suspect' bodies, they should have contributed to the anchoring of the idea of living corpses and bloodsucking vampires among the Western public is another story.[18]

In fact, the military physicians were barely interested in the lives of the frontiersmen themselves.[19] However, Flückinger did also point to the memory of the death of a hajduk, some five years earlier, as a possible origin for the vampire disease. Little is known of the life and fate of this man, who died as the result of a fall and was subsequently turned into a scapegoat by the villagers, but Flückinger offers the following.

Before his unfortunate death, the hajduk claimed to have been visited by a vampire in Kosovo, and to have smeared himself in its blood and eaten the earth from its grave as a defensive measure. Three to four weeks after his death, the hajduk began to visit the inhabitants of the village, attacking both people and cattle. He was held responsible for four deaths. When his body was exhumed forty days after his burial, it was found not to have decomposed. Therefore, in an act of vigilantism that hints at a degree of experience in dealing with such matters, his corpse was impaled and burned.

Flückinger came to the conclusion that the vampire disease had spread as a result of the cattle becoming infected.[20] The repeated involvement of the military authorities could be connected with the increasing domination of the region by the Habsburgs or with the fact that sixteen victims hinted at a mass death that did not seem to stop at the doors of the village elders. Even though little is known about the life of the hajduk, it is possible to establish a few details from his name, which has been preserved in handwritten form in the Austrian State Archives as 'Arnond Paole', but, in the reporting of the time, was often rendered as 'Arnold Paul'. It seems clear that there was a vowel shift in the transferring of a Serbian name into an Austro-Hungarian document. The villagers would probably have called their compatriot 'Arnaut Pavle', referring to the Ottoman designation of 'Arnaut' for Albanians. Pavle's nickname 'the Albanian' corresponded with his clear origin from Kosovo or the Field of Blackbirds, a region that had increasingly been settled by Albanians following the famous battle between the Serbs and the Ottomans in 1389, and where the hajduk had perhaps lived as a herdsman before fleeing to Medveđa.

Unlike with Petar Blagojević from Kisiljevo, no patronym has been handed down for Pavle. Is this perhaps an indication that, without local family attachments, he may have fallen into the role of outsider in Medveđa and maybe even had to earn his keep as a farm labourer? Or does his position as a border soldier recruited from outside perhaps point to the fact that he enjoyed certain privileges in the village, at the expense of the longer-established families? His

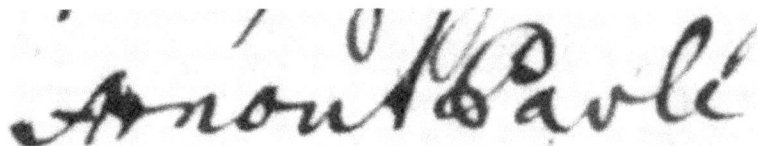

Figure 3.3 Extract from the Flückinger report with the lettering 'Arnond Paole'. There has been a great deal of speculation about the identity of the first known European 'vampire'. The ambiguous spelling means that the name has often been distorted and errors were presumably made in the copying of the first version. The only designation that makes sense is 'Arnaut [i.e. the Albanian] Pavle'.
Used with permission from the Österreichisches Staatsarchiv, Hoffinanz Ungarn, rote Nr. 654, fol. 1138r.

Figure 3.4 'Arnond Paole' as a pandur?
In the first half of the 1740s, the Augsburg copper engraver Martin Engelbrecht (1684–1756) created an illustrated series of exotic soldiers from the Habsburg army. The portrait of a peasant soldier or militiaman – referred to as a *hajduk* on the Military Frontier or a *pandur* in Slavonia – could well reflect the appearance of 'Arnond Paole', who was to be stylized into a vampire following his death.
Source: Martin Engelbrecht, *Théatre de la milice étrangère: Schaubühne verschiedener bishero in Teutschland unbekannt gewester Soldaten von ausländischer Nationen* (Augsburg [1742]), Sheet 2. Used with permission from the Heeresgeschichtliches Museum / Militärhistorisches Institut Wien, Inv. No. BI4849-27.

death, which supposedly resulted from an accident, is suspicious at the very least; why an experienced herdsman should fall from a haycart and break his neck remains unclear. Was he perhaps the victim of violence? Was this a result of social conflicts or did he fall victim to a blood feud? The authorities were carefully not informed about any of this.

When the British physician and writer Herbert Mayo came across the classic vampire case in the mid nineteenth century in his investigation into mesmerism, he could not resist turning it into a tragic romantic tale. Following his discharge from the army in 1727, 'Arnod [sic] Paole' returned from the Levant to his home village with a terrible secret. He then fell madly in love with the seventeen-year-old Nina, who lived in the neighbouring house. However, immediately after their wedding, he confessed to the fact that he had been visited by a vampire in Kosovo, who could come back at any time to claim his tribute. The real mischief only started following 'Arnod's' fall from the haycart.[21]

An Austrian Military Yarn

For all the artistic licence Mayo took, other sources can be found with even more far-fetched theses. The letters from Alexander von Kottwitz, an Ensign in the Württemberg Regiment in Belgrade, to the Director of the Imperial Leopold Academy in Altdorf (Altdorfiana) Johann Friedrich Ettmüller, for example, dated 26 January 1732, can be read as a fairy tale, which reveals the violent fantasies and sexual imaginations of the soldiers stationed in the region. In this, Kottwitz writes of 'vampyres' or 'people-suckers', tracing the term back to the Turkish. He then goes on to outline two cases from 'Kucklina', a settlement neighbouring Medveđa.

First case: two brothers had sought to see through the night by taking it in turns to keep guard, but were nevertheless surprised in their sleep by a vampire. One of the brothers emerged from the incident with a red fleck behind his ear and passed away three days later.

Second case: furthermore, a widow was visited and impregnated by her husband, who had died several days earlier. She reported this to the head of the military in the town and, in relation to the sexual experience, spoke only of the coldness of the semen. Her child was born completely disfigured, without any limbs and with the appearance of a piece of raw meat, and, within three days, had 'wrinkled like a sausage'.

These cases seem to reveal two things. First, from the outset, Western witnesses seemed to take the bite of the vampire quite literally. Second, the issues of adultery and infanticide both seemed to play an enormous role in relation to vampirism.[22]

The scientific journals of the time, by contrast, only published prepared testimonies. On 7 May 1732, for example, the *Commercium litterarium* reported on a vampire case in the Slavonian border town of Požega.

In early 1730, the family of a pandur – as the frontier soldiers were known – were alleged to have poisoned themselves by eating the meat of a sheep that had supposedly had its blood sucked out by a vampire, appearing in the form of a snake. The entire family died and, since their corpses had not begun to decompose after twenty days, they were driven through with a stake, decapitated and burned.[23]

In this version, the vampire disease is reduced to a form of food poisoning, and a snake-bite is seen as the original cause. It is only the posthumous execution that is particularly sensational.

Further evidence for vampiric mischief can be found, by contrast, in Augustin Calmet's handbook on vampirism, first published in 1749, with reference to a letter from the former Captain of Beloz to Ferdinand de Saint-Urbain, the Court Architect of the Dukes of Lorraine. The latter informed Calmet about what Beloz had experienced as part of a delegation from Carl Alexander von Württemburg (see the section entitled 'The Vampire Debate of the Enlightenment' below), which had investigated an alleged case of vampirism in a border town around 1730. Beloz expressed his conviction that vampires generally visited their own relatives and told the following story.

A vampire who had died three years earlier had killed his own brother and three of his grandchildren, as well as drinking the blood of a further granddaughter. The witnesses did not provide any further information about the exact circumstances. Because of the deteriorating condition of the girl whom he had visited, the grave of the vampire, over which will-o'-the-wisps could be seen, was opened up, to reveal a fresh-looking corpse, with half-opened eyes and a still-pulsating heart, which did not give off any particular stench. When the heart was driven through with a stake and the body was decapitated, a great deal of blood was seen to ooze out, along with a whiteish material. Following the renewed internment of the dead man, his granddaughter made a full recovery.

According to Beloz, the spot on the body from which the vampire had sucked blood could be identified by a blueish mark.[24] In the final analysis, what becomes clear from this report is that alleged vampire bites were only ever reported by less than reliable informants. However, by no means was everything that was passed on by rumours written down.

The Vampire Debate of the Enlightenment

The Orientalization of the Balkans at the Academies and Universities

The era of the Enlightenment essentially lasted from the 1680s to the French Revolution of 1789. On the one hand, this was an intellectual movement that had its roots in the decline of feudalism and the rise of the bourgeoisie, and, on the other, it was grounded in the dissolution of the Christian worldview and the triumph of modern rationalism. Alongside the education of the people as responsible, mature citizens, the pushing through of political forms was also central to the Enlightenment agenda. As well as the universities, the scientific academies that were established in London in 1662, Paris in 1666 and Berlin in 1711 provided important arenas for scholarly debate and the construction of public opinion. Reading societies also benefited from the development of the press. The first German daily newspaper appeared in 1650 in Leipzig, and the first German journal in Nuremberg in 1674.

Whereas, up to the French Revolution, the daily newspapers largely restricted themselves to the uncommented reporting of news, the so-called monthlies were quick to discuss current affairs within the broader framework of key societal issues. A further factor that was of great relevance for debates over the vampire phenomenon was the redefinition of the relationship between body, soul and spirit. The soul was understood to be a reflective spirit and at the same time was integrated within the divine mind. This was contrasted by irrational thought and actions, which found their expression in the behaviour of sorcerers and witch doctors, as an expression of demonic ideas or occult natural forces, whose spread can be traced back to the influence of magic upon broad sectors of the population. As a result, the tackling of such superstition was to become a battle cry of the Enlightenment[25] and, accordingly, the subject of vampirism was treated with scorn from the outset. It was telling, for example, that Michael Ranft, the vampire specialist from Nebra, should have stated in his standard work of 1734 that the 'learned scholars of the first rank' had declined to offer any opinions on the subject.[26]

The Habsburg physicians and officers' lack of interest in the lifestyles of the population of the Habsburg Military Frontier region, arising from their misunderstanding of local traditions, was subsequently reflected in the scholarly interpretation of nondecomposed corpses. Nonprejudiced contributions, such as the questioning of the uniqueness of vampires by the Erfurt journal *Neu-eröffnetes Welt- und Staats-Theatrum* (*Newly Opened World and State Theater*), largely remained an exception. In April 1732, the journal did not shy away from equating various fantastical figures such as 'the Slavs' vampires, the Polak's upiertz, and the Germans' chomping dead'.[27] Furthermore, it should also be highlighted that the alleged bloodsuckers gained particular public interest in Western Europe at a time when the talk of the Turkish threat had declined considerably and when the Enlightenment was largely constructing itself on the basis of a criticism of superstition. In this context, we can discern a gradual shift in emphasis in the constitution of 'mental maps'. Whereas spatial perceptions had previously been shaped by the contrast, rooted in antiquity, between a 'civilized' South and a 'barbaric' North, cognitive maps now began to focus primarily on the antagonism between a 'progressive' West and a 'backward' East.[28]

The Rumour Mill and Academic Opinion

Among the most important sources for the spreading of reports on vampirism in the German-speaking lands was Charles Alexander of Württemberg, who, from 1719, served as Commander General and Governor of the Serbian administration in Belgrade. In the winter of 1731/1732, when the vampire disease was being investigated in Medveđa, Charles Alexander was at Schloss Winnental in Württemberg, at the side of his pregnant wife. Following the death of the Crown Prince Frederick Louis of Württemberg in 1731, he immediately seized the chance to press his claims to the throne. Informed at firsthand of the situation at the Military Frontier, he also took the opportunity to instruct the German princely and ducal courts about the emerging phenomenon of vampirism. In the autumn of 1733, he finally assumed control of the government of the Duchy of Württemberg.[29]

In the meantime, the Nuremberg journal *Commercium litterarium* also caused an uproar when, in February 1732, it published the reports of its Vienna correspondents on the vampire cases (see the section entitled 'The Discovery of the Vampire' above). The editors, who largely came from the medical profession, drew on information from twenty-eight towns and furthered the debate in two ways. In keeping with the aim of their journal to disseminate scientific writing throughout Europe (it was published in Latin), they not only included the opinions of other intellectuals, but also popularized the issue by reporting and offering criticisms of the numerous publications on vampirism. In the course of 1732, they therefore published eight reviews, as well a series of commentaries, which discussed cases of revenancy in Silesia, Wallachia and Greece.[30]

However, the demystification of the world being carried out by Enlightenment scholars in cooperation with the state authorities in Vienna had one catch. This was because the Prussian King Frederick William I, in his efforts to roll back political participation and the emancipation of citizens, commissioned the Berlin Society (later Academy) of Sciences to provide an expert opinion on the vampire cases, which even he himself did not really take seriously. In order to preserve their integrity, the Society felt itself obliged to draw up this report, which it duly presented on 11 March 1732. According to a statement from Vienna on 9 March 1732, Johann Jakob Baier, a physician and geologist from Altdorf who had been appointed President of the Leopoldina, the German Academy of the Natural Sciences in Nuremberg, had also been commissioned with drawing up a report on the case. However, against the express demands of the Emperor Charles VI, Baier did not fulfil his duties in this regard before his death in 1735.[31] In his stead, Franz Anton Stebler, later Professor of Medical Sciences at the University of Ingolstadt, published a critical study on vampirism in the publication series of the Leopoldina in 1737.[32]

What was the reason for the compilation of the controversial Berlin report? Following his coronation in 1717, Frederick William I had already expressed his low opinion of scholarship in the state by cutting the funding of the Academy, which had only been established in 1711, and then appointing the historian Jakob Paul Freiherr von Grundling as President in 1718, a man who was also used as court jester. Consequently, in the autumn of 1731, Frederick William went so far as to establish a post in the Academy's budget 'for the numerous court jesters'. On 19 January 1732, he then appointed the Austrian convert and scholar of myths and legends, Otto von Graben zum Stein, as Vice-President of the Academy, despite – or perhaps because of – the fact that in 1731, his two volume-work *Monathlichen Unterredungen von dem Reiche der Geister zwischen Andrenio und Pneumatiophilo* (*Monthly Discussions on the Realm of Spirits between Andrenio and Pneumatiophilo*) had been banned from publication. Among his duties as the effective head of the Academy were the hunting of 'goblins, ghosts and spirits of the night', and the tracing and expulsion of 'Jesuits, and other related bugs and vermin from Rome'.[33]

When Frederick William was informed of the Serbian vampires by Charles Alexander of Württemburg, he must have felt that it presented a perfect opportunity for ridiculing his unloved Royal Prussian Society of the Sciences. He therefore commissioned the Society with drawing up an opinion on Flückinger's report 'Visum et Repertum' of 26 January 1732. On 11 March, the Society presented its 'Honourable Opinion'. This had to be signed by the heads of all the scientific sections, meaning that the entire academy was compelled to participate in the interdisciplinary findings.

Interestingly, no further sources were called upon in drawing up this opinion, which was based entirely on Flückinger's report. In terms of content, it was bound by the spirit of the Enlightenment, with the scholars differentiating between information deriving simply from hearsay and facts that arose from their own investigations. They named several possible natural causes for the sounds that 'Arnond Paole' was supposed to have made upon his impalement, and for the nondecomposed state of several corpses that Flückinger had described. They also pointed out that there had been no actual witnesses to the alleged act of bloodsucking. The explanations they provided for the vampire phenomenon were 'melancholy complexions', or the fantasies of women in their sleep.[34]

Prudently, the Berlin scientists declined to take up any further positions. In Michael Ranft's 1734 bibliographical overview of the literature on vampires, only one work by the disreputable Vice-President of the Society can be found from this time period. However, this was never published and had the somewhat awkward title of 'Otto, Grafens zum Stein unverlohrnes Licht und Recht derer Todten unter den Lebendigen, oder gründlicher Bericht der Erscheinung der Todten unter den Lebendigen, und was jene vor ein Recht in der Obern Welt über diese noch haben können, untersucht in Ereignung der vorfallenden Vampyren, oder so genannten Blut-Saugern im Königreich Servien und andern Orten in diesen und vorigen Zeiten' ('Otto, Graf von Stein's unforfeited light and the rights of the dead among the living, or a thorough report on the appearance of the dead among the living and what rights these might enjoy in the world above, examined on the basis of the cases of vampyres, or so-called bloodsuckers in the Kingdom of Serbia and other places in this and previous times').[35] Clearly, in the rational context of the Enlightenment, only dubious scholars would tackle the occult.

The Vampire as a Transnational Media Event

In Western Europe, it was not only in newspapers and journals that vampires gained a great deal of attention. Remarkably, a baker's dozen of vampire treatises appeared over a very short period of time in the Central German area, focusing both on medical and theological issues.[36] Eleven were published in 1732 and a further two followed in 1733, from both named and anonymous authors (Table 3.1).

Table 3.1 Published works on vampires between 1732 and 1733

Author	Work	Place and date of publication
Anonymous	*Actenmässige und Umständliche Relation von denen Vampiren oder Menschen-Saugern* (A remarkable and unusual account of vampires and bloodsuckers)	Leipzig 1732
Anonymous	*Christliche Betrachtungen über die wunderbarliche Begebenheit mit den Blutsaugenden Todten in Servien* (Christian observations on the miraculous events concerning the bloodsucking dead in Serbia)	Leipzig 1732
Anonymous (under the abbreviation W. S. G. E.)	*Curieuse Und sehr wunderbare Relation, von denen sich neuer Dingen in Servien erzeigenden Blut-Saugern oder Vampyrs* (Curious and very wonderful relation, of which are new things in bloodsuckers or vampires in Serbia)	n.p. 1732
Anonymous	*Schreiben eines guten Freundes an einen andern guten Freund, die Vampyren betreffend* (A letter from one good friend to another, concerning vampyres)	Frankfurt 1732
Anonymous	*Visum & Repertum. Über die so genannten Vampirs, oder Blut-Aussauger* (Proofed Report. On the so-called vampire or bloodsucker)	Nuremberg 1732

Christoph Friedrich Demel	*Philosophischer Versuch, ob nicht die merckwürdige Begebenheit derer Blutsauger in Nieder-Ungarn, A. 1732 geschehen, aus denen principiis naturae, insbesondere aus der sympathia rerum naturalium und denen tribus facultationibus hominis können erleutert werden* (Philosophical investigation into whether or not the remarkable occurrence of bloodsuckers in Lower Hungary in 1732 can be attributed to the laws of nature, in particular to the consensus of natural things and the potential of human possibilities)	Weimar 1732
Johann Christoph Fritsche (anonymously)	*Eines Weimarischen Medici Muthmaßliche Gedancken Von denen Vampyren, Oder sog. Blut-Saugern* (A Weimar physician's thoughts on vampyres, or so-called bloodsuckers)	Leipzig 1732
Johann Christoph Harenberg	*Vernünftige und Christliche Gedancken Uber die Vampirs Oder Bluthsaugende Todten* (Reasonable and Christian Thoughts on the Vampires or Bloodsucking Dead)	Wolfenbüttel 1733
Johann Christoph Meinig (alias Putoneos)	*Besondere Nachricht, von denen Vampyren oder so genannten Blut-Saugern* (Particular report on the vampyres or so-called bloodsuckers)	Leipzig 1732
Johann Christoph Pohl	*Dissertatio de hominibus post mortem sanguisugis, vulgo sic dictis Vampyren* (Dissertation on people who appear after their death as bloodsuckers and are commonly called vampires)	Leipzig 1732
Johannes Christian Stock	*Dissertatio physica de cadaveribus sanguisugis. Von denen so genannten Vampyren oder Menschen-Säugern* (Dissertation on the physic of bloodsucking cadavers. On the so-called vampires or people-suckers)	Jena 1732
Gottlob Heinrich Vogt	*Kurtzes Bedencken Von denen Actenmäßigen Relationen Wegen derer Vampiren, oder Menschen- und Vieh-Aussaugern* (Brief thoughts on the authority's reports on vampires, or human- or cattle-suckers)	Leipzig 1732
Johann Heinrich Zopf	*Dissertatio de vampyribus serviensibus* (Dissertation on the Serbian Vampire)	Duisburg 1733

Figures 3.5 and 3.6 Vampire treatises from the Enlightenment era.

In contemporary treatises, vampires were automatically connected with bloodsuckers, and traced back to the Ottoman influence in the Balkans.

Sources: Title pages of W. S. G. E., *Curious And Very Wonderful Relation, of Which Are New Things in Bloodsuckers or Vampires'* (n.p., 1732), and Johann Christoph Harenberg, *Reasonable and Christian Thoughts on the Vampires or Bloodsucking Dead* (Wolfenbüttel, 1733).

These vampire treatises were based on the protocols of the military authorities, and sought, with the assistance of rationalism and science, to dismiss the statements of those affected as mere superstition. The question of the relationship between the body and the soul, and the theories of Aristotle and Paracelsus related to this moved into the centre of attention. Aristotle divided the soul into three faculties: one faculty of the soul promoting organic growth (*anima vegetativa*), a further sensitive faculty (*anima sensitiva*) and an intellectual faculty (*anima rationalis*). On this basis, the nondecomposition of a corpse can be interpreted as the continued working of the *anima vegetativa*. Paracelsus, on the other hand, developed the doctrine of the three central aspects of man, which returned to their origins upon death; the body to the soil, the soul to God, and the spirit to the elements. He did not consider this so-called astral spirit to be immortal, as the soul was, but he did assume that it had a longer existence than the body. Therefore, the idea of a spirit that lived on for a certain time offered itself as an explanation for phenomena in the grey zone between fantasy and reality.

In this context, those involved in the Protestant discourse in the Central European region neglected to make reference either to the plague that was averted in the Holy Roman Empire around 1700 or to the Habsburg plague order developed in 1728 against a new threat from the Ottoman Empire. So long as the danger of infection with the vampire disease remained restricted to the Orthodox peasants, as the Austrian military physicians claimed, and could therefore be viewed as an endemic phenomenon, Western European scholars' interest in the subject was merely academic.[37] Although the 1728 ban on witch trials in Prussia might have offered a close point of connection, none of the participants in the debate took up a position on the Central European witch trials that might have served to relativize the idea of the archaic conditions of the Southeast European region.[38]

Finally, in 1734, the deacon and writer Michael Ranft from Nebra, who had already distinguished himself with a dissertation on the subject of nachzehrers in 1725, brought together the various debates on the vampires of Medveđa in his *Tractat von dem Kauen und Schmatzen der Todten in Gräbern* (*Treatise on the Chewing and Chomping of the Dead in Graves*). On the one hand, he drew a connection between the previously unknown illness and the anxiety of nightmares and fever. On the other hand, he also traced the alleged nondecomposition of the corpses, the oozing of blood from bodily orifices, and the continued growth of the hair and nails back to climactic conditions and the natural environment. Seen in this light, the phenomenon of vampirism revealed itself to be a product of fantasy and/or superstition, which only played a role beyond Ranft's Protestant horizons in the areas of current or previous Ottoman influence.[39] At the European level, the events in Medveđa found an echo in the Parisian journals *Mercure de France* and *Le Glaneur*, and in London newspapers such as *The Craftsman* and the *Gentleman's Magazine*. In *The Craftsman*, a commentator speculated as to whether the vampirism in the East could be seen as a parable on the state administration and as to whether the hajduk 'Arnold Paul' or 'Paul Arnold', who became known as a vampire in Medveđa in 1732, was perhaps a tax collector, who served the 'blood-sucker of state'. This theory was developed further in English journals, under the motto of 'political vampyres', and bloodsucking was first stylized as a metaphor for a particular form of rule, before then being used to defame specific noble families and particular professions by bringing them into connection with the ill-repute of vampirism.[40]

Beyond this, the terminology of vampires assumed a new re-interpretation as a term of political struggle in the German Imperial domains within the context of the anti-Semitic campaign against Joseph Süß Oppenheimer, the Court Agent of Charles Alexander of Württemberg. Through drawing an

Figure 3.7 and 3.8 Michael Ranft's *Tractat von dem Kauen und Schmatzen der Todten in Gräbern* (*Treatise on the Chewing and Chomping of the Dead in Graves*) and the motto 'Mortuus non mordet' ('The Dead Do Not Bite').

As this handbook on the issue by Michael Ranft demonstrates, the 'chewing and chomping of the dead in their graves' was already a major subject in German-speaking lands, long before one could even begin to talk of bloodsucking Southeast European vampires. In the illustration of a peaceful and orderly graveyard, and referring back to the Latin turn of phrase 'canis mortuus non mordet' ('a dead dog does not bite'), Michael Ranft provides a motto for his book that, from the outset, depicts the alleged vampire bite as absurd.

Source: Title page and frontispiece of Michael Ranft's *Treatise on the Chewing and Chomping of the Dead in Graves, Wherein the True Nature of the Hungarian Vampires and Blood Suckers Have Been Shown, and in Which All the Scholars Who Have Come to the Fore in this Matter Are Also Recensored* (Leipzig, 1734).

analogy between the circulation of money and the circulation of blood, 'Jud Süß' was defamed as a vampire.[41] Nobody was immune from the popularity of this stereotype and, on 14 June 1789, according to the Heidelberg gymnasium director and university lecturer Johann Friedrich Abegg, no less a figure than Immanuel Kant described the Jews as the 'vampyres of society'.[42] The incorporation of the metaphor of the bloodsucker into the canon of anti-Semitic stereotypes demonstrates the popularity of the discourse.

Witch Hunts and 'Magia posthuma' in the Habsburg Empire

In the context of the gradual discontinuation of witch trials in Western Europe from the late seventeenth century onwards – they were outlawed in France in 1628 and in Prussia in 1728 – the 'discovery' of the vampire by the West in the mid eighteenth century provided ample fuel for concerted attempts to portray the Ottoman-dominated Balkans as oriental. Vampirism was seen as a chimera, within whose snare the Habsburg Empire astonishingly also fell. In the provinces of Moravia and Silesia, and especially in the Olomouc Consistory that was part of the Teutonic Order, reports on nachzehrers and poltergeists appeared from the mid sixteenth century onwards, and in particular from the early seventeenth century. In these it seems that being a witch was perceived by the population as a preliminary stage to harm-inflicting revenancy. Just as the authorities knew to instrumentalize witch trials in order to create social discipline, so they also sought to restrict the desecration of the graves of suspected revenants; often, however, they proved to be helpless in the face of the superstitious behaviour of the common people.[43] A typical case was reflected in a note from the parish archives of Engelsberg, dated 30 September 1674.

Following the death in March 1674 in the neighbouring Lichtewerden of Christoph Englisch, a man of disrepute during his lifetime, a poltergeist supposedly began to make its presence felt in the village. On 17 September, at the request of the residents, the authorities ordered an exhumation, and this was carried out on 26 September in the presence of secular and spiritual dignitaries. Since, despite prodding the corpse with a rod, the Freudenthal gravediggers were not in a position to make any concrete statements about its appearance, the procedure was repeated on the following day. The gravediggers from the neighbouring Friedland proved to be much more ruthless in their approach and climbed down into the grave, prodded the body with a sickle and discovered – thus fulfilling their task – that the corpse was still fresh and that there was evidence of a recent loss of blood. Following the Church's banishment of the dead man from the graveyard, the secular commissioners appointed an executioner. On 28 September, the sarcophagus was lifted over the cemetery wall and, along with all the instruments that had previously been used, taken to the parish boundary, where the dead man was burned on a pyre. In the meantime, the empty grave in Lichtewerden was sealed up with stones.[44]

Although such cases were very common in the region, clearly neither the secular nor the Church authorities had come up with any clear rules for dealing with them. In choosing a title for his 1706 work, published in Olomouc, which presented his opinions on the issue from a legal point of view, Carl Ferdinand von Schertz chose a term that was subsequently to become proverbial: 'Magia posthuma'. Schertz outlined the case of a woman who was alleged to have emerged from her grave as a spirit four years after her death, sometimes in human form and sometimes in the form of a dog, choking and afflicting both people and cattle. He also raised the question as to whether the exhumation and burning of a corpse was legal. In a letter to the Bishop of Olomouc, he recommended, in order to ward off such cases in future, that a legal court trial be conducted with posthumous execution as punishment, and also suggested exorcism as a possible alternative.[45] The problem confronting the Bishop of Olomouc was that in the East Central European region, nachzehrer conceptions overlapped with continuing witch hunts. Witch trials were common in Central Europe in the period between 1430 and 1780, and the belief in witches had developed in the fifteenth century from a combination of magical conceptions and Christian theology. The Church accused sorcerers and witches of having entered into a pact with the devil, and they were therefore demonized for having carnal relations with the devil, practising black magic, for levitating and flying, and for holding covens. This conspiracy theory was further fuelled

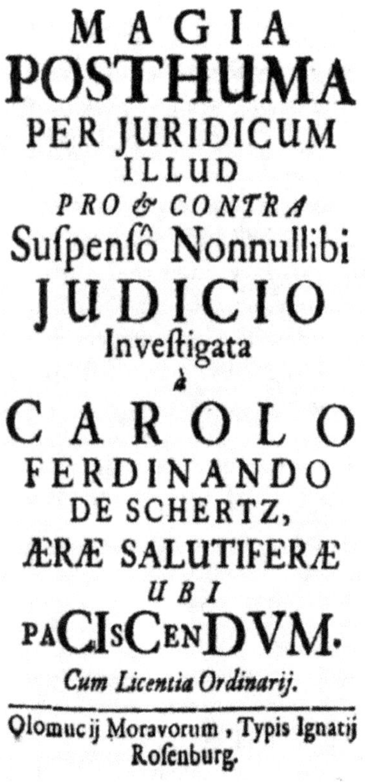

MAGIA POSTHUMA
PER JURIDICUM ILLUD
PRO & CONTRA
Suspensô Nonnullibi
JUDICIO
Investigata
à
CAROLO FERDINANDO DE SCHERTZ,
ÆRÆ SALUTIFERÆ
UBI
paCIsCenDVM.
Cum Licentia Ordinarij.

Olomucij Moravorum, Typis Ignatij Rosenburg.

Figure 3.9 Carl Ferdinand von Schertz's *Magia posthuma* (Post-mortal Sorcery).

At the start of the eighteenth century, in placing the term 'Magia posthuma' on his title page, the legal scholar Carl Ferdinand von Schertz helped to shape a concept that was still causing headlines several decades later during the reign of the Empress Maria Theresa. The terms 'post(h)umus' or 'post(h)uma' actually referred to the sons and daughters of fathers who had died before the birth of their offspring.

Source: Title page of *Magia posthuma per juridicum illud pro contra suspenso nonnullibi judicio investigata a Carolo Ferdinando de Schertz, arae alutiferae ubi paCisCenDUM* (The posthumous magic in this Imperial Report considering the suspension of common sense investigated by Carl Ferdinand von Schertz in the year of our salvation 1706, through which peace should be restored in this respect) (Olomouc, 1706).

by the Inquisition, which made it possible to identify all manner of scapegoats within the context of the expected imminent coming of the Last Judgment. Popular interests therefore went hand-in-hand with the authorities' attempts to ward off black magic and combat troublemakers (see the section entitled 'The Revenant of the Middle Ages' in Chapter 1).

Eastern and Southeastern Europe remained largely unaffected by the witch-hunting hysteria. In Russia, for example, demonology did not play any role in the accusation of sorcerers.[46] By contrast, other conditions dominated in East Central Europe. Because of the weakness of the central authorities, witch-hunts were also very common in the Polish Noble Republic and were only gradually phased out. In Hungary, the appearance of vampiric incidents on the periphery of the kingdom was fairly simultaneous with the end of the witch-trials, which had reached their high point from the late seventeenth century through to the mid eighteenth century. On the basis of this chronology, it therefore seems that the belief in witches travelled from the West to the East, whereas the concept of the vampire moved in the opposite direction around the same period, entering Western Europe from the East (see the section entitled 'The Nachzehrer of the Early Modern Period' in Chapter 1).[47]

Roman Catholic Attitudes towards Vampirism

In the Habsburg Empire, Augustin Calmet, the Abbot of the Benedictine Monastery of Sénones in Lorraine, set new accents in the vampire debate in his *Dissertations sur les Apparitions des Esprits, et sur les Vampires et Revenants de Hongrie, de Moravie* (*Dissertations on the Apparitions of Spirits, and on the Vampires and Revenants of Hungary and Moravia*), which first appeared in 1746 and then, in a revised version, in 1749. In this work, Calmet shifted the emphasis from the Orthodox regions of southern Hungary to the Catholic regions of Silesia and Moravia. Calmet's explanations were based not only on the rediscovery of old reports on the so-called 'chewing and chomping of dead in their graves', but also on his own research and further materials he had gathered on the current vampire cases. His observation of a sequence of hallucinations served as a hook for him; in this respect, pilgrimages, spiritualist movements and witch-hunts were the precursors of the desecration of corpses in his own time.[48] From a theological perspective, Calmet's study is rooted in the Vatican position on the phenomenon of vampirism. It is therefore in keeping both with the four-volume discourse *De servorum Dei beatificatione et beatorum canonizatione* (*On the Beatification of the Servants of God and the Canonization of the Blessed*; Bologna, 1734–1738), written by the later Pope (from 1740) Benedict XIV under his civilian name of Prosper Lambertini, and with the *Dissertazione spora i vampiri* (*Dissertation on Vampires*; Naples, 1774), a manuscript written by the Archbishop of Trani Giuseppe Davanzati in around 1740.

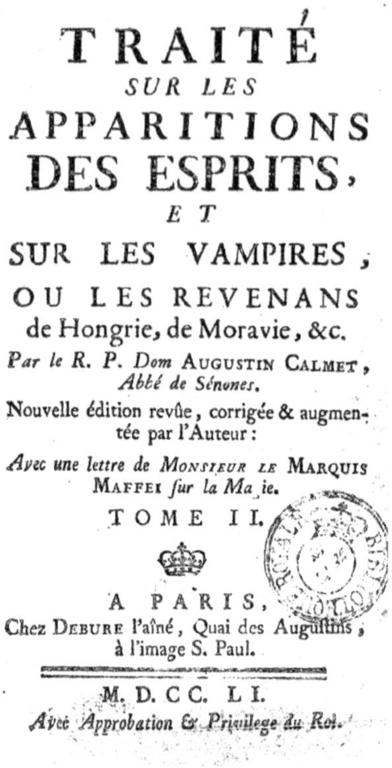

> TRAITÉ
> SUR LES
> APPARITIONS
> DES ESPRITS,
> ET
> SUR LES VAMPIRES,
> OU LES REVENANS
> de Hongrie, de Moravie, &c.
> Par le R. P. Dom AUGUSTIN CALMET,
> Abbé de Sénones.
> Nouvelle édition revûe, corrigée & augmentée par l'Auteur:
> Avec une lettre de MONSIEUR LE MARQUIS MAFFEI sur la Ma_ie.
> TOME II.
>
> A PARIS,
> Chez DEBURE l'aîné, Quai des Augustins,
> à l'image S. Paul.
>
> M. D. CC. L I.
> Avec Approbation & Privilege du Roi.

Figure 3.10 Augustin Calmet's *Traité sur les apparitions des esprits et sur les vampires, ou les revenans de Hongrie, de Moravie, & c.* (*Learned Treatment of Material, on the Appearance of Spirits, and of Vampires in Hungary, Moravia*). In the second volume of his standard work on demonology from the eighteenth century, the French Benedictine Augustin Calmet directed the attention of the reader to the East Central European territories as the place of origin of vampirism. Source: Title page of the second volume of Augustin Calmet's, *Learned Treatment of Material, on the Appearance of Spirits, and of Vampires in Hungary, Moravia* (Paris, 1751). Used with permission from the Bibliothèque nationale de France, signature 8-S-1525 (2).

To a large extent, Lambertini was concerned with pointing out the distinction between magical ideas and divine miracles in order to justify Church teaching on the saints whose bodies, according to tradition, did not decompose. The future pope first addressed the issue of vampires in the fourth volume of the second edition of 1743, making reference to the Nuremberg *Commercium litterarium* (however, the synopsis of the various editions that appeared in 1757 under the editorship of Emmanuel de Avezedo only contains a short note in this respect). According to Lambertini, the coming back to life of dead people can only be conceived of as a divine miracle and, in terms of the laws of nature, is an impossibility. However, in the sanctioning of defensive measures against supposed revenants by the Church authorities, the belief in a possible resurrection of the bodies of normal, sinful mortals in the form of vampires did gain belated approval. Under certain conditions, numerous examples could be found for the incorruptibility of dead bodies. This can only be interpreted as a sign of holiness where the person concerned had previously led an exemplary and pious life. The temporary continued growth of hair and nails after death was also nothing extraordinary, but only divine or demonic forces could be considered responsible for the flowing of fresh blood from a dead corpse.[49]

By contrast, Davanzatti – who was writing at the bequest of the Viceroy of Naples, Cardinal Wolfgang Hannibal Graf von Schrattenbach, the serving Bishop of Olomouc – took up a clear position on the cases of revenancy at the Military Frontier and in the Moravian-Silesian border region. In his view, vampires were an expression of the power of imagination and belonged in the realm of fantasy. The basis for their existence lay in ignorance and fear.[50]

In terms of content, following on from Pope Benedict XIV, Calmet was concerned with questioning the blasphemy that the belief in vampires brought with it on three fronts: the corruption of the doctrine of the Holy Eucharist, the inversion of the belief in the incorruptibility of the bodies of the saints, and the profound questioning of the Church's teaching on the resurrection of the dead. In his view, the central dilemma facing him was the need to negate the existence of ghosts and night-demons, whilst at the same time justifying the existence of angels. In seeking to avoid such contradictions, he drew a clear distinction between the miracles of God and the works of the devil, arguing that, in the final analysis, the world is shaped according to the will of the Almighty.[51]

However, in this regard, Calmet's attempts were not entirely convincing. Thus, in 1772, no less a person than Voltaire, in his *Questions sur l'Encyclopédie*, complained about the inconsistencies in Calmet's works, and depicted the stock-market speculators and traders as the true bloodsuckers, and monks as the real vampires.[52]

A further achievement of Calmet's work was to transfer the South Slavic term of 'vampire' to similar phenomena in East Central Europe, not least through his use of the Polish term 'Upir' (*upiór*). Indirectly, the phenomenon of vampirism was also located firmly within the context of the Greek Orthodox Church.

'Magia posthuma' in the Carpathian Mountains: Georg Tallar versus Dorothea Pihsin

Significantly, at the same time as Calmet's dissertation was being disseminated around the German-speaking lands, new cases of revenancy were once again making the headlines. This began with a case in the settlement of Kapnik near Nagybánia, the present-day Baia Mare close to the Romanian border to the Carpathian Ukraine, known for its gold and silver mines and for a mint. The case had been outlined by an inspector, a master of the mint and a court magistrate – all of whom had German names – in a report to the Imperial Court Administration for Mints and Mining on 28 February 1753. According to this report, an infectious disease had begun to spread in the autumn of 1752, striking down several miners. The idea was to set up an investigation that, alongside the physicians at the mine, would draw in the apothecaries and surgeons from Nagybány, as well as doctors from the neighbouring Felsőbánya, but the cases of death quickly began to decline. For the time being, therefore, the planned investigation was postponed and events thus began to take their course.

Following the death of five further miners between mid January and mid February 1753, all of whom had suffered four days of severe illness, with symptoms of chills, bloody spittle and a burning sensation, a certain Johannes Jablonovski was appointed to conduct the autopsies. Judging by his name, this was a Slav, and he also fell victim to the unknown disease on 16 February. On 17 February, physicians from Kapnik, Nagybánia and Felsőbánya were not able to identify the cause of Jablonovski's death, but, according to the report, they did identify a great amount of water in his bloodless corpse. This in itself was clearly enough to allow for rumours to spread in the neighbourhood about the workings of a bloodsucker.

Tales about nightly visitations by ghosts and nightmares were already doing the rounds at this stage, and the suspicions of the population fell upon two women who had died on 13 October and 8 November, Dorothea Pihsin and Anna Tonnerin. A posthumous investigation was initiated against both. Upon the opening of the graves on 20 February, it was found that, whereas the corpse of the woman who had died later had completely decomposed, the decomposition of the corpse of the former was only partially under way. In contrast to the face, the hands and feet were found not to have decayed at all, but to be fresh and intact, and the corpse appeared to be somewhat bloated. The burial shroud also seemed to be drenched in fresh blood. Thereafter, Anna Tonnerin was declared by the Council to be innocent and an autopsy of the corpse of Dorothea Pihsin was carried out, which revealed her body to still be saturated with blood. Thus, as a result, Pihsin was posthumously convicted of witchcraft and bloodsucking. Her corpse was handed over to the executioner, who burned it under the gallows on a pyre. A great deal of blood was reported to flow from the body at the execution, thereby confirming the correctness of the judgment.

As the report goes on to mention, a further miner had already taken ill before Dorothea Pihsin's execution, but the disease reached its peak with her trial. In order to take the wind out of the sails of any rumours about an infectious scourge, the surrounding districts were also informed of this.

All in all, the report reads like an attempt by the authorities to justify a witch trial, which had been conducted without clerical participation, in which Dorothea Pihsin had been forced to assume the role of scapegoat, and that had been pursued in order to re-establish law and order at the local level and also to demonstrate the functioning of the mining administration to the central imperial authorities. If this impression is correct, then the authorities utilized the belief in revenants simply as a means to pursue their own interests.[53]

Against the backdrop of her policy of settling the thinly populated Habsburg regions of Southeastern Europe with German colonists, the Empress Maria Theresa established a commission, headed up by the surgeon Georg Tallar,

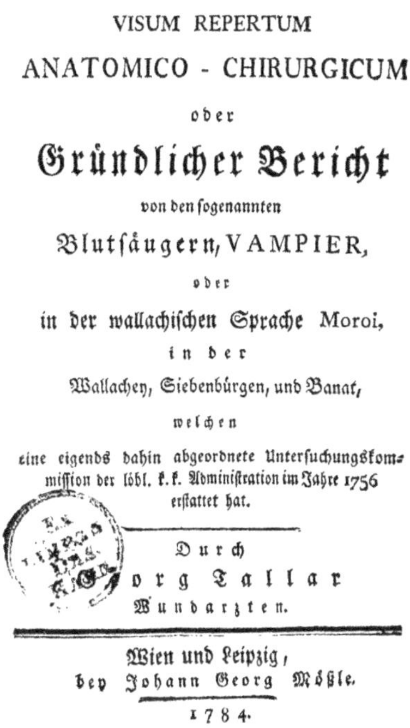
VISUM REPERTUM
ANATOMICO - CHIRURGICUM
oder
Gründlicher Bericht
von den sogenannten
Blutsäugern, VAMPIER,
oder
in der wallachischen Sprache Moroi,
in der
Wallachey, Siebenbürgen, und Banat,
welchen
eine eigends dahin abgeordnete Untersuchungskommission der löbl. k.k. Administration im Jahre 1756 erstattet hat.
Durch
Georg Tallar
Wundarzten.
Wien und Leipzig,
bey Johann Georg Mößle.
1784.

Figure 3.11 Georg Tallar's *Visum repertum anatomico-chirurgicum* (*Anatomical-Chirurgical Report*). In the Latin phrase *Visum repertum* in the title to his 1756 memorandum, Georg Tallar referred back to the famous Flückinger report of 1732 (see the section entitled 'The Discovery of the Vampire' above), but shifted the emphasis away from the South Slavic vampires to the Wallachian *moroi*. Source: Title page of Georg Tallar's *Anatomical-Chirurgical Report or a Thorough Report on the So-Called Bloodsuckers, Vampires or, in the Wallachian Language, Moroi, in Wallachia, Transylvania and the Banat* (Vienna/Leipzig, 1784). Used with permission from the Niedersächsische Staats- und Universitätsbibliothek Göttingen, signature 8 MED PRACT 1736/61.

to investigate the alleged vampires in the peripheral regions of Hungary. The commission's 1756 report, which completely ignored the 'Morbus hungaricus' or typhus fever and its numerous victims, was first published in 1784 under the title of *Visum repertum anatomico-chirurgicum oder Gründlicher Bericht von den sogenannten Blütsaugern, Vampier, oder in der wallachischen Sprache Moroi, in der Wallachey, Siebenbürgen, und Banat* (*Anatomical-Chirurgical Report or a Thorough Report on the so-called bloodsuckers, vampires or, in the Wallachian language, moroi, in Wallachia, Transylvania and the Banat*) (see the section entitled 'Lost Souls in the Danube-Balkan Region' in Chapter 4).

'Magia posthuma' in Moravia: Gerard van Swieten versus Rosalia Polakin

The case of Rosa(lia) Polakin, who was known to be a miracle healer, in (Frei-) Hermersdorf near Bennisch, to the west of Freudenthal on the present-day Polish-Czech border, created a great degree of public interest.

Due to her profession, the woman with the Slavic-sounding name Rosa Polakin was accused by the local population of witchcraft and, after her death on 22 December 1754, of revenancy. She was therefore seen to pose a threat to the other souls reposing in the cemetery who had not yet entered paradise. Accordingly, on 30 January 1755, the Episcopal Consistory of Olomouc responded to the demands of the Hermersdorf population from 19 January 1755 and sanctioned the burning of Rosa Polakin's corpse, which had not yet begun to decompose.

Following this action, and because the local authorities had taken it upon themselves to burn a total of nineteen corpses (although it should be stated that the Vienna newspapers omitted to mention this for reasons of censorship), the scandal spread to the imperial court of Maria Theresa. Behind the scenes, however, the Empress initiated a campaign against the 'Magia posthuma'. On 8 February 1755, she instructed her personal physician Gerard van Swieten, an anatomist and military physician, to undertake an investigation in the area and to draw up a report. On 9 February, she also instructed the Bohemian-Silesian administration to provide assistance to the anatomist Johannes Goser and the military physician Cristian Vabst in their investigations. They were tasked with discovering who 'this so-called vampire or bloodsucker' visited, when and under what conditions. Of particular interest were the forms that the alleged demon was supposed to take, as well as the underlying motivations for the statements of the victims.[54]

According to van Swieten's memorandum, the entire affair was grounded in uncertainty and ignorance. In his view, the physicians who had been commissioned with the postmortem examinations, and whom he referred to as 'Bader' – that is, quack-doctor – were overburdened by their task. There was no reason to expect a body to decay within one month in the heart of winter. The Episcopal Consistory also pointed towards certain signs and marks as evidence, although without describing these in any further detail, and it remains the case that nobody had actually complained about any possible bloodsucking. It is true that the executioner had initially claimed that blood had flown to the floor in streams upon the carving up of the corpse, but he then went on to qualify this by stating that the amount would not have overspilled a spoon. Finally, after the event, the inhabitants of the village may have spoken of nightmares and other anxieties, but they did not testify to any actual apparitions by the dead.

The local authorities clearly identified Marianna Saligerin, who had died eighteen months before Rosa(lia) Polakin, as the originator of all the incidents in Hermersdorf. This woman, known as 'Wenzel Richterin' – that is, a Bohemian soothsayer – was suspected of witchcraft, not only because of her suspicious surname of 'Saligerin', which referred to a mythical figure in the Alpine region, endowed with magical powers, but also because of her thoroughly commendable service as a healer. Following her death and burial, therefore, twenty-eight surrounding graves were opened up and nineteen supposedly nondecomposed corpses were burned. In his report, van Swieten accused the Consistory of having acted too hastily in executing the bodies and disturbing the rest of the dead. He saw it as particularly shocking that the permitted desecration of the bodies clearly had a certain tradition in Olomouc. In his research,

Vampyrismus

von

Herrn Baron Gerhard van Swieten
verfasset,

aus dem Französischen ins Deutsche
übersetzet,

und als ein Anhang der Abhandlung des Daseyns
der Gespenster beigerücket.

Augsburg, 1768.

Figure 3.12 *Vampyrism by Herrn Baron Gerhard van Swieten.*
The French-language memorandum of van Swieten for Maria Theresa appeared, confusingly, thirteen years later, in German in the appendix of *Abhandlung über das Dasein von Gespenster* (*Treatise on the Existence of Ghosts*).
Source: Title page of chapter 'Vampyrism by Herrn Baron Gerhard van Swieten', translated from French into German, and added as an appendix to *Treatise on the Existence of Ghosts*, in [A. Mayer], *Abhandlung des Daseins der Gespenster, nebst einem Anhange vom Vampyrismus* (Augsburg, 1768).

he came across a case from 1731 in which the corpses of two adults and seven children had been burned, since they had been buried in the immediate vicinity of a supposed revenant. On the basis not least of this, in his eyes, blatant injustice, van Swieten called upon the state to take action and demanded a legal resolution.[55] The Empress reacted promptly. On 1 March 1755, she issued an order, stripping the Church of all of its competences in these matters and transferring responsibility for the investigation of 'Magia posthuma' or the illegal burning of corpses, witchcraft, grave-robbing and the obsession with the devil to the secular authorities. So as to avoid the term 'vampire', the order made reference to 'a case of such ghosts'. For the enlightened Empress, the only possible explanations of such phenomena were dreams or imagination. However, she not only held the gullibility of the population to be responsible for this, but also denounced the prejudices of the clergy. In the final analysis, her primary concern was with finding explanations for the underlying deception.[56]

The Directorate for Public Administration, which had been set up in 1749 and that was responsible, among other things, for public sanitation, took a similar approach. In linguistic terms, the minutes of its meeting on 17 March 1755 on the vampire of Hermersdorf, which the Directorate located in Silesia, followed the characteristic style of Maria Theresa's order and, in terms of its content, closely reflected the arguments of van Swieten. The banishment of suspected corpses from a cemetery by clerical and secular authorities and their subsequent incineration were described as arrogant pretension. With regard to the case of Marianna Saligerin, there was an interference in the secular jurisdiction responsible for the examining cases of magic. Beyond this, through their granting of permission for superstitious actions, such as the opening of cemetery walls in order to carry out suspected corpses and the calling up of relatives and friends to act as coffin-bearers, the authorities had also made themselves liable to prosecution. In order to placate the situation, the Directorate recommended that two Jesuits from Troppau and the regional physician be sent to Hermersdorf in order to provide the population with spiritual and medical assistance.[57] The recommended publication of van Swieten's memorandum only happened unofficially, when a German version appeared in 1768 in an appendix to the Augsburg-printed *Abhandlung des Daseins der Gespenster* (*Treatise on the Existence of Ghosts*).

Frederick the Great's Press War against Maria Theresa

In the context of the political struggle for Silesia, the vampire cases represented a perfect opportunity for Prussia to conduct a press war against the Habsburgs, despite the fact that, in principle, Frederick the Great was actually more tolerant than his father Frederick William I in his approach to 'Magia posthuma'. The French writer and philosopher Jean-Baptiste de Boyer, the Marquis d'Argens, who had been living at the Prussian court since the turn of 1741/1742 and who had been appointed as Director of the Historical-Philosophical Class at the Academy of Sciences, was among those who were keen to take up a position on vampirism. In his well-received 'Jewish Letters', which were published in their French original in 1737 and then in German translation, first in 1748 in the journal *Der Naturforscher* and then again in a complete German edition in 1764, he commented on the *Mercure historique et politique*'s 1736 reporting on the cases from Medveđa in an enlightened manner. In his view, the non-decomposed bodies and alleged bloodsucking could be explained by natural phenomena and popular imagination.[58]

Over the subsequent period, the Austro-Prussian conflict over Silesia was to prove one of the most significant factors in the political instrumentalization of the belief in vampires. Following the First Silesian War (1740–42), Austria was forced to hand over Upper and Lower Silesia up to the Opava, as well as the County of Glatz, to Prussia. A so-called Austrian Silesia, the Habsburgs retained only the Duchies of Troppau and Jägerndorf, as well as the Duchy of Teschen on the other side of the Opava. This status quo was confirmed by the Second Silesian War of 1744/1745. In this context, the Berlin press used the incidents in Austrian Silesia in 1755 to confront the Habsburgs with accusations of backwardness. Whilst Maria Theresa attempted to impose silence upon her press organs, Frederick II sought to shape public opinion in his own interests. The *Berlinische privilegierte Zeitung* (*The Privileged Berlin Newspaper*), also known as the *Vossische Zeitung* (*Voss' Newspaper*) after its editor Christian Friedrich Voss, and the *Berlinische Nachrichten von Staats- und gelehrten Sachen* (*Berlin News on State and Scholarly Issues*) both published, in their editions of 3 April 1755, a report from Upper Silesia dated 16 March 1755. This consisted of the news that a 'herb witch', known under her nickname of the 'Tyrolean Doctor', had died in Hermsdorf.

Before her death, the Tyrolean doctor was alleged to have pleaded with her husband to cut off her head before her burial and not to allow her to be interned in the Catholic cemetery. Following her passing, and following a series of further deaths in the village, the residents became persuaded that the herbal healer had become a vampire. Thirty graves were therefore opened, and two-thirds of the bodies that were uncovered were suspected of vampirism and were burned accordingly – according to the Prussian papers 'at the bequest of the very highest authorities'.

In order to dampen somewhat the heightened tensions between Austria and Prussia, the *Vossische Zeitung* did, in its edition of 8 May 1755, print a report from Vienna, dated 23 April, which offered a certain qualification and, in discussing the results of the Habsburg commission of investigation, traced these back to the superstitions and fantasies of the Habsburgs' subjects.[59]

Following the 1755 ban on 'Magia posthuma', vampire reports disappeared from the headlines in the Habsburg Empire. Furthermore, a revision of the legal system also led to the legal marginalization of witchcraft. On 5 November 1766, Maria Theresa enacted the article on sorcery, witchcraft and soothsaying. This only discussed ghosts, ghouls and the possessed, whilst carefully avoiding the term 'vampire' and focusing instead on satanic machinations. In addition, instead of bloodsucking, mention is made only of the mixing of poison. The courts received specific instructions for dealing with investigations into deception and madness. Where the judge did find there to be evidence of actual sorcery or witchcraft, he was to inform both the High Court and the Empress herself. In this way, an official language for such cases was found for the public.[60]

From then on, in the Habsburg Empire, vampire tales were only reported upon at best in a trivial form. The supposed activities of the undead were now seen less to include bloodsucking, which was linked to the risk of contagion, and more the harassing of the community through the playing of all manner of mischievous tricks, such as shape-shifting, choking, participating at meals and festivals, and the acting out of sexuality. Following the Seven Years' War (1756–63), Prussia established itself as the fifth great power in Europe and was later to be confronted with its own vampire problem as an empire in the nineteenth century.

Kasparek's Metamorphosis from Poltergeist to Vampire

A potential missing link between the ghost rider from the Moravian Bennisch (see the section entitled 'The Nachzehrer of the Early Modern Period' in Chapter 1) and the vampires from the Serbian Medveđa (see the section entitled 'The Discovery of the Vampire' above) can be found in a case of revenancy from the Upper Hungarian Lubló (German Lublau), which was alleged to have taken place in Spiš in 1718.[61] Spiš is a region in present-day Northern Slovakia, on the border with Poland. From a historical perspective, settlements with self-administrative rights were important in the area, which belonged in legal terms to the Kingdom of Hungary, but were predominantly controlled, de facto, by the Polish Noble Republic from 1412 to 1772. From the thirteenth century, these settlements were shaped culturally by Germans and populated in part by Gorals, i.e. Slavs from the Polish-Slovakian region of contact. Upper Hungary was never subject to Ottoman conquest; instead, the region was drawn into confessional conflicts in the era of the Reformation and the Counter-Reformation. Against the backdrop of the successful defeat of the Ottomans at the Second Siege of Vienna in 1683 and the eventual restitution of the Kingdom of Hungary at the Treaty of Passarowitz in 1718, the first decade of the eighteenth century saw a temporary emancipation from Habsburg rule following the military revolt of Franz II Rákóczi. However, the partitions of Poland at the end of the century meant that all the towns of Spiš were once again incorporated into Hungary. The state patent of 1781 allowed all confessions to practise their religion unimpeded. The restrictions placed on the guild system from 1783 led to a decline of the German dominance of the Spiš towns. The revolution of 1848 even saw a coalition of interests between the Hungarian and German elites on the basis of their shared socioeconomic interests. A Magyarization of the region then set in following the Austro-Hungarian Compromise of 1867, which reached its zenith in the lifting of civic self-administration and the incorporation of the towns into the Hungarian Komitat (County) of Szepes.[62]

On the basis of the information provided by the responsible notary responsible and a request made by the citizens of Lublau to the Bishop of Krakow, Michal Szembek, it is possible to reconstruct the following about the case of Michael Kasparek (Polish Michał Kasperek).

The resident of Lublau was alleged to have appeared to his servants immediately after his death on 28 February 1718. Interrogations of others who claimed to have been affected confirmed further harassment such as striking, biting and choking. After Kasparek's corpse was found not to have begun to decompose a good forty days after his burial, two townspeople were sent to the Bishop of Krakow in order to ask him to authorize the local priest to take further measures. Their reasoning was, first, that an 'effective antidote' to 'terror' and 'evil' could only be prescribed by 'the highest spiritual doctor' – that is, God – and second, that the 'measures taken in neighbouring localities' had made it clear that only an exhumation could provide a resolution in such situations. It seems clear that there followed a temporary period of peace, before panic then once again broke out among the residents of the town. The Bishop of Krakow granted his permission, whereupon a posthumous execution was carried out on 26 April. First, the heart was extracted and buried beneath a compost heap, and then the corpse was burned. Much to the amusement of the onlookers, the body was seen to croak and flounce with his legs on the pyre – a motif that also appeared in the chronicle entries on the Shepherd of Blow from 1337. After Kasparek's brother had protested against this treatment, the dead man's heart was handed to him. However, the destruction of the corpse did not bring an end to the posthumous activities, and Lublau was visited by a series of fires in May and June. Kasparek's relatives were then forced to swear that, during his lifetime, the dead man had neither owned a magic ring nor undertaken devilish deeds, and had not had any sort of connection with sorcery. Even the religious exorcism, carried out on 27 June and that was perhaps ecumenical in nature, did not produce the desired effect. It was only the burning of Kasparek's heart in the German- and Protestant-occupied town hall that brought an end to the misfortunes.[63]

In the notary's minutes, there is no mention of a consultation with the Starost, who administered the Spiš district on behalf of the Polish king and who resided in Lublau Castle. Clearly the affair was seen primarily as a church and local affair, rather than a secular or supraregional matter. A report received by the editor of the Nuremberg-based *Europäischer Niemand* (*European Nobody*) in July 1718 from the Komitat (County) of Liptau, to the west of Spiš, provides an insight into the workings of the rumour mill. The headline 'Michael Caspareck, who continues to wander following his death in Hungary' was considered sensational enough not only to publish a report (in Latin), but also to print a portrait of Kasparek as a rider on the frontispiece. The text had the following to say about Kasparek.

The dead debt-collector Michael Kasparek had appeared as an 'evil spirit on horseback', knocking on the door of a wedding party and disturbing them with his unseemly behaviour. Thereafter, he impregnated not only his wife but also several maids. He then left the region temporarily in order to collect outstand-

Figure 3.13 'Michael Caspareck, who continues to wander following his death in Hungary'.
In 1719, a decade before the vampire hype, a Nuremberg journal illustrated a report on a revenant in the Upper-Hungarian Spiš, in present-day Slovakia, with a portrait of an eerie rider of death, who was said to be causing unrest in the small town.
Source: Frontispiece of *Der Europäische Niemand* (*European Nobody*), Part II (Nuremberg, 1719).

ing debts that were owed to him in Warsaw, and then reimbursed his creditors in Lublau. At the same time, however, he could not resist playing several mischievous tricks, such as shoving a hop-carrier into the River Poprad. He responded to the posthumous execution of his corpse with an oath of vengeance, in Polish, and subsequently carried out a series of arson attacks. When questioned by his wife about the reasons for his revenancy, he replied that neither the devil in hell nor God in heaven would admit him, since it was not his heart which had been burned, but that of another. Therefore, he was condemned to wander the earth for seven years.

As will be shown later, the solution to this mystery was to lend wings to popular flights of fantasy.[64] First, however, one further witness to the events should be named: the pastor Georg Buchholz, from the Kesmark to the south of Lublau, who informed his son Jakob, who was living in Elbing in Prussia at the time, of the Kasparek affair. In 1754, Jakob then summarized what his father had told him in his continuation of the family chronicle, which his father had written up to 1709. This report, published in 1904, confirms the previously mentioned subjects, thus lending them a certain authenticity, since the writer referred to Kasparek's close contemporaries. What was new were the reasons given for Kasparek's return from the realm of the dead.

Kasparek's revenancy was now traced back to a false oath that he had made in connection with a fraud. On the one hand, the dead man carried out his activities as a choker and a shape-shifter and, on the other, as an apocalyptic rider and a poltergeist, he not only went about his business, but also continued to participate in the social life of the town. He appeared to Jakob Buchholz's father-in-law, among others. The countermeasures taken by a Uniate priest, such as replacing his heart with a sheep's heart, proved to be fruitless. Following his execution and decapitation, Kasparek swore revenge on his own brother, in Polish. (As a judge, his brother was not only responsible for the measures taken, but through his position had also lent the affair a certain symbolic weight.) In contrast to what had been suggested in the *Europäischer Niemand*, Kasparek completely disappeared from the scene following the series of fires. The subject of interest is no longer the revenancy itself, but rather the fate of those left behind. Kasparek's widow later married again.[65]

The main Hungarian witness for the revenant Michael Kasparek was the Slovakian historian Matthias Belius, who also mentioned Lublau in his 1723 work *Hungariae antiquae et novae Prodromus* (*History of Ancient and New Hungary*). In keeping with his characterization as a 'less than respectable' huckster, Kasparek not only slept with his wife after his death, but also paid off her debts. Following 'established popular practice', the corpse was dug up and – in contrast to what was stated by the Lublau notary – after its decapitation, accompanied by a great deal of blood loss, the body was burned. The town had brought down the wrath of God upon themselves for their superstitiousness and was punished with a conflagration of fires that, in turn, were also connected with the dead man. Many believed that an 'evil spirit' with a human appearance was at work here. Others suggested that the phantom had merely donned a mask. Belius, for his part, satisfied himself with the conclusion that this was an edifying 'horror story', worthy of remembrance.[66]

In May 1890, Bertalan Matirko informed the Gesellschaft für Völkerkunde Ungarns (Society for Hungarian Ethnography) about the legend being spread among the common population. According to this, the Lublau resident had exported wine to Poland.

Once, the wife of a Warsaw merchant friend had permitted him to store his full barrels in her house and to take away the empty ones, and Kasparek had taken this opportunity to steal a barrel full of gold. When the Warsaw merchant demanded his property back, Kasparek swore his innocence by stating that the earth should spit out his corpse and the heavens spurn his soul were he to have sworn falsely. In the light of this impertinence, he met with just punishment. After his death three days later, he was forced to wander the earth as a spirit. 'In the night', according to Matirko – reflecting the general interest of ethnographers in the Southeastern European vampire phenomenon – 'he visited the sleeping and drew out their blood.' At the same time, he also used his powers to steal from the rich and give to the poor. However, this did not satisfy him, and at the intercession of his wife it was decided to reduce his suffering. Yet, at the opening of his grave, a bitter truth was then revealed: 'thanks to the human blood he was drinking he had become fitter and fatter from day to day'. Neither the decapitation nor the incineration of his corpse brought the desired redemption and, instead, Kasparek began to appear as an arsonist. It was only finally through an exorcism carried out by the Hungarian and Polish bishops that his machinations were brought to an end. Kasparek was banished to Šariš Castle in the neighbouring Komitat (county) to the east, the ancestral home of the Rákóczis. Bound to the tail of a white horse, from then on, Kasparek was forced to await the hour, which moved closer with the falling of each further hair, when he would stand in judgment before God's throne.[67]

The process of metamorphosis from revenant to bloodsucker can be seen in the reception of the case among the wider German-speaking public. Alongside the Württemberg privy councillor and editor of the *Europäischer Niemand*, Philipp Balthasar Sinold, other persons to have tackled the case of Michael Kasparek included the superintendent of Schaumburg-Lippe, Eberhard David Hauber, compiler of the *Biblioteca sive acta scripta magica* (*The Magic Library or Magic Writings*) and the publicist and esoteric Georg Conrad Horst in his *Zauber-Bibliothek* (*Magic Library*). In the *Europäischer Niemand* of 1719, three scholarly figures ruminated on the reports of revenancy and, in an enlightened manner, traced them back to superstition and the work of the devil. Kasparek's desire for food and sex demonstrate that 'no mere [spirit], but a spirit made flesh' had been at work. In the final analysis, this was no more than an edifying fable, and the most that could be deduced were the actions of a godless 'fraudster' or 'witchmaster'. Hauber's *Biblioteca* of 1738 followed this same interpretation, pointing out that there are no reputable witnesses for this 'ghost tale' and that its creation was consequently the result of 'fantastic impressions'. However, influenced by the debates over the cases from Medveđa that were reaching their zenith at the time, Hauber did make a significant change, through which 'the Upper Hungarian ghost Michael Caspareck' mutated at once into the 'precursor of the vampires and bloodsuckers in Serbia and at the Hungarian frontier'. Horst's *Zauber-Bibliothek* of 1825 pushed this even further, claiming that Kasparek 'was the oldest vampire ... in Hungary' and that 'his so-called vampire status was the most fantastic, adventurous and terrible of all'.[68]

A unique version of Kasparek can be found in Miklós Jósika's 1861 historical novel on *Franz II Rákócz (Második Rákóczi Ferencz)*, which took as its subject the Kuruc Wars against Habsburg rule at the turn of the nineteenth century. Through mixing differing historical epochs, this novel somewhat confusingly interchanges the figure of the Lublau 'sorcerer' and 'warlock' Kasparek with a person of the same name who was a follower of the Kuruc leader Imre Tökölyi, the stepfather of Franz II Rákóczi.

The passage on the ghost commences with the tabooization of the name 'Kasparek'. Speaking it out loud, so the popular belief went, would summon the named person immediately, and mothers commonly admonished their children with the words: 'Don't cry, or Kasparek will come for you!' For the patriotic and Protestant Jósika, Kasparek's exorcism offered an opportunity for polemics against the Catholic authorities. Following a lengthy political discussion, the passage concludes with a ghost story, according to which Kasparek continued to appear as a water spirit at an enchanted spring. On the other hand, reference is also made to the events of 1719, which brought Kasparek honour as a social bandit who stole from the rich and gave to the poor.[69]

Without picking up on this unusual interpretation of his predecessor Jósika, the author Kalman Mikszáth attempted to secularize the case in a humorous manner in his 1892 parable *Kisértet lublon (The Ghost of Lubló)*. Mikszáth combined the ghost story with a criminal case and enriched it with numerous romantic scenes, although overlooking the complex national diversity of everyday life in Upper Hungary. He ignored analogies to vampirism and chose instead to transpose a Hungarian popular culture onto the Polish-influenced Spiš.

According to Mikszáth, the solution to the Kasparek mystery lay in the fact that the Lubló wine-merchant Michael Kasparek and his Warsaw partner Michael Czerniczky were in fact half-brothers, who had fallen in love with the same woman during their youth. Following the funeral of his adversary, Czerniczky then played the role of revenant in order not only to gain the favour and grace of his beloved by paying off her debts, but also to bring forged ducats into circulation. In this, the literary staging of the interrogation of Maria Kasparek takes on an almost grotesque character. It begins with her being questioned about the identity of the alleged revenant, with the alternatives offered being ghosts, spirits, shadows, devils or people of real flesh and blood. The questioning was conducted with a great degree of chauvinistic arrogance and curiosity. Upon being asked whether she had had a romantic rendezvous with the revenant, Maria answered in the affirmative and blushed red. Asked for further details, she gave the response, which sounded both naïve and false to the ears of her male interrogators, that she had never been kissed by another man. She responded to the decisive question of 'whether the figure concerned was a mere vision, a phantom, or a real man and whether he was still her husband, after his death, in truth and everything?' with the reply, which kept all her options open: 'in everything'.

With regards to supernatural forces, Mikszáth's work shows several references to Central Europe fairy tales on sorcerers and witches, but none to Southeast European vampire legends. The tale therefore finds a completely new denouement: whereas the rumours of the visitations gradually disappear following the execution of Kasparek's corpse, the tearing down of his former home and the banishment of his widow to a convent, it is only the activities of the forgerer that continue to generate interest. Michael Czerniczky, the fake Kasparek, is finally caught red-handed when the trail of false ducats lead him to the gates of the convent to which the love of his youth had been banished. Without once again making explicit reference to Michael Kasparek, the narrator, who drew upon case files from the Warsaw archives, relates that an eight-strong forger band was executed in 1720.[70] Mikszáth's tale was filmed in 1976 and appeared in East German cinemas the following year under the title of *The Phantom Rider*.

It should be noted that, in terms of cultural studies, the Kasparek legend is less a vampire story than a ghost story of historical value. Reference points for a pan-European perspective are not only the 'Turkish threat' and the Enlightenment, but also confessionalization and nationalism. An anthropological interpretation can only be undertaken with due reference to the ethnic and religious upheavals at the time and in the region where the incidents allegedly took place. These factors are already reflected in the designation of the town itself: despite being formally subject to Polish rule up to the end of the seventeenth century, Lublau was dominated by German and Protestant burghers. In the course of the major socioeconomic reorganization and transformations of the eighteenth and nineteenth centuries, the town underwent a Slovakization and re-Catholicisation in quantitative terms, which justified the name Lublov. From the Compromise of 1867 onwards, and as a result of the politically motivated Magyarization of the town, it was then officially called Lubló, despite the considerable Goral or Ruthenian population.

After his death, the 'Polish Catholic' Mihal Kasperek had to cater for all the clichés related to revenancy cases, first in a German environment as Michael Kasparek and then, as Kaszperek Mihály, in a Hungarian one. The phenomenon of the nightmare as an individual experience intertwined, at the level of social relationships, with the problems that financial obligations brought with them. The result was a public scandal, in which the relationship between Eros and Thanatos, Love and Death, added fire to the fuel of contemporary fantasies. On the one hand, the dead man had to serve as a scapegoat and bear the accusation of witchcraft, whilst, on the other, a charlatan was also constructed, capable of tricking the authorities. Whereas the enlightened public consigned the case to the realms of fraud and superstition, the sensational reporting and fantastical literature ensured that it became considered as an early example of urban vampirism. Through secularization and Magyarization, Hungarian literature then came to the genial conclusion of portraying it as a criminal case. The bugbear Michael Kasparek was thus completely robbed of any prospect he may have had of entering into competition with Bram Stoker's Dracula. In reference to social activities, the impression very much remains at the end that Kasparek was a modern vampire in Voltaire's sense, that is a tax collector and a usurer.

Notes

1. 'Copia eines Schreibens aus dem Gradisker District in Ungarn', *Wienerisches Diarium* (July 21, 1725, no. 58): 11/12. Cf. the reprint from the '*Hamburgischer Correspondent* (1725, no. 121)', in Eberhard Buchner (ed.), *Das Neueste von gestern: Kulturgeschichtlich interessante Dokumente aus alten deutschen Zeitungen*, vol. II: 1700–1750 (Munich, [1912]), no. 242, 147/148.
2. Michael Ranft, *De Masticatione mortuorum in tumulus (Oder von dem Kauen und Schmatzen der Todten in Gräbern), Liber Singularis: Exhibens Duas Excercitationes, Quarum Prior Historico-critica Posterior Philosophica est* (Lipsiae, 1728), § 26, 73; § 52, 93/94; Michael Ranft, *Tractat von dem Kauen und Schmatzen der Todten in Gräbern, Worin die wahre Beschaffenheit derer Hungarischen Vampyrs und Blut-Sauger gezeigt, Auch alle von dieser Materie bißher zum Vorschein gekommene Schrifften recensiret werden* (Leipzig, 1734), § 26, 124/125; § 52, 157/158; reprint: *Traktat von dem Kauen und Schmatzen der Toten in Gräbern: Michael Ranft in einer Bearbeitung durch Nicolaus Equiamicus* (Diedorf, 2006), § 26, 67/68; § 52, 83/84. In the original version there are no details in this respect. See Michael Ranft, *Dissertatio historico-critica de masticatione mortuorum in tumulis: Oder von dem Kauen und Schmatzen der Toten in Gräbern* (Leipzig, 1725).
3. Jutta Nowosadtko, 'Der "Vampyrus Serviensis" und sein Habitat: Impressionen von der österreichischen Militärgrenze', *Militär und Gesellschaft in der Frühen Neuzeit* 8 (2004): 153–70; Peter Mario Kreuter, 'Vom "üblen Geist" zum "Vampyr": Die Darstellung des Vampirs und seines kulturellen Hintergrunds in den Berichten österreichischer Militärärzte zwischen 1725 und 1756', in Julia Bertschik and Christa Agnes Tuczay

(eds), *Poetische Wiedergänger. Deutschsprachige Vampirismus-Diskurse vom Mittelalter bis zur Gegenwart* (Tübingen, 2005), 113–27; Thomas M. Bohn, 'Vampirismus in Österreich und Preußen: Von der Entdeckung einer Seuche zum Narrativ der Gegenkolonisation', *Jahrbücher für Geschichte Osteuropas* 56(2) (2008): 161–77, reprinted in *Kakanien Revisited*, 20 January 2009; Stéphanie Danneberg, '"Vampire sind äußerst unordentliche Untertanen": Überlegungen zur Funktion und Instrumentalisierung des Vampirphänomens', *Zeitschrift für Siebenbürgische Landeskunde* 33(2) (2010): 177–92; Leo Ruickbie, 'Evidence for the Undead: The Role of Medical Investigation in the 18th-Century Vampire Epidemic', in Barbara Brodman and James O. Doan (eds), *The Universal Vampire. Origins and Evolution of a Legend* (Plymouth, 2013), 75–90; Leo Ruickbie, 'Memento (Non)mori: Memory, Discourse and Transmission during the Eighteenth-Century Vampire Epidemic and after', in Simon Bacon and Katarzyna Bronk (eds), *Undead Memory. Vampires and Human Memory in Popular Culture* (Oxford, 2014), 31–58.
4. See Karl Kaser, *Freier Bauer und Soldat: Die Militarisierung der agrarischen Gesellschaft an der kroatisch-slawonischen Militärgrenze (1535–1881)* (Vienna, 1997).
5. See Fikret Adanır, 'Heiduckentum und osmanische Herrschaft: Sozialgeschichtliche Aspekte der Diskussion um das frühneuzeitliche Räuberwesen in Südosteuropa', *Südost-Forschungen* 41 (1982): 43–116.
6. See Kurt Wessely, 'Neuordnung der ungarischen Grenze nach dem großen Türkenkrieg', in *Die k. k. Militärgrenze: Beiträge zur ihrer Geschichte* (Vienna, 1973), 29–93; Gunnar Hering, 'Das Jahr 1683 und die orthodoxen Völker Südosteuropas', *Römische Historische Mitteilungen* 26 (1984): 361–85, reprinted in Gunnar Hering, *Nostos: Gesammelte Schriften zur südosteuropäischen Geschichte*, ed. Maria A. Stassinopoulou (Frankfurt, 1995), 149–76.
7. See Karl Kaser, *Familie und Verwandtschaft auf dem Balkan: Analyse einer untergehenden Kultur* (Vienna, 1995), 265–416; Karl Kaser, *Macht und Erbe: Männerherrschaft, Besitz und Familie im östlichen Europa (1500–1900)* (Vienna, 2000), 166–79.
8. See Michael Hochedlinger, *Austria's Wars of Emergence: War, State and Society in the Habsburg Monarchy, 1683–1797* (London, 2003); Harald Heppner and Damiela Schanes, 'The Impact on the Treaty of Passarowitz on the Habsburg Monarchy', in Charles Ingrao, Nikola Samardžić and Jovan Pešalj (eds), *The Peace of Passarowitz, 1718* (West Lafayette, IN, 2011), 53–62.
9. See Paul Sauer, *Ein kaiserlicher General auf dem württembergischen Herzogsthron: Herzog Carl Alexander von Württemberg 1684–1737* (Filderstadt, 2006), 98–132.
10. See Official Langer, 'Serbien unter der kaiserlichen Regierung 1717–1739', *Mitteilungen des k. k. Kriegsarchivs* NF 3 (Vienna, 1889), 155–247, at 192/193, 218–20, 242–43.
11. See Tiberius von Győry, *Morbus Hungaricus. Eine medico-historische Quellenstudie, zugleich ein Beitrag zur Geschichte der Türkenherrschaft in Ungarn* (Jena, 1901), 17/18, 114. See also Josef Stitzl, 'Der Morbus Hungaricus im Banat', *Medizinische Zeitschrift. Fachblatt der deutschen Ärzte in Rumänien* 11 (1937): 96–106, 147–56; Anton Peter Petri, *Beiträge zur Geschichte des Heilwesens im Banat* (Marquartstein, 1988), 241–49.
12. See Erna Lesky, 'Die österreichische Pestfront an der k. k. Militärgrenze', *Saeculum* 8 (1957): 82–106; Gunther E. Rothenberg, 'The Austrian Sanitary Cordon and the Control of the Bubonic Plague: 1710–1871', *Journal of the History of Medicine* 28 (1973): 15–23; V. Bazala, 'Kroatisch-slawonische Militärgrenze als Gesundheitsfaktor mit besonderer Berücksichtigung des sog. Pestkordons', in J. Antall and G. Buzinkay

(eds), *Acta Congressus Internationalis XXIV Historiae Artis Medicinae: 25–31 Augusti, Budapestini* (Budapest, 1976), vol. I, 527–41. See also Daniel Panzac, *La peste dans l'Empire ottoman: 1700–1850* (Leuven, 1985).
13. Gunther E. Rothenberg, *Die österreichische Militärgrenze in Kroatien 1522 bis 1881* (Vienna, 1970), 84–91.
14. Klaus Hamberger (ed.), *Mortuus non mordet. Dokumente zum Vampirismus, 1689–1791* (Vienna, 1992), 46–49.
15. *Commercium litterarium ad rei medicae et scientiae naturalis in crementum institutum* (Noremberg, 12 March 1732), 82–84.
16. Ranft, *Tractat von dem Kauen und Schmatzen der Todten in Gräbern*, 194; 2006 edn, 101. Cf. Oliver Hepp, 'Vom Aberglauben hin zur "magischen Würckung" der Einbildung. Michael Ranffts Tractat von dem Kauen und Schmatzen der Todten in Gräbern', in Christoph Augustynowicz and Ursula Reber (eds), *Vampirglaube und magia posthuma im Diskurs der Habsburgermonarchie* (Vienna, 2011), 105–23.
17. Hamberger, *Mortuus non mordet*, 49–54.
18. Andreas Leithner and Christian Reiter: 'Vampirismus aus medizinischer Sicht', in Rainer M. Köppl (ed.), *100 Jahre Dracula* (Vienna, 1998), 147–53; Christian Reiter, 'Der Vampyr-Aberglaube und die Militärärzte', *Kakanien Revisited*, 17 August 2009, reprinted in Christoph Augustynowicz and Ursula Reber (eds), *Vampirglaube und magia posthuma im Diskurs der Habsburgermonarchie* (Vienna, 2011), 125–46.
19. See Vlado Vlačić, 'Militärberichte und Vampirmythos', in Augustynowicz and Reber (eds), *Vampirglaube und magia posthuma im Diskurs der Habsburgermonarchie*, 69–87.
20. Hamberger, *Mortuus non mordet*, 49–54, at 49/50.
21. Herbert Mayo, *On the Truths Contained in Popular Superstitions with an Account of Mesmerism* (Edinburghm, 1849), 24–29. Cf. Clemens Ruthner, 'Undead Feedback: Adaptions and Echoes of Johann Flückinger's Report, Visum et Repertum (1732), until the Millennium', in Barbara Brodman and James O. Doan (eds), *The Universal Vampire: Origins and Evolution of a Legend* (Plymouth, 2013), 91–108.
22. Ranft, *Tractat von dem Kauen und Schmatzen der Todten in Gräbern*, 183–85; Hamberger, *Mortuus non mordet*, 56/57. See also Marion Mücke, 'Wissenschaft im Netz: Die Deutsche Akademie der Naturforscher (Leopoldina) und ihre Verbindungen nach Wien um 1750', in Sonia Horn, Gabrielle Dorfner and Rosemarie Eichinger (eds), *Wiener Gespräche zur Sozialgeschichte der Medizin: Wissensaustausch in der Medizin des 18. Jahrhunderts* (Vienna, 2007), 25–44; Marion Mücke and Thomas Schnalke (eds), *Briefnetz Leopoldina: Die Korrespondenz der Deutschen Akademie der Naturforscher um 1750* (Berlin, 2009).
23. *Commercium litterarium ad rei medicae et scientiae naturalis in crementum institutum* (Noremberg, 5 May 1732), 146/147; German translation in Hamberger, *Mortuus non mordet*, 57/58.
24. Augustin Calmet, *Dissertations sur les Apparitions des Esprits, et sur les Vampires et Revenans de Hongrie, de Moravie, etc.*, new revised and improved edn, 2 vols (Einsiedeln, 1749), vol. II, 54–58 (the entry is missing from the version of 1746); English translation: *Dissertations upon the apparitions of angels, daemons, and ghosts and concerning the vampires of Hungary, Bohemia, Moravia, and Silesia* (London, 1759), 215–17.
25. See Gabriele Dürbeck, *Einbildungskraft und Aufklärung: Perspektiven der Philosophie, Anthropologie und Ästhetik um 1750* (Tübingen, 1998); Andreas Würgler, *Medien in der frühen Neuzeit* (Munich, 2009). Cf. Köpeczi, Béla, 'Un Scandale des Lumiéres. Les Vampires', in Raymond Trousson (ed.), *Thèmes et figures du siècle des Lumières.*

Mélanges offerts à Roland Mortier (Geneva, 1980), 123–35; reprint: 'Les vampires de Hongrie: un scandale des Lumières', *Artes populares*. *A Folklore Tanszék Evkönyve* 7 (1981): 87–105; Milan V. Dimić, 'Vampiromania in the Eighteenth-Century: The Other Side of Enlightenment', *Man and Nature. Proceedings of the Canadian Society for Eighteenth-Century Studies* 3 (1984): 1–22; Charles Porset, 'Vampires et Lumières', *Studies on Voltaire and the Eighteenth Century* 266 (1989): 125–50; Antoine Faivre, 'Du vampire villageois aux discours des clercs. (Genèse d'un imaginaire à l'aube des Lumières.)', in *Les Vampires. Colloque de Cerisy* (Paris 1993), 45–74; Benjamin Durst, '"... da sie in den närrischen Wahn gestanden, daß es Vampyren gebe": Dimensionen des Aberglaubensbegriffs und Strategien der Aberglaubenskritik in gelehrten Beiträgen zur Vampirdebatte der 1730er Jahre', *Mitteilungen des Instituts für Europäische Kulturgeschichte* 19 (2010): 32–104; Peter Bräunlein, 'The Frightening Borderlands of Enlightenment: The Vampire Problem', *Studies in History and Philosophy of Biological and Biomedical Sciences* 43(3) (2012): 710–19.

26. Ranft, *Tractat von dem Kauen und Schmatzen der Todten in Gräbern*, 185; 2006 edn, 97.
27. 'Von dem Königreich Servien in Ober-Hungarn', in *Neu-eröffnetes Welt- und Staats-Theatrum, welches die in allen Theilen der Welt, sonderlich aber in Europa vorfallende Staats-[,] Kriegs- und Friedens-Affairen, wie auch andere merckwürdige Begebenheiten in einem deutlichen Auszuge vorstellet. Vierdte Eröffnung* (Erfurt, 1732), 224–36, at 233.
28. See Larry Wolff, *Inventing Eastern Europe: The Map of Civilization on the Mind of the Enlightenment* (Stanford, 1994).
29. See Sauer, *Ein kaiserlicher General auf dem württembergischen Herzogsthron*, 167–89.
30. *Commercium litterarium ad rei medicae et scientiae naturalis in crementum institutum* (Nuremberg), 12 March 1732, 82–84; 19 March 1732, 90–92; 30 April 1732, 138–44; 5 May 1732, 146–52; 28 May 1732, 170–76; 11 June 1732, 190/191; 25 June 1732, 206–8; 9 July 1732, 219–24; 23 July 1732, 234–40; 6 August 1732, 250–56; 10 September 1732, 291–93. Cf. Tilman Rau, *Das Commercium Litterarium: Die erste medizinische Wochenschrift in Deutschland und die Anfänge des medizinischen Journalismus* (Bremen, 2009) 60, 159–64.
31. See the report in the 'Vossische Zeitung (1732, Nr. 37)', in: Buchner, *Das Neueste von gestern*, vol. II, no. 579, 271/272, reprint in: Eberhard Buchner (ed.), *Medien, Hexen und Geisterseher. Kulturhistorisch interessante Dokumente aus alten deutschen Zeitungen und Zeitschriften (16.–18. Jahrhundert)* (Munich, 1926), no. 207, 307/308.
32. Franciscus Antonius Ferdinandus Stebler, 'Sub vampyri, aut sanguisugae larva a verae philosophiae et rationalis medicinae placitis detectum ac dejectum depravatae imaginationis spectrum', in *Acta physico-medica Academiae caesarae Leopoldino-Carolinae naturae curiosorum*, vol. IV (Nuremberg, 1737), Appendix, 89–112.
33. Adolf Harnack, *Geschichte der Königlich Preussischen Akademie der Wissenschaften zu Berlin*, vol. I, part 1: *Von der Gründung bis zum Tode Friedrich's des Großen*, vol. I, part 2: *Vom Tode Friedrich's des Großen bis zur Gegenwart*, vol. II: *Urkunden und Actenstücke zur Geschichte der Königlich Preussischen Akademie der Wissenschaften* (Berlin, 1900). Reprint: (Hildesheim, 1970), vol. I, 215–35, in particular 223, 234; vol. II, 233–35; Werner Hartkopf and Gert Wangemann, *Dokumente zur Geschichte der Berliner Akademie der Wissenschaften von 1700 bis 1990* (Heidelberg, 1991), 233–35.
34. Hamberger, *Mortuus non mordet*, 111–14.
35. Ranft, *Tractat von dem Kauen und Schmatzen der Todten in Gräbern* (1734), 272/273; Edition 2006, no. XII, 144.

36. See a selection of the reviews in the publications of anonymous Eudoxus, 'Bericht von einigen Schriften, so bishero wegen der Vampyren herausgekommen', in *Auserlesene theologische Bibliothec, oder Gründliche Nachrichten von denen neuesten und besten theologischen Büchern und Schriften* (Leipzig, 1732), no. 62, 143–152; Eudoxus, 'Nachlese von den Schriften wegen der Vampyren', in *Auserlesene theologische Bibliothec, oder Gründliche Nachrichten von denen neuesten und besten theologischen Büchern und Schriften* (Leipzig, 1732), no. 69, 870–81. See also further reactions to the vampire debate: *Remarquable Curieuse Brieffe, oder deutliche Beschreibung Alter und Neuer merckwürdiger Begebenheiten, die sich hin und wieder, guten Theils im Churfürstenthum Sachsen und incorporirten Landen zugetragen* (Leipzig, 1732), no. 201, 899–909; *Geistliche Fama, mitbringend Einige Neuere Nachrichten von Göttlichen Erweckeungen, Wegen, Führungen und Gerichten. Achtes Stück* (Sarden, 1733); Joh[ann] Daniel Geyer, *Müßiger Reise-Stunden, Gute Gedancken, Von denen Todten Menschen-Saugern, An die Hochpreißlichen Praesidem und Collegas S. R. I. Academicae Naturae Curiosorum. Neundter Discours* (Dresden, 1735); Christian Ludwig Charisius, *Medicinisches Bedencken Von denen Vampyren, oder sogenannten Blutsaugern, Ob selbte vorhanden, und die Krafft haben, denen Menschen das Leben zu rauben?* (Königsberg, 1739). Cf. also Anja Lauper, 'Die "phantastische Seuche": Johann Christoph Harenbergs Theoretisierung der vampiristischen Einbildungskraft', in Christian Begemann et al. (eds), *Dracula Unbound: Kulturwissenschaftliche Lektüren des Vampirs* (Freiburg im Breisgau, 2008), 51–73.
37. See Edward A. Eckert, 'The Retreat of Plague from Central Europe, 1640–1720: A Geomedical Approach', *Bulletin of the History of Medicine* 74 (2000): 1–28.
38. See Gustav Hennigsen, 'Das Ende der Hexenprozesse und die Fortsetzung der populären Hexenverfolgung', in Sönke Lorenz and Dieter R. Bauer (eds), *Das Ende der Hexenverfolgung* (Stuttgart, 1995), 315–28.
39. Ranft, *Tractat von dem Kauen und Schmatzen der Todten in Gräbern*, 206–92; 2006 edn, 106–59.
40. See 'Question Physique sur une espéce de Prodige duëment attesté', *Le Glaneur historique, moral, litteraire, galant & calotin* 2 (La Haye, 3 March 1732), no. 18, 1–4; 'Appendice au Vampyrisme', *Le Glaneur historique, moral, litteraire, galant & calotin* 2 (La Haye, 17 March 1732), no. 22, 4–6; 'Courtes Reflexions Physiques sur le Vampyrisme', *Le Glaneur historique, critique, politique, moral, littéraire, galant et calotin* 3 (La Haye, 23 April 1733), no. 18 (Supplement), pages not numbered; 'Wampirs, fait singulier et de plus extraordinaires, s'il est vrai', *Mercure de France* (Paris, May 1732), 890–98; 'Extract of a Private Letter from Vienna', *London Journal*, no. 663, March 11, 1732, 2; [Caleb D'Anvers (= Nicholas Amhurst), 'Political Vampyres',] *The Craftsman: Being a Critique of the Times*. (London, 20 May 1732), no. 307, 120–29, at 124/125; 'Political Vampyres', *The Gentleman's Magazine: or, Monthly Intelligencer* 2 (London, May 1732): 750–52; 'Political Vampyres', *The London Magazine, or, Gentleman's Monthly Intelligencer* 1 (London, May 1732): 76/77. See also 'A Confutation of the Stories about Vampires, or Dead Bodies Sucking the Living in Hungary etc.', *The London Magazine: and Monthly Chronologer* 6 (London, May 1737): 236–38; 'Travels of Three English Gentlemen, from Venice to Hamburgh, Being the Grand Tour of Germany, in the Year 1734', *The Harleian Miscellany; or, A collection of scarce, curious, and entertaining Pamphlets and Tracts, as well in Manuscript as in Print, found in the Earl of Oxford's Library* 11 (London, 1810): 218–355. Cf. Sara Libby Robinson, *Blood Will Tell: Vampires as Political Metaphors before World War I*. (Boston, 2011).

41. 'Jud Süß', in *Curieuser Nachrichten aus dem Reich der Beschnittenen. Erste Unterredung: Zwischen Sabathai Sevi, einem in dem vorigen Seculo in den Morgenländern höchst-berüchtigt gewesenen jüdischen Ertzbetrüger, und dem fameusen Württembergischen Avanturier, Jud Joseph Süß Oppenheimer* (Frankfurt and Leipzig, 1738), 91–94, reprint in *Einhundertundzehn Volks- und Gesellschaftslieder des 16., 17. und 18. Jahrhunderts mit und ohne Singweisen. Nach fliegenden Blättern, handschriftlichen Quellen und dem Volksmunde*, collected and edited by Franz Wilhelm von Ditfurth (Stuttgart, 1875), 74–78, reprint in *Die historischen Volkslieder vom Ende des dreißigjährigen Krieges, 1648 bis zum Beginn des siebenjährigen, 1756: Aus fliegenden Blättern, handschriftlichen Quellen und dem Volksmunde*, collected by Franz Wilhelm von Ditfurth (Heilbronn, 1877), 291–94. Cf. Anne von der Heiden, *Der Jude als Medium: 'Jud Süß'* (Zürich and Berlin, 2005), 63–87; Anne von der Heiden, 'Der Zerstörer allen Lebens: "Jud Süß" als politischer Vampir', in Alexandra Przyrembel and Jörg Schönert (eds), *'Jud Süß': Hofjude, literarische Figur, antisemitisches Zerrbild* (Frankfurt, 2006), 325–36.
42. Johann Friedrich Abegg, *Reisetagebuch von 1798*, ed. Walter and Jolanda Abegg, 2nd edn (Frankfurt, 1977), 190.
43. See Vaclav Medek, 'Vom Satanismus auf dem nordmährischen Herrschaftsbesitz des Deutschen Ordens', in Klemens Wieser (ed.), *Acht Jahrhunderte Deutscher Orden in Einzeldarstellungen* (Bad Godesberg, 1967), 387–93; Winfried Irgang, 'Die Stellung des Deutschen Ordens zum Aberglauben am Beispiel der Herrschaften Freudenthal und Eulenburg', in Udo Arnold (ed.), *Von Akkon bis Wien. Studien zur Deutschordensgeschichte vom 13. bis zum 20. Jahrhundert. Festschrift zum 90. Geburtstag von Althochmeister P. Dr. Marian Tumler O. T. am 21. Oktober 1977* (Marburg, 1978), 261–71.
44. 'Ein Dokument zur Geschichte der schles. Hexenprozesse', prepared by A. Schmidt, *Zeitschrift für Geschichte und Kulturgeschichte Österreichisch-Schlesiens* 2 (1906/7): 193/194.
45. *Magia posthuma per juridicum illud pro contra suspenso nonnullibi judicio investigata a Carolo Ferdinando de Schertz, arae alutiferae ubi paCisCenDUM* (Olomouc, 1706), quoted from Calmet, *Dissertations sur les Apparitions des Anges* (1746), 271/272, revised edn: *Dissertations sur les Apparitions des Esprits* (1749), vol. II, 27–28; English version: *Dissertations* (1759), 195–97. See also Maiello, Giuseppe, *Vampyrismus a Magia posthuma: Vampyrismus v kulturních dějinách Evropy a Magia posthuma Karla Ferdinanda Schertze (první novodobé vydání)*, 2nd enlarged edn (Prague, 2014), 192–216.
46. See W.F. Ryan, 'The Witchcraft Hysteria in Early Modern Europe: Was Russia an Exception?', *Slavonic and East European Review* 76 (1998), 49–84; W.F. Ryan, *The Bathhouse at Midnight: An Historical Survey of Magic and Divination in Russia* (University Park, PA, 1999), 68–93.
47. See Gábor Klaniczay, 'Decline of Witches and Rise of Vampires in 18th Century Habsburg Monarchy', *Ethnologia Europea* 17 (1987), 165–80; Karen Lambrecht, 'Wiedergänger und Vampire in Ostmitteleuropa – Postume Verbrennung statt Hexenverfolgung?', *Jahrbuch für deutsche und osteuropäische Volkskunde* 37 (1994): 49–77, at 49/50, 68; Karen Lambrecht, *Obrigkeiten und Hexenverfolgungen. Zaubereiprozesse in den schlesischen Territorien* (Vienna, 1995), 383–401, in particular 383/384, 401.
48. Calmet, *Dissertations* (1746), 247/248; *Dissertations* (1749), vol. II, pages not numbered (p. II); English version: *Dissertations* (1759) 179/180. Cf. Louis Vax, 'Dom Calmet et les Vampires', in Alain Cullière (ed.), *Aspects du Classicisme et de la Spiritualité. Mélanges en l'onneur de Jacques Hennequin* (Paris, 1996), 423–36; Marie-Hélène Huet, 'Deadly Fears: Dom Augustin Calmet's Vampires and the Rule over Death',

Eighteenth-Century Life 21 (1997): 222–32; Fernando Vidal, 'Ghosts, the Economy of Religion, and the Laws of Princes: Dom Calmet's Treatise on the Apparitions of Spirits', in Claire Gantet and Fabrice d'Almeida (eds), *Gespenster und Politik. 16. bis 21. Jahrhundert* (Munich, 2007), 103–26.

49. Prospero Lambertini, *De servorum dei beatificatione et beatorum canonizatione*, 4 vols (Bologna, 1734–38 (no vampires mentioned); 2nd edn, Passau, 1743, vol. I, 199/200; 3rd edn, *Benedicto XIV. doctrinam De servorum dei beatificatione et beatorum canonizatione. Redactam in synopsim Emmanuel Azevedo* (Rome, 1757); 391; 4th edn, *Benedicti decimiquarti De servorum dei beatificatione et beatorum canonizatione*, 4 vols, newest edn, in all parts corrected and enlarged (Venice 1764), vol. I, 155. Cf. David Keyworth, 'The Aetiology of Vampires and Revenants: Theological Debate and Popular Belief', *Journal of Religious History* 34(2) (2010): 158–73; Marco Frenschkowski, 'Die Unverweslichkeit der Heiligen und der Vampire: Eine Studie über kulturelle Ambivalenz', in Christoph Augustynowicz and Ursula Reber (eds), *Vampirglaube und magia posthuma im Diskurs der Habsburgermonarchie* (Vienna, 2011), 53–68.

50. Giuseppe Davanzati, *Dissertazione sopra i vampiri* (Napoli, 1774); 2nd edn Napoli, 1789); revised edn: Giuseppe Davanzati, *Dissertazione sopra i vampiri: A cura di Giacomo Annibaldis* (Bari, 1998). Cf. Francesco Paolo Ceglia, 'The Archbishop's Vampires: Giuseppe Davanzati's Dissertation and the Reaction of "Scientific" Italian Catholicism to the "Moravian Events"', *Archives internationales d'histoire des sciences* 61 (2011), nos. 166–67, 487–510.

51. Calmet, *Dissertations* (1746), 252, 451/452; *Dissertations* (1749), vol. II, in Preface (pages not numbered [p. V]) and 216; English version: *Dissertatons* (1759), 181/182.

52. Voltaire, 'Vampires', *Œuvres complètes de Voltaire. Nouvelle édition.* [Vol. 42:] *Dictionnaire philosophique*, Vol. VII (Paris, 1827), 406–13.

53. Hamberger, *Mortuus non mordet*, 88–93.

54. *Codex Sanitario-Medicinalis Hungariae*, vol. I, compiled by Franciscus Xav. Linzbauer (Buda, 1852–56) [sic], 722.

55. Ibid., 728–37; 'Vampyrismus von Herrn Baron Gerhard van Swieten verfasset, aus dem Französischen ins Deutsche übersetzet, und als ein Anhang der Abhandlung des Daseyns der Gespenster beigerücket', in [A. Mayer], *Abhandlung des Daseins der Gespenster, nebst einem Anhange vom Vampyrismus* (Augsburg, 1768); Reprint: 'Vampyrismus von Herrn Baron Gerhard van-Swieten verfasset, aus dem Französischen ins Deutsche übersetzet', in Rainer M. Köppl (ed.), *100 Jahre Dracula* (Vienna, 1998), 37–46. Cf. Daniel Arlaud, 'Vampire, Aufklärung und Staat: Eine militärmedizinische Mission in Ungarn, 1755–1756', in Claire Gantet and Fabrice d'Almeida (eds), *Gespenster und Politik. 16. bis 21. Jahrhundert* (Munich, 2007), 127–41.

56. *Sammlung aller k. k. Verordnungen vom Jahre 1740 bis 1780, die unter der Regierung des Kaisers Joseph des II. theils noch ganz bestehen, theils zum Theile abgeändert sind, als ein Hilfs- und Ergänzungsbuch zu dem Handbuche aller unter der Regierung des Kaisers Joseph des II. für die k. k. Erbländer ergangenen Verordnungen und Gesetze in einer chronologischen Ordnung*, vol. III (Vienna, 1786), no. 385, 172/173.

57. *Codex Sanitario-Medicinalis Hungariae*, 723–25.

58. [Jean Baptiste de Boyer], 'Lettre Cent-Vint-Cinquieme', in *Lettres juives ou Correspondance philosophique, historique et critique entre un Juif voyageur à Paris et ses correspondans en divers endroits* (La Haye, 1737), vol. V, 49–66; English translation: 'Letter CXXXVII', in *The Jewish Spy: Being a Philosophical, Historical and Critical Correspondence, by Letters which lately pass'd between certain Jews in Turkey, Italy, France, &c. Translated*

from the Originals into French, by the Marquis d'Argens, and now done into English (London, 1744), vol. IV, 122–32.
59. Eberhard Buchner, *Das Neueste von gestern. Kulturgeschichtlich interessante Dokumente aus alten deutschen Zeitungen*, vol. III: *1750–1787* (Munich, [1912]), no. 93 and 93a, 66–68; reprint in Buchner, *Medien, Hexen und Geisterseher*, no. 214 and 214a, 312/313. Cf. Bernhard Unterholzner, 'Vampire im Habsburgerreich, Schlagzeilen in Preußen: Wie Mythen zu politischen Druckmitteln werden', in Christoph Augustynowicz and Ursula Reber (eds), *Vampirglaube und magia posthuma im Diskurs der Habsburgermonarchie* (Vienna, 2011), 89–103.
60. *Constitutio Criminalis Theresiana oder der römisch-kaiserl. zu Hungarn und Böheim k. k. königl. apost. Majestät Mariä Theresiä Erzherzogin zu Oesterreich k. k. peinliche Gerichtsordnung* (Vienna, 1769), 167–73; *Codex Sanitario-Medicinalis Hungariae*, 776–85.
61. See Thomas M. Bohn, 'Das Gespenst von Lublau. Michael Kaspereks/Kaspareks Verwandlung vom Wiedergänger zum Blutsauger', in *Kakanien Revisited*, 29 October 2009; reprinted in Augustynowicz and Reber (eds), *Vampirglaube und magia posthuma im Diskurs der Habsburgermonarchie*, 147–61.
62. See Wynfried Krieglieder, Andrea Seidler and Jozef Tanzer (eds), *Sprache und Kultur in der Zips* (Bremen, 2007).
63. Bertalan Matirko Jr., 'Die Zipser Volkssage von Kasparek', *Ethnologische Mitteilungen aus Ungarn* 2 (1890–92): 162–164, at 164.
64. 'Extractum Litterarum ex Comitatu Liptoviensi in superiori Hungaria 1718, mense Julio', *Der Europäische Niemand, Welcher niemanden zu beleidigen, Jedermann aber nützlich zu seyn, beflissen ist; Wie er solches in allerhand vertraulichen Gesprächen von neuen und alten Staats-Angelegenheiten, Hof-Intriguen, Kriegs- und Friedens-Begebenheiten, gelehrten. Sachen, und vielerley andern sonderbaren Materien, zu erkennen gibt*, Part II ([Nuremberg], 1719): 972–80; reprinted and translated in Eberhard David Hauber, *Biblioteca sive Acta et Scripta Magica* (Lemgovia, 1738), 709–14; reprint of the translation in Georg Conrad Horst, *Zauber-Bibliothek oder von Zauberei, Theurgie und Mantik, Zauberern, Hexen, und Hexenprocessen, Dämonen, Gespenstern, und Geistererscheinungen. Zur Beförderung einer rein-geschichtlichen, von Aberglauben und Unglauben freien Beurtheilung dieser Gegenstände*, 6 parts (Mainz, 1821–26), Part V, 387–90; reprinted in Hamberger, *Mortuus non mordet*, 62–64.
65. *Historischer Geschlechtsbericht (Familienchronik) von Georg Buchholtz, dem Älteren, nebst einem Auszuge aus dem Tagebuch seines Sohnes Jakob Buchholtz. Nach den hinterlassenen Handschriften*, prepared by Rudolf Weber (Budapest, 1904), 368–70.
66. Matthias Belius Pannonius, *Hungariae antiquae et novae Prodromus* (Nuremberg, 1723), 108.
67. Matirko, 'Die Zipser Volkssage von Kasparek', 162/163.
68. 'Extractum Litterarum ex Comitatu Liptoviensi', 975–80; Hauber, *Biblioteca sive Acta et Scripta Magica*, 714–18; Horst, *Zauber-Bibliothek*, Part V, 386, 391.
69. Miklós Jósika, *Második Rákóczi Ferencz*, 6 vols (Pest, 1861); German translation: Nicolaus Jósika, *Franz Rákóczi II*, 6 vols (Pest, 1862), vol. VI, 119.
70. Kálmán Miskszáth, *Kisértet lublon* (Pest, 1892); German translation: Koloman Mikszáth, *Das Gespenst von Lublau* (Leipzig, 1899), 2/3, 48/49, 59–63, 130/131, 141.

CHAPTER 4

Vampirism in Popular Belief

Demonic Figures in East and East Central Europe

The Partition of Poland

The Polish Noble Republic (Rzeczpospolita Polska) was founded upon the monopolization of the legislative by the nobility (*Nihil novi*, 1505), the practice of the free election of kings (*Articuli Henriciani*, 1573) and the principle of unanimity in parliamentary decisions (*liberum veto*, 1652). The Union of Lublin of 1569 brought Poland and Lithuania together in state legal terms, and the Union of Brest of 1596 placed the sizeable Orthodox Churches in the territory under the supremacy of the Pope. The subsequent period witnessed a Polonization of the Ruthenian nobility and a concentration of power in the hands of the magnates. The era of the Northern Wars, fought over domination of the Baltic region, which began in the mid sixteenth century and was brought to an end with the Treaty of Nystad in 1721, contributed greatly to the downfall of the Noble Republic. The partition of the Polish-Lithuanian Commonwealth between the great powers of Prussia, Russia and Austria-Hungary, undertaken in three stages between 1772 and 1795, led to the disappearance of the Polish state from the political map of Europe for more than a century.[1]

In the Russian zone of partition, the Kingdom of Poland, the so-called Congress Poland, was established as a result of the Congress of Vienna in 1814/1815. Formally, this territory was granted its own constitution, but in reality it remained firmly connected to the Tsarist Empire through a personal union. The two uprisings against despotic Tsarist rule – initiated in 1830/1831 by the cadets of the Warsaw Military Academy and in 1863 by the government-in-exile in Paris – were met with harsh repressions and a vigorous programme of Russification. The term 'Poland' was replaced by the designation 'Vistula Land', and the Polish language was outlawed in Lithuania and Belarus.

In contrast to the Russians, the Habsburgs were keen to incorporate the local elites into the state administration. In particular, following Austria's exit from the German Confederation and the Compromise with Hungary in 1866/1867, the autonomy of the provinces of Galicia and Lodomeria were further extended. In administrative terms, therefore, the Austrian zone of partition was in the hands of the Polish upper classes.

Up to the 1863 uprising of the Poles in the Tsarist Empire, the Prussian state implemented a policy of imperial – that is, informal and indirect – rule in relation to its eastern provinces, which conceded self-administration and instruction in the Polish language whilst, at the same time, emphasizing the dominance of Prussian patriotism. After 1863, there then followed a transition to a policy of colonial – that is, repressive and assimilatory – rule, which was characterized by the Germanization of education and the government and the settlement of German colonists.[2]

In the context of the weakness or absence of the central powers, vampirism in Poland was tackled primarily by the clergy in the eighteenth century, by romantic and patriotic-minded writers in the first half of the nineteenth century, and by nationally-minded ethnologists in the second half of the nineteenth century. Striking cases of revenancy were documented from the eighteenth century onwards in the Ukrainian territories of the Polish-Lithuanian Union. Otherwise, until the emergence of the threat of cholera in the 1830s, Polish vampire cases were still largely overshadowed by events on the territory of the Habsburg Military Frontier (see the section entitled 'The Vampire Debate of the Enlightenment' in Chapter 3).

Murder and Manslaughter on the Peripheries of Poland-Lithuania

In 1738, there was a lynching in the Ukrainian village of Humińce (Ukrainian Humentsy). This case has been handed down through the records, written in both Latin and Polish, of the interrogation of witnesses conducted in the town court of Kamianets-Podilskyi (Polish Kamieniec Podolski) in 1745/1746. These made reference to an 'upyr' (*upier*) as a possible motivation for the crime. The events transpired as follows.

When the residents of the village made a nightly procession across the fields, hoping thereby to bring an end to an outbreak of plague, they chanced upon Michał Matkowski (Ukrainian Mykhailo Matkovsky) from the neighbouring village of Przewrocie (Ukrainian Pryvoróttya), who, with his bridle in his hand, was searching for his runaway horse. It is unclear whether he appeared to the villagers as the devil incarnate or whether the procession was in any event following pagan rituals. Without further ado, the people of Humińce beat Matkowski senseless and left him there to die. When they later heard that Matkowski had made his way back home, they reconsidered their position. The village community made its way to the neighbouring community before the break of dawn in order to demand that the local squire hand over the alleged evildoer.

Around midday, the leaders of the mob seemed to believe that they had received his permission, at least secondhand, and broke down Matkowski's door and seized him, hoping to place him on trial in Humińce. Later interrogations showed that only a few of the villagers seemed to be aware of the dubious light in which the nearby regional court viewed such acts of vigilantism. So as to spread doubt about the legality of the act, one witness even claimed that he had been prepared, as a precaution, to pay the potential criminal damages of 100 złoty in advance in order to avoid the punishment that might come in the wake of their extrajudicial sentencing. Even the priest who took Matkowski's confession is supposed to have said that he was responsible only for his soul and not for his body. In a painful procedure, Matkowski's eyes, ears and mouth were sealed up with tar and stones prior to his burning at the stake.

The questioning of the witnesses leaves the impression that the villagers, in an intoxication of fear and violence, only incidentally justified by the activities of an upyr, merely seized upon a random scapegoat, whom they could offer up to the gods as a sacrificial lamb.[3]

Beyond this, the upyr also played an important role in the discrediting of unpopular persons. For example, a Polish military tribunal established in Kodnya in the east of the present-day Western Ukraine in the wake of the Haidamak or Vagabond Uprising of the Orthodox Cossacks of 1768/1769 also addressed the murder of an Orthodox priest in 1770. The accused was a 26-year-old peasant named Lesko Kołbasiuk (Ukrainian Kovbasyuk) from the village of Wujtowce (Ukrainian Vijtivtsi).

At his interrogation, Kołbasiuk claimed that, because of a plague, a rumour was being spread around the village that a demon had been provoking the deaths by breathing his poisonous breath upon the houses. Some claim to have seen an upyr who had been attacked by human dogs and from whom the cattle had fled in fear. On the basis of the description of his clothing, the priest Vasyl was identified as the culprit. Understandably, the priest denied all the accusations about his nocturnal machinations. In the meantime, his wife stated, in his presence, that he often went about in the company of his departed sister and other dead persons, making a great hullabaloo and gnashing their teeth. Potential doubts about these claims were dispersed by a cook, who made similar assertions. Thirteen men therefore dug a grave at the cemetery, kidnapped the priest, beat him half to death and then, finally, having driven an aspen stake through his back, buried him alive.

Although Kołbasiuk was the only one of the executioners to survive the plague, he claimed that, through their actions, they had succeeded in banishing the threat. Since he had nothing to do with the rebellious Haidamaks and since he had only struck the priest three times, he claimed to be innocent and, against the backdrop of the massacres that the Haidamaks had perpetrated upon Catholics and Jews, he did in fact escape without further punishment.[4]

Vampirism as an Issue for Polish Theologians

An interesting reference to vampirism in Poland comes from Augustin Calmet, who, in his standard work on vampires in Hungary, Moravia and Silesia from

1749, mentions a letter, dated 3 February 1745, written by the Warsaw priest Piotr Hiacynt Śliwicki. The Visitator of the Polish Mission had clearly conceived a dissertation on vampirism, although without reaching a conclusion. According to Calmet, Śliwicki claimed that the belief in vampires was firmly rooted among the Polish population, even though he was not aware of any eyewitnesses.[5] Unfortunately, Calmet did not have any further information to offer from this source.

Of greater substance were the remarks made by the priest Benedykt Chmielowski in 1755 in the second edition of his famous Polish-language encyclopaedia *Nowy Ateny* (*New Athens*). Under the term 'upier' (*upiór*), he described dead persons, of whom the devil had taken possession, and who brought about disease, not only among people but also among cattle. In this regard, though, he admitted, publications on the issue spoke more in terms of sorcerers and witches. People claimed to see these spirits at night. Particularly suspect were midwives, who were accused of having entered into a pact with the devil and of peddling the souls of newborn babies. Adults, it is true, were protected by baptism, but they were also endangered at death, when the soul left the body. In order not only to disempower the devil, but also to bring about the salvation of an upiór, Chmielowski recommended that traditional popular customs be followed, meaning the driving of a stake through the heart of a suspicious body and the burning of the corpse. Further protection against posthumous activities was provided, in his view, not only by the laying of reliquaries in the grave but also through exorcisms.

In Chmielowski's opinion, upiór conceptions were particularly widespread among the Ruthenians, that is, the Orthodox Belarus and Ukrainian population. In terms of Polish popular belief, Chmielowski referred to elements similar to those which could be found in Central European *nachzehrer* conceptions, namely the supposed devouring of the burial shroud and the alleged swelling of the bloodfilled corpse. In the final analysis, the phenomenon could be traced back to a punishment from God, intended to force the population to repent and to change their ways.[6]

In 1752, the Polish poet Elzbieta Drużbacka wrote a polemic pamphlet against this view, directed from an enlightened perspective against 'certain monks'.[7] Supposedly, Pope Benedict XIV – who had written in the mid eighteenth century, as a theologian, on the canonization of the saints (see the section entitled 'The Vampire Debate of the Enlightenment' in Chapter 3) – also took a similarly ironic stance on the Polish vampires. It remains open to question how reliable the information is presented in this regard by the French writer Louis Antoine Caraccioli in his 1783 biography of the pontiff. What is clear, however, is that Caraccioli derived his knowledge on the Polish vampires not only from a reading of Augustin Calmet's handbook (see the section entitled 'The Vampire Debate of the Enlightenment' in Chapter 3), but also from his own firsthand experiences in Lublin.[8]

According to Caraccioli, the Pope responded to a query from a Polish archbishop in a missive, recommending that measures be undertaken against this superstition. Initially, writing in a polemic manner, he drew a connection between Poland's proverbial 'Golden Freedom' – understood here as anarchy – and the custom of posthumous revenancy. Then, moving on to discuss the Ruthenian regions of the Polish-Lithuanian Union, he denied the claims recognizing the mummification of the Orthodox saints at the Monastery of the Caves in Kiev as a miracle. With reference to the cases of vampirism in Poland and very much in keeping with Maria Theresa's views (see the section entitled 'The Vampire Debate of the Enlightenment' in Chapter 3), he then bemoaned the abuse of office by priests, who sought to supplement their income by offering additional masses and exorcisms for a fee. In the final analysis, he felt that the underlying causes behind cases of revenancy lay in the fantasies of the living.[9]

In 1772 and 1777, in a wide-ranging two-volume study *Diabeł w swoiey postaci* (*The Devil in His Own Form*), the priest Jan Bohomolec provide the definitive Polish answer to the question of vampirism, decisively confronting the issue of ghostly apparitions, as well as that of witches, soothsayers and sorcerers, in the style of Augustin Calmet. In Bohomolec's opinion, an upiór was nothing more than a product of fantasy, grounded in the disreputable reputations of the dead and the spreading of rumours. Particularly interesting is Bohomolec's listing of the various defensive measures undertaken by the populace. Where a dead person was suspected of revenancy, pig manure was stuffed in his mouth. Second, the corpse would also be decapitated and a stake driven through his heart. Furthermore, Bohomolec also discussed preventative measures that did not necessarily aim at the destruction of the upiór. When the dead person was turned on his stomach and his hands were bound behind his back, he could supposedly only carry out his activities under a full moon. Moreover, it was possible to identify the resting place of an upiór by leading an innocent young boy through the cemetery on a stallion, which had not yet mated with a mare. The horse would struggle and fight against having to cross over the grave of an upiór. Bohomolec did not focus solely upon Poland in his considerations, but also drew upon discussions from the wider pan-European debate. Unintentionally, therefore, he also transferred certain common, yet superficial, vampire definitions onto the upiór.[10]

Polish Revenants as an Expression of Fraud and Deceit

At the end of the eighteenth century, reports began to pile up documenting the instrumentalization of the belief in vampires in frauds and rackets. In his diary, published in 1854, the theologian and writer Wojciech Wincenty Bagiński, who was active in Belarus and Lithuania, wrote about a criminal case from 1782: in the town of Płock, located on the Vistula between Toruń and Warsaw, an infatuated girl had murdered her aunt, since she had thwarted her relationship with a servant. In order to cover up her crime, the girl had then invented an upiór and accused him of the murder.[11]

In 1783, the Warsaw journal *Pamiętnik polityczny i historyczny* (*Political and Historical Monument*) then also published an article about a 'curious upiór'. The author first pointed out that tales about upiórs had receded somewhat into the background during the era of the Enlightenment, but then went on to outline a curious case, which only indirectly related to revenancy. Thus, in order to escape his creditors, a merchant had faked his own death and his wife had then remarried. The unexpected return of the merchant twenty years after his death brought joy to his creditors, but distress to his wife. In order to avoid a court case, he was advised not to draw too much attention to his return.[12]

A report in the *Schlesische Provincialblätter* (*Silesian Provincial Papers*) from 1801 also had a similar undertone. This concerned a *strzyga* ('witch') from Großgorschütz (today Gorzyce) near Ratibor (today Racibórz), which at the time still belonged to Austrian Silesia. Following the death of a woman named Marynna Warlin, rumours began to spread that she could be expected to return in the form of a vampire, since a mark in the form of shears had been discovered on her back. Therefore, the priest placed a so-called *Lukaszettel* (a piece of paper covered with pious phrases) on her tongue, stuffed her nostrils with soil and ordered that she be buried on her stomach. Subsequently, the daughter of the dead woman, who worked as a servant at the court of the local ruler, also fell into disrepute. Thereafter, following the intervention of the Church authorities, the body of the dead woman was exhumed. This revealed the alleged mark of the shears to have been a misinterpretation and the woman was then finally given a proper Christian burial.[13]

The Vampire as a Subject of Polish Literature

At the turn of the eighteenth and nineteenth centuries, the upiór does not seem to have been a familiar category of thought for the common people. Rather, the figure increasingly developed into a popular literary character among the reading public. Early evidence of this can be found in the works of the travel writer and publicist Count Jan Potocki, and those of the literary historian and patron of the arts Joseph Maximilian Ossolinski. Interestingly, both of them were inspired by Ukrainian demonology. The popularization of the vampire figure in Polish national poetry and messianic literature goes back as far as Adam Mickiewicz. Furthermore, the writer Kazimierz Władysław Wójcicki also pursued an interest in popular culture.

Potocki began working on his novel *Le manuscrit trouvé à Saragossa* (*The Manuscript Found in Saragossa*) as early as 1794. Through an artistic device, he later attributed the text to a fictitious editor, who had supposedly unearthed it during the Napoleonic Wars in the form of a Spanish manuscript. The novel is composed of several interwoven tales, which are structured around the background plot of a traversal of the Sierra Morena. In late 1804, one hundred copies were published in French. At the end of his life, Potocki withdrew to his estates in Podolia and Volhynia, but presented a revised edition of his text in 1810. A Polish translation first appeared posthumously (*Rękopis znaleziony w Saragossie*).

As far as 'vampires' are concerned, in one part of the novel, a cabbalist is encouraged, in the light of rumours about the nocturnal activities of two recently hanged men, to tell the protagonists a revenant story from ancient Athens. In this, referring to the debates of his own time, the Jewish mystic comes to the conclusion that, whereas Hungarian and Polish vampires were corpses that left their graves at night and drank the blood of the living, Spanish vampires were impure spirits who reanimated dead bodies.[14] In fact, Potocki had little to offer on the subject and the word 'upiór' does not appear once in the text. The figures who fuelled the author's imagination and delusions seem rather to have been 'revenants' or 'vampires'. Plagued by depression, he committed suicide in tragic circumstances.

In 1800, Ossolinski composed an anthology on his country estate close to Vienna, entitled *Wieczory badeńskie czyli powieści o strachach i upiorach* (*Baden Evenings or Tales about Fears and Upiórs*), which was published posthumously in Kraków in 1852. In the sole piece that justified the choice of the title, Ossolinski reported on rumours of revenancy in a village near to the settlement of Terebovlia in Western Ukraine. However, it emerged that no such rumours had been going around the village. A young nobleman, who had been attacked on his way through the village, had come to the conclusion that this had been the work of an upiór, but was then informed by his mother that his assailant had in fact merely been a mentally disturbed servant who had been carrying out mischief in the region.[15] Ossolinski therefore contented himself with compiling a collection of edifying horror stories, without developing the ambition of pre-empting John William Polidori's 1819 classic *The Vampyre*. At this stage, the Polish 'upiór' could still very much have offered a literary alternative.

In his unfinished drama *Dziady* (*Forefathers' Eve*), which appeared in 1823 (parts 2 and 4), 1832 (part 3) and, posthumously, 1860 (part 1), as well as in his *Lectures on Slavic Literature and the Condition of the Slavic Nations*, delivered at the Collège de France between 1840 and 1842, Adam Mickiewicz tackled the subject of vampirism.

The drama *Forefathers' Eve* draws upon a combination of the Christian holiday of All Souls with the pre-Christian cult of the dead, anchored in popular culture, and sees a banquet celebrated by both the living and the departed. The second part, which actually appeared first, is prefixed with a poem about the 'upiór', which is at least the equal of Gottfried August Bürger's 'Lenore' (1773) or Johann Wolfgang von Goethe's 'Braut von Korinth' ('Bride of Corinth') (1793) in its importance for the vampire subject. In the scene following the poem, which takes place in a chapel, the *guslar* or master of ceremonies conjures up the spirits of the departed. Inevitably, the lord of the manor, who had died three years earlier and who had not been able to find rest, appears at the window in the form of an upiór. However, things first become really dramatic when an upiór, described as a hermit, enters the home of an Orthodox priest, who had invited several children to dinner. The hermit reveals himself to be Gustav, the dead son of the priest who, in defiance of his father's instructions, makes the case for the pagan feast of the dead.

Between the publication of the first two parts of *Forefathers' Eve* and the final two, Mickiewicz composed the patriotic epic *Konrad Wallenrod* about the Grand Master of the Teutonic Order of the same name from the fourteenth century. In this poem, Mickiewicz portrays the Grand Master as a kidnapped Lithuanian boy who, instead of betraying his heritage, leads the order to its doom. This act balances thoughts of revenge with the motif of self-sacrifice. In this context, the poet refers in a hallucinatory ballad to the execution of the dead as a means for banishing the threat of plague. With reference to the resurrection of corpses it is stated, succinctly, that the bones will rise up from their graves on the day of judgment to the sound of trumpets.

The final part of *Forefathers' Eve* (part three), published by Mickiewicz personally, once again takes up the leitmotif of victimhood and revenge, and enriches this with the vampire *syuzhet*. In a reference to 'Wallenrodism', the original hero Gustav is now reincarnated as Konrad, and reveals himself in a vampiric manner, and as was still in keeping with popular belief in the second half of the nineteenth century, as the bearer of two souls. Where, as Gustav, he had chosen suicide as the result of an ill-fated love, as Konrad he reappeared as an angel of vengeance, bound to the national cause and fiercely opposed to the Russian Tsar. In a less than godly ballad, Konrad offers a vivid celebration of bloodlust very much in keeping with the Gothic tone of the novel.

Whereas, according to Mickiewicz, the vengeance of the repressed Polish people had to be satisfied, it was also necessary to prevent the physical reappearance of their dead enemies through the chopping up and impaling of their corpses. Departing from the inherent temptations of vampirism, therefore, *Forefathers' Eve* thus metamorphosed from a romantic drama into an epic of national freedom, in which the resurrection of the heroes can be read as an allegory for the endurance of the nation following the downfall of the state.[16]

In his *Lectures on Slavic Literature and the Condition of the Slavic Nations*, Mickiewicz saw the belief in vampires as a part of the cultural heritage of the Slavic peoples, and whilst he did seek to understand the Serbian term in the sense of a 'bloodsucker', he also remarked that this figure had yet to find its way into poetry. Drawing upon the thoroughly Western-inspired vampire discourse of the time, Mickiewicz defined the upiór, with reference to Polish popular belief, as a person with two hearts. When evil grows to dominate within this type of person and provokes their metamorphosis into a demon, this opens up the possibility of a sort of witches' sabbath, at which the upiór community discussed scourges such as hunger and the plague.[17]

The further transmission of the upiór term is connected with the author Władysław Wójcicki, who made a considerable contribution to the documentation of popular belief in the nineteenth century. In his three-volume collection *Przysłowia narodowe* (*Proverbs of the People*), he discussed the phrase 'red like an upiór' (*czerwony iak upior*). As his starting point, he took the Western debates of the eighteenth century, in which vampires were portrayed as bloodsuckers and chokers, who infect their victims through biting them. Fatally, he drew upon the fictitious motifs of the alleged Illyrian or South Slavic anthologies of Prosper Mérimée and Wilhelm Gerhard from 1827 and 1828 (see the Introduction); by contrast, Wójcicki did not name any specific Polish case. On the one hand, he claimed to have made a sojourn in Słupi in the district of Sandomierz in 1826 and to have heard from a peasant who claimed to have been beaten, through the night, by a young man who had transformed himself into an upiór. On the other hand, he also related that, in the administrative district of Kraków, a piece of paper with verses from the Bible was placed in graves in order to prevent posthumous activities; the evocation of suspicious persons did, it is true, help to banish demonic evildoers, but primarily it served to placate the nerves of the population. Finally, he also reported that in Red Ruthenia, a province in the Polish-Ukrainian border region, all the bodily orifices of a corpse were stuffed so as to prevent the escape of an upiór that might possibly be present, and that could otherwise arise and threaten the livestock. Wójcicki did admit that the Polish phrase 'red like an upiór' derived from the rosy complexion of the harmful revenant's cheeks, but at the same time he also highlighted the corresponding expression 'red like a Toruń brick' (*czerwony iak Toruńska cegła*), which made reference to the red brick castles of the Teutonic Order. In both instances, the red colour of the face demonstrated itself to be suspicious: it revealed either shame or a guilty conscience.[18]

Several years later, in 1837, Wójcicki again made mention of the upiór in the preface to his two-volume anthology *Klechdy, starożytne podania i powieści ludu Polskiego i Rusi* (*Fairy Tales, Ancient Traditions and Legends of the Polish and Ruthenian People*). However, in light of the lack of empirical evidence, it was not provided with its own piece. Nevertheless, in journals such as *Kłosy* (*Ears of Wheat*), Wójcicki did discuss related phenomena such as the *zmora* ('nightmare') or the *strzyga* ('witch'), which fuelled the fantasies of ethnographers in the final third of the nineteenth century; however, these articles from 1865 were not finally published until the reissued edition of *Klechdy* of 1972.[19]

Fear in Times of Cholera

Reports by Polish ethnographers on harmful revenants in the second half of the nineteenth century repeatedly refer back to cholera. This plague was introduced for the first time in 1830 by Russian soldiers, who had been deployed in the repression of the Polish Uprising, and then subsequently reappeared in several waves in East and East Central Europe up to the First World War, bringing countless deaths in its wake. As always, where supernatural forces were raised in the struggle against potential causes of disease, the population turned to similar measures to those undertaken in times of plague.[20] Ethnographers subsequently took account of this in the terminological distinction between upiór and *strzyga* (fem.) and *strzygoń* (masc.). Whereas the classic upiór receded into the background as a phenomenon of the upper classes, among the common people the strzyga or strzygoń gradually took on the role of the harmful revenant.

In his 1856 anthology *Archivum domowe* (*Domestic Archive*), Kazimierz Wójcicki published several explanations that the agronomist and ethnographer Józef Gluziński had offered on the customs and traditions of the Polish rural population, based on material that he had gathered in the period before 1847 in the region around Zamość und Hrubieszów in southeastern Poland, close to the border with Ukraine. In these, the upiór is portrayed as a harmful revenant, who would conduct his activities up to the first crow of the cock, but who, in contrast to the strzyga, did not suck blood. Since signs of later revenancy could already be discerned during a person's lifetime, a series of defensive measures were carried out upon dead suspects. Should these prove to be unsuccessful, a posthumous execution would be undertaken.[21]

A truly pioneering study in this regard was the article on superstition among the Slavic population by the Upper Silesian publicist Józef Lompa, which appeared in the *Schlesische Provinzialblätter* in 1862. This did not discuss the belief in vampires, and the designation 'upiór' was thus demoted to a term of scholarly disputes of the late eighteenth century. Instead, Lompa discussed the terms 'zmora' – referred to in the German translation as 'Alp' and in the general Slavic designation as *mora* ('nightmare') – and 'strzyga'. In popular belief, the zmora was a mythical female creature who sat herself down either upon the chests of sleeping people or on treetops in the forest. When people sought to defend themselves, the zmora would send them into a state of sleep through her breath or would take flight by transforming into a straw or a mouse. The zmora was accused of competing with newborns for their mothers' milk. One could only rid oneself of them by speaking their name out loud. As for the strzyga, Lompa claimed that, according to popular belief, people born with a full set of teeth were in possession of two souls and were therefore predestined to transform into strzyga after their death. This was because one of the two souls would remain in the corpse, thus ensuring its reanimation. The strzyga could leave its grave at midnight and climb the church spire, so as to cast its sight over the environment. Those who found themselves within its field of vision, and who were of the same age that the strzyga had been at the time of their passing, would then also meet their own death. As a precaution, it was recommended that pebbles be placed in the mouth of the dead person, that they be turned onto their stomachs or that their head be cut off and placed between their feet.[22]

All these Polish reports on revenancy were brought together in a large compilation, published in over thirty volumes from 1857 by the ethnographer and composer Oskar Kolberg: *Lud: Jego zwyczaje, sposób życia, mowa, podania, przysłowia, obrzędy, gusła, zabawy, pieśni, muzyka i tańce* (*The People: Their Customs, Lifestyles, Language, Legends, Proverbs, Rituals, Curses, Songs, Music and Dances*). The 1874 volume, dedicated to the administrative region of Kraków, tackles both the 'strzygoń' and 'zmora'. Thus, in higher circles, a strzygoń is referred to as an upiór. He becomes apparent during his lifetime through nightly walks and first becomes harmful after his death. Each strzygoń has both a good and an evil soul. Believers claimed, among other things, that a strzygoń provides for the household of those he has left behind, and was even capable of siring children with his widow, but that he had to return to his grave by the first crow of the cock. A child conceived by a strzygoń turned out to be weak and would not survive into adulthood. In return for a few złoty, some priests evidently offered to sprinkle the house with holy water in order to drive out the strzygoń. Elsewhere, it was said of the strzygoń that he tormented relatives with bites and blows; those who succumbed had to die. With regards to the upiór, there was a widespread belief that this species had retreated back to Russia (in the Tsarist Empire, specifically to Ukraine).[23] Alongside the zmora, the volumes dealing with the administrative districts of Poznań and Lublin from the years 1882 and 1884 also touched upon the *wieszczy* ('seer'). Whilst zmora were understood to be persons who, following their death, would break into the homes of their neighbours in the form of a midge or a butterfly, causing nightmares, the wieszczy was a revenant who would call out names from the church tower or cast his glance around in order to bring about the deaths of those he thus ensnared.[24] Due to the contradictory claims present in the various witness statements, it remains very difficult to come to any general conclusions about the specific characteristics of these expressions of Polish popular belief.

Polish Vampire Tales

In 1893, the teacher and ethnographer Otto Knoop published a collection of *Sagen und Erzählungen aus der Provinz Posen* (*Tales and Stories from the Province of Posen*) in which he referred to both the vampire and the upiór. Vampire was the title he gave to a story from the district of Wirsitz (today Wyrzysk). According to this tale, a person born with an embryonic skin covering his face, a so-called caul, is able to call upon his relatives and associates living with earshot of the church bells to follow him into the grave. If this caul is not removed after his birth and fed to him in a dried and powdered form with milk, the only remaining defence against the plague that will inevitably result from his death is the decapitation of the corpse.

A dead spirit, referred to as an upiór, was the subject of a story related by Śroka, a village doctor from Biskupitz (today Biskupice) in the district of Schildberg (today Ostrzeszów). This tells of the death of a young man, named Szymanek, who already had teeth upon birth.

In the region around Biskupitz, the belief prevailed that a person born with a full set of teeth was in possession of two souls, one of which would act as a dead spirit for a period of one year after their death, endangering the lives of all those who came into his line of sight. Therefore, after Szymanek's death, numerous villagers claimed that they had been harassed by a spirit at night. Soon, the number of deaths of people who claimed, during their illness, to have been choked by Szymanek began to pile up, and his grave was therefore opened. Predictably, the corpse gave the impression of not being decomposed and a growth of facial hair could even be detected. In order to destroy the dead spirit, the head was severed from the torso, with great care being taken that none of the life-threatening blood spurted onto those present. Following this posthumous execution, the unusual series of death came to an end.[25]

In 1905/1906, Knoop followed up on this in the *Zeitschrift des Vereins für Volkskunde* (*Journal of the Ethnographic Society*) with 'Sagen aus Kujawien' ('Tales from Kujawy'), a region in the east of the province of Poznań in north-central Poland. From a Polish source, he shared an incident from Rogoźno, which was alleged to have taken place in a forester's lodge, somewhere between Gniezno and Wresznia.

On the night following the death of the forester's adult son, a dreadful wailing sound could be heard outside the house at midnight. At the same time, a knocking on the window panes could also be heard. Spooked by this, the sister, who was praying alongside the corpse, saw a horrible figure with long teeth. The spirit demanded, in Polish, that the body be surrendered to him, but it proved possible to ward him off with the use of a rosary. The following day, passing gypsy travellers stated that the apparition was an upiór. He would appear three times following a person's death, in order to devour the heart of the deceased. As well as the rosary, candles consecrated at Candlemas could also be used as a defence.[26]

Knoop also shared the following case from Brudzyn, which had been reported to him from a German source by the teacher Szulczewski.

Shortly after the death of the eldest son of a peasant family, all the other family members also passed away, with the exception of the father. A night-watchman came to the conclusion that this could be the work of a vampire. He convinced the peasants to open the grave of the eldest son. The corpse gave the impression of not having decomposed and, at the same time, the flesh seemed to have been eaten away. As an explanation, it was pointed out that a vampire could find no rest after death and that he therefore devoured himself, and dragged his closest relatives with him into the grave. The placing of a coin between the vampire's teeth was intended to prevent him from biting.[27]

According to a report published by the Varsovian ethnographer Stanisław Ciszewski in his 1887 book *Lud rolniczo-górniczy z okolic Sławkowa w powiecie Olkuskim* (*The Agricultural and Mining Population in the Vicinity of Sławkow in the District of Olkusz*), the following case of revenancy was supposed to have taken place in the settlement of Bukowno, between Kraków and Katowice.

Following his death, a man who was believed to be in possession of two souls, and had therefore been designated as a strzygoń, began to visit his widow at night, threatening her not to betray him. Once, when leaving his wife in the morning, he chanced upon an old acquaintance, who first struck him and then forced him to flee. When the priest was informed of this episode, he ordered that the grave of the strzygoń be opened, a piece of paper with his name on placed under his tongue, and the corpse turned on its stomach. With a smack on the dead man's posterior and the reburial of the coffin in the earth, the ceremony was successfully completed.[28]

In a tale published in the geographic-ethnographic journal *Wisła* (*Vistula*), which most likely came from the area around Sieradz to the southwest of Łódź, a sleeping man was allegedly abused in his sleep by a zmora. Transformed into a small creature, the zmora sat on the chest of the sleeping man, drew his tongue from his mouth and sucked blood out of it. The following night, in order to get rid of her, the man placed his clothes in the bed and then lay down to sleep elsewhere. Furious at this trick, the zmora then stabbed him with a knife.[29]

Whilst the first story recorded by Ciszewski sees a widow harassed by an alleged revenant, who is then put back in his place through not exactly Christian means, the second tale sees a righteous man fall into the clutches of a witch, who first extracts his life force and then brings about his doom. Whereas the first story implicitly tackles sexual assault, the second represents a reaction to the threat of cholera. In both cases, the tongue plays a central role, as an expression of language and an instrument of communication.

Taking into account the personalization of the causes of disease evident in these examples, as well as the stylization of scapegoats as poltergeists, the journalist *Stanisław Wasylewski* was able, with reason, to claim in his article in the journal *Lud*, 'W sprawie wampiryzmu' ('On the Matter of Vampirism'), that there were no vampires in Poland, because the upiór is not a bloodsucker.[30]

Vampirism as an Issue in Prussia's Eastern Provinces

After vampirism had played a role in the debates of Western physicians and theologians in the final third of the eighteenth century, it then found its way, as a tragic motif, into the poetry of the Sturm und Drang movement. Gottfried August Bürger's 1773 ballad on the undead soldier and his bride Lenore and Johann Wolfgang von Goethe's 1797 poem on the dead bride of Corinth constituted two of the most prominent examples of this. In the English horror novel, through the mediation of Lord Byron, the figure of the bloodsucker underwent a definitive transformation from a Southeast European demon of disease to a British dandy or a Styrian sadist, in John William Polidori's *The Vampyre* of 1819 and Sheridan Le Fanu's *Carmilla* of 1872. Polidori's figure even found his way onto the German stage in Heinrich Marschner's opera of 1828.

Independently of this, the second third of the nineteenth century also saw the development of a separate vampire discourse in Prussia as part of a broader interest in superstition in the fields of ethnology, mythological studies and criminal studies. When one focuses upon the partitioned Polish lands in Western and Eastern Prussia and in Poznań, and on the debates surrounding the 'rebirth' of the Polish state, several striking findings emerge.

In the mid nineteenth century, the proportion of the Polish population in Prussia's Eastern provinces was around 25%, and in Poznań alone it was over 60%. Minority groups included Catholic Kashubians, Protestant Masurians and Protestant Lithuanians. Daily life in the region was shaped by cosmopolitan trading relationships and religious ecumenicism. Alongside socioeconomic backwardness, a further central structural characteristic was the intensity of piety and superstition. Significantly, the belief in bloodsuckers, nachzehrers and the nightmares seems to have been present in equal measure in Catholic and Protestant areas. Revenants could be identified by the red facial colour of the corpse in the grave, and countermeasures against them included the placing of a coin under the tongue and of aspen crosses on the chest and under the armpits of the corpse. The furnishing of the coffin with poppies and nets was seen as a further precaution, decapitation as a defence, and the consumption of flour enriched with vampire blood as a medicine.

On the part of the German national movement, the period between the first Polish Uprising against Russian rule in 1830 and the German Revolution of 1848 saw a transition from a Romantic enthusiasm for Poland to a more functional friendship. The aftermath of the revolution led to an increasing polarization of worldviews between Protestant-Conservative Germans on the one

Figure 4.1 The execution of a vampire in a booklet for enlighteners and non-enlighteners.

In *Taschenbuch für Aufklärer und Nichtaufklärer auf das Jahr 1791 (Booklet for Enlighteners and non-Enlighteners for the the year 1791)*, Carl von Knoblauch zu Hatzbach ironically focused on different kinds of superstition. The opening of a grave of a supposed vampire is described as a public event. While the attendant nobles are sceptical about the planned impaling, the priest is desperately praying to god. The assistant of the executioner is protecting his nose, even though the corpse still looks like the body of a living person.

Source: Carl von Knoblauch zu Hatzbach (ed.), *Taschenbuch für Aufklärer und Nichtaufklärer auf das Jahr 1791* (Berlin, 1790), between 18 and 19.

hand and the Catholic-Democratic Poles on the other. The transformation in Germany, in the period leading up to unification, from a perception of Russia as the primary enemy to one of France as the main foe, inevitably led to a rapid deterioration in German attitudes towards the Polish national movement. After 1871, antagonism peaked in a two-sided polemic debate over the theory of the nation as a bearer of culture, which attempted to present the 'eastward colonization' of the German Middle Ages as a major cultural accomplishment, and the myth of the Germans as conquerors, which assumed a continuous German 'Drang nach Osten'.[31]

A comparison of the German and Polish sense of mission is instructive. Polish messianism was inspired by Adam Mickiewicz's *Księgi narodu polskiego i pielgrzymstwa polskiego* (*Books of the Polish People and of the Polish Pilgrimage*), published in 1832, which is shot through with the idea of liberty. In this, the temporary disappearance of the Polish state from the political map of Europe is equated, metaphorically, with the crucifixion, burial and resurrection of Christ, with the Polish nation being presented as the 'Christ of nations'. In contrast, German historicism took up the categories of historic and nonhistoric nations, differentiating between state-building nations and stateless ones. Accordingly, in his 1860 novel *Geschichte der Revolutionszeit 1789–1800* (*History of the Revolutionary Period 1789–1800*), Heinrich von Sybel referred to the partitions of Poland at the end of the eighteenth century as 'political and moral suicide'. Therefore, he laid the blame for the denial of entry into paradise for Poland firmly at the feet of the failings of the Noble Republic.[32] In other words, whereas the Polish national movement focused on the foreign domination by Prussia, Austria and Russia and sought to provide historical legitimization for the Noble Republic's right to existence, the German elite and rulers saw themselves as the bearers of culture and utilized history to question the durability and viability of a Polish state. Whereas the 'rebirth' of their nation constituted a collective vision for the Polish elite, derived from the biblical Passion story, from the perspective of German publicists, superstition among the Slavophone rural population, as evidenced by the vampire cases, was merely an expression of a wider 'Polish threat'.

The existence of the belief in 'bloodsuckers' among the German population was first mentioned in Wilhelm von Tettau and Jodocus Temme's 1837 *Volkssagen Ostpreußens, Litthauens und Westpreussens* (*Folk Tales of East Prussia, Lithuania and West Prussia*). This pointed towards the dangers that threatened the family members of dead persons who retained a rosy complexion following their death. Defensive measures that could be undertaken against potential cases of revenancy included the decapitation of the corpse, accompanied by a huge loss of blood and, bizarrely, the drinking of this blood by those left behind as a sort of medicine.[33] Whereas the writer and librarian Ludwig Bechstein had already touched upon the 'vampire' in his *Deutsches Sagenbuch* (*German Fairy-*

tale Book) of 1853, the theologian and publicist Adolf Wuttke still claimed, in the 1860 first edition of his encyclopaedic work *Der deutsche Volksaberglaube in der Gegenwart* (*German Popular Superstition in the Present*), that the motif of posthumous activities only appears 'in a very few cases' in his homeland and also that the term 'vampire' was not in widespread use among the people.[34]

The term 'vampire' did not really receive any traction in the Prussian context until the mythologist and scholar of religion Wilhelm Mannhardt began to tackle the issue at greater length in 1859 in the *Zeitschrift für deutsche Mythologie* (*Journal of German Mythology*). At this time, Mannhardt still clearly located the belief in vampires in 'regions of the former Slavic population', but in the same breath he also referred to traces and witnesses in 'regions of purely German heritage'. In contrast to his later works, it still seemed to be important to him to accentuate the German contribution to the wealth of popular tales and, tellingly, Poland still constituted a *terra incognita* for Mannhardt. Whereas the Kashubians in Western Prussia spoke about 'vieszczy' ('seer') or 'stryz' ('witch'), as described by Mannhardt, the Germans in Pomerania used the terms 'Gierhals', 'Gierrach', 'Begierig' and 'Unbegier' (descriptions of greedy persons, derived from German *gierig*). According to Kashubian popular belief, people born with teeth, a caul or a red mark were considered to be condemned to posthumous bloodsucking. Those who were unable to find their peace with this world before their deaths also fell under this curse. A bloodsucker could be identified by the red colour of the corpse's face, as well as the fact that the left eye remained open. He would leave the grave at night in order to plague the living. However, the only evidence of his nightly visitations was a scarcely discernible bite wound on the left side of the breast. Nevertheless, the people whom he had visited would inevitably fall victim to a fatal disease.[35]

Following the growth of an anti-Slavic mood among the Prussian public, the omens in Mannhardt's work were turned on their head. In his 1878 treatise on *Die praktischen Folgen des Aberglaubens* (*The Practical Consequences of Superstition*), he expressed his outrage at the desecration of corpses that had led to a furore in the courts following German unification. This dreadful state of affairs was to be found in particular 'among the Polish-speaking sections of the population'. Under this premise, Mannhardt came to the conclusion – paraphrasing a statement from the second edition of Wuttke's 1869 work[36] – that the belief in vampires was spread 'in parts in the German', but 'everywhere in the Slavic world'. On Russian territory, it was less an epidemic and more an endemic 'evil', which stood in direct opposition to the moral and scientific consciousness of the German people. Thus, in Mannhardt's argumentation, the vampire, or the belief in him, had transformed over the course of two decades from a component of German mythology to an element in the anti-Polish polemic.[37]

The debate at the turn of the twentieth century concentrated on the Slavic origins of the belief in vampires. The participants in this debate drew, on the one hand, upon medieval chronicles and, on the other hand, upon contemporary press articles. Stefan Hock, for example, in his 1900 dissertation *Die Vampyrsagen und ihre Verwertung in der deutschen Literatur* (*Vampire Tales and Their Utilization in German Literature*), differentiated between the 'sucking vampire' and the 'chomping Gierrach'. He located the vampire among the South Slavs and their neighbours, and the Gierrach among the West Slavs and 'the Germans living among them'. In this, Hock interpreted vampirism as a phenomenon which had been reimported in the course of German 'Eastern colonization'.[38] Further, in the first volume of his work *Schlesische Sagen* (*Silesian Tales*) from 1910, the ethnographer Richard Kühnau addressed 'Spuk- und Gespenstergeschichten' (Horror and Ghost Stories) in which, having tackled poltergeists and tormenting spirits (*quälgeist*), he moved on to discuss 'vampire tales'. In so doing, he initially attributed the belief in vampires to the Slavs, but also conceded that the Germans, too, had fallen under the influence of the witch-hunts of the sixteenth and seventeenth centuries. However, by the start of the twentieth century, the belief in vampires in Silesia had largely disappeared; in the popular conception, 'the figure of the vampire has become a poltergeist or a quälgeist'. In this context, Kühnau also claimed that the *scheiga* or *strzyga*, derived from Polish mythology, still played a role as the cause of diseases in the 'Upper Silesian Polish regions'.[39]

Incidents of Vampirism in the Courts on Prussia's Peripheries

An incident among the Wollschläger family from the second half of the eighteenth century, mentioned for the first time by Tettau and Temme, was to go on to become a classic of Prussian vampirism. In the 1830s, Wilhelm von Tettau was a district administrator in the Prussian Konitz (today Chojnice). The incidents that he has passed on to us correspond in their central aspects to what the ethnologist Leo Gerschke reported from the Wollschläger family chronicle in the *Westpreußen Jahrbuch* (*West Prussian Annual*) in 1962.

Following the burial of a member of the Wollschläger family at Jakobsdorf Monastery, several other relatives also passed away unexpectedly. Those left behind came to the conclusion, based on the fresh facial colour that the dead body seemed to reveal, that bloodsucking was at play. Therefore, the family instructed a nephew of the dead man, namely the later County Director Joseph Wollschläger, to cut off the head of the alleged evildoer. The nephew visited the dark vault where the body lay in the company of a monk, but was left high and dry by his companion who had been terrified upon the opening of the coffin. When the nephew chopped off the head of his dead uncle, a stream of blood spurted out, extinguishing the candles. Nevertheless, he managed to gather up some of the blood in a cup and take this with him. However, he emerged from this escapade with a life-threatening disease that left him bedridden for half a year.[40]

As late as 1916, Leo Gerschke was able to take a close look at this so-called Uhier von Jakobsdorf ('Monster of Jakobsdorf'). As he outlined half a century later, in 1940, he had only just missed out on the opportunity to take a photograph. Furthermore, in his youth, Gerschke had also heard the following version of the incidents surrounding the alleged revenant from the elderly people of his home region.

Following the death of the elderly Wollschläger, apparitions began to be seen in the monastery. Doors would open and close for no apparent reason, and the monastery's St Bernard dog would yelp and whimper as if struck by an unseen hand. In order to combat the revenant, several men lay in hiding with a lantern and a spade. When they felt that the uhier was beating the dog again, they lit the lantern and threw open the trapdoor to the burial vault. Thereafter the uhier retreated back down into the grave. When the men inspected the grave, they saw that the hands of the dead person, lying by his side, were covered in dog hairs. After his head had been buried between his legs, the dead man no longer appeared as a revenant.[41]

Due to the underlying nationalist and xenophobic mood, and in contrast to the case of the respected family of the later County Director Joseph von Wollschläger, it was largely Polish-sounding names that appeared in a court case handling grave desecrations in the late nineteenth century. According to the commentary published in the collection of the high state prosecutor Friedrich Oppenhoff, *Die Rechtsprechung des Königlichen Ober-Tribunals und des Königlichen Ober-Appellations-Gerichts ins Straf-Sachen* (*The Judgements of the Royal High Tribunal and the Royal Court of High Appeal in Criminal Matters*), the background to this case can be outlined as follows.

Since the forester Gehrke and his children fell gravely ill immediately after the death of his wife, the belief began to spread in the family that the dead woman wanted to 'come back to claim' her relatives. Thereafter, accompanied by several friends, the forester's brother opened the grave in order to place a rope and some linseed in the coffin. Since the corpse had been found to have reddish cheeks, they came to the decision that they should immediately chop off her head and place it under her arm.

At the third instance in front of the courts, in February 1871, the accused could finally prove that the grave desecration was not the result of mischief making, but had been authorized by the family members. At no stage did they feel any guilt, since they had decided upon a 'measure which was felt to be beneficial by all sides'.[42]

A death in the Poblocki family from Kantrzyno or Kantrschin (today Kętrzyno) in the West Prussian district of Neustadt (today Wejherowo) – a family that had its roots in the Polish nobility, but had since fallen on hard times – once again caused headlines in 1870, at least according to the popular writer and eyewitness Ernst Krause alias Carus Sterne.

On 5 February 1870, the churchwarden Franz von Poblocki died of 'emaciation' at the age of sixty-three. His funeral took place on 9 February in the neighbouring village of Roslasin in the Pomeranian district of Lauenburg (today Lębork). On 18 February, the dead man's oldest son fell victim to a disease similar to that of his father, diagnosed by the physician as 'galloping consumption'. Since several further family members seemed to have become afflicted in the meantime and fears of a general wasting away had begun to spread, it was decided that the two bodies identified as the cause of the disease should be decapitated. The second eldest son Josef, who had also fallen ill, assumed responsibility for this. The unskilled labourer Johan Dzigcielski was tasked with the decapitation of the brother, who had not yet been buried. He received instructions to gather the blood from the corpse in order that this could be given to the living as medicine. The burial was to take place on 22 February, in the father's grave in Roslasin (today Rozłazino).

The Roslasin gravedigger was bribed so as to gain access to the father's coffin at night. However, plagued by doubt, he informed the priest, who forbade the desecration of the body, ordered that the more recently departed person should be buried in a different grave and summoned guards to watch over the coffin. Nevertheless, Josef von Poblocki succeeded in carrying out a decapitation of the corpse. However, he was disturbed in this by the village innkeeper, who had been woken by the noise. At this, the three men involved immediately took flight, without having managed completely to refill the grave with soil. They were identified the following day thanks to the work tools that they had left behind. The priest then carried out a proper Christian burial, addressed the consciences of his congregation in his sermon, and filed a complaint against Josef von Poblocki and his accomplices.

On 28 February, the mother of the chief suspect, Josephine von Poblocki, fell victim to a nervous fever, according to the physician's diagnosis. However, the family were convinced that she had died because she had declined to take the medicine that had been made from the blood of the previously departed revenant.

In October 1870, the district court imposed a prison sentence upon the grave desecrators, but this was rescinded by the Court of Appeals in May 1872 on the grounds that they had essentially acted out of self-defence, 'without knowledge of the lacking authorisation.'[43]

In 1887, in reference to a notice in the *St Petersburger Zeitung* (*St Petersburg News*), Friedrich Salomon Strauss, the Austrian publicist and expert on Southeastern Europe, mistakenly drew a connection between the belief in vampires in Serbia and that in Prussia-Lithuania in the *Mittheilungen der Anthropologischen Gesellschaft in Wien* (*Notifications of the Anthropological Society in Vienna*). This related to the court case on a charge of grave desecration brought against the Lithuanian Robert von Gostowski in Danzig (today Gdańsk).

Since the father of the accused, who was suffering from consumption, had raised concerns among his family about the unusual manner of his impending death, he had begged that his head be chopped off before burial and laid separately from the torso in the sarcophagus. Witnesses did indeed confirm that the father was convinced he would become a vampire. However, since the accused had himself fallen ill, despite undertaking these preventative measures, he convinced a gravedigger, by offering him alcohol, to lift out the coffin. With his own hands, he then turned over the corpse onto its stomach and hurled the head into a thicket.

Since Robert von Gostovski and his aides had acted out of superstition, the court found him to be only partially guilty and, he was handed only a short-term prison sentence.[44]

In a brochure on *Verbrechen und Aberglaube* (*Crime and Superstition*) from 1908, the criminologist Albert Hellwig presented a vampire case, which was supposed to have taken place at the start of the nineteenth century in the eastern region of the Prussian province of Pomerania.

Following the death of an illegitimate child, who had not yet reached his first birthday, his mother also passed away. Since her sister, who was living in the same house, subsequently became seriously ill, the other remaining family members became convinced that they had to destroy a vampire who, to use a term adopted by Hellwig, was going about in the form of the illegitimate child so as – in the words of the accused – to prevent a further gathering up of the dead. The coffin was therefore opened up and the head of the child was separated from his body with a spade. The blood that spurted out was gathered up and given to the diseased aunt. Since this seemed to result in the containment of the plague, those involved were all convinced that they had taken the appropriate measures.[45]

A further desecration of a corpse, which took place in 1913 in the fishing village of Putzig (today Puck) in the west of Danzig Bay (today Gdańsk), was also discussed by Hellwig in 1914 in the *Archiv für Religionswissenschaft* (*Archive for Religious Studies*).

According to the statement made to the district court by the chief suspect, who was living in Polchau (today Połchowo), seven further people had died in his family following the death of his mother two and a half years previously. Many people had suggested to him that his mother had not been able to find peace and was thus calling her relatives after her into the grave. Particularly in Protestant circles – that is, among members of the unofficial Prussian state Church – it was recommended that the woman, who had been buried in a Catholic cemetery, be decapitated. In view of the increasing physical decay that he himself had begun to feel, the accused overcame his initial doubts and agreed to undertake this act, together with his brother-in-law. The men were aided by two other men, whom the father of the accused had called upon for assistance.

The two strangers opened the coffin, cut off the head of the dead woman and placed it between her legs. This seemed to bring about an improvement in the health of the accused, who thus became convinced that this action had saved his life. Nevertheless the district court of Danzig (today Gdańsk) sentenced the chief suspect to six weeks imprisonment, and the others to one month.[46]

Cases of Revenancy in Fairy Tales and Legends on Prussia's Peripheries

Alongside a distinctive terminology, a further peculiarity of the area settled by the Elb Slavs in the early Middle Ages is the radicalization of nachzehrer conceptions, known from the Central German region. The *Sagenbuch der Lausitz* (*Book of Tales from the Lausitz*), published in 1862 by the priest and ethnographer Carl Haupt, describes the 'Alp' ('nightmare'), 'Mähre' or 'Drutte' (Wendish or Elb Slavic 'Murava'), leaning upon Polish traditions, as an evil spirit who arises from a person with a monobrow and harasses the sleeping in the form of an ugly hag. A 'vampire' or bloodsucker, by contrast, appeared for the last time in the area of Sorb settlement in the person of a noblewoman from the sixteenth century with the ominous name of Countess Villambrosa.[47] Whether this was a play on the legend of the Hungarian 'Blood Countess' Elisabeth Báthory, who went on trial on the territory of present-day Slovakia in 1611 for the murder of domestic servants and young maids, remains open to question.[48]

By contrast, the *Wendische Sagen* (*Wendish Tales*), published in 1880 by the teacher and ethnologist Edmund Veckenstedt, offered many examples of 'Alpdrucks' ('nightmares'), 'Aufhockers' ('shape-shifters') and bloodsuckers from Lower Lusatia, in particular from the region around Cottbus. According to Veckenstedt the 'murawa' or nightmare particularly set upon elderly people. One example reported on the case of a farmhand who was subject to permanent physical harassment by an alpdruck and who had claimed that his dead mother visited him at night. On her deathbed, she confessed to having carried out arson attacks in the village on several occasions. Following the revelation of this secret, the apparitions came to an end. In a similar manner, in a passage on aufhockers, Veckenstadt also provided a solution to the mystery that had confronted a night-watchman. During his watch, he had felt an unusual and heavy burden upon his back. When he came home, he discovered that his wife had died. Veckenstedt's explanation of this nocturnal occurrence was that the night-watchman had carried the weight of death. Finally, Veckenstedt also gave a passage in his anthology the title of 'vampyre'. In this he described golums as weasel-like figures who, at night, not only ransacked the graves of recently departed people and ate their corpses, but also sucked the blood of the living. Two tales from the vicinity of Cottbus are similar to Serbian vampire tales and represent a reaction to unusual cases of death.

First case: a peasant had broken his neck falling from a wagon and, following his burial, emerged from his grave to drink the blood of his son. Following the death of his son, the village community decided to burn both corpses as a precautionary measure.

Second case: a murdered peasant was accused of going about at night, extinguishing candles, thumping on doors and drinking people's blood. In order to put a stop to this, his grave was opened twice. The driving of a nail through the head and a stake through the heart did not have the desired effect, and it was only after the corpse was burned that peace was re-established.[49]

In 1885, the teacher and ethnographer Otto Knoop published a collection of *Volkssagen, Erzählungen, Aberglauben, Gebräuche und Märchen aus dem östlichen Hinterpommern* (*Folk Tales, Legends, Superstitions, Customs and Fairy Tales from Eastern Pomerania*), that is, from those areas lying to the east of the River Oder in present-day Poland. Alongside the 'Mahrt', he also discussed the 'Unhier', that is, a monster. When infants were born covered by a caul, popular belief held that countermeasures needed to be taken against the properties of an unhier connected to this. Midwives were instructed secretly to burn the caul and to feed it to the baby in powdered form. Where this was not done, one family member would be dragged to the grave every year following the death of the affected. As a further precaution, a coin could also be placed in the mouth of the dead unhier and cabbage seeds or peas could also be strewn during the procession of the coffin from the village to the churchyard. Upon his annual return, the dead man would then have to ensure that all these seeds or peas were gathered up before he could fall upon his victims. A final defensive measure was decapitation. The unhier could not begin to decompose until the death of his final relative.[50]

A further West Prussian vampire case from the period before the First World War was outlined in Hans B. Meyer's 1956 representation of *Das Danziger Volksleben* (*Danzig Popular Life*). Here an eyewitness admitted that he had participated in warding off a 'Nohier' (another variant of the monster described previously) in 1907 in the district of Karthaus (today Kartuzy).

After a woman from Niedersommerkau (today Ząbrsko Dolne) had died during childbirth, along with her child, both were buried together in one coffin in the cemetery at Schaplitz (today Czapielsk). Shortly thereafter, further family members began to fall ill and to pass away. Initially the new mother was suspected of going about as a nohier and her father decided, with the help of several men, to open the coffin. This revealed a sitting child, who thus exposed himself as the supposed origin of the disease. The men therefore cut off his head and placed this at the end of his torso, face down between his legs. Much of the blood that had spurted out was gathered up and all the family members were smeared with this. Thereafter, there were no further cases of disease.[51]

After the *Schlesische Provinzialblätter* had already reported in 1801, in an ironic manner, on the alleged Polish strzyga in the district of Ratibor (today

Raciborz), it published a further report in 1873 on the same phenomenon, this time in a German environment. Against the backdrop of a cholera epidemic, fears had begun to spread in a suburb of the town of Ratibor, which had fallen under Prussian control in 1742, about the rampaging of a 'Seiga' (or 'Scheiga'), a demon of illness in the Slavic world who had, in the meantime, become Germanized.

The tragic heroine was a well-regarded widow named Karoline, who had served the community as a nurse, tending to the dying and keeping wake following their deaths. When her own sister died, Karoline had discovered to her horror, during the preparation of the body, that a mark in the form of shears could be found on her neck, the mark of the seiga. In the knowledge that a mass dying would set in one year after her sister's death, Karoline found herself in a moral dilemma, but could not bring herself to decapitate the corpse. According to the newspaper, the series of death did in fact come to pass at the expected time. Initially the victims were all women, among them Karoline. The menfolk could breathe easy for a little longer. However, when death began to come for them – the report concludes – they reached the decision to exhume and decapitate the seiga.[52]

In 1904/1905, the Berlin school director and poet of the Silesian dialect Karl Klings presented a literary interpretation of this material in the *Oberschlesien* (*Upper Silesia*) journal. His heroine is the infirm Martha, whose elder sister was killed by a lightning strike. Martha recognized the fact that the mark of shears on her body was in fact a burn mark. A year after her sister's death, to the astonishment of the community, she offered herself as a sacrifice to the alleged seiga.[53]

Vampirism in the Tsarist Empire

In the framework of the discrediting of East Central and Southeastern Europe in the German vampire discourse, and in light of the worsening political relationship under Bismarck's successors, the incorporation of the Tsarist Empire into this discourse was a logical consequence. Drawing upon the 1897 study *Superstition and Criminal Law* (*Sueverie i ugolovnoe pravo*) by the St Petersburg lawyer August Löwenstimm, the jurist and publicist Albert Hellwig also identified a distinction between the 'Western Cultural States' (Kulturstaaten) and the 'East of Europe' in his 1908 brochure *Verbrechen und Aberglaube* (*Crime and Superstition*).[54] The cases that Löwenstimm referenced in his chapter on 'Upyrs and the Opening of Graves' focused on Lithuania and Belarus, and on Volhynia and Podolia, i.e. on the territory of 'Old Poland' or the heart of East Central Europe. Löwenstimm compared the juridical treatment of cases dealing with the desecration of bodies in the German and Russian Empires, finding fault in both cases with the absence of clear regulations that would have taken superstition into consideration to a suitable degree in the determining responsibility. In the Tsarist Empire, he identified particular motivations for the opening of graves, in the use of body parts as talismen and medicines on the one hand, and in the search for scapegoats for epidemics and periods of drought on the other.[55]

In fact, the figure of the upyr only received a very limited resonance in Russian fairy tales. In the eight-volume fairy tale collection of the Moscow archivist Alexander Afanasyev, known as the 'Russian Grimm', which appeared between 1855 and 1863, there were only a very few revenant stories. However, one tale can be found in the sixth volume, from 1862, most likely of Ukrainian origin, entitled *The Impure (Nechistyi)*. This tale, brimming with magical elements, combines two motifs: that of the vampire bride and that of the flower-child. In this, the 'Impure' is depicted as an evil spirit and eater of people.

The beautiful Marusya meets a stranger at a dance, who proposes to her. In order to discover more about his background, her mother advises her to attach a ball of yarn to him at their next meeting. Having done so, Marusya follows the stranger to the church, where she discovers, to her horror, that he turns out to be a cannibal, when she sees him chewing on a dead body. She cannot bring herself to tell anyone what she has seen. When she refuses to admit her guilt to the stranger, whom he meets again in the company of friends, he kills first her father, then her mother and, finally, the girl herself. Before her death, on the counsel of her grandmother, Marusya pleads with the priest to carry her coffin out beneath the threshold and to bury it at the crossroads.

The passing son of a boyar – a nobleman – is so infatuated with the flower that grows on her grave that he plucks it and replants it in his own garden. At night, the flower reveals itself to be Marusya, and she enchants the prince. When he makes her an offer of marriage, Marusya consents, on condition that she does not have to visit any church for four years. However, under duress, her groom forces her to the church before time.

At the gate to the churchyard, she again encounters the impure man. Once again, he takes Marusya to task and threatens her with the death of her husband and her son, who has been born in the meantime. At this, she gathers a bottle of holy water and a bottle of living water from her grandmother. Armed with these, she confesses to the impure man what she knows, and then douses him with the holy water, following which he perishes and turns into dust. With the living water, by contrast, she is able to bring her two dead relatives back to life.[56]

Although Afanasyev discussed the phenomenon of Central and Eastern European vampirism in 1869 in the third book of his multivolume *Poeticheskie vozzreniia slavian na prirodu* (*The Poetic Outlook on Nature by the Slavs*) as an ethnologist, he had never considered the term 'vampire' to be fit for Russian popular culture. He recognized the existence of this phenomenon in the realm of the Tsarist Empire exclusively in relation to the Ukrainians and Belarusians.[57] Only the editor of the third part of the second edition of Afanasyev's *Narodnye russkie skazki* (*Russian fairy tales*), which appeared posthumously in 1873, chose to replace the title of 'The Impure' with that of 'Upyr'. Under this unusual title the tale is famous still today.[58]

Already in 1872, William Ralston Shedden-Ralston, alias William Ralston, publicist and librarian of the British Museum, had considered the problem of vampires in his publication *The Songs of the Russian People*, based on Russian fairy tales and South Slavic vampire tales. He confirmed that vampirism in the Tsarist Empire was primarily a Ukrainian and Belarusian issue. Thus, the Ruthenians – the Eastern Slavs in the territory of the former Polish-Lithuanian Union – would burn or drown women who had been suspected of witchcraft in order to combat cattle disease, and Ukrainians and Belarusians in the Russian Empire would typically seek to ward off cholera by burning the first victim, who was considered to be the source of the disease. In popular belief, according to Ralston, 'vampires' were recruited from among the ranks of the cursed, sorcerers and witches, heretics, suicide victims, nonbaptized children and alcoholics. They were accused of possessing the power to cause famine through storms, drought and cattle diseases.[59]

With regard to Ukrainian demonology, the ethnographer Oleksandr Malinka claimed in 1886 that harmful revenants not only acted as poltergeists or bloodsuckers, but also that it was said of them that they would tear out and eat their victims' hearts. Generally, an upyr is characterized as having a reddish facial colour. A distinction should also be drawn between the 'dead upyr', a nondecomposed corpse who leaves his grave up to the first crow of the cock, and the 'living upyr', a person of a strong build who carries a 'dead upyr' on his back. A further peculiarity were the *odminy* ('changeling', or children swapped at birth), who entered the world as deformed babies, without bones, and with only a head, and long arms and legs, but who enjoyed the gift of prophecy.[60]

Ukrainian Vampire Tales

The first documented case of a Ukrainian vampire (*upyr*) in the Tsarist Empire was presented in 1883, with an ironic undertone, by the Ukrainian ethnographer and social critic Petro Yefymenko in the Russian-language journal *Kievskaia starina* (*Kievan Antiquities*). Drawing upon archival sources, Yefymenko recounted how the Kievan colonel Anton Tanski had summoned the peasant Semyon Kalenichenka to the military chancellery in 1727, since the latter had claimed to be an upyr and to have unleashed epidemics. However, the chancellery was not deceived and declared the peasant to be insane.[61]

Later, a revenant narrative was to develop around the figure of Tanski himself. Rumour had it that he had derived his fortune, in part, from an inheritance, and in part from a bequest from Peter the Great, but also, predominantly, through his greed. Therefore, the following story emerged.

Since Tanski had occasionally donated to religious causes, as a good Christian should, a group of passing monks had identified his house, in good faith, as a good place to store the donations intended for their monastery. Overcome by avarice, Tanski attempted to kill the monks. One, however, managed to escape. As a consequence, the bishop excommunicated the sinner. Unexpectedly, Tanski died shortly thereafter, but he was alleged to have reappeared time and again at night, and to have wandered about as a revenant up to the first crow of the cock, with flaming eyes, a fiery mouth and a knife in his left hand. When the son of the dead man exhumed his father, in the presence of the bishop, a fresh corpse was revealed, with long nails and a long beard. Therefore, with beseeching prayers being recited over the grave, the corpse was driven through with an aspen stake. Thereafter, around midnight, a distressing moan could occasionally be heard coming from the grave.[62]

One year after the publication of this entertaining vampire story, the journal *Kievskaia starina* followed up with a file from the district court in Berdychiv. This covered a bizarre struggle against alleged vampires that had taken place in the Ukrainian village of Podosy, against the backdrop of an epidemic. From the file, the following sequence of events can be pieced together.

Following a growing number of deaths, which neither blessing the waters of the local springs and wells nor naked women walking around the perimeters of the village had been able to stop, the inhabitants of Podosy turned to the healer-peasant Maksim Mazurenko from the neighbouring village of Stepanok. Mazurenko explained that the source of the disaster emanated from the grave of the recently departed sacristan and his wife. Both supposedly emerged from the grave at night and infected the local peasants by breathing on them, or brought about their deaths by drinking their blood. Furthermore, a dubious eyewitness was also found who raised fanciful and frankly absurd accusations about nocturnal poltergeist activities. Nevertheless, these seemed to hit the audience's nerve and, on this basis, Mazurenko suggested that the corpse's head be chopped off in order to prevent further deaths in the village. Carrying this measure out himself, he also claimed that the blood spurting from the corpse was in fact that which the revenant had sucked out of his victims. Finally, Mazurenko also impaled the corpses on an aspen stake. He was rewarded for this classic vampire fighting with a silver rouble, a cartload of rye and the services of helpers to help him with his harvest. In front of the court, he pointed out that he had been born with innate abilities and that, as a 'living upyr', it was his calling to help people.

As punishment for his un-Christian behaviour, the vampire hunter Mazurenko was merely instructed to perform penance for half a year.[63] The fact that the authorities more or less tolerated the desecration of bodies was clearly rooted in their desire, in dealing with the plague, not to further inflame local tempers through unpopular sanctions.

From the 1880s, alongside the documentation of historic vampire cases in the *Kievskaia starina*, there developed a growing interest in Ukrainian superstition in ethnological journals, pursued by both Polish and Ukrainian authors. In 1880, Andrzéj Podbereski presented an article on demonology among the Ukrainian people in the Kraków journal *Zbiór wiadomości do antropologii krajowéj* (*Collection of News on Regional Anthropology*). In this he drew upon tales from the district of Chyhyryn on the left bank of the Dnieper. Alongside the usual tales of witches and revenants, more prosaic motifs also appeared, and the tales had a didactic tone. Podbereski thus points out that, in the popular conception, a dead person could be brought back to life as a *pereľèsnik* when he is grieved over too much. As an *obojàsnik*, he then leaves the grave and – invisible to all others – drinks the blood of those left behind. There is also a sarcastic tale in which a boy digs up a corpse in order to scare a girl, only to then himself fall victim to the man he had dug up, who turns out to be an upyr (upiór). A further story also seems somewhat bizarre.

An executed man, hanging from the gallows, and who had already decomposed down to his skeleton, calls upon a passer-by to take him down. However, rather than showing his gratitude, he instead follows the man to his house. At the door, though, the hanged man is surprised to encounter an upiór, who was already inside the house. Thereafter, the two dead men began to fight each other up to the first crow of the cock. The outcome remains unclear, since neither of them is able to cross the threshold, which is considered to be magic.[64]

In his collections of ethnographic material from the region of Chernihiv, published in 1895 and 1900, the populist and anti-Tsarist author and publicist Borys Hrinchenko included several striking tales about the dead. The style and manner in which the tales of revenancy are presented is somewhat picaresque, and even has a hint of social critique in parts. The vampire motif, at least, is entirely distorted. The tale 'Upyr', written in 1895, is about a soldier who returns to his home village following the receipt of a notification of death.

Upon his arrival in the village, the soldier first becomes aware of fiery eyes looking out at him from the undergrowth and then, in his parents' house, unexpectedly encounters his father, whom he believed to be dead. Following the description of a meal, at which the father does not take part, the tale continues with a report of a coach ride to a wedding in a neighbouring village. Nobody wants to believe that the soldier has arrived accompanied by his dead father. After everyone has gone to bed, the father begins to drink the blood of the guests. Furthermore, he also hides a couple of tufts of hair from the bride and groom under the wall of the house.

Questioned by his son as to the meaning of his actions, the father explains that, unlike the other wedding guests, the married couple will not wake up the following day. Having convinced himself that he cannot report any of this to anyone, since he has to return to the army, the son asks how it might be possible to save the married couple. His father responds that he would have to slaughter a black calf, smear the married couple with its blood and also reattach the tufts of hair to each of them. His aim is to drive the residents out of his home village; this was why he had made the fiery glances that his son had perceived at the edge of the village, in order to scare people off. Asked how his activities can be reined in, the father confesses that he normally sleeps in his grave during the day, but that he can also seek out shelter under the oven if necessary. It is only possible to draw him out of this hiding place with twelve pokers and twelve pairs of bulls, and he can only be buried under the oaks in the open fields. If the action is not completed by sunset, his evil nature would cause him to kill anyone who had been involved in the attempt.

Either way, the village residents now knew what had to be done and they set out to tackle the evildoer in the manner he himself had outlined. Thereafter, hairs from both people and cattle were found in his house, providing evidence of the harmful effects of his activities.[65]

In a popular tale, recorded by Hrinchenko in 1900, the central role is played, according to the title, by a 'Vampire Count' (Pan-Upyr) from Chernihiv. The tale goes as follows.

A rich man continues to run his household after his death. When his servants complain about this, he beats them up, and a bishop takes the man into his prayers. Immediately, the dead man finally goes down into the earth. When he is exhumed, he emerges with open eyes and a stake of aspen wood is therefore driven into his heart, bringing the apparitions to an end.[66]

Alongside the revenancy, bloodsucking is only really hinted at in the margins of Hrinchenko's tale. On the one hand, this reflects the fear of black magic and, on the other hand, can also be read as a protest against corporal punishment. All the same, the possibility of warding off the evil eye and the threat to the community is offered both by magical measures and by the performance of Christian rituals.

In 1897, in the Russian journal *Zhivaia starina* (*Living Antiquity*) and in 1904 in the German-language *Zeitschrift des Vereins für Volkskunde* (*Journal of the Ethnographic Society*), the Lviv publicist Juljan Jaworskij published an article containing tales, in the style of Hrinchenko, told about the 'vampire' respectively the *opyr* among the South Russians, that is, the Ukrainians in Polish Galicia. In terms of content, these range from farcical Jewish tales about nachzehrer legends through to the Lenore materials, which went back to August Ludwig Bürger's ballads about the bride of an undead soldier.

First case: a tale from a village in the district of Bóbrka (Ukrainian Bibrka) near Lviv concerns a Jewish innkeeper whose vampiric nature is revealed when a black cat, into which he transforms at night, has its ear cut off. The following day, the Jew appears with a bandaged ear. He complains that he was laughed at by the living and mistaken by vampires as one of their own.

Second case: a tale from a village in the district of Skole deals with a series of fatalities following the death of an old man. A rich peasant gains permission from the Catholic clergy to destroy the supposed people-eater. With the help of the old man's widow, the peasant exhumes the corpse to reveal a vampire, sitting up, with a blood-red face and resting on his hands. He had clearly already drunk a great deal of human blood. His widow curses him, and the rich peasant sees that the body is removed from the grave and chopped into bits. Wrapped in a shroud, it is then thrown into a thornbush and burned. A strong wind blows the participants, still crying, back to the village.

Third case: in a further tale from the village of Skole, the head of a household returns four days after his death in order to exhort his wife to leave their children and come and join him. At the cemetery, he commands the grave to open itself and then orders the hesitant woman to climb down into it. Cunningly she allows the revenant to go in first and then tosses in a bundle of clothes behind him. She then flees into a house, in which a recently deceased person has been laid out before his funeral. The revenant, who had now taken up pursuit, attempts to fraternize with the dead man from outside the window. On three occasions, the woman is able to stop the latter from rising up by binding him with pieces of clothing. The spooky scene comes to an end with the first crow of the cock, with the deceased man giving himself over to death and with the revenant falling into a torpor.[67]

Popular Galician tales in which ghosts or revenants played a role could often be found in the journal of the Lemberg Society for Ethnography, *Lud* (*People*), appearing from 1895. For example, in 1902, the Kraków professor Bronisłav Gustawicz published reports which he had gathered in the 1870s during his exploration of the flora and fauna in the region around the town. With the exception of a few Catholics and a few Jews, almost all the villagers belonged to the Uniate Church and were therefore Ukrainians. A tale from the village of Dźwinogród (Ukrainian Zvenihorod) to the southeast of Lviv was given the title 'Upiórs spread a plague'. Here, two revenants appear in the form of dogs, who attempt to kill each other, thus bringing about a plague among the cattle. The tale 'Upiórs', from the village of Janów (Ukrainian Yaniv; today Ivano-Frankove) to the northwest of Lemberg concerns a cholera epidemic in 1831. After sunset, revenants in various forms gather together at a cemetery and wander around together up to the first crow of the cock. So as not to bring about any further mischief, the population considered it taboo to name the source of the infection.[68]

In 1906, Antoni Siewiński, a teacher from the small town of Buczacz (Ukrainian Buchach) to the southwest of Lviv, published a series of popular tales. According to a story entitled 'On the Upiór', an alcoholic father continued to beat his wife and child following his death. To bring an end to this, his grave was opened up, the heart of the dead man was driven through with a stake of aspen wood, and his head was chopped off and placed between his legs.[69]

Belarusian Vampire Tales

According to a study by the St Petersburg lawyer Löwenstimm, within the context of a mid nineteenth-century cholera epidemic in the district of Novogrudok (Belarusian Navahrudak) in the western part of the present-day Belarus, not only was there a series of corpse desecrations, but also a number of human sacrifices. He outlined the following case from 1848.

A priest informed the judge responsible that, against his will, the peasants had made an example of a dead and already buried woman, so as to combat the cholera. In the resulting court case, the peasants related that the woman concerned had been the first victim of the disease. The village community attempted to convince the army doctor, Rubtsov, that the woman had led a profligate lifestyle and that she had died in a pregnant state. Rubtsov investigated the grave in order to test for any irregularities and, in fact, the unborn child was no longer in the womb, but rather lying separately in the coffin. Since the mouth of the dead mother was also open, her corpse was driven through with a stake of aspen wood.[70]

In 1896, the Belarusian teacher Pavel Demidovich also wrote on the popular beliefs of his homeland in the journal *Etnograficheskoe obozrenie* (*Ethnographic Survey*). In his view, it was important to distinguish between a revenant, who appears in dreams or in reality when his eternal rest is disturbed, and a *vupr*, a dead charlatan who has sold his soul to the devil and who brings harm to the living. A tale from the village of Nikolsk near Minsk about a dead woman who comes back from the afterlife in order to breastfeed her child comes across as particularly bizarre.

Although the dead woman continues to perform the housework, it is not possible for her widower to communicate with her. The old wives of the village advise him to go to the cemetery, along with the priest, to open the grave and to chop off the head of his wife, who was found in the coffin with her eyes open. On his journey back home, the husband has the impression that someone had hurled an earthenware pot after him. Upon closer inspection, he discovers that his wife is close behind and that she had thrown her severed head after him. Thereafter the grave is opened once again and her corpse is driven through with a stake of aspen wood, bringing an end to the apparitions.

This tale clearly related to the issue of revenancy. First, it is suggested that a mother is providing for her child, and the impression is then given that a woman is defending herself against ill-treatment by her husband. The man behaves towards the ghostly apparition in a dismissive manner and the curse that is mentioned, 'Go into the afterlife as a vupor!', is also revealing.[71] The vampire experiences a secularization in the context of the fairy-tale world and is transformed into a figure of terror through whom conflicts are resolved.

Lost Souls in the Danube-Balkan Region
'The Eastern Question' and the 'Turkish Yoke'

In the history of European diplomacy, the so-called 'Eastern Question' arose from the decline of the Ottoman Empire and the growing opposition between the Great Powers of Britain, France, Prussia, Austria and Russia, but also from the emergence of nationalist movements on the Balkan Peninsula. The collision of interest between these powers arose not only from the second, unsuccessful siege of Vienna by the Ottomans in 1683, but also from Russian claims in the Balkans following the Treaty of Küçük Kaynarca of 1774. It was not until the Congress of Berlin in 1878 and the Treaty of Lausanne of 1923 that binding solutions for the 'Eastern Question' were put in place, through the provision of autonomy for a range of Balkan nations on the one hand and the creation of the modern Turkish state on the other.

From the sixteenth century, the Ottoman Empire had undergone a period of internal decentralization and, from the seventeenth century onwards, it could no longer keep up with the competitive pressure within the European-dominated global economy. Against the backdrop of the gradual decline of the Ottoman Empire, the eighteenth century saw a shift in focus, from a geopolitical perspective, from the conflict with the Habsburgs to that with Russia. The long nineteenth century saw the emergence of the Concert of Europe, that is, the dominance of Britain, France, Prussia, Austria and Russia, on the basis both of the preservation of the balance of powers and of the preservation of the territorial status quo in the Balkans. Geopolitically, this was a fragile system. Furthermore, from 1774 onwards, the question of 'The Straits' also advanced to the forefront, i.e. the Russian 'striving for a place in the warm seas' and the competition with Britain over control of the Bosphorus and the Dardanelles.[72]

Parallel to these developments, clerics and scholars in the Balkans, referring back to their own medieval history and the cultural value of their own languages since the eighteenth century, began to call for an epoch of national 'rebirth', seeking to focus their attentions in the course of the nineteenth century on shaking off the 'Turkish yoke'. Through a series of uprisings, Serbia was able between 1804 and 1817 to gain the status of a tribune-paying principality before, in 1878, achieving complete sovereignty. Shortly thereafter, the Greek War of Independence of 1821–29 led to the creation of a rump state there. The union of Moldavia and Wallachia in 1858 led to the constitution of Romania, which achieved autonomy in 1878. The tribute-paying principality of Bulgaria, constituted in 1878, gained independence in 1908.

From 1878 onwards, as a result of the rivalry between the Greek, Serbian and Bulgarian national movements, the 'Macedonian Question' emerged as a new flashpoint. The European solution, formulated at the Congress of Berlin in 1878, promised reforms within the Ottoman Empire, in the interests of maintaining the territorial status quo, but also took into consideration ethnic disparities in drawing up the borders between the newly constituted national states. As a result, following the unsuccessful military conflicts of 1912/1913, the Balkans continued to constitute a 'powderkeg' that was even to be held responsible for the outbreak of the First World War.[73]

Rites of Passage and the Cult of Souls in the Danube-Balkan Region

Thanks to a combination of imperial transformations and military confrontations, as well as traditional ways of life and multicultural entanglements, the population of the Danube-Balkan region were confronted with extreme conditions in their daily existence. It is perhaps thanks to the fears and needs arising from these circumstances that conceptions of revenancy have remained lively up to the present day.

If one follows the claims made by ethnologists at the turn of the nineteenth and twentieth centuries, then the death customs of the Orthodox Christians, which sought to ensure a peaceful transition into the afterlife, can be summarized as follows: the relatives of the dying seek reconciliation on their deathbed. Death was immediately followed by the ritual washing of the body. There then followed a period of the laying out of the body, with the face of the corpse directed towards the east, accompanied by lamentations. In this manner, the community marked their taking of leave from their former member. Thereafter, the house in which the person had died was considered to be impure for a period of three days, requiring cleansing and a re-establishment of the distinction between the realms of the living and the dead. In order to draw a symbolic barrier between life and death, the water was poured away and the fire extinguished. The funeral took place after one day and one night. At the internment, the feet of the deceased were laid out facing the east, and several symbolic objects were placed in the grave, which were meant to ease the passage of the dead into the afterlife. This was followed by the cleansing of the attendants and the house of the dead person, as well as the celebration of a funeral banquet. Over the following forty days, women were expected to guard the house. In memory of the dead and in order to fortify their souls, funeral banquets were also celebrated on the seventh and the fortieth day after death, as well as on the anniversary and half-anniversary of their passing, and on All Souls' Day. At these, a place was also laid out for the deceased, since it was assumed that

Figure 4.2 Festival of Souls in Bosnia.
The commemoration of the dead continued to play a significant role for the Orthodox population of Southeastern Europe. Alongside funeral banquets, there were also regular celebrations that involved the cleansing of the bones of already fully decomposed bodies at the cemeteries by the companions of the departed. The opening of graves and reburials were therefore nothing unusual.
Source: Friedrich S. Krauss (ed. and trans.), *Tausend Sagen und Märchen der Südslaven* (Leipzig, 1914), vol. I, 324.

his soul would participate. The actual period of mourning came to an end one year after death, with the entry of the dead person onto the register of departed family members.[74] Since the conclusive entry of the soul was only assumed to have taken place with the complete decomposition of the corpse, exhumations were common. Three to seven years after burial, the grave was opened. The bones were taken out, cleansed in wine, draped in white shrouds and reburied, documenting that the soul had now found eternal rest. Departures from the norm caused consternation among those left behind, such as where the process of decomposition was not complete or where a process of mummification had set in, since this was not in keeping with Greek-Orthodox doctrine, in particular with regard to excommunication (see the section entitled 'The Vrykolakas among the Greeks in the Ottoman Empire' in Chapter 2).

Among the faithful, official doctrine intermingled with heathen elements to create a syncretic cult of souls. This constituted a precondition for corresponding conceptions of ghosts, such as the belief that the soul of a dead person did not arrive at its destination immediately, but hung around in the grave or in the house for forty days. According to popular belief, it could take on the form of a bird or butterfly, but also that of a dead spirit. When the soul of the dead lingered in the house for longer than expected, this was interpreted as a sign that they were not able to find eternal rest. Either those left behind had not managed to find their peace with the departed or the cause of their death had not yet been satisfactorily determined. Popular tradition also believed that a person's soul could leave the body while they were sleeping.

If, in considering this cult of the dead, one also takes into account phenomena such as the *mora* or witches, then it is necessary to relativize the supposed uniqueness of the vampire. A mora is a young woman, whose evil spirit afflicts men, women and children at night through crushing and bloodsucking. Old women, in particular, were often considered to be witches, and both people and animals had to suffer as a result of their black magic. In the period where the soul of a witch or a mora, given to the devil, would leave the body, oral testimonies showed that a sort of rigor mortis would set in. In such cases, the switching of the positions of the head and feet would ensure that the impure soul could no longer return and that the demonic forces could no longer emerge.[75]

When one summarizes the bizarre emphasis on demonic conceptions among the common people, a banalization of the belief in vampires emerges. According to the observations, which the Slovenian gymnasium teacher, ethnologist and historian Emilijan Lilek in 1899 published in the *Glasnik Zemaljskog muzeja u Bosni i Hercegovini* (*Messenger of the National Museum of Bosnia and Herzegovina*), the belief in vampires arose from sufficiently well-known elements: in South Slavic conceptions, the vampire is a corpse that is reanimated, seven or forty days after death, by a spirit, and that then inflicts harm upon its relatives or neighbours. Either an evil person or a dead person over whom an animal has jumped or flown can be transformed into a vampire. In order to feed itself, the vampire drinks the blood of humans and animals, as a result of which it appears in the grave to be nondecomposed and bloated.

It is only the amendments that Lilek contributed to this well-known picture, on the basis of his experiences in Sarajevo, which are of particular interest: the vampire leaves the grave through a mouse-hole, sometimes even in the form of a mouse. His metamorphosis can be traced back to the fact that his body does not have any bones. He generally only encounters the living in human form, but in this he appears to be unkempt and animalistic in appearance, revealing himself, if at all, through his shroud. In order to find a vampire's grave and destroy the evil spirit, it is therefore necessary to search for mouse-holes or to look out for a stallion's shunning of a grave. Lilek's interpretation is simultaneously suggestive and absurd. It mixes the archetypical element of the fear of the vampire, fantastical ingredients derived from rumours, and surreal embellishments drawn from a portrait of manners. This particularly concerns the suggestion that a vampire can bring about vampirization by holding the soil from his grave under people's noses, thus causing them to sneeze. So as to prevent this, it is necessary to wish the afflicted person good health. Either way, this trivial description of everyday vampirism appears to be more authentic than the poor imitation of the vampire motif in Bram Stoker's Dracula legend.[76]

The Greek Revolution

It was not only the Ecumenical Patriarchate of Constantinople, i.e. the Greek clergy, which benefited from the toleration of non-Muslim faith communities in the Ottoman Empire, which was grounded in cultural autonomy and joint responsibility, but also the Phanariotes, i.e. the Greek merchants from the Istanbul district of Phanar. The Greek elite therefore had an interest in maintaining a constant understanding with the Ottoman rulers; revolutionary ideas tended to emerge from foreign colonies set up by long-distance Greek traders, for example, in the form of the Revolutionary Committee Filiki Etaria (Society of Friends), established in Odessa in 1814. When a rebellion broke out on the Peloponnese in 1821, the Patriarch of Constantinople therefore threatened the rebels with excommunication, on the order of the Ottoman government, the Sublime Porte. However, this threat had little effect, since the revolutionaries proclaimed the independence of Greece from the Ottoman Empire as early as 1822, at the First National Assembly of Epidaurus. From 1823/1824, there followed a civil war between the opposing camps within the revolutionary party – between the elite and the peasants.

The Greek revolutionary movement was greeted by a wave of sympathy among the broader European public, known as philhellenism. However, the recognition of Greek independence by the Ottoman Empire was not achieved until the Russian-Turkish Wars of 1828/1829 and the Peace of Adrianople. At the London Conference of 1830, England, France and Russia declared themselves to be Greece's protective powers and promised a monarchical form of government. In 1832 the Kingdom of Greece gained full sovereignty under Otto I von Wittelsbach, and in 1844 the parliamentary constitution provided the path to a constitutional monarchy. This state incorporated the Peloponnese, as well as a small section of central Greece, and united less than a third of all the Greeks in the Ottoman Empire. From this constellation emerged the 'Great Idea' (*megali idea*) of the unification of all Greeks. In 1833, the 'Church of Greece' declared autocephaly, but were not to gain recognition of their independence from the Patriarch of Constantinople until 1850.[77]

Greek Vampires in Travel Writing of the Premodern Period

In the first third of the nineteenth century, against the backdrop of the growing philhellenism, vampirism no longer played the role in reports by travellers to Greece that it had in the second half of the seventeenth century. In the period from 1794 to 1798, for example, the Italian adventurer and global citizen Saverio Scrofani travelled across Greece twice. His *Viaggio in Grecia* (*Travels in Greece*), which only covered the period between 1794 and 1795 and that was drawn up for commercial reasons, appeared in 1799. In this, in a popular style, Scrofani sought to portray superstitious beliefs and practices in Greece as a matter of ridicule. With a view to the consequences of excommunication in the Orthodox Church, he shifted the perspective from the phenomenon of the incorruptibility of the corpse to the murderous activities of the dead souls, who fed off human blood. As Scrofani ironically commented, the measure of excommunication had led to a situation where the cemeteries were full of spirits ('uricolacas'). The ecclesiastical authorities therefore willingly allowed themselves to be drawn into the struggle against vampires, so long as their physical wellbeing was provided for.

To eradicate posthumous mischief, congregations would turn to the bishop with a generous donation. Thereafter, the family of the deceased or, on a temporary basis, the richest landowner were expected to lay out a table at the cemetery. At the ceremony, outlined by Scrofani on the basis of his own observations, the bishop initially invited the deceased to participate in a meal. If this was rejected, this was taken as proof that the excommunication had been effective. The bishop would then prepare a beverage that he would first drizzle over the corpse and then drink himself. Finally, he would eliminate all problems with the renewed internment of the dead person and the celebration of a funeral banquet.

At the heart of Scrofani's consideration was less the sensational phenomenon of vampirism itself and more the rarely discussed state of the Greek Church.[78] With reference to vampirism, the Greek theologian Nikodimos Agioreitis therefore accused his compatriots, in his *Christoitheia ton christianon* (*The Good Customs of Christians*), published in 1803 in Venice, of making themselves the subject of ridicule; apart from the Orthodox, no other 'nation' (*ethnoz*) continued to believe in vampires.[79] Clearly, the triumphal march that had been made into the Latin discourse and into Catholic Poland by the vampire had escaped Agioreitis' attention.

Later, following the blossoming of philhellenism, the reporting on such issues was transformed. Therefore, the *vrykolakas* (here 'vrukolakas') only played a peripheral role in William Martin Leake's *Travels in Northern Greece*, which he published between 1835 and 1841, serving at best as a parody of the lower clergy. The Bishop of Larissa imposed a financial punishment on a priest who had allegedly destroyed two revenants, and threatened to cut off his beard, which was a symbol of his godly existence. Thereafter, there were no further reports of vrykolakas in all of Thessalia.[80]

A legend of a different kind, clearly intended to bear witness to the more exotic elements of Greek popular belief, can be found in the 1837 book *Travels in Crete* by the English traveller and economist Robert Pashley. According to this legend, the village of Kalikráti in the region of Sfakiá was visited by a 'katakhanás'.

Since the dead person concerned had been a respectable figure during his lifetime, an arch had been erected over his grave. One day his godson, a wandering shepherd, sought shelter from the rain under this. Since he had laid down his arms in the form of a cross, it was not possible for the dead man to leave his grave. However, he did speak repeatedly to the shepherd. In keeping with traditional beliefs, the shepherd did not answer until the fourth time, and got his godfather to give an oath that he would remain unharmed.

After this, the dead man left the cemetery, having first asked for a further conversation at a later date. He took advantage of his temporary absence to send a young married couple to their destruction, and then returned with a freshly-extracted liver in his bloodsoaked hands, which he fried with his breath alone. Understandably, the shepherd sought to decline the invitation to join him in eating this, and contented himself secretly with eating dry bread. Upon his departure, the dead man had threatened to tear apart the shepherd's entire family with his bare hands should he reveal anything of what had happened. However, the shepherd did inform the village of what he had seen and immediately thereafter, the community burned the dead man at the stake. Going through the ashes, they discovered a fingernail, which was again consigned to the flames.[81]

From a contemporary perspective, this story appears to be an expression of a syncretism of Christian and magical conceptions in the defence against evil spirits. Not only the ruined happiness of the marital pair, but also the relationship between godfather and godson and his kin seem to hint at the fact that all families have bodies in the basement, in a metaphorical sense, or carry unresolved conflicts around with them.

Less profound, by contrast, was the British archaeologist Charles Thomas Newton, who had taken up the post of Vice-Consul in Mytlini on Lesbos in 1852. In his 1856 book *Travels and Discourse in the Levant*, he recorded that the curse 'may the vampire claim you' was often uttered during heated interpersonal arguments. Newton also underlined that a hidden, transcendental level lay behind this expression. According to him, the islanders would bury the bones of those who had not been able to find posthumous rest on a neighbouring island, in the belief that they could not cross saltwater.[82]

Ancient and Modern Greek Vampirism

In his 1871 book *Das Volksleben der Neugriechen und das hellenische Altertum* (*Common Life among the Modern Greeks and Hellenic Antiquity*), the classicist Bernhard Schmidt, in listing numerous terminological variants among the Southern Slavs, argued that the Greek term 'bourkalakas' (*vrykolakas*) was a loan word from the Slavic 'vukodlak', at the same time highlighting that the conception of the bloodsucker, dominant in Western reporting, only played a minor role among the Greeks. Originally, the dominant belief had been that the soul of a dead person who was unable to find peace would agitate for the reanimation of a nondecomposed body. However, due to the influence of the Church, the idea gradually established itself that the devil would take possession of the human body and bring ruin in its form. The argument for the independent development of a Greek belief in vampires was supported, on the one hand, by the presence of certain precursors in ancient mythology and, on the other hand, by the fact that it was much stronger on the islands than on the mainland. Yet, in the demons of classic mythology, such as *lamiai* and *empusae*, bloodthirsty beasts who, usually in the form of beautiful young women, would bring ruin to young men, we are not dealing with revenants in a strict sense.[83]

Drawing upon the idea that there had been a continuation of ancient traditions, the British scholar John Lawson established a connection between murderers and their victims in his 1910 *Modern Greek Folklore and Ancient Greek Religion*. Here he offered the daring thesis that there was a direct continuity between classical times and the contemporary period: ultimately, both the perpetrator, weighed down by the heavy burden of their crime, and the victim, punished by an unnatural death and the inability to find eternal rest, were confronted with the same destiny. Where a murdered person seeks revenge as a revenant, the murderer's soul is also unable to find peace of mind.[84] However, this view, seemingly obvious at first glance, should be treated with caution. Since our knowledge of antiquity derives only from what had been handed down by educated elites and since modern popular beliefs have usually been reported on from an external perspective, it is debatable whether there has truly been a continuation of traditions. The motivation of revenge as a key factor in revenancy is common across all cultural spaces and did not find its first expression in classical philosophy.

Symptomatic of this is a story published by Schmidt in his 1877 collection *Griechische Märchen, Sagen und Volkslieder* (*Greek Tales, Legends and Popular Ballads*). The talk is of the tale 'The Vampire', from the central Greek settlement of Arachova.

A man is murdered in an open field and left there to die. Eventually his body is discovered and buried in his home village. Thereafter, in a curious manner, eggs, chickens, goat and sheep begin to disappear repeatedly. One night, the priest discovers a demon climbing out of the grave of the murdered man and breaking into the barn. When the demon arrives at the house of his widow, he calls out: 'Oh, woe is me! Why did you murder me? I will gobble people up for this!' On the following day, an old man explained that the dead man had transformed into a vrykolakas (here 'vroukalakas'), and that the lives of his relatives and friends were now under threat. Salvation could only be brought by someone born on a Saturday.

As it happens, just such a person arrives at the grave, also on a Saturday, shortly before sunrise. First, he fills a coat with rags and hangs this on a tree close by, before then opening the grave. This reveals a well-fed figure with a rosy complexion, rolling wildly with his eyes. Asked by the vrykolakas who had betrayed him, the Saturday-child points towards the coat, hanging on the tree. Immediately, the vrykolakas scorches the coat with a burst of flame. Whilst the fiend thus expounds his powers, the Saturday-child cuts out his heart, drives a stake through it and boils it in a pot of vinegar. Thereafter, he pours the vinegar on the 'vampyre', lying in his grave.[85]

It is striking that, in this story, the vrykolakas did not, as Lawson presumed, visit his murderer, but rather his relatives. Initially he seems only to have been searching for food. He then complains to his widow, at the same time threatening the village community with vengeance. However, instead of going into this interesting aspect, the perspective of the story switches: from that of the revenant or victim unable to find peace to that of the vampire hunter or fearless hero, who promises salvation for the guilty conscience of the village. Thanks to the experience of an old man, a specialist is called upon, whose supernatural powers derive from the fact that he was born on a day – Saturday – where vampires did not leave their graves. The trick with the coat again hints clearly at the motif of revenge. Through the destruction of the corpse, the village community had eventually arrived at a solution to the problem they found themselves confronted with. In the end, nobody had to face punishment for the original crime.

Greek Vampires in Observations from the Interwar Period

George Horton, the former U.S. Consul at Smyrna, characterized the isles of Greece in his memoirs, which he published in 1929 as *Home of Nymphs and Vampires*. He distinguished a harmless Hellenic conception from a malignant Slavic grafting and mentioned a couple of stories from common people about corpses from which the spirit has no fled. On the one hand, they had been described as possessing supernatural strength; on the other hand, vampire stories contained a romantic element.[86]

In his 1996 book *Vampires. The Occult Truth*, an author writing under the pseudonym of Konstantinos reported, at second hand, a rather more realistically constructed vampire episode from the early 1920s. The mother of a Greek woman who had emigrated to the United States in the mid 1970s had borne witness to the following incident in Pyrgos in the Western Peloponnese.

A young farmer had succumbed to depression and alcoholism and had mistreated his wife. One evening, while she was serving on guests, her husband disappeared. The following morning, it emerged that he had hung himself from an olive tree. Since suicide brought with it excommunication and the refusal of a Christian burial, the dead man, thus robbed of his eternal rest, was condemned to continue his existence in this world in a twilight state. Within two months, eight cases of disease arose in the village, two of which proved to be fatal.

As a result, the widow confessed that the dead man had been appearing to her at night – clearly, she wanted to rid herself of an evil spirit. Therefore, a priest was consulted and the grave was opened, accompanied by prayers. Whilst the corpse did not appear to be rosy and fresh-looking, as was expected of a vrykolakas (here vroukalakas), but was rather shrunken and mummified, it was discovered, following the dissection of the corpse, that the remains of his internal organs had fused together and that his heart was still beating(!). Immediate assistance was offered by the holy water that they had brought with them, and then the body of the alleged vrykolakas, as well as those of his two supposed victims, were disposed of by burning. Thereafter, the other sick people made a rapid recovery. An unexpected consequence of the vampire case was also the pregnancy of the widow.

Perhaps it was his wife's pregnancy, never entirely explained, which was responsible for the young man's depression. However, after the baby's stillbirth, the problem disappeared from the agenda in both a literal and a metaphorical sense.[87]

The persistence of the belief in vampires among Greek emigrants in the United States is demonstrated in B. Demetracopoulou Lee's 'Greek Accounts of the Vrykolakas', which was published in the *Journal of American Folklore* in 1942. This was based primarily on a series of tales, gathered in 1934 from former residents of Arcadia on Crete. One of the witnesses claimed that the devil was behind the vrykolakas, highlighting the fears stirred up by the Church. In fact, it was the lack of a Christian burial that was responsible for a dead person's metamorphosis into a revenant, and he had never heard anything about any bloodsucking. A further witness pointed at the presence of an animal during the laying out of the body as the cause of revenancy. He had heard of a family father, who had been suspected of vampirism because of his habit of disappearing on Saturdays and giving renditions of songs at village fetes, using the voices of the dead. A further witness recollected a dead troublemaker who had repeatedly stolen food. However, it had been possible to ward him off by holding liturgies and conducting other common measures at the grave. The vrykolakas resembled a living person, but was only a 'phantasma', like a breath in the air his corpse was intangible.[88]

Similar observations were also made by Georg Eckert and P.E. Formozis, who researched Greek popular belief during German occupation in the Second World War. Their 1943 volume *Mazedonischer Volksglaube. Magie, Aberglaube und religiöse Vorstellungen in Saloniki und der West-Chalkidiki (Macedonian Folklore. Magic, Superstition and Religious Conceptions in Salonica and Western Chalkidiki)* documents various claims made by refugee families. The forty-year-old Angelika Houmanidou from Vilia, a Greek-Albanian village in Attica, who had worked for a time in Athens as a factory worker before moving to Salonica, where she made a living from manufacturing artificial flowers, had a whole range of stories to offer.

First case: initially, Houmanidou reported that there had been a cemetery in Vilia, in which revenants had carried out their misdeeds, as a result of which boiling water had been poured over their graves. The bishop instructed that two twin calves be bound to a silver plough and that the village be furrowed, in the pattern of a cross, with iron crucifixes being erected at the end of the furrow tracks.

Second case: Houmanidou also recounted how a shoemaker had left the village to seek work elsewhere and had subsequently died, without anybody hearing about it. When the missing man did appear again to his wife, she began to become suspicious. Sending a message to the town where her husband had died, she discovered the horrible truth. Thereafter, the apparitions came to an end, with the grave being filled with boiling water and petroleum.

Third case: finally, Houmanidou also reported about a shepherd from a village in the Peloponnese, who had a wife and two children. After the shepherd had discovered a treasure, his wife and her lover, a customs official, attempted to kill him. Since one of the children woke up, he too had to die. Thereafter, their bodies were buried in the cellar, where they began to act as ghosts. In the meantime, his wife was enjoying herself with her lover and her other child in Italy. Eventually a stranger summoned up the courage to waylay the revenants in the haunted house. After the dead man's demands for a Christian burial had been satisfied, his wife was apprehended in Italy and handed a prison sentence.[89]

In their 1943 book *Geister- und Dämonenglaube im Pontos (Belief in Ghosts and Demons in the Pontos)*, Eckert and Formozis published tales they had gathered from Greeks, who had been expelled from the southern Black Sea coast by the Turkish government in the 1920s. Witnesses coming from the region around Trabzon reported, unanimously, that stray white dogs and cats revealed themselves at night to be the incarnation of deceased Turks who, as evil spirits, would inflict harm upon the living. As a rule, Islamic dignitaries were generally handed the responsibility for the destruction or re-interment of this type of vrykolakas (here 'wrikolakas'). The statements in this respect are contradictory and, among other things, it was admitted that Christian Greeks could also be transformed into vrykolakas if they had taken a wrong turn in their lives. In this context, Turks were also accused of placing Christian symbols on their graves in order to ward off demons. Elsewhere it was also claimed that canny Turks would use revenancy on the one hand as an argument when it came to put off friends and associates by suggesting repayments after death. On the other hand, they would also discipline their debtors by leading them to believe that they would return from the beyond, as had already happened in the case of one creditor, who posthumously visited a defaulting Greek.[90] Here the vampire represented multi-ethnicity and cultural transfer, and acted as a means for the conduct of conflict.

Illyrianism and Yugoslavism in the Western Balkans

Whereas Serbia and Bosnia fell under Ottoman rule following the battle at the 'Field of Blackbirds' (Kosovo) in 1389 and were incorporated into the Ottoman Empire in 1459 and 1463, respectively, the Kingdom of Croatia became a part of the Habsburg Empire following the 1526 Battle of Mohács, which proved to be devastating for Hungary. However, parts of Istria and Dalmatia remained under the influence of the Venetian Republic up to the end of the eighteenth century. Furthermore, Dubrovnik was able to maintain its independence. However, following the Congress of Vienna in 1814–15, all of Istria and Dalmatia fell under Austrian rule. Finally, in the wake of the Austrian-Hungarian Compromise of 1867, the Kingdom of Croatia and Slavonia was allocated to the Hungarian half of the Empire, whilst the Crown Lands of Dalmatia and Istria remained in the Austrian half.

The Serbs fought successfully for their sovereignty in the uprisings of 1804–13 and 1815–30. In the context of the Greek struggle for independence and thanks to Russian pressure, the Serb leader Miloš Obrenović won for himself the hereditary rank of prince and, for his territory, the status of an autonomous principality, tributary to the Ottomans. The Serbs first gained full independence at the 1878 Congress of Berlin, and the Kingdom of Serbia was established in 1882. The Ottoman provinces of Bosnia and Herzegovina fell under Austrian administration in 1878 and were formally annexed in 1908.

A collective national movement of Croats, Serbs and Slovenes had already coalesced in the second third of the nineteenth century, and Illyrianism, the idea of a common descent from the ancient Illyrians, found its way onto the European political agenda. In the era of national states, the idea of Yugoslavism, of bringing together the 'South Slavs', retreated into the background in the final third of the nineteenth century. Nevertheless, the Kingdom of Serbs, Croatians and Slovenes did emerge from the aftermath of the First World War and, from 1929 as the Kingdom of Yugoslavia, was to survive up to the Second World War.[91]

Against the backdrop of this political turbulence, it becomes clear why vampirism among the South Slavs should have been primarily recorded by late nineteenth-century ethnologists in the dry statistical listing of rumours concerning the preventative measures undertaken before burials or the desecration of graves, whereas it was recorded by philologists in more or less profane legends and fairy tales concerning the activities of revenants. In light of the fact that superstition and ghost stories seem to have fired the imaginations of large parts of the population, the marginalization of scapegoats and the sensationalist reporting of horrific visions seem to have been the norm. However, concrete cases of vampirism were only rarely documented.

Vampirism in Dalmatia

By 1322, Dubrovnik had developed into an independent noble republic, but it was subsequently to fall under the cultural influence of Venetian hegemony in the Adriatic. By the early fifteenth century, Dubrovnik's territorial growth incorporated not only the islands off the coast, but also the coastal territory to the northwest of the city. From 1430, Dubrovnik enjoyed the privilege of free trade in the dominions of the Ottoman Empire, but was expected to pay tribute from 1458 onwards. Following an economic and cultural high point in the fifteenth and sixteenth centuries, a gradual decline set in from the seventeenth century onwards, particularly after the devastating earthquake of 1667. The republic was eventually abolished following its conquest by the French in 1808.[92]

A fascinating criminal case from Dubrovnik, from the period 14 October 1737–30 June 1738, was recorded by the Croatian historian Ante Liepopili in 1918 in the journal *Zbornik za narodni život i običaje južnih slavena* (*Collection on the Popular Life and Manners of the South Slavic People*).[93] This case tackled the desecration of graves on the island of Lastovo, which were alleged to have taken place during the hunt for a revenant. As far as the living conditions on the island are concerned, it should be pointed out the nine-kilometre-long island is predominantly hilly. Alongside the cultivation of vines, olives and fruit, the only other industry on the island was fishing. The present-day settlements of Lastovo, Skrivena Luka, Pasadur, Zakopatica and the harbour of Ubli are not mentioned in the files.

On 14 October 1737, the chief financial officer of Dubrovnik, Prince Petar Sori, sent a report to the Archbishop of Dubrovnik, Fra Anđjel Franchi. The rumour had been spreading around the town that the residents of the island of Lastovo had been opening up graves in order to search for 'a certain kind of dead person', who remained in his grave during the day and would wander about at night, killing people, until he was destroyed by impaling. Since these superstitious actions challenged Christian beliefs and the authority of the Church, a criminal investigation was set up. In this, the Archbishop ordered that various witnesses be interrogated. Interestingly, the witnesses questioned here provided several different designations for the vampire: 'kosac', 'prikosac', 'tenjac' and 'vukodlak'. It is particularly striking that the term 'vampir' – the media event of 1732 – should be missing from this list.

The files have the following to report on the incidents behind the investigation. On 14 October 1737, two people from Lastovo currently living in Dubrovnik were interrogated: Antun Mikuš (aged fifty) and Antun Šagor (aged thirty). Mikuš claimed that he had been harassed by a group of excitable young men, some of them also watchmen, whilst he was keeping watch close to St Rochus Church. They had insisted on the necessity of searching the graves of the island for revenants, since they believed these to be responsible for the spread of dysentery (*serdobol*). The group then decided to investigate the Church of St Michael on the coast, where a drowned man had been buried a year before. Luka Fulnis (aged thirty) emerged as a ringleader and, mindful of the tried and tested defensive measures, he warned against precipitous actions, and particularly against handling the corpse. However, only bones were found in the grave. Their next target was the Church of the Mother of God, which lay in the fields, and where they opened the grave of a man who had died eight months previously. Again, however, nothing unusual was revealed. Mikuš did not offer any comments on the islanders' conceptions in themselves. Šagor claimed that he had not participated in the opening of the grave at St Michael's, since he was aware of a ban imposed by the Church a year previously. However, he had not been able to avoid participating in the action at the Church of the Mother of God. With reference to conceptions of revenancy, he merely admitted that such occurrences were common on the island, although he did not provide any further details in this regard.

The following day, 15 October, two Dubrovnik residents, Pero Celefa and Lovro Lucenta, both fifty-seven years old, were questioned. Celefa claimed that he had visited Lastovo both that year and the year before, but had not been aware of any epidemic. Many Lastovo residents believed that revenants could cause harm to the living and that reanimated men could even have intercourse with their widows. He had also heard that priests would participate in combatting revenants. In the current case, for example, Don Marin had carried a paschal candle. With reference to a visit to the island he had made sixteen years before, Lucenta reported that there had been an epidemic. Interestingly, his statements are recorded in the third person in the file. He also reported that the revenants were reported to eat the hearts and internal organs of the living and to drink their blood, and that, in this, they preferred to attack people with whom they had been in conflict during their lifetime.

Following the aforementioned witnesses, several of those who were accused of having participated in the grave desecrations were also called to Dubrovnik for interrogation in the period up to 24 October. Ivan Antun Rešić (aged thirty-two) stated that a dead person would be brought back to life when a spirit took possession of his corpse, or when something evil resided within. Marin Kolendić Kozić (aged twenty-six) justified the actions by saying that someone had claimed that five deaths in one day demanded an explanation. Just as Marin Nika Kokot (aged thirty) had done, Kozić also denied the participation of a priest at the exhumation. Antun Pavlović's son Pavo, known as Pizzin (aged thirty-seven), claimed that Luka Fumis, who had previously been described by another witness as the ringleader, had warned the group not to go to the Church of the Mother of God. He had wagered his life on the belief that nothing would be found there, since it was all a myth. A few days later, on 28 October, Lovro Fulmis made the following admission of guilt to the deans of Lastovo: he, and not his brother Luka, had participated in the actions. Luka had wanted to wash his hands of the whole affair and had warned the group not to believe this nonsense. Furthermore, Lovro Fulmis also testified that no Church employee had taken part in the grave openings. Building upon this, Luka Fulmis was once again personally interrogated on 16 December and he again strongly denied having had anything to do with the exhumations. Rather, he had expressed his conviction to the other accused that the Church knew best how to tackle revenants, insofar as they existed. By contrast, an unauthorized grave opening should not be carried out. According to Fulmis, the watchmen had assembled in his name without his knowledge.

Alongside these suspects, a number of priests were also interrogated. On 26 November, the priest Don Marin (aged twenty-six), the son of Antun Pavlović, stated on recorded that he had known about the grave opening at the Church of the Mother of God in early August. He had been surprised by the behaviour of the mourners at a subsequent funeral at the Church of St Cosmas and St Damian, where he had been told, in confidence, that several of those present had wanted to take advantage of the burial in order to identify the graves of possible revenants. Whatever the case may have been, he was aware of previous impalings of corpses, and twelve years earlier a priest had been alleged to have participated in one of these. On 2 December, Don Luka Dundović (aged thirty-two) stated that he had been informed that his dead mother was moving about as a revenant (*kosica*), but had then found her grave, in contrast to the others, to be untouched. Don Marin Borovinčić (aged eighteen) had taken part in the desecration of the body. On 3 December, Don Marin Pavlović (aged sixty-three) was also interrogated. According to the protocol of his hearing, his statements are rendered in a tone that was critical of Church authority and divine omnipotence. Stating first that he had become infected by the dysentery that was affecting nearly everybody during the summer, he claimed that popular rumours held the cause of this epidemic to be either flu, the infection of the air through a plague, a punishment from God or the workings of a revenant. As far as his experience with revenants was concerned, he stated that a priest, who was convinced of the existence of supernatural powers, had informed him that he himself had destroyed a revenant half a century earlier. This revenant had initially fled upon the grave being opened, but had then been brought back by the use of a gun. Furthermore, Don Marin also confessed that he had been an unwilling witness to the opening of a grave seventeen years earlier, but that he had only been made aware of the impalement of the corpse the following day. Here he also denied that he had been present at the recent exhumations.

Following the conclusion of the investigation, on 11 February 1738, the Archbishop provided the eighteen accused (all men aged between twenty and fifty, including the young Don Marin Borovinčić) with one final opportunity to give statements upon the case. The vicar of Lastovo summarized their positions on 6 March. Whilst several of the accused did appear in person in Dubrovnik over the course of April and May, the governor of Lastovo once again read out all their statements on 26 April. All admitted their guilt, had nothing to offer in their defence and were prepared to submit to the judgment of the Church. On 23 May, the Archbishop informed the accused that they should come to his residence to hear his judgment, which was finally announced on 30 June. All were found 'more or less' guilty of opening graves and desecrating bodies. Accordingly, one and the same punishment was found to be suitable for all. They were sentenced to process around the churches of the island with a stone hanging from their necks. All then had to repeat this penance the following year and twelve of them once again the year after that. Otherwise, they would be excommunicated. Finally, they also had to pay twelve ducats each to cover the costs of the court case.

In the context of the hysteria that the bloodsuckers had caused throughout Europe in the mid eighteenth century, in both theological and literary circles, it is surprising that the vampire terminology should have made way for other terms on the Adriatic coast and that it was therefore clearly little known. For the Dubrovnik authorities, this case of revenancy on the margins of their sphere of influence seems to have represented something of a novelty. From their point of view, the 'incursion of the vampire' was the result of a rumour. Since the authority of the Catholic Church had been immediately challenged by the desecrations of graves and corpses, the Archbishop attempted to create a clear distance to all forms of superstition and to discipline the faithful through financial punishment. In the files there is no evidence of any religious struggle or rivalry with other confessions. In their conflicts with the Ottomans and the Venetians, the prime concerns of the port and trading city of Dubrovnik appear to have lain elsewhere.

For their part, the islanders of Lastovo were fully aware of the illegality of their actions. Either the Christian authorities had set down clear moral boundaries or they were aware of the prohibitions handed down by the Church in earlier cases. Since the witnesses largely maintained their silence during the hearing, the authorities had to assume that the last 'vampire hunts' had already come to an end a decade earlier. It appeared that only a few of the grave desecrators arrested in October 1737 had had any previous experience in this field. It is also striking that they should have undertaken these actions, despite there being no new cases of death. The dysentery that was going around the island could not have taken on epidemic proportions, and all the victims appear to have made a full recovery. The only burial that was mentioned in the files clearly concerned a usual death and had nothing to do with the 'vampire disease'. Therefore, the impression remains that this was a form of public entertainment, through which the eternal rest of long-dead persons was forced to suffer, but in which only one case taken into consideration was justified by any sense of suspicion, namely the death of the drowned man.

It was only outsiders who had anything to offer on the role of vampirism and, on the part of the Lastovo residents themselves, there is no more than a vague hint about the understanding of revenancy as the possession of a corpse by an evil spirit or the continued activities of a restless soul. Two Dubrovnik sailors and traders described the activities of the harmful dead as follows: returning to sexual impulses, it was said of male revenants that they would have intercourse with their widows. With regard to the motivation of revenge, they mentioned the posthumous visitation of an adversary by his erstwhile opponent. In the first instance, harmful revenants would act as people-eaters, who particularly set their sights on the heart and liver; only in the second instance would they act as bloodsuckers.

Since the people of Lastovo largely kept their silence, we also learn nothing about the case itself. After all, the drawing of the innocent Luka Fulmis into the court case provides clear evidence that the islanders were by no means united. All in all, the most that we can reconstruct are the actions of the grave desecrations, and even then only in vague terms. Clearly, in August 1737, against the backdrop of an outbreak of disease, several watchmen and a few adventure-seekers had set off an unsuccessful hunt for a harmful dead person in the vicinity of two churches on the island. An actual desecration of a corpse, or the impaling of a dead person, can only have taken place, if at all, on the margins and in all secrecy. However, instead of conducting a thorough investigation into the sensibilities of the common population after the event, the Church authorities were primarily concerned with finding out about the possible involvement of the clergy. This was where the real sacrilege was seen to have taken place. The insubordination of the old Don Marin Pavlović at the hearing demonstrates the insolence of the clergy. The episcopal consistorium's conviction of the young Don Marin Borovinčić seems, by contrast, to have been a makeshift solution.

An unusual interpretation of the young vampire phenomenon can be found a quarter of a century later in the description of the region by the Italian scholar Alberto Fortis, published in Italian in 1774 under the title *Viaggio in Dalmazia* and in 1778 in English under the title *Travels into Dalmatia*. Beyond his interest in the natural sciences, Fortis was primarily concerned with the political and economic interests of Venice, and with sounding out the economic potential of Dalmatia. As an Italian, he focused predominantly on the Morlaks, a predominantly Romance population group that had gradually become assimilated with the Slavs.

In his work, pointing to the heroic folk songs performed by bards, Fortis attempted to popularize South Slavic folk literature (see Introduction). Alongside this, he also discussed the superstition that he felt was still prevalent in the region and that he connected with the supposed Transylvanian conceptions of revenancy on the one hand, but also with the local term *vukodlak*. Similar to the *strix* in Roman antiquity, in Fortis' portrayal the vukodlak drank the blood of young children. The strength of this belief among the Morlaks, the name Fortis gave, without exception, to all the inhabitants of the coastal region, can be read from the measures that they undertook to ward off revenants. In suspect cases, they attempted to hinder revenancy through cutting the hollows of the knees or sticking pins into the corpse in question. Fortis was also impressed by the suggestion that the dead sometimes pleaded with their relatives, before their death, to take the appropriate measures to prevent them from coming back and harming their own children.[94]

Regardless of the fact that Fortis did not provide much information, he did attribute an archaising significance to the vukodlak. This serves to relativize the motif of child abuse, the finding of which underlies Fortis' depiction in a latent manner. What remains, therefore, is the figure of a harmful revenant, whose delinquency had already become clear during their lifetime and whose corpse had to be incapacitated and prevented from bloating, in order to stop it leaving the grave and to hand it over to decomposition.

After all, superstition also remained widespread among the population over the course of the nineteenth and twentieth centuries. Thus, in 1882, in the *Archiv für slavische Philologie* (*Archive for Slavic Philology*), the Croatian linguist Vatroslav Jagić published an article from the Trieste newspaper *L'Indipendente* about a court case in the coastal resort of Abbazia (Croatian Opatija) in the Kvarner Gulf. Three men had desecrated the grave of Giovanni Verlien with the justification that he was a 'stregone' (warlock), referred to in the Croatian coastal region, according to Jagić, as *kodlak* or *kudlak*, and in inland Istria as *štrigun*. His posthumous activities could already have been expected during his lifetime through external signs, such as his birth in an embryonic skin (see the section entitled 'The Nachzehrer of the Early Modern Period' in Chapter 1). One defensive measure was the driving of a nail into the dead person's mouth.[95]

Also worthy of mention are the tales dedicated to the 'vampire' (vukodlak), published by the Croatian teacher and journalist Stjepan Banović in 1928 in the Zagreb *Zbornik za narodni život i običaje Južnih Slavena* (*Collection on the Popular Life and Manners of the South Slavic People*).

First case: someone reported that, during a business trip to Constantinople, his father had encountered his uncle, who had died several years earlier, in front of a butcher's shop. He lured his uncle into the shop and got the butcher to chop off his finger, causing him to lose blood and collapse into himself.

Second case: another witness claimed that an associate of his father had been transformed into a vampire in Neretva in the Dalmatian hinterland. He understood this to be a punishment from God and had asked his friend for a favour, which he promised to repay with money and clothing – he requested that his corpse, which was lying in its grave, be impaled on Good Friday, in order that his soul might find salvation.[96]

In these stories, the vampire appears as an evil spirit or a monster, devoid of any meaning in itself. After all, references such as that made to the Passion of Jesus Christ point to the fact that the question of the afterlife, with the two options of heaven and hell, played a major role in everyday life.

Vampirism in Serbia

The belief in vampires also emerged repeatedly in the course of the establishment of state administrative structures and the gathering of popular songs and fairy tales in the Principality of Serbia under the leadership of Miloš Obrenović in the first third of the nineteenth century.[97] In 1820, for example, community leaders and traders reported to the Prince that the residents of Ub had taken to convening in their houses at night and refused to go out into the streets for fear of vampires. Since neither the Bishop nor the local administrator had permitted graves to be opened, they now sought permission from the Prince. Miloš did permit the exhumations, but forbade the participants from undertaking any actions on the corpses themselves, instead recommending prayer as a preferable measure against revenancy. However, the administrator responsible later reported that the residents carried out their struggle against vampires, on their own initiative, in the tried and tested manner.

In 1839, the regional court in the so-called Black River Valley (Crnorečka kotlina), i.e. on the River Crni Timok, was informed by the ecclesiastical consistorium that nine people had died within one week in the village of Šarbanovac, that they had been declared to be vampires and that their corpses had been desecrated as a result. The village assembly had accused them of choking first the cattle and then women and children. The alleged vampires were exhumed, and their hearts were torn out and cooked in wine. Then they were laid back in the grave.[98]

The existence of the belief in vampires in Serbia could therefore not be denied. However, it was not perceived to be a matter of public concern. This was perhaps down to the fact that bloodsucking did not play any role in the reports. Rather, in the context of a politics primarily focused on the nation state, the problem of superstition was largely marginalized and cannot be researched directly over the entire course of the nineteenth century. Symptomatic in this regard is the work of the dramatist Joakim Vujić, who was to become known as the 'father of Serbian theatre'. In his 1828 book *Putešestvije po Serbiji* (*Travels through Serbia*), he recorded a discussion with two monks at the Monastery of Klisura in western Serbia, south of Požega.

According to Vujić, the monk Gerasim, who was visiting from the Monastery of Dečani, south of Peć, in present-day Kosovo, claimed to have seen a vampire with his own eyes. In response to the question of what it looked like, he described a dug-up corpse, which had not decomposed, had bulging, staring eyes and had bared its teeth. When Vujić inquired about the activities of the vampire, he was told that he had visited the village at night, terrifying the people and strangling them, and had even slept with his own wife. She had not put up any resistance, for fear of physical violence. After the exhumation, a priest had placed a whitethorn twig between the teeth of the dead man and poured three drops of holy water into his mouth.

Before allowing the monk to go on, Vujić asked in an ironic tone why the vampire had not sought to defend himself, and pulled the priest's beard. Gerasim pointed out to his conversation partner that vampires did not possess any powers during the day. It was only at night that their corpses became animated by the 'impure', allowing them to wreak havoc. With regard to the destruction of the vampire, Gerasim also reported that the village elder had driven the aforementioned whitethorn branch into the breast of the corpse, causing fluid to spurt out of its mouth. Following the reburial of the corpse, nothing more was heard of any posthumous activities.

In Vujić's striking pastiche, it is not only his empirical findings that are striking, but also the mindset of the author. On the one hand, the lack of a direct eyewitness to the nondecomposed corpse seems to have been symptomatic for all vampire reports. On the other hand, given that Vujić is writing about an essentially prototypical Serbian 'vampire', the lack of any mention of bloodsucking seems surprising. Were it not for the religiously inspired reference to the reanimation of the dead body by the devil, the impression could arise that this merely concerns the description of a nightmare. The harmful magic that is only indirectly referred to in this tale is thus super-elevated through the reference made to the breach of sexual taboos. In this monastic context, the destruction of the animated corpse through the use of a thorn branch also adds a further

Figure 4.3 'Vujić discusses vampires with monks from the Monastery of Klisura'.
This illustration of a discussion about vampires in the Serbian Monastery of Klisura shows the discrepancy between an educated townsman and an Orthodox hermit, and is meant to represent the backwardness of the rural lifestyle and the lack of common education in the Serbian provinces.
Source: Joakim Vujić, *Putešestvije po Serbiji* (Buda, 1828), between 180 and 181.

New Testament connotation, since it can be read as a corruption of the Passion of Christ, who had a crown of thorns placed upon his head during his flagellation. In this context, it is also telling that there should have been no mention of a funeral pyre, a popular method in the posthumous execution of witches. Vujić's target audience is therefore not so much the common people and their traditional conceptions as it is the lower clergy, and those sections of society that would ideally constitute the basis of a national awakening, but that, in practice, represented more or less syncretic positions.

Bringing his depiction of the conversation to a conclusion, Vujić could not resist commenting that the Almighty should grant Prince Miloš Obrenović a long life, so that he could establish schools during his reign, in which talented teachers could work towards the eradication of superstition. In order to demonstrate clearly the absurdity of popular beliefs, Vujić also mentioned a further trivial vampire case that was supposed to have taken place in southern Hungary in his home town of Baja, not far from the Danube. This reflects the Enlightenment spirit of secularized Europe in a peculiar way, in that the murder of her husband by a woman and her lover, appearing as a vampire, is staged in a carnivalesque manner, so as to scare off the other residents of the house during their lovers' tryst.[99]

In spite of this, the common people, bound to their traditional values and norms, held fast to their belief in vampires during the nineteenth and twentieth centuries. At the beginning of the 1880s, Vule Vukotić, a leading official in Niš, wrote a letter in which he documented several incidents in his district.

First case: in 1880, a disease had broken out among the sheep. The villagers had suspected a peasant who had died two months earlier of devouring the sheep as a vampire and had therefore burned his corpse.

Second case: a dead soldier had returned from the frontier in Bosnia as a vampire, because his friends had brought his horse back. At first, he had presented himself to his wife and then quartered himself in the attic. However, he had then begun to attack the sheep. Paradoxically, a wolf then began to offer him competition in this respect, and this wolf eventually devoured a sheep into which the vampire had entered.[100]

In both cases, vampirism represented nothing other than a threat to the sheep, which constituted the basis of the village communities' livelihood.

Alongside this, in an essay published in 1923 in the journal *Srpskij knijževni glasnik* (*Serbian Book Messenger*), the Serbian classicist and religious scholar Veselin Čajkanović referred to an article in the Belgrade newspaper *Vreme* (*The Times*) about an incident in the Bosnian village of Tupanari. The incident goes as follows.

Shortly after the funeral of a peasant, his widow began to complain that he had been returning to the house and wreaking havoc. Initially, the villagers were divided in their opinions about the events. However, when the sons of the dead man began to concur with their mother's opinion one month later, the village community eventually came to the conclusion that they should destroy the vampire. Therefore, the grave was opened, and the body was impaled with a whitethorn branch and burned on the funeral pyre.

Čajkanović was of the traditional opinion that the impaling was meant to prevent the dead man from leaving the grave, whereas the burning was intended to eliminate all body parts into which the spirit could have entered. A mixture of both customs was used in combating vampires, with impaling being the older of the two traditions.[101]

Krauss against Karadžić

Alongside the specialists mentioned above, it was particularly the Austrian ethnologist and researcher into sexual behaviour Friedrich Salomon Krauss who contributed to the popularization of peculiar vampire tales from Southeastern Europe. During his travels through Bosnia and Herzegovina and Dalmatia, he adopted a sceptical position towards the idea of a Greater Serbia. In 1883/1884, he published *Sagen und Märchen der Südslaven* (*Legends and Fairy Tales of the Southern Slavs*) and in 1914 *Tausend Sagen und Märchen der Südslaven* (*One Thousand Legends and Fairy Tales of the Southern Slavs*). Further unpublished material appeared in 2002, under the title *Volkserzählungen der Südslaven* (*Popular Tales of the Southern Slavs*). In part, these works are translations of material from the collections of South Slavic ethnologists and philologists into a late-Romantic literary German, and in part they are the artistic interpretation of oral traditions. Interestingly, vampires do not appear at all in the two-volume *Sagen und Märchen der Südslaven*. Rather, this collection follows the model of Vuk Stefanović Karadžić, the Serbian philologist and ethnologist who, in 1853 and 1854, in the style of the Brothers Grimm, published *Narodne srpske pripovijetke* (*Volksmärchen der Serben – Popular Tales of the Serbs*) in both Serbian and German. Here, while the *vila*, a female spirit of nature, does have a role to play as a peculiarity of the Balkans, the undead are not mentioned at all.[102]

Krauss presented only two examples. The tale 'Die Spinnerin und der Tote' ('The Spinner and the Dead Man') constitutes a simplified version of a motif, the more radical variants of which have been handed down from other regions (see the section entitled 'Demonic Figures in East and East Central Europe' above). Krauss told the story as follows.

The womenfolk of a village gather at a widow's house to spin cloth. All of them have a lover, apart from the daughter of the house. When she expresses, with a sigh, that she would even take a dead man, her impious wish is fulfilled. After the dead suitor appears to have become a permanent guest by the fourth evening, the girl turns to the priest for advice. He recommends that she should tie a thread from a ball of wool to the intruder so that she can track him back to the grave. However, because of her being bound up in these demonic intrigues, the priest felt the girl to be irrevocably lost and advises her parents to carry her out of the house through an opening in the wall, avoiding the door and windows, and to bury her alive at a crossroads. The parents follow the priest's advice and, as a result, when the dead man appears again, seeking after the girl, he cannot do anything more than issue vague threats.

After a period of time, a rose springs up from the girl's grave, which is then plucked by a passing count, who takes it with him. At night, this rose transforms back into the girl, who consumes the count's supper. When he discovers the girl, he immediately decides to marry her. However, because of the curse weighing down upon her, the girl demands a three-year period of concealment and silence. One evening, though, the count attends a feast, at which he is brought to break his vow of silence. Unexpectedly brought back on the girl's trail, the dead suitor then suddenly appears among the guests. All that remains for the girl is to beg the count to make a confession in the church, after which she perishes into dust.

In the second tale, a king's daughter falls in love with a common soldier. When her father seeks to bring an end to the relationship by stationing the soldier in another country, his daughter dies from grief. In a wise premonition, the king orders a guard to be placed over her grave and, in fact, the dead woman does leave her grave every evening, devouring the soldiers on guard. The king therefore orders her former lover to keep guard. When he begins his watch, the church door opens miraculously and God himself enters in the form of a beggar, offering wise advice. On the first night, the soldier hides behind the altar and on the second behind the organ. He is not discovered by the greedy woman until the hour that she has for her nocturnal activities is already over. On the third night, the beggar advises the soldier to lie in the grave and avoid any conversation with her. Once the ghostly hour has ended, the beggar appears at the grave and awakens the girl with the promise of renewed life, should she remain together with the common soldier until they are parted by death. The king therefore no longer has any choice other than to arrange the marriage.

In depicting the forging of familial ties, Krauss restricts himself in both cases to depicting a game of temptations in which societal taboos are broken. Undead persons or spirits appear here as messengers for the devil, promising just punishment, or as 'poor souls' who experience an unhoped-for mercy. The reference to the Serbian nobility, which had fallen victim centuries before to the Ottomans, and to the organ, which is not present in Orthodox churches, seem to show that what was being offered here was a particular interpretation for a Western public.[103]

Remarkably, beyond the mention of a *mora*, a nightmarish and bloodsucking night-demon, which is pinned to a door by a tailor's apprentice in a tale of the same name from 1884,[104] the vampire in a true sense does not appear until Krauss' collections from 1914 and 2002. Freed from the constraints of a classic collection of fairy tales, trivial motifs appear to have entered somewhat belatedly into his work. These concern stories about hauntings and apparitions, in which the vampire appears either as a profane revenant or as a fantastical figure of horror. The tale 'Der Jux eines Totenwärters' ('The Frolics of a Warden of the Dead'), for example, concerns a comedy of errors.

During a death watch, a young man leaves his companion in order to pick grapes. In the meantime, the man who had remained behind sits the dead man on a chair, and lies down in the coffin himself. When the grape-picker returns, he thinks that the dead man is his partner, and when the latter begins to throw his voice, taunting him from the coffin, his companion flees to the village to gain help in fighting the supposed vampire.[105]

In the tale 'Wie zwei Vampire miteinander um einen Riesenknochen raufen' ('How Two Vampires Fight Each Other over the Bone of a Giant'), the bloodsucker serves as a frightful ghost and is also rendered abstract through the anecdotal framework. Two merchant friends place a wager on the loyalty of their servants. Their allegiance goes so far that they wrestle at night in the morgue over the primeval tibia bone of a supposed cyclops, although each takes the other to be a vampire.[106]

The tale from Istria 'Von einem Vampir, der den Obstgarten des Ortspfarrers heimzusuchen pflegte' ('On a Vampire, Who Visited the Orchard of the Local Priest') is a further curious distortion of the vampire motif.

Following the repeated plundering of his fruit orchard, a priest commissions a bell-ringer to keep watch. On the night from Saturday to Sunday, he makes out a dead man, dressed only in trousers and socks, as the mischief-maker. Since the latter removes his socks before climbing a pear tree, the bell-ringer is able to play a trick on him. When the dead man notices that his socks have been stolen, he threatens his taunter, who has in the meantime retired to the safety of the bell-tower, uttering the threat 'just as you have done to me, so I will do to you'. The fruit thief then rapidly climbs the bell-tower in the form of a snake, but is stopped in this by the ringing of the bell. The following day, the community find the dead man lying in a pool of blood. At this, the priest declares that the blood came from the victims of the revenant, who had gone about as a 'strigo' or a 'vila', pointing in this regard to numerous recent cases of death in the village.[107]

Whereas this subject, centred around the bell-tower, is known from Central European nachzehrer tales (see the section entitled 'The Nachzehrer of the Early Modern Period' in Chapter 1), the excursion at the end of this story concerning harmful revenants comes across as a little artificial. The bloodsucking is overshadowed by the stolen fruit, and the destruction of the bloated corpse by the fall from the church tower.

No less confusing is the tale in Krauss' collection, entitled 'Der Vampir von Leskovac' ('The Vampire of Leskovac'), from a small town in Southern Serbia known for its textile industry.

The narrator begins the tale by claiming that he had heard, at the age of five or six, about the vampirization of a Muslim. Following his death, he had visited the homes of the rich, spreading terror. Out of fear, several families had taken to sleeping in shared quarters at night. In the meantime, the vampire rampaged through the abandoned houses, breaking crockery and staining the bedsheets. The narrator then goes on to relate how, in his childhood, he had also seen with his own eyes how another vampire, fully bearded and clothed only in a turban-like cloth, had ridden around on a buffalo cow. This dead man was said to have entered into a relationship with his widow. Eventually, a so-called vampire-son put an end to the monster with a rifle. Furthermore, the narrator also reported that a vampire was a creature of flesh and blood, albeit one without skin and bones.[108]

What is striking in these stories, taken from the craftsmen community, is the multicultural environment on the one hand and the cautious social criticism on the other. In fact, there is no reason why the vampire should appear predominantly to the local Ottoman elite, recruited from the merchant community. These tales discuss contraventions of the norms, not only directed against the moral codes of a patriarchal society but also contravening the purity laws of the Islamic religion. In some places, the vampire appears as a bearded devil and in others as a boneless gnome. Here, Christian conceptions are mixed with the superstitions of the Roma and in this way, find their way into Islamic culture.

In his 1908 essay *Slavische Volksforschungen* (*Slavic Ethnological Research*), Krauss shared two further reports on vampirism, which he had heard of at second hand. His mother had been told a story that was supposed to have taken place in 1873 in the Croatian city of Pleternica, in the Slavonian region of the former Military Frontier.

Two days after her funeral, an old woman had begun to wreak havoc by chucking stones against the house door and kicking up dust. The family that she had left behind now only dared to sleep in the company of a group of men. However, the dead woman did not allow herself to be put off by this. One man had his skull fractured and another injured his hand. The apparitions only came to an end ten days later.

This tale had nothing to do with vampiric bloodsucking and it seems, rather, that the phenomenon of the poltergeist was also known in Croatia. Whether we can make conjectures here about an evil stepmother remains open to question. The fact that the actions of those affected should not be taken ever so seriously is made clear through the reference to the extraordinary cost of lighting the house.[109]

The tale of a peasant from the northeast of Bosnia, which Krauss had heard of from a gendarme, appears to be more refined. One hundred and fifty years earlier, following the death of a priest's wife, a series of deaths had occurred in the village of Čengić, which had also affected the family of the contemporary witness.

The gendarme's great-grandfather, Pero, had set a fire in the church at night and waylaid the priest's dead wife. When she appeared, he attempted to hunt her with a log of hawthorn wood taken from the house. After she responded to her assailant with threats, Pero went to the priest the following day, along with the village administrator, in order to report the incident. Since the priest denied his wife's revenancy, Pero took his accusations to the court – in the village of Zvornik, at that time still Ottoman – claiming that he had left soot marks on the funeral shroud with the plank of wood. He received permission to open the grave and they uncovered a bloated corpse, which was then incapacitated with a hawthorn stake and burned on a funeral pyre. Before this, a snake attempted to flee from the grave, but was struck down immediately on the spot and, after this, the series of deaths in the village came to an end.

This report once again reflects a classic vampire tale. Affected this time was an Orthodox community, which had been authorized by the Ottoman authorities to take their own measures in combating supposed vampires. The great-grandfather appears as a hero, capable of asserting himself in the face of all opposition. The snake seems to represent a demonic figure, which had temporarily taken possession of the corpse.[110]

The Orthodox Patriarchate and the Sublime Porte as Bogeymen in the Central Balkans

In the second half of the eighteenth century, pious monks in the Central Balkans, on the territory of present-day Bulgaria, began to glorify the tradition of medieval Bulgarian statehood. In this they instrumentalized cultural memory for nationalist purposes and aimed to repudiate the Ottoman social order. At the turn of the nineteenth century, the dissolution of the confessional administrative authority was further aided by the conflict between the Sublime Porte, i.e. the Ottoman government, and the Ottoman regional administrators. Against this background, Bulgarian educators began, from the 1830s onwards, to resist the spiritual patronage of the Orthodox Patriarchate in Constantinople. From the 1860s, inspired by the struggles for independence in other regions of Southeastern Europe, Bulgarian emigrants dedicated themselves to an armed struggle against Ottoman rule and to throwing off the 'Turkish yoke'. Significantly, neither the liberation of the peasants nor agricultural reform was considered to be a key component of this national 'rebirth', which was characterized by an idealization of the Bulgarian nation. Its key representatives were drawn from the mountainous regions of Central Bulgaria and the Bulgarian diaspora in the Danube principalities. They were initially recruited from the ranks of long-distance traders, then from craftsmen and, finally, from among political exiles.

Over the course of this national movement, Bulgarian communities sought to emancipate themselves from the Greek bishops, demanded the introduction of their own language into the Greek liturgy and denied the recognition of the Orthodox patriarchs in Constantinople. Eventually, in 1870, the Sultan ordered the establishment of a Bulgarian diocese, an exarchate, which constituted the foundation for church autonomy. At the same time, the confessionally structured schools also furthered the spread of the Bulgarian language among the Slavic population of Macedonia.

The establishment of a literary public and the development of secret societies created the preconditions for the path to state independence. In the decades leading up to the April Uprising of 1876 and the founding of the Bulgarian state in 1878, thanks to Russian military and German diplomatic intervention, the Bulgarian elite, in their conviction that they represented the nation in their attempts to shake off the 'Turkish yoke', held an exaggerated opinion of themselves. On the one hand, the village communities were reliant upon the patterns of identification created by an urban literary public and, on the other hand, regardless of their generational and social status, the educated elites also belonged to various interest groups.[111]

Macedonia, for which the Congress of Berlin in 1878 had only called for reforms on the part of the Ottoman government, was, fatally, to develop into a territorial object of conflict in the process of nation-building in the Balkan countries of Bulgaria, Serbia and Greece. The unresolved 'Macedonian question' was to be the match which would ignite the 'powderkeg' of the Balkan Wars of 1912/1913.[112]

Vampirism in Macedonia

Thanks to the integration of the Central Balkans into the Ottoman Empire and the subjugation of the Christian communities to the Greek-Orthodox Patriarchate in Constantinople, the documentation of vampire cases among the Balkan Slavs remained fairly rare, due to the absence of administrative structures. Nevertheless, it is possible to find entries from the years 1836 to 1839 in the 'Registry Books' (*sicillāt*) of the Kadis of Manastir (Macedonian Bitola), which detail the payment of fees to specialists in the defence against 'spirits' (*cādūcılar*). Since the relevant files were designed for accounting purposes, they merely make reference to the fact that these specialists were recruited from the region of Tikveš and the town of Köprülü (Macedonian Veles). However, since these vampire specialists were evidently operating under the instruction of the authorities, it can be conjectured that rumours concerning harmful revenants represented a significant threat to the social order and were by no means restricted to village communities, although it can also be assumed that exhumations were by no means a regular occurrence. On the basis of the sources, the relationship to the plague, which was raging in Macedonia at this time, can only be guessed at.[113]

The belief in vampires is more graphic in the tales of Marko Cepenkov, a tailor and teacher from Prilep (Turkish Perlepe), who gathered together legends and songs from the artisanal community in 1856/1857, and published these in 1889, following his move to Sofia, in the journal *Sbornik za narodni umotvoreniia, nauka i knizhnina* (*Collection of Folk Wisdom, Science and the Art of Books*).[114]

One story here is about the fatal affair of a bride of a dead man, whose mother spends one night from Saturday to Sunday far away in the town. So as not to be alone, the girl invites a friend from the neighbourhood to come and spin with her. During their conversation, she expresses her regret that her dead husband was buried with his ring on. The two friends decide to dig up the body, but are then forced to cut off the ring finger and boil it. However, at midnight, before it is possible to slip off the ring, the dead man arrives down the chimney in the form of a vampire. When he discovers that millet is being cooked in the pot, he wants to take part in the meal, during which the neighbour manages to slip out. Fate then takes its ominous course. Before the first crow of the cock, the vampire kills the girl and drinks her blood, stuffs the dead corpse with straw and dresses her in her bridal costume. When her mother returns, she is initially outraged, but then has to come to face to the facts.[115]

In another tale, a vampire slips into his best clothes and suitors a poor woman for the hand of her daughter in marriage, whilst at the same time offering his services in finding suitable partners for her two youngest daughters. He then leads his bride to the cemetery and into his dwelling, a cave hidden beneath a stone slab. He orders his wife to fry human flesh, which is hanging there from a hook. When the girl refuses, she is immediately slaughtered on the spot. The vampire then clothes himself as a merchant and seeks to tempt the second daughter into his cave, appealing to her that she is required as a carer for her older sister. She then meets the same fate. Finally, refusing the mother's offer of help, the vampire claims the youngest daughter. The youngest daughter attempts to escape through prayer, but she is heard doing so, and discovers a hidden coffin in the corner that she takes out into the nocturnal forest. From God, she solicits a trunk, which can only be opened with a hair, climbs into this and feeds herself for a while with fruit. The vampire's search for her proves to be unsuccessful.

Instead, the son of a Tsar, passing by on a hunt, catches sight of the girl, whom he takes to be a *vila* (here Bulgarian *samovila*), a nymph-like creature.

However, he is not able to capture her, nor can he open the trunk, in which he suspects there to be a treasure. Upon their arrival at the palace, the trunk is placed in the prince's room. Thereafter, the girl begins to eat his food, until she is discovered leaving the trunk by a servant. As a result, the prince waylays the girl and takes her spontaneously to be his wife. The trunk is hidden in a dungeon.

However, since envious persons hire a murderer, the marriage comes to an unhappy end. Instead, the girl finds herself in some stinging nettles, bound by her abductors, but luckily, before she starves to death, she is discovered just in time by a herb-woman. In the meantime, the prince has been taken ill and orders food from his subjects in order to aid his recovery. Together with the old woman, his bride prepares a herbal dish and garnishes it with one of her own hairs. After eating it, the prince asks for the meal again and expresses his desire to visit the herb-woman. There he discovers his bride hiding in a baking trough, and takes both her and the old woman back with him.[116]

A third tale outlines the fate of a patchwork family. A widower with a daughter marries a widow, who also has a daughter. The father owns a mill, inhabited by evil spirits.

One time, when he is away, the mother attempts to throw her stepdaughter to the vampires to eat. The girl bakes a pita, a flat-bread from leavened dough, and visits the mill, where she feeds a dog, a hen and a cat. Grateful, the cat then warns her not to sleep before the first crow of the cock and not to open the door. When there is a knock on the door, the dog says that it is a vampire. Before opening the door, the cat advises her to instruct the vampire first to gather all the wealth of the richest man in the region, which she does. Following his return, the cock crows and the vampire disappears. On the second night, the same scene repeats itself. However, this time, as well as money, she instructs the vampire to also bring the rich man's produce.

Jealous of this, the stepmother then sends her own daughter to the mill. However, this girl eats her food alone, without giving anything to the animals and, because of this, they refuse to provide her any assistance. As can be expected, the vampire enters and drinks the girl's blood. The stepmother then recognizes the error of her ways and pays penance. Finally, the mill is torn down and a church is erected in its place.[117]

In these tales, the vampire no longer plays a central role. He appears as a monster in human form, who is referred to once as a revenant, once as an eater of humans, but is otherwise only distinguished from other demons, at best, through his bloodsucking. The central characters in these stories are humans, with all their passions and faults. Both tales concern family constellations in which the man is not at home, and the roles of the widow and the stepmother therefore become central. The hero is always the daughter who has been left alone and who has to prove herself, in a domestic context, as a suitable bride, in things such as spinning or baking. Innocently placed in danger, it is always a good deed or a prayer that offers her salvation. By contrast, the stories present the bite of the vampire as just punishment for the breaking of taboos or committing of crimes, such as murdering someone or disturbing the peace of the dead.

The narrator offers all manner of worldly words of advice, whether this be the maxim 'clothes make people' or the motto 'eating alone makes you fat'. Reflecting concerns about securing the daily bread, the mill at night appears to be an enchanted place. The inclusion of numerous horrific visions, such as the consumption of human flesh or the stuffing of corpses, is also down to public tastes. The excursion about the Tsar's son is to be understood as a literary embellishment, and the appearance of animals that can communicate with humans is taken from the realm of fables. In the final analysis, the fate of the small people always seems to depend upon the possibility of securing for themselves, through a trick or ploy, a portion of the riches of the wealthy.

Vampirism in Ottoman Bulgaria

Despite the sparsity of mentions in written documents, the vampire question is not entirely unknown among the Slavic subjects of Ottoman rule in the Central Balkans. Whereas the authorities still had fundamental difficulties in dealing with such cases in the seventeenth century, a certain routine was established over the course of the eighteenth century, in which there was an increasing toleration of the desecration of graves and corpses by the local population (see the section entitled 'The Vrykolakas among the Greeks in the Ottoman Empire' in Chapter 2). Furthermore, from a reading of the Ottoman sources, the impression arises that the subjects, legally deprived of the freedom of movement, sought – whether because of the tax burden, security concerns or concerns for their health – for ways to justify their desire for migration. For example, the first Turkish newspaper, appearing from 1831, *Takvim-i Vekayi* (*Calendar of Facts*), informed its readers on 6 September 1833 of a report that an Ottoman officer from the former Bulgarian capital of Veliko Tarnovo (Turkish Tırnovo) had submitted to the Sublime Porte. According to this, the following had taken place.

The residents of Veliko Tarnovo were allegedly subject to nightly attacks by monsters (*cadi, hortlak*) and felt themselves compelled to leave their homes. In this case, the authorities were forced to fall back on the assistance of a Christian, who claimed to be on the hunt for vampires. He exhumed the bodies of two janissaries and interpreted their nondecomposed state as evidence of their nocturnal activities. Eventually, the vampire hunter was able to bring an end to the dreadful state of affairs, first by impaling the dead men, then by pouring boiling water over them and, finally, by burning them.

Clearly, this tale also sought further to discredit the reputation of the former elite unit of the janissaries, which had originally been recruited from Christian offspring and that had been abolished in 1826 as a result of their increasing interference in the affairs of state.[118]

The first vampire tales from Central Bulgaria have been preserved in a prominent place, namely in the memoirs of the revolutionary Zahariy Stoyanov, which were published in three volumes between 1884 and 1892 under the title *Zapiski po bŭlgarskite vŭstaniia* (*Memoirs of the Bulgarian Uprisings*). Having attended elementary school, Stoyanov first became a shepherd in the area around Kotel, the 'Cradle of the Bulgarian Rebirth', in the Eastern Balkan highlands. During his apprenticeship to a tailor in the town of Ruse on the Danube, he educated himself autodidactically and joined a revolutionary committee. After participating in the Bulgarian Uprising of 1875/1876 against Ottoman rule, he emerged as a liberal publicist and legal official.[119]

In Stoyanov's 'eyewitness reports', vampires (Bulgarian *vapir*) are mentioned in two places. He relates that the shepherds of Kotel would pass the time on long winter evenings with discussions about heaven and hell and the recounting of horror stories. They were convinced of the existence of evil spirits, witches, fairies and vampires. However, it is never explained what stance the later revolutionary took on these issues. Retrospectively, Stoyanov only found the belief in vampires to be relevant insofar as it was connected to anti-Turkish sentiment. Thus, a *haji*, a Christian figure who, drawing on Islamic tradition, was considered worthy of respect as a result either of their religious experiences or their having been on pilgrimage to Jerusalem, was supposed to have claimed that the souls of dead Christians would enter into paradise, whereas those of Muslims were condemned to damnation. Also, when a Christian sinner was transformed into a vampire, he would nevertheless retain human form. A Turk, by contrast, was predestined to reincarnation as a pig, that is, as a member of a species considered to be impure in Islam. In this context, another shepherd recounted a mishap with a slaughtered wild boar, whose meat had turned out to be impossible to cook. Upon closer inspection of the quarry, it emerged that the wild boar's ears were stuffed with cotton and that a silver ring was hanging from his foreleg. This was taken to be the finger-ring of a recently deceased Turk. Whether, in the context of the complicated Turkish–Bulgarian relationship, this might even have been a Pomak, a Bulgarian Muslim, remains open to question.[120]

During his time as a village teacher in Northern Bulgaria, Stoyanov learned in 1873 of a self-designated vampire hunter in Pirgovo, a neighbouring community of the Danube town of Ruse, on the border to Romania. This was a priest called Marin, whose supposed special abilities Stoyanov commented upon ironically.

According to the priest two gypsies had complained several days after the funeral of their father that the dead man had left his grave and had slipped into the house through a keyhole, where he had then thrown pieces of bread at his relatives and had not departed until the first crow of the cock, taking with him a bag of flour. Apparently, the priest had declared himself prepared to burn the vampire, before he could choke anybody, for a fee of 200 groschen. At noon, a crowd of people had gathered at the cemetery to witness this act.

On the fortieth day after the death of the suspect, the priest had appeared, dressed in his liturgical vestments and carrying an icon, and paced around the graves until he discovered a mouse-hole. The dead man buried at this location was revealed to be as black as a charred piece of wood and bloated like a barrel. First his breast was driven through with a sharp stake and then his body was covered in boiling wine. Finally, the grave was filled with embers and wood. Whilst the people were driven away by the stench, the priest had continued to chant his prayers in a calm manner.

Clearly, Stoyanov's intention with this report was to deride the lower clergy. The priest had instrumentalized the superstitions of the people in order to make money for himself. The only remedy to this was rational understanding or secular reason, which could only be spread through the expansion of the school system.[121]

Vampire Hunters in an Independent Bulgaria

Following the achievement of Bulgarian independence, serious references to vampire hunters can be found in the works of foreign experts, namely those of the Czech historian and politician Konstantin Jireček, and the Hungarian ethnographer and journalist Adolf Strausz. Jireček gained fame on the back of his 1876 book *Dějiny bulharského národa* (*History of the Bulgarians*). He was appointed to the Bulgarian government in 1879 and, from 1881/1882, assumed the position of Minister for the Economy. In 1884, he was appointed Director of the National Library, but took up a professorship at the Charles University in Prague in the same year, a post he was to hold until his transfer to the University of Vienna in 1893. In his book *Das Fürstentum Bulgarien: Seine Bodengestaltung, Natur, Bevölkerung, Wirthschaftliche Zustände, geistige Cultur, Staatsverwaltung und neueste Geschichte* (*The Principality of Bulgaria: Its Territory, Nature, Population, Economic Conditions, Spiritual Culture, State Administration and Recent History*), published in 1891, he traced the belief in vampires back to concerns for the cattle. In the area around Provadia in the northeast of Bulgaria, there was a 'sorcerer' (*dzhadadzhiia*, derived from the Turkish *džadá*) or exorcist of devils, who specialized in hunting vampires. He was one of the descendants of children who had been sired by a vampire (*fürkuliák*) and who had the ability to recognize vampires, who were otherwise invisible for normal people.[122]

In this context, Jireček made reference to a village in which a bout of the sleeping sickness had broken out.

A vampire hunter, or dzhadadzhiia, had chased an evil spirit from one animal to another with an icon. The spirit first entered into the bells, and then into the wool of a sheep, before disappearing into the mouth of a dog. When he was eventually discovered in a wooden pipe, this was stuffed up and burned, thus bringing an end to the disease.

A case of disease in another village also led to the summoning of a dzhadadzhiia. The evil spirit was chased from one yard to another, until the icon that was being used for this began to tremble to the touch. After this, the dzhadadzhiia followed the spirit into the freshly dug grave of a gypsy. The corpse was immediately exhumed and burned, with the crowd present being able to make out the whimpering of the vampire. Within two weeks, the plague had been overcome.[123]

Following his studies in Pest and Vienna, Adolf Strausz worked as a war correspondent in Bosnia and Herzegovina, and later travelled across the Balkans on numerous occasions in the service of the Hungarian government. From 1892, he instructed ethnography and commercial geography at the Privileged Oriental Company in Budapest, which in 1921 was reorganized as the Economic University. His 1898 book *Die Bulgaren: Ethnographische Studien* (*The Bulgarians: Ethnographic Studies*) made only vague references to the phenomenon of vampirism. On the one hand, he outlined the custom of sticking a needle in the stomach of a suspect before their burial. On the other hand, he also outlined the belief that a vampire retains its human form, but is made only of skin and blood, and has no flesh or bones. Strausz went into further detail on the 'vampire conjurer' (*vampiridzhi*). In some places, a vampire, lying in its grave, would be burned on the night from Saturday to Sunday. The vampiridzhi, by contrast, professional vampire conjurers, specialized in shooting vampires. When they burnt a cane at a cemetery and swung their rifle, the vampire would emerge and flee for his life. In order to prevent the emergence of a new vampire from the blood of one who had been shot, either boiling water was poured over the corpse or it was covered with glowing coals. Should it not be possible to destroy the vampire, he would be chased off to another district.[124]

The vampire cases outlined by Strausz are suitably bizarre.

Half a century earlier, two vampires had been responsible for the outbreak of a plague. They had corrupted foodstuffs and shattered the night-time peace, tucking into the cheese and butter, and making music and a racket in the barns and spinning rooms. It had not even proved possible to stop them with a rifle. A monk from Kalugerovo in Central Bulgaria had then advised that bottles of wine and oil be thrown into the water in order to restore the peace of the dead. These measures did in fact lead to the gradual disappearance of the vampires.

In a further case, Strausz also referred to a vampire by name. This tale concerned the tailor Timon from the district around Prilep in the south of present-day Macedonia.

Because of a plague, the bishop had sung psalms for forty days in forty houses and sprinkled holy oil. Eventually he visited the cemetery, sprinkled holy water on Timon's grave and then instructed the body to be dug up. The dead body revealed itself in a bloated form, which, interestingly, Strausz traces back to water rather than blood. Only after the bishop had poured water into the mouth of the dead man did the corpse finally collapse in on itself, becoming as thin as a rake. After this, nothing more was heard of the vampire, although the new owner of the house did begin to complain that he was still active and was carrying out his evil tricks even more aggressively than before, angered by the holy water. He then allegedly called upon a professional vampire hunter.[125]

From Jireček's perspective, the vampire merely played the role of a demon of illness. His focus is on the phenomenon of the supposed vampire offspring and their descendants (dzhadadzhiia), who performed a bizarre sort of exorcism in a shamanic staging of Christian rituals. It surely cannot be a coincidence that, in one of these tales, it was a representative of the Roma community who was identified as the scapegoat. Interestingly, the vampire merely functions as an evil ghost, invisible to normal people. Therefore, the burning of a bloated corpse appears to be the only possible form of combating vampires. Strausz also outlined two different variants of vampire – one a human figure and the other an evil spirit. According to his depiction, professional vampire hunters stood in direct competition with the ecclesiastical authorities, with muskets and boiling water offering themselves as alternatives to icons and holy oil. The talk is no longer of bloodsuckers, but merely of plaguing-spirits.

From the Danubian Principalities to the Kingdom of Romania

From the twelfth century, the Romance-language speaking population of the Danube-Balkan region, largely composed of wandering shepherds, were referred to in the West as Vlachs. At the start of the fourteenth century, they constructed two voivodships, i.e. principalities, Wallachia and Moldavia, which, in the period of the 'Middle Ages', reaching up to the eighteenth century, were in part in a joint vassal relationship to the surrounding Great Powers, whether this was the Habsburgs, the Ottomans or the Poles-Lithuanians. In the eighteenth century, so-called 'Phanariote Rule' was established in the Danubian principalities, named after the Greek merchants, set up as princes by the Ottomans, who had originally come from the Istanbul district of Fener (Greek Phanar). The only pillar of a sense of united identity was the Orthodox Church, whose numerous monasteries owned considerable lands. At the turn of the 1820s and 1830s, the Russian Tsarist Empire appeared on the scene as a protective power, winning internal autonomy and freedom of trade for the Danubian principalities. Following the establishment of a customs union in 1846, the double election of Prince Alexander Cuza led to the union of Moldavia and Wallachia as the Principality of Romania. The Congress of Berlin of 1878 finally brought independence from the Ottoman Empire, and the Kingdom of Romania was proclaimed in 1881. A 'Greater Romania' was then established in the course of the First World War, incorporating Bessarabia, Bukovina, Transylvania and parts of the Banat.[126]

Transylvania played a special role within the Kingdom of Hungary, since settlers from the German-speaking lands, referred to simply as 'Saxons' and who had settled in the area since the thirteenth century, had been granted numerous privileges and enjoyed considerable autonomy. The Orthodox Vlachs were excluded from the medieval 'university of nations', constituted on a corporative basis in 1437 and composed of the Hungarian nobility, the association of Saxon towns and the frontier-guard population of Szeklers. In the sixteenth century, the Reformation established itself among the Saxons. In the wake of the division of the historical Hungary between the Ottoman Empire and the Habsburg Empire, the Principality of Transylvania achieved a degree of independence in 1541 with the incorporation into the Habsburg Empire in 1690 confirming the privileges of the Saxons. Although the Romanians constituted the majority of the population, they did not enjoy any political rights until the 1860s. The Austrian-Hungarian Compromise of 1867 led to the loss of Transylvanian autonomy, and the administrative reforms of 1876 were the starting gun for a policy of Magyarization, directed above all against the Romanians.[127]

The historical region of the Banat, located where present-day Serbia, Hungary and Romania meet, became a part of the Habsburg Empire following the Peace of Passarowitz of 1718. As a crown territory, the sparsely populated region, dotted with fortified towns, was a part of the Military Frontier. One part of the Banat was integrated into the region of the Habsburg Military Frontier, but its core area was incorporated into Hungary from 1778. Alongside Hungarians and Vlachs, Serbian refugees also settled in the region around Temesvar (Romanian Timișoara) following the Second Siege of Vienna by the Ottomans in 1683, as did colonists from the southwest German region in the so-called 'Schwabenzug' (Swabian migration) of the 1720s. Thanks to the 'Banat fever' (malaria) and the 'morbus hungaricus' (typhus), the region became known in the eighteenth century as the 'Graveyard of Nations' or the 'Coffin of the Germans'. After all this, slightly over half of the population were Romanians by the mid nineteenth century and, disregarding the national minorities, one-fifth each were Serbians and Germans.[128]

Bloodsuckers in Transylvania and the Banat

Regardless of the fact that, since Bram Stoker's *Dracula*, Transylvania has been seen in the Western media as the homeland of the vampire, the first reports on 'bloodsuckers' in the region came not from among the indigenous population, but rather from the German minority living there. According to contemporary Romanian understanding, alongside the historical region Siebenbürgen, other parts of the Kingdom of Hungary such as the Banat and the regions of Crişana, Satu Mare and Maramureş all belonged to Transylvania. In general, the question can be raised as to whether vampires had already been brought into Romania by the Saxon colonists in the Middle Ages in the form of nachzehrers or whether they first entered the region in the course of the Swabian migrations of the 1720s. In any event, the first traces of them in Transylvania are to be found in the late seventeenth and early eighteenth centuries.

In his work *Pestis Dacicae anni MDCCIX* (*The Transylvanian Plague of 1709*), for example, published in the same year as the plague, the theologian, physician and historian Samuel Köleseri reported on the belief in harmful dead persons among the population. According to Köleseri, in the neighbouring villages of Kis-Kerék and Pókafalva, lying between Fehérvar and Hermannstadt (Romanian Sibiu), desecrations of corpses were regularly undertaken as a measure against the plague. In one case, a man, two women and a girl were exhumed. Since the corpses of the women were found to be in a nondecomposed state and seemed to be devouring their funeral shrouds, stones were forced down their throats before they were burned, but this did not stop the epidemic. In a further case, the corpses of a Romanian villager and his grandson were dug up and deemed to be suspicious. Köleseri also refers here to a late-eighteenth century case from Hermannstadt (Romanian Sibiu) in which a dead officer of the guards had caused various people to have nightmares. The opening of the grave revealed the dead man and his grandchild to have been chomping on their shrouds, and they were therefore decapitated, bringing an end to the harmful magic. As an explanation for the disease, Köleseri pointed towards the possible impact of the devil through 'witches and sorceresses' (*sagae et veneficae*). However, in his view, either fantasy or a false diagnosis were really responsible.[129]

On 7 May 1732, in the context of the debates around the vampire cases of Medveđa (see the section entitled 'The Discovery of the Vampire' in Chapter 3), the *Commercium litterarium* (*Literary Correspondent*) reported on a plague in the no-longer-identifiable Wallachian village of Merul, on the border to Transylvania, which claimed the lives of eighty residents between November 1717 and April 1718. The journal's correspondent, who is not referred to by name but who was possibly living in Vienna, called upon an eyewitness, who had worked as a quartermaster in the army and was living in the locality at the time in question. The correspondent reported the following on the plague.

The disease, accompanied by delusions and an increased redness of the face, led to death within three days. Those affected hinted at the influence of witches and sorceresses, but there was no talk of bloodsuckers. However, shortly before the disappearance of the plague, the eyewitness had seen how several bodies were dug up in a cemetery, from those graves that a black horse had shied away from. Among the dead who had been dug up were found the nondecomposed corpses of an old man, a woman and two children. According to established custom, the suspects were decapitated and burned, and thereafter the disease no longer re-emerged.

Whether the witnesses of the time had transposed the news from the north Bosnian cases onto the earlier experiences in Merul remains open to question. What is interesting in this context is that the Vienna correspondent should have emphasized that only the villagers had been taken ill, but not the soldiers. From this he concluded that this was something endemic and had nothing to do with evil forces emerging either from the living or the dead. The normal revenant, at least one from the ranks of the local population, would surely also have attacked the hated soldiers who were stationed in the village.[130] With this statement, the reporter made clear that the question of posthumous activity was already known to him from his own cultural background.

The first concrete case of vampirism on the territory of present-day Romania was outlined by Joseph Teutsch, the pastor of the community of Nussbach (Romanian Măieruș), close to Kronstadt (Romanian Brașov) in his work, begun in 1754, *Nachlese zu den kurzgefassten Jahresgeschichten von Ungarn und Siebenbürgen* (*Postscript to the Summary Annual Histories of Hungary and Transylvania*), which was published in 1903 in the *Quellen zur Geschichte der Stadt Brassó* (*Sources on the History of the Town of Brassó*). In 1719, according to Teutsch, during an outbreak of plague and in the wider context of the Counter-Reformation, a dead woman had been impaled and burned in Nussbach because her grave, lying in a garden, had sometimes appeared to be open in the morning, and she was therefore suspected of being a 'vampire or a bloodsucker'.[131] Teutsch also noted a further report from 1756 about a 'plague physician'. In the upper suburb of Kronstadt, i.e. the Romanian district, the body of a Vlach woman who had died three months earlier was exhumed. She was allegedly found lying on her back with her hands thrust behind her back, wearing a torn headscarf. One ear was bleeding and an oozing wound disfigured her breast. Although nothing was reported in either case about possible countermeasures, there is a clear parallel with the nachzehrer ideas familiar from the Central German area in times of plague. The unusual cases of death at least posed a puzzle that, in the era of the Enlightenment, continued to animate the fantasies of the Transylvanian Saxons. However, the appearance of vampirism in the Transylvanian environment was firmly denied. Therefore, in a later addition to Teutsch's chronicle, calling upon common sense, the suspicion was stated that, due to the body's unusual position, this might have been a case of someone being buried alive.[132] Also symptomatic is the fact that, in a Vienna dissertation, the Transylvanian Saxon Martin Martinus should have referred back to a case of vampirism from Medveđa, even though he could instead have called upon more local examples in his discussion of the various types of demon.[133]

In his 1894 article 'Beiträge zur Geschichte des Vampyrismus in Südungarn' ('Contributions to the History of Vampirism in Southern Hungary'), which appeared in *Ethnologische Mitteilungen aus Ungarn* (*Ethnological Reports from Hungary*), the Budapest teacher Lajos Baróti presented further cases of grave desecrations in the Banat from 1725/1726 and from the first half of the 1750s. According to this, the administrator of the Lugos-Facsád (Romanian Lugoj and Fäget) district was commissioned on 31 March 1725 with opening the grave of an alleged sorceress in Herinbiesch (Romanian Herendeşti), who had been accused of posthumous activities. His report of 3 April 1725 recorded that no signs of decomposition could be found, three months after the woman's death. One hand was found to be at the height of her head and, from the discovery of a pool of blood under her head, it was determined that she was, indeed, a 'bloodsucker'. A notification from 10 April 1725 authorized the administrator to proceed in the usual manner. Clearly, the military authorities largely gave the population free rein in the desecration of suspect corpses, whereas the Church was vehemently opposed. For example, on 1 August 1725, the sub-administrator of the Lugos-Facset district called for the revocation of the excommunication that the local bishop had previously imposed upon the community of Babscha (Romanian Babşa) for destroying an alleged bloodsucker on its own initiative.[134]

The struggle against vampires seemed, temporarily, to gain a new impetus as a result of the plague which struck the Banat during the Turkish Wars of 1736–39. In any event, the orientalist Anton von Hammer, who had occasionally worked as an interpreter in the area of the Banat Military Frontier, outlined a case of bloodsucking in his *Temeswarer Pestchronik* (*Temesvar Plague Chronicle*) of 1839. This case took place in the settlement of Neu-Arad, separated by the River Mureş from the town of Arad, and that had been settled since the early 1720s not only by Serbian refugees but also by Germans from Franconia and from Alsace-Lorraine.[135] According to a euphemistically formulated Prussian press release, disseminated by a Viennese correspondent on 25 June 1738, vampires did certainly seem to appear from time to time in the Banat, but, up to that point, they had not bothered 'to pester a single member of the German nation'.[136]

Lajos Barótis' information hints at a further high point in the struggle against vampires at the end of the 1740s and in the first half of the 1750s. Thus, on the orders of the Orthodox bishop, the priest in Karansebesch (Romanian Caransebeş) locked up his church, since the community there had recently desecrated eleven corpses. Other independent actions against supposed vampires were also registered in several further places. In 1751, in the small town of Kovin in the Vojvodina, today part of Serbia, representatives of both the local church community and the military stationed there burned the corpse of a man with a Slavic-sounding first name (Marinko Káláritt), and in 1753, corpse desecrators in Schebell (Romanian Jebel) were taken into custody for a period of fourteen days.[137]

Against this backdrop, and in the context of the ban she had imposed on 'Magia posthuma', Empress Maria Theresa sent a commission of investigation under the leadership of the surgeon Georg Tallar to the peripheral southern areas of Hungary in 1756 (see the section entitled 'The Vampire Debate of the Enlightenment' in Chapter 3).[138] After some delay, Tallar's report was published in 1784 under the title of *Visum repertum anatomico-chirurgicum oder Gründlicher Bericht von den sogenannten Blütsaugern, Vampier, oder in der wallachischen Sprache Moroi, in der Wallachey, Siebenbürgen, und Banat* (*Anatomical-Chirurgical Report or a Thorough Report on the So-called Bloodsuckers, Vampires or, in the Wallachian Language,* Moroi, *in Wallachia, Transylvania and the Banat*). In view of the settlement of German-speaking colonists in the region, the Empress seems to have been keen not to allow further horror stories to spread among the public, alongside the 'morbus hungaricus'. Tallar, who claimed to speak both Hungarian and Romanian, pointed out that he had already personally been witnesses to three cases of supposed vampirism, that is, to posthumous executions: in 1724 in the Transylvanian Deva, in 1728 in the Wallachian Oburschta, and in 1753 in the settlements of Schebell and Klein Dikva (Romanian Ticvaniu Mic), lying to the south of Timișoara, as well as in the village of Kallatsa (Romanian Călacea) to the north of the same town.[139]

For the vampires, Tallar employed the Wallachian or Romanian designation of *moroi*. This designated a dead man or woman who was believed to appear to the living not only in their sleep, but also when they were awake. These visits were then followed by an illness, which lasted for two to three days, and was accompanied by the symptoms of heart pain, headaches and gastrointestinal problems, all of which led to feverish fantasies. For this reason, in direct opposition to the authorities, the village communities often demanded the exhumation of dead corpses. In this context, the habit of using the blood of the alleged revenants as an ointment also became widespread, in the hope of preventing further contagion.

All things considered, Tallar concluded that the supposed vampire disease could be traced back to the unbalanced diet of the rural population and to the rules on fasting in the Orthodox Church. From his perspective, the Serbian refugees who had made their home in the Banat from the 1690s proved to be much more resistant to this disease due to their healthy consumption of ample amounts of red pepper, which strengthened their immune system. In conclusion, Tallar advanced the prognosis that superstition would lose its power when those who had fallen ill could be healed through medication.[140] Regardless of the fact that Tallar's primary interest was in the disease itself, his statements do provide an early example for the emergence of the undead in Romanian popular culture, even if the problem is not specified.

The *Osservazioni storiche naturali e politiche intorno la Valachia e Moldovia* (*Natural and Political Historical Observations on Wallachia and Moldova*), published in 1788 by Stefan Raicević, from Dubrovnik, following an eleven-year stay in the country, are constructed somewhat differently. Raicević had experienced the conditions under Phanariote rule at first hand. For the enlightened Catholic, the belief in 'vampiri' or 'vampyres' only made sense in connection with the instrument of excommunication. According to Raicević, for a fee, priests and bishops were prepared to undertake an exorcism of nondecomposed bodies and to renounce excommunications. As a lower-class phenomenon, vampirism was also a means employed to discipline the rabble in the interests of the Church. Since it was the punishment imposed for perjury by the church courts, excommunication became so inflationary that the Greek patriarchs were requested to grant a general absolution in favour of avoiding vampirism. On a lengthy visit, the Patriarch of Jerusalem, for a fee, issued letters of absolution and held masses for the souls of the dead. The problem hardly occurred among the nobility, and unpopular police officers and traders seemed to be accused particularly often.[141] In his work, Raicević does not speaks of bloodsuckers, but limits himself to highlighting the contradiction between Church doctrine and the conceptions of the common people when it came to dealing with evil spirits, thus revealing the consequences of Greek-Orthodox theology and the instrument of excommunication. Affairs in Wallachia and Moldavia in this respect were portrayed as being very different from those in the Habsburg Empire.

Transylvanian Superstition

Whereas, thanks to Bram Stoker's novel, the name of the vampire count 'Dracula' and that of his species, known as *nosferatu*, became interlinked in the Western imagination with Romania, due to fantastical embellishments and erroneous descriptions, the ominous landscape of Transylvania came to be seen as an almost fictitious location. Stoker's sources included country descriptions of the Danubian principalities and travel books on Transylvania. For example, in his 1820 book *An Account of the Principalities of Wallachia and Moldavia*, the British Consul William Wilkinson mentioned that the Voivod Dracula crossed the Danube in 1462 and fought the troops of Mehmed II, the conqueror of Constantinople. However, Wilkinson mistakenly derived the name from the Romanian word for devil, thus seeing in it an expression of particular cruelty.[142] In fact, the Voivod known in Romania as Vlad III Țepeș ('the Impaler') used the name Dracula in diplomatic correspondence as an honorary title. It was a diminutive form of the term 'Dracul', which his father had taken on as a member of the Order of the Dragon, founded by the Emperor Sigismund II. Stoker took the description of the vampire, as well as the term 'nosferatu', from the Scottish writer Emily Gerard, who, as the wife of a Polish officer in the Austro-Hungarian army, originally from Galicia, had resided from 1883 to 1884 in Hermannstadt (Romanian Sibiu) and Kronstadt (Romanian Braşov). In 1885, Gerard published an article on 'Transylvanian Superstitions' in the journal *The Nineteenth Century*, which she then published again in her 1888 book *The Land beyond the Forest*. Since Gerard could not herself speak the local language, she mistakenly used the term later adopted by Stoker, 'nosferatu', as a designation for vampires, the belief in which she claimed was just as widespread in Romanian popular culture as the belief in heaven and hell.[143] Therefore, through the combination of two falsely understood terms, Stoker's dubious achievement lay in having turned the Impaler Prince into the Vampire Count.

Although German-speaking settlers and colonists in Transylvania and the Banat were aware of bloodsuckers in the eighteenth century, Romanian 'vampires' were not widely known among a public readership until the mid nineteenth century. Information on this is provided in the appendix to the *Walachische Märchen* (*Wallachian Fairy Tales*), published by the Stuttgart gymnasium teacher Albert Schott and his brother Arthur, drawing upon Romanian informants. The Schott brothers only mentioned *moroi* and *strigoi* in passing, as evil spirits, but did cover the 'murony' and the 'wampyr' at greater length. These are the illegitimate offspring of two parents, themselves born out of wedlock, or the victim of a bloodsucker. The immortal 'murony' would leave his grave at night and could take on any number of animal forms, from that of a dog to that of a flea. According to the Schott brothers, its calling card was the bite that could be made out on the victim's throat – a provocative thesis that is not mentioned elsewhere in Romanian folklore. If one opened a grave, one could identify a 'murony' by the fact that he lay the wrong way round and had a rosy complexion. He could be destroyed by driving a nail through his forehead or a wooden stake through his heart, or by burning him. As a preventative measure, a thorny rose-branch would be lain in the grave before burial. The fact that 'murony' is an artificial word suggests that a bloodsucking demon may have been integrated into the world of Romanian superstition, without this having very much to do with the actual beliefs of the peasants.[144]

Regardless of this, the mythologist and scholar of religions Wilhelm Mannhardt was clearly inspired by the Schott brothers in his 1859 article 'Die Vampyre' ('The Vampires'), published in the *Zeitschrift für deutsche Mythologie und Sittenkunde* (*Journal for German Mythology and Research into Customs*). In this piece, Mannhardt already anticipated Stoker's combination of the Dracula name and the vampire term in claiming that, in Moldavia, the evil spirit *dracul* could reanimate excommunicated persons after their death. Those thus possessed did not decay, but rather chomped in their graves, and left the graveyard at night in order to inflict harm on their relatives and to suck their blood. The priest therefore had to absolve the dead from their excommunication. In reference to the Vlachs of the Banat, Mannhardt used the term 'murony', employed by the Schott brothers.[145] However, in his theologically tinged interpretation, Mannhardt portrayed the phenomenon of bloodsucking in the recently united Romania in a more vivid manner than they had done.

Also drawing upon the Schott brothers in terms of content, Emily Gerard, who had a command of German, differentiated between a living vampire and a dead one in her representation, which was to prove so decisive for Stoker. However, she was not able to portray this in a comprehensible manner. Rather, she largely stuck to the view, which played upon the purity of blue blood or upon sexual taboos, that a 'living vampire' was the illegitimate offspring of two parents who had also been born out of wedlock.[146] In 1926, the English ethnologist and zoologist Agnes Murgoci attempted a typological specification in her article that appeared in the journal *Folklore*, 'The Vampire in Roumania'. Witches and sorceresses are to be distinguished from reanimated corpses. These were persons whose future posthumous vampirism is already evident during their lifetime and whose souls or corpses, possessed by evil spirits, would become a law unto themselves.[147]

Again, according to Gerard, even a spotless family tree could not guard against vampiric attacks upon the family vault. However, in projecting the puritanism of the British nobility upon the peasant world of Transylvania, Gerard rather overshot the mark. Nevertheless, the motif of vampiric reproduction, which had never before been so clearly formulated, proved to be of great significance for Stoker: anyone killed by a 'nosferatu' would themselves in turn become transformed into a vampire and would also drink the blood of innocent people until the evil spirit could be driven out. The form of exorcism that Gerard describes seems greatly secularized: following the opening of a suspect's grave, either a stake would be driven through the corpse or a pistol shot fired at it. In particularly difficult cases, it was advisable to cut off the head and to fill the mouth with garlic, or to tear out the heart, burn it and scatter the ashes over the grave. In this, Gerard transferred the literary conceptions of the vampire from the West onto Romanian folklore, thus distorting her seemingly authentic information.[148]

Nevertheless, Gerard's controversial theses did find a degree of confirmation in the work of the Transylvanian-Saxon pioneer of Roma research Heinrich von Wlislocki. In 1896, in *Am Ur-quell. Monatsschrift für Volkskunde* (*At the Source. Monthly Journal for Ethnology*), he wrote about the 'Quälgeister im Volksglauben der Rumänen' ('Tormenting Spirits in Romanian Popular Culture'). In this piece he differentiated between the 'varcolac' (*vârcolac*), a term borrowed from the Greek by seventeenth-century Wallachian theological literature (see the section entitled 'The Vrykolakas among the Greeks in the Ottoman Empire' in Chapter 2), and the 'nosferat'.

According to Wlislocki, varcolac was the name given to unbaptized children who were stolen by witches, or to unbaptized youths and adults, whose mothers had neglected their Christian duties after giving birth. And in popular belief (again, according to Wlislocki), the moon was inhabited by varcolaci (plural), and they would cause lunar eclipses through their greed. They lay in their graves for seven years during the day, but would emerge at night, in the form of little black children, in order to drink people's blood. The victims would only die after the ninth visit of the varcolac. Protection was offered by incense, fennel, garlic or holy water. If one stuffed up the hole through which the varcolac gained entry into the house, he would lose his powers and transform himself into something in the form of straw. When this was burned, the varcolac would enter the afterlife. However, if this did not happen within a period of seven years, the varcolac would be banished to the moon and thrown into hell at the first lunar eclipse. Furthermore, there was also a belief that the seventh child of a family would transform into an animal at night and act as a bloodsucker.

A nosferat, by contrast, was the illegitimate child of a couple who themselves had been born out of wedlock. The nosferat would come to the world stillborn and would first become animated in the grave. A male nosferat visited women, and a female nosferat visited men. The nosferat would rob victims of their life force through sexual intercourse. Particularly endangered in this respect were newly married couples. The nosferat was held responsible both for unwanted pregnancies and for unexplained infertility, and would only drink the blood of older people.[149]

In contrast to Wlislocki, Elias Weslowski, the director of a technical school from Kimpolung (Câmpulung), which today lies in Northern Romania, on the border to Ukraine, but that at the time was in the Habsburg part of the Bukovina, focused entirely upon the *strigoi* (or 'strige' or 'strigoane'). According to his collection 'Die Vampirsage im rumänischen Volksglauben' ('Vampire Tales in Romanian Popular Belief'), published in 1910/1911 in the *Zeitschrift für österreichische Volkskunde* (*Journal for Austrian Ethnology*), the appearance of such a figure was to be expected in families in which either seven sons or seven daughters had been born consecutively. They would behave as humans during the day, but at night they would transform themselves and carry out harmful magic. Like the devil, the strigoi went about with a shaggy tail. Bound by magic and the art of sorcery, he possessed the abilities of a sightseer. On the night of St George, 23 April, he would participate in a witches' coven. He threatened the harvest, summoning either hailstorms or drought and also jeopardized marital harmony, seducing spouses. The strigoi was responsible for milk and eggs going off, and the female variant in particular would suck the blood of infants. To protect themselves, people would rub their stable doors with garlic and daub their houses with crosses of tar. Dead vampires were to be buried with their faces down, and further preventative measures included filling the mouth with garlic, piercing the heart or decapitation. Seven weeks after the burial, and then again after seven years, the dead person was to be exhumed and checked for any change in their position, so that the relevant measures could be undertaken where necessary. As with Wlislocki, Weslowski's synthesis seems to mix profane old wives' tales with real scenarios of threat.[150] In this context, the strigoi had to serve as an explanation for violations of the canon of moral values, for the death of newborns and for the failure of harvests. However, from an anthropological perspective, the title of 'vampire tales' does not seem to be justified.

Tales of Revenancy from Romania

Against the backdrop of this independent creation of a terminology, the Romanian tales of revenancy written down over the course of the twentieth century are also of interest, even though they have little to do with vampires in a direct sense.[151] Weslowski's recordings from the years 1910/1911 have two fundamental variants at their core: on the one hand, revenancy as a solution to social conflicts and, on the other hand, revenancy as a means for disciplining girls of a marriageable age. One story, set in the town of Sereth (Romanian Siret), bears the title 'Der Vampir und der Schmiedgeselle' ('The Vampire and the Blacksmith's Apprentice').

When a blacksmith's apprentice begins to lose weight, a soothsayer claims that the smith's wife is acting at night as a vampire and is using him as a saddle horse. The apprentice therefore throws a saddle over the woman and turns the tables. At night, at the edge of the village, he comes across a witches' coven, which finishes before the first crow of the cock. When the smith sees the horse in his garden the following morning, he initially wants to drive it away, but then agrees to shoe it, and to use it as a work animal. Due to the master of the house's concerns about his wife, the apprentice finally throws the halter over the horse once again, causing the missing wife to reappear, wearing horseshoes. Regardless of the fact that the couple have children, the woman is finally burned at the stake.[152]

Another tale from the region around Kimpolung (Romanian Câmpulung) is entitled 'Der Vampir als Kamel' ('The Vampire as a Camel').

A rich, but hard-hearted peasant is found dead in a forest. On the seventh day after his funeral, the local cattle begin to die. The source of this distress is revealed to be the devil, going about in the form of a bloodthirsty camel, and a stake of yew-wood is therefore driven into the corpse.

Whereas the first story characterizes a sneaky wife as a witch, the second denigrates an egotistical exploiter as a camel.[153]

The next two tales from Weslowski's collection are somewhat more profound. The title of the first is 'Das heiratslustige Mädchen' ('The Girl who was Eager to Marry').

In a deserted mountain village, a soothsayer announces a suitor to a girl. However, the gallant young man disappears abruptly at midnight. At their next meeting, marriage is already a topic of discussion. The young man then abducts the willing girl, taking her on horseback to an open grave in the cemetery. Only now does the girl attempts to free herself from the clutches of her abductor, who suddenly transforms into a skeleton. Having reached a chapel, the girl collapses to the floor, exhausted. Whilst the skeleton can still be seen outside the church, the girl is discovered inside, half-dead. Following a temporary recovery, she is able to relate what has passed, but she then wastes away before a year has passed. In his funeral eulogy, the priest warns the congregation to take care in dealing with young men.[154]

The second tale is entitled 'Das schöne Mädchen' ('The Beautiful Girl'). It is a narrative that also has a Slavic tradition (see the earlier section entitled 'Demonic Figures in East and East Central Europe'), and Kimpolung's proximity to Ukraine could have been instrumental in this transfer of motifs.

A distrustful girl will only accept a bridegroom 'from the other world'. One day, a handsome young man appears and converses with her up to midnight, placing an engagement ring on her finger before departing. Since the girl has her suspicions, she attaches a thread to him and, using this, is able to follow him back to the cemetery, where she throws the ring into the grave out of disappointment. At their next rendezvous, the revenant threatens that if she does not admit to this crime, her father will die, which, following her refusal, immediately comes to pass. At their next meeting, the same scenario is repeated, this time with the mother as the victim. In expectation of her own death, the girl takes her leave from her friends and asks to be buried outside of the cemetery. Following her death, these wishes are fulfilled and, shortly after her burial, a rose bush shoots up from the grave. At the patron festival of the Church, the rose is placed in front of the icon of the Mother of God, and is transformed back into the girl, who then retires to spend the rest of her life in a convent.

According to Weslowski, in a more brutal version of this tale, the girl's grandmother points out that, while a 'living vampire' is harmless, a 'dead vampire' is extremely dangerous.

This time, on the advice of her grandmother, the girl follows her suitor's tracks through the snow up to a chapel, where she discovers her potential lover chewing on a human bone. Since he recognizes the girl, he attempts to force a confession out of her on the following two nights, and causes first her father and then her mother to die. Seeing that there is no way out of this situation, the girl then takes her leave from her grandmother and begs the gravedigger that he not carry her body out of the door, but rather through a hole in the house wall, and that he bury her in a flowerbed in front of the house.

Shortly thereafter, a lily shoots up from the grave. Because of its beauty, the son of a prince who was passing plucks the flower and places it in his chambers. At night, the lily transforms into the girl. The prince awakes, liberates her and takes her as his wife. Their joy is only tarnished by the fact that the bride refuses to go to a church service. When the prince is finally able to convince her to do so, the revenant appears once again at the church portal, and kills the husband and their children. However, a village witch is able to bring the dead back to life using an elder-branch.[155]

The moral of these stories is at the same time both complicated and simple. All of them concern a girl of a marriageable age, who has not only been taken in by a perfect stranger, but who has also turned down unserious suitors from her own environment. Temptation by the demon always has a role to play, and in one case there is a radicalization of this figure as a cannibal. Furthermore, in the representation of the crossing of the threshold into the afterlife and back, the narrator is undertaking a daring manoeuvre between Church norms and the fantasies of the believers that depart from these. In this, priestly warnings and death stand on the one side, and reanimation and the renunciation of the world on the other. Since she wishes to avoid her own future revenancy, the girl views the cemetery as taboo. The dream visions are just as much about the desire for eternal rest as they are about the fulfilment of secret desires.

In 1926, in the journal *Folklore*, Murgoci cited several reports and tales taken from the journal *Ion Creangă* that had been published before the First World War by the Romanian writer Tudor Pamfile. These also echo motifs such as that of the evil stepmother. However, other horror stories were also spun around provocative girls. For example, at the turn of the twentieth century, an old woman who allegedly posed a posthumous threat to her relatives had died in the Oltenian village of Amărăști.

Several months after her death, an old woman was accused of having come back to attempt to claim first the children of her oldest son and then those of her younger one. Her sons therefore opened up the grave and carved up the old woman's corpse, but this did not prevent the children from continuing to waste away. When, at the next exhumation, the body was revealed not to have decomposed, they took it into the woods, tore the heart out, quartered it and burned it to ashes. They mixed these ashes with water and gave them to the children to drink in a potion, in order to bring about their recovery. Finally, they burned their mother's corpse.[156]

A tale from the town of Botoșani, which today lies in northeastern Romania, on the border with Ukraine and Moldova, offers a different variant of the motif of the girl with the ball of wool.

At a convivial gathering, an uninvited guest appears, who beguiles the girls present. Only one young woman remains suspicious. When she discovers a tail on the stranger's lower back, she flees into the forest with several sheets of linen. In a rage, the stranger kills the other girls, drinks their blood and tears apart their bodies, playing tricks with their body parts. He then hunts down the girl who has fled into the wood and orders her to go down into a cave with him. The girl allows him to go first, and then flees again, although not before stuffing the entrance to the cave with the sheets she had brought with her.

Lured by a light, she comes across a house, inhabited by a dead man who – unseen by the girl – comes to life at midnight. Whilst the exhausted girl sleeps through to the first crow of the cock, the bloodsucker, having discovered the girl's trail and followed her, enters into a struggle with the dead owner of the house. In this, the girl is initially able to escape with her wits intact. Enchanted by the beauty of nature, she returns unharmed to her parents and only then, in a mysterious manner, does she begin to suffer the fate of an undead person.[157]

In his 1982 article on 'The Romanian Folkloric Vampire' in the journal *East European Quarterly*, the American Slavist Jan Louis Perkowski cited numerous examples gathered from the material that the Romanian linguist Emil Petrovici had collected in the 1930s for an atlas of dialects, published in 1943. Alongside the documentation of all manner of preventative measures against vampires, two seemingly authentic cases stand out in particular due to their brutality.

In the Oltenian village of Ohabă, a dead person was accused in 1932 of having transformed themselves into a *strigoi* and of harassing women. The police did in fact find a bloated corpse. Attempts to reduce this back to a human size did not bear fruit, and neither a skewer nor a prod with a rifle could bring about any transformation. It was only eventually the mistreatment of the corpse with a knife by a woman who had been hired especially for the task that yielded any results. However, the informants remained silent about the extent of the desecration of the corpse.

In 1936, by contrast, a wedding with a vampire was supposed to have taken place in the village of Nucșoara in Muntenia, in the south of Romania. When the bride organized a church wedding, the secret vampire showed his teeth in front of the house of God. Naively, however, her mother interpreted this as a sign of love. Shortly thereafter, whilst visiting their daughter, the parents happened to see their son-in-law through the window, drinking her blood. As a result, he was shot.[158]

Whereas concerns for the chastity of girls of a marriageble age seem to have been the underlying theme of nineteenth-century Romanian revenancy tales, there also seems to have been a shift in focus at the beginning of the twentieth century towards issues of domestic violence. In this, the 'vampire' is given a sexual connotation, as impure and a violator. Thus, it was possible to express revenge and self-justice, at least in fantasy.

Vampirism among the Roma

The term 'gypsy', which has pejorative connotations, referred and refers to very heterogeneous populations groups, originating from northwestern India, and divided partly by clan and partly by profession, who settled in the Danube-Balkan region in the thirteenth and fourteenth centuries. In common practice, however, the self-designation of Roma (singular Rom, i.e. 'person') gradually established itself. Depending upon the respective form of rule, the Roma were marginalized to varying degrees by the societies of Southeastern Europe. Whereas they were situated on the bottom rung of the social hierarchy in the Kingdom of Hungary and the Ottoman Empire, at the same time they were also of use as craftsmen and taxpayers, whereas in Wallachia and Moldavia, up to the mid nineteenth century, they essentially had the role of slaves, forced to hire themselves out into the service of local large-scale landowners or the state. Under Maria Theresa, great attempts were undertaken in the 1760s to make the Roma of the Habsburg Empire sedentary and to assimilate them into the wider society. In fact, however, only a minority of Roma led a travelling existence. They often settled down on the margins of towns, where they were forced to perform so-called 'dishonourable' professions. Although, over time, they gradually assumed the religion or confession of their social environment, they nevertheless preserved their established customs.[159]

The Transylvanian-Saxon Heinrich von Wlislocki, who, following his studies at the University of Klausenburg (Romanian Cluj), worked as an educator, agriculturalist and writer, was considered to be the foremost expert on the Transylvanian Roma in the late nineteenth century. In 1883, this pioneer of modern Romani studies accompanied a group of travelling Roma in Transylvania and the Banat over a period of many months. He presented his observations in his works *Vom wandernden Zigeunervolke: Bilder aus dem Leben der Siebenbürger Zigeuner. Geschichtliches, Ethnologisches, Sprache und Poesie* (*On the Travelling Gypsy People: Scenes of the Life of the Transylvanian Gypsies. History, Ethnology, Language and Poetry*, 1890), *Volksglaube und religiöser Brauch der Zigeuner vorwiegend nach eigenen Ermittlungen* (*Popular Belief and Religious Customs of the Gypsies, Largely Based upon my Own Investigations*, 1891) and *Aus dem inneren Leben der Zigeuner: Ethnologische Mitteilungen* (*On the Inner Life of the Gypsies: Ethnological Reports*, 1892). In 1890, in his collection *Volksdichtungen der siebenbürgischen und südungarischen Zigeuner* (*Popular Literature of the Transylvanian and Southern Hungarian Gypsies*), he demonstrated the existence of a unique and orally transmitted popular folk literature among the gypsies.

As far as the conceptions of the afterlife among the Transylvanian Roma were concerned, Wlislocki identified a differentiated categorization of souls at the start of their journey into the realm of the dead: the souls of people who had died a natural death wandered the earth until the dissolution of the flesh from their bodies; the souls of those who had drowned were kept in pots by water spirits until their bodies decayed; and the souls of those who had been murdered entered into wild animals, and remained there so long as their murderer was still alive (the murderer's soul would then experience the same fate, but would be lost for centuries). Earlier, according to a no longer practised ritual, the dead had been decapitated after a certain period of time, and their head removed from their burial place and buried elsewhere, with a stake being driven into their empty grave. At the same time, a single post, just about peering over the surface of the earth, was driven into the soil above the dead skull. Wlislocki assumed that this was in order to keep a check on the decomposition of the corpse.

With regard to the fixation of the Roma on the human flesh in their conceptions of death, Wlislocki pointed out that the Transylvanian Roma had at times been confronted with accusations of cannibalism.[160] Against this backdrop, Wlislocki also outlined a type of revenant who was reminiscent in many ways of general vampire conceptions, but who largely avoided bloodsucking: the *mulo*. This would emerge from stillborn children and would not enter the realm of the dead until the age of thirty. He was composed entirely of flesh and did not have any bones, and had had to leave behind the middle finger of each hand in the grave. The mulo-folk lived in the mountains, where they hoarded the treasure they looted on their nightly raids. The mulo wreaked a great amount of havoc, in that they sat on the chests of the sleeping or threw stones at them. The mulo would also boil up the flesh of his fellow mulos once a year in order to maintain his powers. This was clearly connected with the belief that the flesh of a body without a skeleton could be conserved and stabilized.[161]

A fairy tale recorded by Wlislocki under the title of 'Das Mulo-Volk' ('The Mulo-Folk') went as follows.

A wise man offers the advice to a childless married couple, hoping to start a family, that they should drink water from a pumpkin during a waxing moon. However, the woman experiences a stillbirth, with the dead child condemned to an existence as a mulo. One year later, the couple climbs up into the mountains in order to liberate their child from the mulo-folk. Finally, they are led by a white mouse into a cave, which turns out to be a house. A mulo invites them to a dinner, which consists of the flesh of the child. The child is rescued when the mulo lifts him from the boiling pot and hands him to the father, safe and sound, except for a piece of flesh missing from the buttocks.[162]

Another story is entitled 'Die Hochzeit des Mulo' ('The Mulo's Wedding').

An orphaned girl grows up with her relatives – travelling gypsies – but is treated badly by them. One day, while he is searching for food in the woods, a family member disappears, and his wife therefore orders the girl to look for him. She loses her way, but sees a light, which is coming from a house in which it turns out a mulo wedding is taking place. On New Year's Eve (the only possible night), a mulo had abducted a woman, who he wishes to boil up, so that she loses her bones and herself becomes a mulo. By using jimson seeds, which have medicinal properties and are able to cause hallucinations, the young girl is able to drive the mulos away.[163]

At the heart of both tales is the motif of concern for the fate of young offspring, in one case in the form a married couple's childlessness and in the other in relation to the fate of an orphaned girl. When one considers that, in mulos, we are dealing with stillborns, the horror stories no longer seem coincidental. In contrast to vampires, mulos are given the status of a social group and are granted the right to a private life, and the grave therefore mutates from a treasure-cave into a cosy home. Whilst their life on earth is structured around the frictionless functioning of all parts of the skeleton, their existence in the transition to the other side centres upon the activities of the soul, clothed in the mantle of fresh flesh. In this, the boiling seems to take on the function of preservation. In the first tale, the mulo child is rescued by the pilgrimage of the father, and the consumption of the flesh provides life on a symbolic level – as in the Christian Eucharist – therefore raising the possibility of the reincarnation of the candidate of death. In the second tale, adult mulos enter the action. Like a creator God, in the boiling up of human flesh, they see a possibility to overcome their loneliness through creating a partner – just as, in the Old Testament, God created Eve from Adam's rib. The winding path that the transmission of such metaphors has taken has undoubtedly led to cultural misunderstandings, extending to accusations of cannibalism. The existence of a longer tradition in this respect is hinted at by the Transylvanian-Saxon Dracula stories of the late fifteenth century, in which gypsies were portrayed as victims, who were forced to eat their companions.[164]

Against this background, it should be questioned whether the 'Vampire' tales that the English writer Francis Hindes Groome published in 1890 in the *Journal of the Gypsy Lore Society* – that is, at the same time as Wlislocki's mulo tales – did in fact derive from the Romanian Roma. Groome translated the title of his story 'Čohano' (Romanian *ciohano*, actually 'sorcerer' or 'witch') as 'Vampire'.

A group of young people spend a convivial evening in a hut with an elderly woman. All manner of couples come together, with only Nina, the daughter of rich parents, remaining alone. Eventually, a young man shows up who proceeds to flirt with her up to the first crow of the cock. However, before he leaves the house, the old woman notices his horse-hooves. When the young man appears for a second time, the woman points out this peculiarity. The following night, Nina attaches a spindle of thread to the suitor, with the help of which she is able to follow him back to his grave the following morning. Terrified by what she has seen, she then remains away from the old woman's hut. After this, the čohano visits the house of Nina's parents and takes them to task. Since he cannot allow them to reveal his secret, the čohano kills first the father and then the mother. Before Nina's turn arrives, she gives her riches to the servants of the house and requests a burial in the woods, underneath an apple tree. So as to prevent its return after death, the body is not carried out through the door, but rather through a hole in the wall.

When a prince comes by on a hunt half a year later, he plucks a flower that has shot up from the grave in the meantime, and takes it with him. In his chambers, the flower transforms into the girl who, without his knowledge, lays down alongside him in the bed. At dawn, she transforms back into a flower. When the prince awakes in a trance time and again, his father begins to get suspicious and waylays the girl the following night. When she is discovered, she allows herself to be kissed by the prince and is thus liberated from her fate. They marry and she gives birth to a lovely child.

However, the čohano reappears, and kills both the prince and the child. However, it proves possible to destroy him by uttering the curse 'God send you an outbreak'. As he explodes, the stepfather tears out his heart, with which the girl, her child and her husband are all brought back to life, as, through the revenant's blood, are the girl's father and mother too.[165]

As is not difficult to make out, the motifs underlying this story are also evident in the Slavic and Romanian traditions (see the section entitled 'Demonic Figures in East and East Central Europe' above), and Groome was therefore likely to have doubted their Roma origins. However, the motifs of the flower-girl who, following her reawakening by a member of the elite, meets her downfall through the premature attendance of a church service, and that of the steadfast girl who first loses her own parents and then, following her own death, is carried out of the house under the threshold by the gravediggers are both already mentioned in the tales of a Hungarian Rom, who was stationed in Vienna as an infantry soldier in the 1860s. His tales were included in an anthology published as a draft version by the Vienna Professor Friedrich Müller in 1869 in the proceedings of the Imperial Academy of the Sciences.[166] In all these variants, the juxtaposition of clear and direct arguments on the one hand and the rough and indirect statements on the other is striking. This is true both with reference to family cohesion and social critique, and in relation to sexual innuendo and acts of brutality.

Either way, in the 'Čohano', Groome introduced a term into the expert literature that was also taken up by the Serbian ethnologist Tihomir Djordjević in his dissertation, submitted in Munich in 1902, on 'Die Zigeuner in Serbien' ('The Gypsies in Serbia'). Like their Orthodox cousins, the Roma believed that an honest man would be granted a peaceful death. Nevertheless, revenancy could be motivated by the need to put the affairs of this world in order posthumously, for example, by doing good deeds or by enacting vengeance. Alongside this, the conception also dominated that evil deeds carried out during a dead person's lifetime could hinder the separation of soul and body. However, in these cases, no reference is made to the lack of decomposition; rather, the belief was that the earth would spit great sinners back out.

Djordjević found a further peculiarity of the Roma belief-world in the preconditions for 'vampirization' or for the transformation of a dead person into a čohano. Alongside the underlying reasons, such as wicked acts conducted during their lifetime, and external causes such as an animal crossing a dead person's body, Djordjević also saw the affiliation to a so-called 'vampire-clan' as decisive for posthumous activities. In the first forty days after his death, a potential vampire would leave his grave in the form of another creature. When this creature had not been eaten by wolves before this time had passed, the vampire would then return as a human. According to an alternative interpretation, 'vampirization' signifies the rebirth of a man as a butcher, who does not require any scales to weigh his produce, being able to do so using his hands alone (see the section entitled 'Investigations in Eastern Europe' in Chapter 5). This echoes the falling-away of the flesh from the skeleton, which is consumed, in the case of humans, by Mother Earth or, in the case of animals, serves as food.[167]

In relation to these portrayals, one limiting element that can be highlighted is that there is not a clear enough distinction made between the vampire conceptions of the titular nation (that is, the Serbs) and the revenancy beliefs of the minority (in this case, the Roma). Regardless of this, the belief-world of the Roma has not been taken into consideration enough by modern vampirologists. Their conceptions of revenancy have played an important role in the transport network of cultural transfers that is undoubtedly deserving of further attention.

Notes

1. See Daniel Stone, *The Polish-Lithuanian State, 1386–1795* (Seattle, 2001).
2. See Alix Landgrebe, 'Wenn es Polen nicht gäbe, dann müßte es erfunden werden': *Die Entwicklung des polnischen Nationalbewußtseins im europäischen Kontext von 1830 bis in die 1880er Jahre* (Wiesbaden, 2003); Christian Pletzing, *Vom Völkerfrühling zum nationalen Konflikt: Deutscher und polnischer Nationalismus in Ost- und Westpreußen 1830–1871* (Wiesbaden, 2003); Thomas Serrier, *Provinz Posen, Ostmark, Wielkopolska: Eine Grenzregion zwischen Deutschen und Polen 1848–1914* (Marburg, 2005).
3. V.B. Antonovich, *Koldovstvo. Dokumenty – protsessy – issledovanie* (St Petersburg, 1877), 17/18, 105–12.
4. Ja. Sh. 'Ubiistvo upyria v Kievshchine vo vremia chumy 1770 goda', *Kievskaia starina* 28 (1890): 338–41.
5. Augustin Calmet, *Dissertations sur les Apparitions des Esprits, et sur les Vampires et Revenans de Hongrie, de Moravie, etc.*, newest revised and improved edn, 2 vols (Einsiedeln, 1749), vol. II, 218/219 (no entry in the edition of 1746); English translation: *Dissertations upon the apparitions of angels, daemons, and ghosts and concerning the vampires of Hungary, Bohemia, Moravia, and Silesia*, translated from the French (London, 1759), 326/327.
6. Benedykt Chmielowski, 'O upierach', in *Nowe Ateny albo akademia wszelkiej sciencyi pełna*, Part [1–]2 (Lwów, 1745–46), Part 3–4, 1754–56, at Part 3, 247–57.

7. Elzbieta Drużbacka, 'Sprzeczka z rożnymi zakonnikami o upirach, którym autorka tych wierszow wiary niedaie', in *Zbior rytmow duchownych, panegirycznych, moralnych y swiatowych W. JMci Pani Elzbiety Druzbackiey z Kowalskich skarbnikowey zydaczewskiey*, vol. I: *Zebranie rytmow przez wierszopisow żyiących lub nászego wieku zeszłych pisanych* (Warsaw, 1752), 297–304.
8. See [Louis Antoine Caraccioli,] *Lettres à une illustre mort décédée en Pologne depuis peu de temps: Ouvrage du sentiment, ou l'on trouve des Anecdotes aussi curieuses qu'intéressantes* (Paris, 1771), 92–99.
9. Louis Antoine Caraccioli, *La vie du pape Benoît XIV, Prosper Lambertini* (Paris, 1783), 192.
10. Jan Bohomolec, *Diabeł w swoiey postaci z okazyi pytania, jeśli są Upiory, ukazany*, Part I (Warsaw, 1772; 2nd edn Warsaw, 1775), 1–9; Jan Bohomolec, *Diabeł w swoiey postaci albo o upiorach, gusłach, wróżkach, losach, czarach, z przydatkiem o ukazywaniu się Duchow y odpowiedzią na zarzuty przeciwko pierwszey Części czynione*, Part II (Warsaw, 1777), 1–184.
11. *Rękopism X. Bagińskiego, dominikana prowincyi litewskiéj (1747–1784 r.)* (Wilno, 1854), 123.
12. 'Upior osobliwszy', *Pamiętnik polityczny y historyczny* 2 (1783): 74–77.
13. 'Aberglaube', *Schlesische Provincialblätter* 34 (1801): 186/187.
14. [Jan Potocki,] *Rękopis znaleziony w Saragossie. Romans wydany posmiertnie z dzieł Jana Potockiego*, vol. I. (Lipsk, 1847); French reconstruction in two volumes: *Manuscrit trouvé à Saragosse* (1804) and *Manuscrit trouvé à Saragosse* (1810), edited by François Rosset and Dominique Triaire (Paris, 2008), Version de 1804, 65/66, 222; Version de 1810, 65, 214.
15. 'Upiór', in *Wieczory badeńskie czyli powieści o strachach i upiorach Józefa Maksymiliana Hrabi z Tenczyna Osssolińskiego* (Kraków, 1852), 86–89; reprint: Warsaw, 1970, 87/88.
16. Adam Mickiewicz, *Die Ahnenfeier. Ein Poem. Zweisprachige Ausgabe*, ed. Walter Schamschula (Cologne, 1991), 41–47, 58/59, 92/93, 186/187, 240–43.
17. Adam Mickiewicz, *Les slaves: Cours professé au Collège de France (1840–1841)*, 5 vols (Paris 1849), vol. I, 202–4, 308–10; German edn: *Vorlesungen über slawische Literatur und Zustände: Gehalten im Collège de France in den Jahren von 1840–1842*, 4 vols (Leipzig/Paris, 1843–45), vol. I, 171/172, 279–81.
18. Kazim[ierz] Wład[ysław] Wójcicki, 'Czerwony iak Upior', in *Przysłowia narodowe*, vol. I (Warsaw, 1830), 143–63.
19. See *Klechdy, starożytne podania i powieści ludu Polskiego i Rusi: Zebrał in spisał Kazimierz Władysław Wójcicki*, 2 vols (Warsaw, 1837), 8; extended version: *Wybór i opracowanie Ryszarda Wochciechowskiego, słowo wstępne Juliana Krzyżanowskiego* (Warsaw, 1972), 249–52.
20. See Barbara Dettke, *Die asiatische Hydra: Die Cholera von 1830/31 in Berlin und den preußischen Provinzen Posen, Preußen und Schlesien* (Berlin, 1995); Olaf Briese, *Angst in Zeiten der Cholera*, vol. I: *Über kulturelle Ursprünge des Bakteriums: Seuchen-Cordon I. I*, vol. II: *Panik-Kurve: Berlins Cholerajahr 1831/32. Seuchen-Cordon II*, vol. III: *Auf Leben und Tod: Briefwelt als Gegenwelt. Seuchen-Cordon III*, vol. IV: *Das schlechte Gedicht: Strategien literarischer Immunisierung. Seuchen-Cordon IV* (Berlin, 2003).
21. Józef Gluziński, 'Włościanie polscy uważani pod względem charakteru, zwyczajów, obyczajów i przesądów z dołączeniem przysłowiów powszechnie używanych (z rękopismu)', in Kazimierz Władysław Wójcicki (ed.), *Archiwum domowe do dziejów i literatury krajowej z rękopismów I dzieł najrzadszych* (Warsaw, 1856), 393–575, at 521–26.

22. Joseph Lompa, 'Schlesien in slavisch-mythologischer Hinsicht', *Schlesische Provinzialblätter* 1 (1862): 393–96.
23. Oskar Kolberg, *Lud: Jego zwyczaje, sposób życia, mowa, podania, przysłowia, obrzędy, gusła, zabawy, pieśni, muzyka i tańce*, Series VII, *Krakowskie*, Part III (Kraków, 1874; reprint 1962), 63–75.
24. Oskar Kolberg, *Lud: Jego zwyczaje, sposób życia, mowa, podania, przysłowia, obrzędy, gusła, zabawy, pieśni, muzyka i tańce*, Series XV, *W. Ks. Pozańskie*, Part VII (Kraków, 1882; reprint 1962), 35–44; Series XVII, *Lubelskie*, Part II (Kraków, 1884; reprint 1962), 94–100.
25. *Sagen und Erzählungen aus der Provinz Posen*, collected by Otto Knoop (Posen, 1893), 138/139.
26. Otto Knoop, 'Sagen aus Kujawien', *Zeitschrift des Vereins für Volkskunde* 15 (1905): 102–5; 16 (1906): 96–100, at Nr. 16, 96.
27. Ibid., 96/97.
28. *Lud rolniczo-górniczy z okolic Sławkowa w powiecie Olkuskim*, described by Stanisław Ciszewski (Kraków, 1887); another edition in *Zbiór Wiadomości do Antropologii Krajowej* 10 (1886): 187–336; 11 (1887): 1–129, at Nr. 16, 12.
29. Ignaja Piątkowska, 'Jak sobie lud wyobraża istoty świata nadprzyrodzonego', *Wisła. Miesięcznik gieograficzny i etnograficzny* 15 (1901): 501–4, at 504.
30. Stanisław Wasylewski, 'W sprawie wampiryzmu', *Lud. Organ Towarzystwa Ludonznawczego w Lwowie* 12 (1907): 291–98, at 296/297.
31. See Philipp Ther, 'Deutsche Geschichte als imperiale Geschichte: Polen, slawophone Minderheiten und das Kaiserreich als kontinentales Empire', in Sebastian Conrad and Jürgen Osterhammel (eds), *Das Kaiserreich transnational. Deutschland und die Welt 1871–1914* (Göttingen, 2004), 129–48; Helmut Walser Smith, 'An Preußens Rändern oder: Die Welt, die dem Nationalismus verloren ging', in Sebastian Conrad and Jürgen Osterhammel (eds), *Das Kaiserreich transnational: Deutschland und die Welt 1871–1914* (Göttingen, 2004), 149–69.
32. Adam Mickiewicz, *Księgi narodu polskiego i pielgrzymstwa polskiego* (Paris, 1832), 23; English translation: *The Books and the Pilgrimage of the Polish Nation* (London, 1833), 21; Heinrich von Sybel, *Geschichte der Revolutionszeit von 1789 bis 1795* (Düsseldorf, 1860), vol. 3, 313; reprint: *Geschichte der Revolutionszeit 1789–1800* (Stuttgart, 1898), vol. 5, 158.
33. W.J.A. von Tettau/J.D.H. Temme, *Die Volkssagen Ostpreußens, Litthauens und Westpreußens* (Berlin, 1837; revised edn Berlin, 1865; reprint Hildesheim, 1994), 275–77.
34. Ludwig Bechstein, *Deutsches Sagenbuch* (Leipzig, 1853), 214–17; Adolf Wuttke, *Der deutsche Volksaberglaube der Gegenwart* (Berlin, 1860), 221.
35. Wilhelm Mannhardt, 'Über Vampyrismus', *Zeitschrift für deutsche Mythologie und Sittenkunde* 4 (1859), 259–82, at 260, 265, 274.
36. Adolf Wuttke, *Der deutsche Volksaberglaube der Gegenwart*, 2nd edn (Berlin, 1869), 257, 261, 449; 3rd edn by Elard Hugo Meyer (Berlin, 1900), 274, 278, 479; 4th edn (Leipzig, 1925), 274, 278, 479.
37. Wilhelm Mannhardt, *Die praktischen Folgen des Aberglaubens, mit besonderer Berücksichtigung der Provinz Preußen* (Berlin, 1878), 6, 11, 28.
38. Stefan Hock, *Die Vampyrsagen und ihre Verwertung in der deutschen Literatur* (Berlin, 1900; reprint Hildesheim, 1977), 24.
39. Richard Kühnau, *Schlesische Sagen*, vol. I: *Spuk- und Gespenstersagen*, vol. II: *Elben-, Dämonen- und Teufelssagen*, vol. III: *Zauber-, Wunder- und Schatzsagen*, vol. IV: *Regis-*

ter (Leipzig, 1910–1913), vol I, XXXII/XXXIII. See also 'V. Vampirsagen' in vol. I, 148–99.
40. Tettau/Temme, *Die Volkssagen Ostpreußens, Litthauens und Westpreußens*, 275–77.
41. Leo Gerschke, 'Vom Vampirglauben im alten Westpreußen', *Westpreußen-Jahrbuch* 12 (1962): 89–94.
42. F[riedrich] C[hristian] Oppenhoff (ed.), *Die Rechtsprechung des königlichen Ober-Tribunals und des königlichen Ober-Appelations-Gerichts in Strafsachen* (Berlin, 1871), vol. 12, 78–80.
43. Carus Sterne, 'Der Vampyr-Schrecken im neunzehnten Jahrhundert', *Die Gartenlaube. Illustrirtes Familienblatt* 34 (1873): 555–558; 35 (1873): 569–571; 37 (1873): 598–600, at (1873): 555–57; Mannhardt, *Die praktischen Folgen des Aberglaubens*, 17. See also F[riedrich] C[hristian] Oppenhoff (ed.), *Die Rechtsprechung des königlichen Ober-Tribunals und des königlichen Ober-Appelations-Gerichts in Strafsachen* (Berlin, 1872), vol. 13, 310.
44. Friedrich S. Krauss, 'Vampirglaube in Serbien und Lithauen', *Mittheilungen der Anthropologischen Gesellschaft in Wien* 17 (1887): 67/68.
45. Albert Hellwig, *Verbrechen und Aberglaube: Skizzen aus der volkskundlichen Kriminalistik* (Leipzig, 1908), 26/27.
46. Albert Hellwig, 'Deutscher Volksglaube vor Gericht', *Archiv für Religionswissenschaft* 18 (1915): 287–300, at 293/294.
47. Karl Haupt, *Sagenbuch der Lausitz*, Part I: *Das Geisterreich*, Part II: *Die Geschichte* (Leipzig, 1862–63; photomechanical reprint Bautzen, 1991), 66–68.
48. See Michael Farin (ed.), *Heroine des Grauens: Wirken und Leben der Elisabeth Báthory in Briefen, Zeugenaussagen und Phantasiespielen*, 3rd, corrected and extended edn (Munich, 2003).
49. *Wendische Sagen, Märchen und abergläubische Gebräuche*, collected and retold by Edmund Veckenstedt (Graz, 1880), 131–38, 327–331, 354/355.
50. *Volkssagen, Erzählungen, Aberglauben, Gebräuche und Märchen aus dem östlichen Hinterpommern*, collected by Otto Knoop (Posen, 1885), 82–85.
51. Hans B. Meyer, *Das Danziger Volksleben* (Würzburg, 1956), 165.
52. 'Choleramärchen aus Oberschlesien'. Presented by Konst. Baster, *Schlesische Provinzialblätter* 77/New Series 12 (1873): 448/449.
53. Karl Klings, 'Die Seiga', *Oberschlesien, Zeitschrift zur Pflege und Kenntnis und Vertretung der Interessen Oberschlesiens* 3 (1904): 27–45.
54. Hellwig, *Verbrechen und Aberglaube*, 22–28, quote at 24.
55. A. Levenstim, *Sueverie i ugolovnoe pravo* (St Petersburg, [1897]), 69–79.
56. A.N. Afanas'ev, 'Nechistyi', in *Narodnye russkie skazki*, vol. VI (Moscow, 1862), no. 66, 326–31.
57. A.N. Afanas'ev, *Poeticheskie vozzreniia slavian na prirodu. Opyt sravnitel'nogo izucheniia slavianskikh predanii i verovanii v sviazi s mificheskimi skazaniiami drugikh rodstvennykh narodov*, 3 vols. (Moscow, 1865–1869), vol. III, 557–587.
58. A.N. Afanas'ev, 'Upyr', in *Narodnye russkie skazki*, Book III, 2nd edn (Moscow, 1873), no. 206, 274–79.
59. W.R.S. Ralston, *The Songs of the Russian People, as illustrative of Slavonic Mythology and Russian Social Life* (London, 1872), 290–324, in particular 309, 320–21.
60. A.N. Malinka [Oleksandr Nikiforovič], *Ukrainische Dämonologie: Überlieferte Ursprünge und kultisches Brauchtum der Hexen und Hexer über das Leben der Toten, der Geister, Werwölfe und Vampire*, 2nd edn (Leipzig, 2005), 71–75.

61. P.S. Efimenko, 'Upyri. (Iz istorii narodnykh verovanii)', *Kievskaia starina* 6 (1883): 371–79, at 374/375.
62. Ibid., 375/376.
63. K. Koshovik, 'Zhivoj upyr' v bor'be s umershimi upyriami', *Kievskaia starina* 8 (1884): 169–71.
64. Andrzéj Podbereski, 'Materyjały do Demonologii ludu ukraińskiego. Z opowiadań w powiecie Czehryńskim', *Zbiór wiadomości do antropologii krajowéj* 4 (1880): 3–82, at 9–29.
65. B.D. Grinchenko, *Etnograficheskie materialy, sobrannye v Chernigovskoi i sosednikh s nei guberniiakh*, vol. 1: *Raszkazy, skazki, predaniia, poslovitsy, zagadki i pr.* (Chernigov, 1895), no. 86, 52–56.
66. B.D. Grinchenko, *Iz ust naroda. Malorusskie rasskazy, skazki i pr.* (Chernigov, 1900), no. 170, 133/134.
67. Iul'jan Iavorskii, 'Galitsko-russkie poveriia ob opyrjakh', *Zhivaia starina* 7(1) (1897): 107–10, at 107/108.
68. [Bronisław Gustawicz,] 'Kilka szczegółów ludonnawczych z powiatu bobreckiego. Zebrał Bronisław Gustawicz', *Lud. Organ Towarzystwa Ludonznawczego w Lwowie* 8(1) (1902): 265–74, at 270/271.
69. Antoni Siewinski, 'Opowiadania ludu w powiecie sokalskim i buczackim', *Lud. Organ Towarzystwa Ludonznawczego w Lwowie* 12(1) (1906): 250–63, at 252/253.
70. Levenstim, *Sueverie i ugolovnoe pravo*, 73/74.
71. P.P. Demidovich, 'Iz oblasti verovanii i skazanii belorussov', *Etnograficheskoe obozrenie* 8(1) (1896): 91–120; 8(2/3) (1896): 107–45, at 140–42.
72. See Suraiya Faroqhi, *Geschichte des Osmanischen Reiches* (Munich, 2000), 84–111.
73. Edgar Hösch, *Geschichte des Balkans* (Munich, 2004), 55–61.
74. See Friedrich S. Krauss, 'Der Tod in Sitte, Brauch und Glauben der Südslaven. Vorwiegend nach eigenen Ermittlungen', *Zeitschrift des Vereins für Volkskunde* 1 (1891): 148–63; 2 (1892): 177–89; Emanuel Lilek, 'Familien- und Volksleben in Bosnien und in der Herzegowina', *Zeitschrift für österreichische Volkskunde* 6 (1900): 23–30, 53–72, 164–72, 202–25, at 61–68; G.F. Abbott, *Macedonian Folklore* (Cambridge, 1903; reprint Chicago, 1969), 192–210; E[dmund] Schneeweis, *Serbokroatische Volkskunde*, Part I: *Volksglaube und Volksbrauch* (Berlin, 1961), 83–99; Christo Vakarelski, *Bulgarische Volkskunde* (Berlin, 1969), 301–12.
75. See Julius Negelein, 'Die Reise der Seele in Jenseits', *Zeitschrift des Vereins für Volkskunde* 11 (1901): 16–28, 149–58, 263–71; Julius Negelein, 'Macedonischer Seelenglaube und Totenkultus', *Zeitschrift des Vereins für Volkskunde* 14 (1904): 19–35; Milenko S. Filipovič, 'Die Leichenverbrennung bei den Südslawen', *Wiener völkerkundliche Mitteilungen* 10/New Series 5(1–4) (1962): 61–71.
76. Emilijan Lilek, 'Etnološki pabirci po Bosni i Hercegovini', *Glasnik Zemaljskog muzeja u Bosni i Hercegovini* 11 (Sarajevo, 1899): 700–21, at 702–5.
77. See Ioannis Zelepos, *Kleine Geschichte Griechenlands: Von der Staatsgründung bis heute* (Munich, 2014).
78. *Viaggio in Grecia di Saverio Scrofani siciliano fatto nell'anno 1794, 1795*, 2 vols (Londra, 1799), vol. 1, 156–58.
79. Ioannis Zelepos, 'Vampirglaube und orthodoxe Kirche im osmanischen Südosteuropa: Ein Fallbeispiel für die Ambivalenzen vorsäkularer Rationalisierungsprozesse', in Andreas Helmedach et al. (eds), *Das osmanische Europa: Methoden und Perspektiven der Frühneuzeitforschung zu Südosteuropa* (Leipzig 2014), 363–79, at 377.

80. William Martin Leake, *Travels in Northern Greece*, 4 vols (London, 1835–41; reprint (Amsterdam, 1967), vol. IV, 216/217.
81. Robert Pashley, *Travels in Crete*, 2 vols (London, 1837; reprint Athens, 1989), vol. II, 196–219.
82. C.T. Newton, *Travels and Discoveries in the Levante*, 2 vols (London, 1865), vol. I, 212/213.
83. Bernhard Schmidt, *Das Volksleben der Neugriechen und das hellenische Altertum*, Part I (Leipzig, 1871), 159–71.
84. John Cuthbert Lawson, *Modern Greek Folklore and Ancient Greek Religion: A Study in Survivals* (Cambridge, 1910; reprint New York, 1964), 435, 461/462.
85. *Griechische Märchen, Sagen und Volkslieder*, collected, translated and explained by Bernhard Schmidt (Leipzig, 1877), 139/140.
86. George Horton, *Home of Nymphs and Vampires: The Isles of Greece* (Indianapolis, 1929), 109–21.
87. Konstantinos, *Vampires: The Occult Truth* (St Paul, MN, 1996), 52–58.
88. B. Demetracopoulou Lee, 'Greek Accounts of the Vrykolakas', *Journal of American Folklore* 55(21) (1942): 126–32.
89. Georg Eckert and P.E. Formozis, *Mazedonischer Volksglaube: Magie, Aberglaube und religiöse Vorstellungen in Saloniki und der West-Chalkidike* (Thessaloniki, 1943), 46–48.
90. Georg Eckert and P.E. Formozis, *Geister- und Dämonenglaube im Pontos* (Thessaloniki, 1943), 5–11.
91. See Ludwig Steindorff, *Kroatien. Vom Mittelalter bis zur Gegenwart* (Regensburg, 2001); Holm Sundhaussen, *Geschichte Serbiens. 19.–21. Jahrhundert* (Vienna, 2007).
92. See Robin Harris, *Dubrovnik: A History* (London, 2003).
93. Ante Liepopili, 'Vukodlaci', *Zbornik za narodni život i običaje južnih slavena* 23 (1918): 277–90; English translation in Jan L. Perkowski, *The Darkling: A Treatise on Slavic Vampirism* (Columbus, 1989), 85–102.
94. Alberto Fortis, *Viaggio in Dalmazia*, 2 vols (Venezia, 1774; reprint Munich, 1974), vol. I, 63–67; English translation: *Travels into Dalmatia. Containing General Observations on the Natural History of that Country and the Neighboring Islands; the Natural Productions, Arts, Manners and Customs of the Inhabitants: in a Series of Letters* (London, 1778), 61–64.
95. V. Jagić, 'Vukòdlak – Kodlàk vor Gericht', *Archiv für slavische Philologie* 6 (1882): 618–20.
96. Stjepan Banović, 'Vukodlaci', *Zbornik za narodni život i običaje Južnih Slavena* 26 (Zagreb, 1928): 347–57.
97. See Leopold Ranke, *Die serbische Revolution: Aus serbischen Papieren und Mittheilungen* (Hamburg, 1829), 32; 2nd edn (Berlin, 1844), 63/64.
98. See Tihomir R. Đorđević, 'Gradja za srpske narodne običaje iz vremena prve vlade kneza Miloša (Druga zbirka)', *Srpski etnografski zbornik* 19 (1913): 443–67, at 464–65; John V. A. Fine Jr., 'In Defense of Vampires: Church/State Efforts to Stop Vigilante Actions against Vampires in Serbia During the First Reign of Miloš Obrenović', *East European Quarterly* 21 (1987): 15–23, in particular 16/17; reprinted in Alan Dundes (ed.), *The Vampire. A Casebook* (Madison, WI, 1998), 57–66, in particular 58/59.
99. Joakim Vujić, *Putešestvije po Serbiji* (Buda, 1828), 181–87; reprint (Gornji Milanovac, 1999), 116–121.

100. M.Đ. Milićević, *Kraljevina Srbija. Novi krajevi* (Beograd, 1884), 154–58.
101. Veselin Čajkanović, 'Ubijanje vampire', *Srpski književni glasnik* 9 (1923): 268–84, reprinted in Veselin Čajkanović, *Sabrana dela iz srpske religije i mitologije*, Book I: *Studije iz srpske religije i folklore* (Beograd, 1994), 221–39; translation: 'The Killing of a Vampire', *Folklore – Forum* 7 (1974), 260–71, reprinted in Dundes (ed.), *The Vampire*, 72–84.
102. See *Narodne srpske pripovijetke*, collected and edited by Vuk Stef. Karadžić (Vienna, 1853).
103. Friedrich S[alomon] Krauss, *Sagen und Märchen der Südslaven: Zum Teil aus ungedruckten Quellen*, vol. I (Leipzig, 1883), Nr. 70, 293–96.
104. Ibid., vol. II (Leipzig, 1884), no. 146, 383.
105. *Tausend Sagen und Märchen der Südslaven*, collected and rendered in German by Friedrich S. Krauss, vol. 1 (Leipzig, 1914; reprint Paderborn, 2012), no. 211, 384.
106. Friedrich Salomo Krauss, *Volkserzählungen der Südslaven: Märchen und Sagen, Schwänke, Schnurren und erbauliche Geschichten*, ed. Raymond L. Burt and Walter Puchner (Vienna, 2002), no. 88, 178–80.
107. Ibid., no. 136, 254–58.
108. Ibid., no. 137, 258/259.
109. Friedrich S. Krauss, *Slavische Volksforschungen: Abhandlungen über Glauben, Gewohnheitsrechte, Sitten, Bräuche und die Guslarenlieder der Südslaven* (Leipzig, 1908), 118.
110. Ibid., 134/135.
111. See Hans-Joachim Härtel and Roland Schönfeld, *Bulgarien. Vom Mittelalter bis zur Gegenwart* (Regensburg, 1998).
112. See Fikret Adanır, *Die Makedonische Frage. Ihre Entstehung und Entwicklung bis 1908* (Wiesbaden, 1979).
113. See Michael Ursinus, 'Osmanische Lokalbehörden der frühen Tanzimat im Kampf gegen Vampire? Amtsrechnungen (masārıf defterleri) aus Makedonien im Lichte der Aufzeichnungen Marko Cepenkovs (1829–1920)', *Wiener Zeitschrift für die Kunde des Morgenlandes* 82 (1992): 359–74.
114. See Marko K. Cepenkov, *Makedonski narodni umotvorbi vo deset knigi*, Book 9: *Narodni veruvanja. Detski igri*, ed. Kiril Penušliski and Leposava Spirovska (Skopje, 1972), nos. 523–29, 112–22.
115. Quoted from Adolf Strausz, *Die Bulgaren: Ethnographische Studien* (Leipzig, 1898), 190–92.
116. Quoted from August Leskien (ed.), *Balkanmärchen: Aus Albanien, Bulgarien, Serbien und Kroatien* (Jena, 1925), no. 12, 48–54.
117. Quoted from ibid., 192–94; Wolfgang Eschker (ed.), *Mazedonische Volksmärchen* (Düsseldorf, 1972), no. 25, 93–97. See also a simplified version in *Tausend Sagen und Märchen der Südslaven*, vol. II, no. 77, 147.
118. Zeynep Aycibin, 'Osmanlı Devleti'nde Cadılar Üzerine Bir Değerlendirme', *OTAM* (Ankara Üniversitesi Osmanlı Tarihi Araştırma ve Uygulama Merkezi Dergisi) 24 (2008), 55–70, in particular 59. See also R[obert] Walsh, *A Residence at Constantinople During a Period Including the Commencement, Progress, and termination of the Greek and Turkish Revolutions* (London, 1836), vol. I, 464. In another report, Walsh even asserts that the Sultan accused janissaries, who were buried in Constantinople, to be vampires. See Thomas Allom and Robert Walsh, *Constantinople and the Scenery of The Seven Churches of Asia Minor*, 2 vols (London, c. 1839).

119. See Zakhari Stoianov, *Zapiski po bŭlgarskite vŭstaniia*, vols I–II, *Razkaz na ochevidtsi. 1870–1876*, vol. III, *Zatvorite* (Plovdiv, 1884–92).
120. Ibid., vol. 1, 28–30.
121. Ibid., 160/161. See also S[ain]t Clair, S[tanislas] G [Graham] B[ower] and Charles A. Brophy, *Twelve Years' Study of the Eastern Question in Bulgaria*, a revised edition of *A Residence in Bulgaria* (London, 1877), 29–33.
122. Constantin Jireček, *Das Fürstentum Bulgarien: Seine Bodengestaltung, Natur, Bevölkerung, Wirthschaftliche Zustände, geistige Cultur, Staatsverwaltung und neueste Geschichte* (Prague, 1891), 99/100.
123. Ibid., 100.
124. Strausz, *Die Bulgaren*, 188/189.
125. Ibid.
126. See Ekkehard Völkl, *Rumänien. Vom 19. Jahrhundert bis in die Gegenwart* (Regensburg, 1995).
127. See Harald Roth, *Kleine Geschichte Siebenbürgens*, 4th edn (Cologne, 2012).
128. Josef Stitzl, 'Der Morbus Hungaricus im Banat', *Medizinische Zeitschrift. Fachblatt der deutschen Ärzte in Rumänien* 11 (1937): 96–106, 147–56, at 98. Cf. Ingomar Senz, *Die Donauschwaben* (Munich, 1994).
129. Samuel Köleséri de Kereseer, *Pestis Dacicae anni M.DCC.IX. scrutinium et cura*. (Sibiui, 1709), 111–20. Cf. László András Magyar, 'Die siebenbürgische"Vampir-Krankheit"', *Communicationes de historia artis medicinae* 186–87 (2004): 49–62, at 53/54.
130. *Commercium litterarium ad rei medicae et scientiae naturalis incrementum institutum* (Nuremberg, 7 May 1732): 146–52.
131. Joseph Teutsch, 'Nachlese zu den kurzgefassten Jahrgeschichten von Ungarn und Siebenbürgen', in *Quellen zur Geschichte der Stadt Brassó*, vol. IV: *Chroniken und Tagebücher*, Part 1 (1143–1867) (Brașov, 1903), 403–89, at 409.
132. Ibid., 468.
133. Martini Martinus, *Dissertatio inauguralis practico-medica de daemonomania et variis ejus speciebus* (Vienna, 1782), 40–57.
134. L[udwig/Lajós] Baroti, 'Beiträge zur Geschichte des Vampyrismus in Südungarn', *Ethnologische Mitteilungen aus Ungarn* 3(1–2) (1893/1894): 219–21; Anton P. Petri, 'Zur Volkskunde der Banater Rumänen und Serben."Blutsauger" (Vampire) in den Aktenauszügen der Temeschburger Landesadministration 1725–1753', *Südostdeutsches Archiv* 4 (1961): 140–143.
135. Anton von Hammer, *Geschichte der Pest, die von 1738 bis 1740 im Temeswarer Banate herrschte. Ein aus glaubwürdigen Quellen geschöpfter Beitrag zur Geschichte dieses Landes* (Temeswar, 1839), 47. See also Anton Peter Petri, *Heimatbuch der Marktgemeinde Neuarad im Banat* (n.p., 1985), 30/31, 41–43, 410–13; Anton Peter Petri, *Beiträge zur Geschichte des Heilwesens im Banat* (Marquartstein, 1988), 273–78.
136. See '*Vossische Zeitung* (1738, Nr. 79)', in Eberhard Buchner, *Das Neueste von gestern. Kulturgeschichtlich interessante Dokumente aus alten deutschen Zeitungen*, vol. II: *1700–1750* (Munich, [1912]), no. 726, 344, reprinted in Eberhard Buchner, *Medien, Hexen und Geisterseher: Kulturhistorisch interessante Dokumente aus alten deutschen Zeitungen und Zeitschriften (16.–18. Jahrhundert)* (Munich, 1926), no. 211, 311.
137. Baroti, 'Beiträge zur Geschichte des Vampyrismus in Südungarn', 220.
138. Cf. Valeriu L. Bologa, 'Raportul din 1756 al unui chirurg german despre credițele românilor asupra moroilor', *Anuarul arhivei de folklor* 3 (1935): 159–68; László

András Magyar, 'Über die siebenbürgische Vampir-Krankheit: Ein Bericht des deutschen Chirurgen Georg Tallar aus dem Jahre 1755', *Zeitschrift für siebenbürgische Landeskunde* 25 (2002): 161–64; Ádám Mézes, 'Visum Repertum: Georg Tallar és az 1753-as Vámpírvadászat', in Gábor Klaniczay and Éva Pócs (eds), *Boszorkányok, varázslók és démonok Közép-Kelet-Európában* (Budapest, 2014), 109–54.

139. Georg Tallar, *Visum repertum anatomico-chirurgicum oder Gründlicher Bericht von den sogenannten Blutsäugern, Vampier, oder in der wallachischen Sprache Moroi, in der Wallachey, Siebenbürgen, und Banat, welchen eine eigends dahin abgeordnete Untersuchungskommission der löbl. k. k. Administration im Jahre 1756 erstattet hat* (Vienna, 1784), 15/16.

140. Ibid., 42, 54–56, 82. See also David Gömöry, *Dissertatio inauguralis physico-medica, sistens tentamen de indole aeris Hungarici* (Vienna, 1765), 61–66; Hußty, Zacharias Gottlieb (ed.), *Diskurs über die medizinische Polizei*, vol. 1 (Preßburg/Leipzig 1786), 157–65.

141. [Stefan Ignaz Raicević,] *Osservazioni storiche, naturali e politiche intorno la Valachia a la Moldavia* (Napoli, 1788), 234–39.

142. William Wilkinson, *An Account of the Principalities of Wallachia and Moldavia: with various Political Observations relating to them* (London, 1820; reprint New York, 1971), 17–19.

143. Emily Gerard, 'Transylvanian Superstitions', *The Nineteenth Century* 18(101) (1885): 130–50, at 142; Emily Gerard, *The Land beyond the Forest: Facts, Figures, and Fancies from Transylvania*, 2 vols (Edinburgh, 1888), vol. I, 319/320.

144. Arthur Schott and Albert Schott (eds), *Walachische Mährchen: Mit einer Einleitung über das Volk der Walachen und einem Anhang zur Erklärung der Mährchen* (Stuttgart, 1845), 297–99.

145. Mannhardt, *Vampyre*, 269–271.

146. Gerard, 'Transylvanian Superstitions', 142; Gerard, *The Land beyond the Forest*, 319.

147. Agnes Murgoci, 'The Vampire in Roumania', *Folklore. A Quarterly Review of Myth, Tradition, Institution and Custom* 37 (1926): 320–49, at 321, reprinted in Dundes (ed.), *The Vampire*, 12–34, at 13/14.

148. Gerard, 'Transylvanian Superstitions', 142; Gerard, *The Land beyond the Forest*, 319/320.

149. Heinrich von Wlislocki, 'Quälgeister im Volksglauben der Rumänen', *Am Ur-quell. Monatsschrift für Volkskunde* 6 (1896): 17–19, 60–62, 90–92, 108–10, 142–44, at 91/92, 108.

150. Elias Weslowski, 'Die Vampirsage im rumänischen Volksglauben', *Zeitschrift für österreichische Volkskunde* 16 (1910): 209–16; 17 (1911): 67–78, at 16 (1910): 209–11.

151. Cf. extracts from Raymond T. McNally, *A Clutch of Vampires: These Being among the Best from History and Literature* (Greenwich, CT, 1975), 189–194, as well as the retellings, directed at the American popular taste, to be found in Adriana Groza, *Transylvanian Vampires: Folktales of the Living Dead Retold* (Jefferson, NC, 2014).

152. Weslowski, *Vampirsage*, vol. 16, 211/212.

153. Ibid., 213/214.

154. Ibid., 214–16.

155. Ibid., vol. 17, 68–72. See an alternative version of the story 'The White Flower' in Groza, *Transylvanian Vampires*, 116–21.

156. Murgoci, 'The Vampire in Roumania', 324.

157. Ibid., 341–43.

158. Jan Louis Perkowski, 'The Romanian Folkloric Vampire', *East European Quarterly* 16 (1982): 311–22, at Text I, 312, and Text XII, 314, reprinted in Dundes (ed.), *The Vampire*, 35–46, at Text I, 36, and Text XII, 38/39.
159. See Viorel Achim, *The Roma in Romanian History* (Budapest, 2004). See also Dennell Spencer Wilson, 'The Gypsies' Belief in Vampires: A Historical Perspective', *Roma. Half-Yearly Journal on the Life, Language and Culture of Roma* 3(2) (1977): 8–13.
160. Heinrich von Wlislocki, 'Gebräuche der transsilvanischen Zeltzigeuner bei Geburt, Taufe und Leichenbestattung', *Globus* 51(16/17) (1887): 249–51 and 267–70, at 268/269, reprinted in Heinrich von Wlislocki, *Zur Ethnographie der Zigeuner in Südosteuropa: Tsiganologische Aufsätze und Briefe aus dem Zeitraum 1880–1905*, ed. Joachim S. Hohmann (Frankfurt, 1994), 245–59, at 253–55; Heinrich von Wlislocki, *Vom wandernden Zigeunervolke: Bilder aus dem Leben der Siebenbürger Zigeuner. Geschichtliches, Ethnologisches, Sprache und Poesie* (Hamburg, 1890), 296–99.
161. Heinrich von Wlislocki, *Volksglaube und religiöser Brauch der Zigeuner vorwiegend nach eigenen Ermittlungen* (Münster, 1891), 35, 39.
162. *Volksdichtungen der siebenbürgischen und südungarischen Zigeuner*. Collected from non-edited original texts translated by Heinrich von Wlislocki (Vienna, 1890), no. 27, 245–47.
163. Ibid., no. 28, 247–49.
164. See the Nuremburg print of 1488 and the undated Lübeck print (between 1488 and 1493) in Dieter Harmening, *Der Anfang von Dracula: Zur Geschichte von Geschichten* (Würzburg, 1983), 32–36, 118–26.
165. Francis Hindes Groome, 'The Vampire: A Roumanian Gypsy Story', *Journal of the Gypsy Lore Society* 2(3) (1890): 142–48, at 142–46, reprinted in Francis Hindes Groome, *Gypsy Folk-Tales* (London, 1899), 14–19.
166. Friedrich Müller, 'Beiträge zur Kenntniss der Rom-Sprache', *Sitzungsberichte der Kaiserlichen Akademie der Wissenschaften. Philosophisch-Historische Classe* 61(1) (Vienna, 1869): 149–206, at 152–59, 161–67; reprint: (Munich, 2011) (Lincom facsimile collection 1), 10–17, 31–37.
167. Tihomir R. Gjorgjević [Đorđević], 'Die Zigeuner in Serbien. Ethnologische Forschungen', part I, PhD. dissertation, Ludwig Maximilian University of Munich 1902 (Budapest, 1903), 68–71.

CHAPTER 5

Vampirism in the Modern Period

Investigations in Eastern Europe
Vampirism after the Second World War

Despite the comprehensive processes of modernization brought about, in particular, by state socialism, with its focused acceleration of industrialization and urbanization, it is possible to identify regions in Eastern Europe in which, after 1945, the traditional belief in vampires remained very much alive, beyond the Dracula stereotypes spread by the American film industry in Hollywood or the British Hammer Horror productions in London. However, in the vestiges unearthed by ethnologists, it becomes clear that harmful magic now only plays a role as an engaging subtext. In oral traditions, there was a shift in emphasis in terms of content, away from the fears about life-threatening plagues and catastrophes, and towards educational anecdotes about human transgressions and temptations. Through an exemplary depiction of certain cases, the following chapter will illuminate these developments from a variety of perspectives.

Greece

The transmission of Greek vampire tales beyond the horizon of the Second World War is covered in the 1970 work *The Dangerous Hour: The Lore of Crisis and Mystery in Rural Greece* by the ethnologists Richard H. and Eva Blum. In the reports by the public, the vrykolakas (here *vrikolakos* or *vrikolax*) appears as a harmful revenant, who sullied households and drank the milk from cows. Someone reported the following, which they had heard from word of mouth.

Following her death, a single woman had transformed into a vrykolakas and returned regularly at night in order to keep house. However, before leaving the house, she always urinated on the freshly baked bread. An associate of the narrator claimed that the dead woman had sat behind him on his horse at night.

When the rider sought to calm himself by lighting a cigarette, the dead woman disappeared again. Later a hole was discovered at her grave. So as to prevent further damage, a fire was lit upon her grave, and the priests also carried out various ceremonies.

The following tale was also doing the rounds.

A dead man visited his widow at night in order to conduct sexual relationships with her, and she subsequently conceived two children. However, the woman proved to be a gossip, who enjoyed nothing more than discussing others' infidelity. One night, she told her husband about the indecent behaviour of a bride who, in the absence of her groom, had had sex with the best man. Shocked, the vyrkolakas cried out 'This world is immoral ... may the earth swallow us all!', following which the entire family immediately disappeared.[1]

In both cases, the 'moral of the story' is extremely simplistic. The portrayals of harmful magic cover all the ambivalences that the performance of everyday family duties and the maintenance of Christian values entail.

Bulgaria

The vampire also carries out his nefarious deeds in the Bulgarian tales about demonic figures, collected from the 1970s by Evgeniia Mitseva from the Institute for Folklore in Sofia and published in 1994 under the title *Nevidimi noshtni gosti* (*The Invisible Night-Time Guests*). Among other things, he appears in the variant of the *talasŭm*. Mitseva claimed that she could identify the following stages in the development of the vampire: a young, still weak vampire disturbs the peace of a house by making a great deal of noise; in the next stage, he harasses and suffocates the sleeping, blowing on them like a bellows; finally, in the form of an animal, he destroys objects and drinks blood. All in all, however, because of their variety and contradictory nature, the statements cannot be reduced to a common denominator. Thus, in 1978, the mine-worker Stoian Dimitrov Saiakov, born in 1923, from a village near Blagoevgrad, informed Mitseva that a dead person, over whom a cat has sprung, usually begins to wander about as an invisible mischief-maker forty days after their death. By contrast, in 1981, Zdravka Dimitrovna Nesheva, an agricultural worker born in 1916 from a village near Svilengrad, informed her that vampiric machinations are the result of the confused wanderings of the soul, which can last for up to forty days after death. Within this timeframe, it is necessary to pierce the corpse through in order to prevent a return of the deceased person.[2] Beyond the contradictions between them, these statements reflect a certain banalization of the problem. In the depictions of contemporary witnesses, the vampire has been reduced to a fiend, who is only occasionally brought into connection with visions of horror.

Macedonia

In Macedonian popular culture, two species of vampire can be identified: the invisible spirit of a dead person and a corpse possessed by a foreign spirit. This emerges from the collection of interviews conducted in the 1970s and in the first half of the 1990s by the Institute for Folklore in Skopje and the Institute for Old Slavic Cultures in Prilep. These were published in 1988 and 1995 by Tanas Vrazhinovski under the title of *Vampirite vo makedonskite veruvania i predaniia* (*The Vampire in Macedonian Beliefs and Traditions*) and *Narodna demonologiia na makedontsite* (*National Demonology among the Macedonians*). The sources of posthumous activities are a wicked life or a disturbance in the transition to the afterlife, for example, through the responsibility to meet debts or the duty of social care. The belief in vampires therefore creates a bond between 'this world' and 'the other'. Under these preconditions, five types of vampire can be made out: the spouse or sexual partner, the good housewife or housekeeper, the harmful revenant person, the butcher, marked by his affinity to blood (see the section entitled 'Lost Souls in the Danube-Balkan Region' in Chapter 4), and the vampire who sometimes takes on animal form.

For example, Stoina Giorgiiova, born in 1894, from a village to the northeast of Prilep, recounted in 1969 the tale of a young man who had died at the age of seventeen or eighteen and had subsequently been transformed into a vampire.

Instead of drawing attention to himself in his home village, the alleged vampire joined up with a stranger and went to seek work abroad. There he found a job as a butcher and made a name for himself by slaughtering animals and carving up pieces of meat without either using scales or losing a drop of blood. One day he was recognized by visitors from his home village. They outfoxed the vampire by pricking his finger as he handed them their meat, and he then bled to death.

Also worthy of mention is the report, written down in 1987 in Toronto, told by Aleksandr Giamos, born in 1919 in Trnava – today a Serbian settlement on the border to Macedonia.

A stranger, suspected of vampirism, appeared in a village and offered his services to the villagers. It was only when he declared his intent to marry that the villagers began to worry, since this imperiled the salvation of the souls of the community's daughters. In order to catch the vampire and chase him off, they fell back upon a ruse, sending a woman into an open field with a wheat pitta bread, so as to entice him. However, before he revealed his true face, the appearance of wolves brought a premature end to the proceedings. A second attempt was therefore made and the son of a vampire was summoned from a neighbouring village to identify the revenant and render him harmless. He staged a wedding ceremony at which he shot the vampire, who had appeared to dance. However, the vampire did not bleed to death, but rather survived.

These tales are not about harmful magic. Rather, the first tale is, in the first instance, about the temptation to which a young person succumbs upon leaving the village, and the revelation of the identity that he had established for himself in his new place of residence. Whether or not the young man would have caused any harm in his home village seems to be irrelevant, given the shift of emphasis on to the depiction of his peculiar skills as a butcher. In the second tale, the vampire does not even appear as a fiend, and the concern is solely for the unmarried girls of the village. Clearly, the vampire, who is invisible for mere mortals, can only be destroyed when it is possible to extract his blood. Here then, the common depiction of the bloodsucker is turned on its head.[3]

Serbia

In the villages of southeastern Serbia, the belief in vampires also remained alive up to the collapse of the Yugoslavian state. At least, there is still quite a deal to be found in this respect in the collection *Kazivanja o nečastivim silama* (*Tales of Evil Forces*), gathered between 1967 and 1989 by the literary scholar and ethnologist Radoslav Radenković and published in 1991. In a story entitled 'Two Vampire Sons', a village community traces an outbreak of deaths among the local cattle back to the revenancy of a woman who had recently died in a neighbouring settlement. To help them, they hired two vampire sons, who were able to recognize and combat vampires. Armed with a rifle, they chased the revenant woman up a tree. As soon as she was shot down, she transformed immediately into manure, and thereafter the series of death among the cattle came to an end.

In the tale 'A Vampire Pilfers a Sack of Flour', a miller confronts an invisible thief. Since the miller was convinced that a sack had moved at night, as if moved by an invisible hand, he took the precautionary measure of marking a second sack with a cross. However, in so doing, he involuntarily drew down the curse of a vampire upon himself, although he could not be harmed directly. When the miller discovered traces of blood a short time later, this was traced back to a kid goat. Thereafter, the miller strung up garlic at the entrances to the mill, thus banishing the vampire.[4]

In these tales, the vampire merely represents a personification of the plague threatening the cattle or the harvest. Nevertheless, the people fall back upon traditional defensive measures, whether this was the use of sacred symbols, the administration of tried and tested household remedies or the use of modern weapons.

In 2009, in an investigation into *Banatsko selo* (*The Village in Banat*), conducted precisely in the neighbouring settlement to Kisiljevo in Vojvodina, in northeastern Serbia, where the existence of bloodsuckers had first been reported on in 1725 (see the section entitled 'The Discovery of the Vampire' in Chapter 3), the Serbian ethnologist Nikola F. Pavković stated that the belief in vampires was still alive. 'Nobody has seen them, but they do exist' seems to have been the generally stated conviction in Gaj and Dubovac on the opposite bank of the Danube to Kisiljevo. It is true that the threat of the vampire as such had disappeared in the meantime, and people thus restricted themselves in the prevention of revenancy to laying poppy seeds in the grave as burial objects, but tales were still rife that, whilst deliberately avoiding the term 'demon', discussed the despicable conduct of dishonourable dead persons.[5]

Croatia

Alongside ethnologists, other writers also testified to the vampire belief in the villages of Southeastern Europe resisting socialist modernity. For example, in the 1980s, vampire motifs also appeared in the work of the Croat Drago Orlić, from Istria, *Štorice od štrig i štriguni* (*Stories of Witches and Sorcerers*), a collection of tales written in the colloquial idiom.

In the tale 'Mother and Daughter Štrige and Ivan Krsnik', first published in 1986, the two women suck the blood of their son and brother.

When the wicked mother and daughter can no longer find any victims, because of the precautions taken by the village community, they fall upon Ivan, an army comrade of their relative who had come to visit. However, Ivan, whose Slovenian name 'Krsnik' means vampire-hunter, proves himself to be invulnerable, thanks to the remedies that he carries with him in his bag. Furthermore, he is also able to extract from the witches the secrets of the healing powers that might counter their bloodsucking. After he has gathered together the village community, the witches disappear up the chimney, never to be seen again.[6]

Orlić was interested in the horror stories of his home region as a literary subject and therefore referred to the motif of the Slovenian 'vampire hunter' (*krsnik*) (see the section entitled 'The Nachzehrer of the Early Modern Period' in Chapter 1).

Albania

In his autobiographical novel of 1993, *Të gjallët dhe të vdekurit e një fëmijërie: Botimi i dytë i plotësuar* (*There was a Village in Kosovo: The Living and the Dead of My Childhood*), the Albanian author Arid Demolli devoted himself both to the everyday idyll and to the horror stories of his Kosovan home town of Gllogovicë, lying on the border to Serbia. For him, vampirism was a matter for old wives' tales. A 'vampire' (*vampiri*; Albanian actually *lugát*) who emerged from its grave as a poltergeist was seen as threatening by Demolli precisely because it only existed in tales, and thus remained invisible. Whenever an old woman died, people would whisper about their transgressions during their lifetime and about changes to the state of their corpse. Happily, a 'vampire hunter' (*vampiraçi*; Albanian actually *dhampir*), the son of a lugát, armed with a firearm, would always promise assistance.[7] In his childhood memories, Demolli was primarily concerned with working through interpersonal conflicts and traumatic experiences.

Romania

In her 1986 Münster dissertation, which went further in terms of substance, but remains unpublished, Ioana-Maria Ionescu demonstrated, on the basis of interviews from the first half of the 1970s, that the farmers in a substantial part of Wallachia were still not aware of the term vampire in the Ceauşescu era. Instead, Ionescu cited the terms *strigoi* (masc.) and *strigoică* (fem.), derived from 'striga' (Latin 'witch'), as well as *moroi* (masc.) and *moroaică* (fem.), derived from 'mort' (Romanian 'death' or 'dead'). These are to be distinguished from the colloquial term *striga*, which designates a female demonic creature, which at times would rob domestic animals of their life force and at times torment suckling babies and make them cry. The turn of phrase 'living moroi' (*moroi viu*) denoted a person who, intentionally or unintentionally, had an 'evil eye', whereas the turn of phrase 'dead moroi' (*moroi mort*), by contrast, referred to a revenant in the strict sense.

Ionescu identified the 'attachment of the soul to the earthly' as the source of revenancy, whether this became evident through omens such as being born with a caul, whether through harmful magic or the evil eye, or whether through devilish possession and wicked deeds. As a consequence, the 'fate of the affected soul' demonstrated itself to be cruel in that its entry into paradise following death was impossible. Rather, the soul was forced to return into its nondecomposed body from sunrise to sunset. It remained dependent upon nourishment, which consisted either of the blood of humans or animals or their 'breath of life', or of certain seeds, in particular millet. The fatal consequences for those left behind are the spreading of infections or plagues, and the threatening of the harvests through drought or parasites, or the revenant returning to drag them into the grave. Hints that revenancy was at play were provided by nocturnal noises in the house, the subsiding of the soil on the grave and the appearance of a hole next to the cross on top.

To prevent the revenancy of suspected persons, it is necessary to stab through the navel or heart of the corpse with a pin – a measure that was only rarely practised, due to Church sanctions – or to stuff the mouth, nose and ears with gravel. The dropping of millet seeds behind the funeral procession also rendered the deceased person's posthumous activities difficult, as did the placing of garlic or thorny branches in the grave. Beyond this, there also existed the possibility of liberating the soul through summoning a brother or sister of fortune. Alongside garlic, the crucifix and calling on the name of Jesus also offered protection against revenants, as did guarding the house at night. A suspect could be identified by the shying away of a white horse (in other cases a black horse is mentioned), ridden over the grave on the night from Friday to Saturday by a person born on a Saturday. Where exhumation revealed a non-decomposed body, the heart was either stabbed through with a pin or taken out and either burned separately or with the entire body. The coffin was then sealed up again, with the mortal remains once again being doused with holy water.[8]

The popularity of such horror stories in socialist Romania is also demonstrated in the book *Were-Wolf and Vampire in Romania* published in 1982 by the American ethnologist Harry Anthony Senn on the basis of field research that he had conducted in 1977. One of the people he interviewed, in the settlement of Vîntere on the Hungarian border, in the west of the country, had the following anecdote to relate.

A notary's employee was accused of stealing milk. Initially, he declared his innocence and was outraged at the suggestion. He then lay in hiding at the alleged scene of the crime, hoping to catch the real culprit red-handed. In this manner, he discovered a strigoică who, in the form of a dog, had sucked the milk out of the cows. The man therefore rammed a pitchfork into the dog, which fled back, wounded, to his home, where he then died. Thereafter, the priest called upon the clerk to give a report. He commissioned him to buy new clothes, without concern for the price, to bury the strigoică (that is, the dog) and to keep watch for three days. On the first night, the strigoică left the grave without discovering the watchman, who had hidden behind a cross. On the second night, the watchman was able to hide behind an altar. On the third night, three witches showed up who, by combining their powers, were able to discover the clerk, but then had to return to their graves since the clock had already struck three o'clock. The man then fled back into the house and thus found salvation. He married and established a family.[9]

It is clear that this tale of the notary's assistant is an old wives' tale. A scapegoat is searched for in the undead person, upon whom the blame for a theft can be pinned. In this case, revenants were not bloodsuckers, but milk-drinkers. The references to a lawyer and a priest are striking, since through this, the unusual actions gain both state and Church sanction. The adventure in the church reveals an entertaining motif that is familiar from other vampire stories. Finally, fears about the nightly machinations of witches is a further central theme.

Poland

In the course of field research conducted in the 1980s in the northeast of Poland, in the context of a planned ethnographic atlas, it emerged that traditional conceptions about upióRs and strzygons were still very much alive, even if the modern mass media had brought about a certain dilution of this. Thus, those asked stated that a man who possesses two souls is predestined to become a vampire. A defence can be provided by giving a second name at birth or baptism. In the recital of suspicious factors, reference was also made to the stain of suicide and to unbaptized children, as well as to portents such as birth with a full set of teeth or with a full-cheeked and rosy face. Known defensive measures against revenancy included the placing of items in the grave, holy water and decapitation of the corpse. Less relevant, but nevertheless still alive, was the memory of the *zmora*, usually a woman who would transform her form at night and pester the living with choking and bloodsucking. The seventh daughter of a family was suspected of future mutation into a zmora, as were children whose baptismal vows had been spoken out incorrectly. One countermeasure was to keep the zmora away from the bed using sharp objects, and others were to smear the breasts with excrement, cause confusion through switching beds or bribe an evil spirit by preparing them breakfast.[10]

Belarus and Ukraine

A recently published book on *Narodnaia demonologiia Polesia* (*The Popular Demonology of Polesia*) mentioned 'walking dead' (*khodiachyj pokoinik*), who were supposed to have lived in the marshy region along the River Prypiat between Belarus and Ukraine. The editors Liudmila N. Vinogradova and Elena E. Levkievskaia summarize the results of an ethnological investigation undertaken at the end of the Soviet period, claiming that, in contrast to vampire beliefs, there was an absence of the demonic in Polesian revenancy conceptions. In view of the fact that Polesia is a region that, as the original homeland of the Slavs, is often attributed archaic characteristics, these results carry a certain political explosiveness. This was because, during the Brezhnev era, the marshes on the Belarusian side were drained on a large scale, whereas nuclear power stations were built on the Ukrainian side. Was this type of Soviet modernization in fact intended to bring about an end to superstition or a Russification of daily life in the region?

According to the editors of the Moscow anthology, it was less the 'bloodsucker' and much more the 'nachzehrer' that animated the minds of the Polesians. Strikingly, there is no term for the troublemaker among the locals. Those who had had contact with witches and sorcerers during their lifetime, or who had died before their time, or died an unnatural death were particularly suspected of acting as nachzehrers. As a rule, the affair was generally reduced to a dreamtime apparition, but it was also admitted that the phenomenon posed a direct threat to body and life. Usually the activities depicted were those of poltergeists, but revenants also appeared who aided their families. Alongside the widower, who sexually harassed his wife, the bridegroom who sought to carry his beloved with him into the afterlife also appears in these statements.[11]

The Roma in the Western Balkans

In a series of articles by Tatomir P. Vukanović on the belief in vampires among the Roma of Kosovo in Old Serbia and in the Sanjak of Novi Pazar, which appeared in the *Journal of the Gypsy Lore Society* at the end of the 1950s, as well as in Elwood B. Trigg's 1973 monograph *Gypsy Demons and Divinities*, the observations made by Heinrich von Wlislocki in the late nineteenth century concerning the boneless mulo (here mullo) were once again confirmed. Whereas Vukanović traces the variety of beliefs in the walking dead to animism – that is, to the belief that all phenomena in nature possess a soul – and saw in the 'vampire son' (Albanian *dhampir*) an institutional defence against evil spirits, Trigg speculates on the cult of ancestry in India as a factor motivating the belief in vampires.[12]

Attributions in Germany

The Depiction of 'Dark Forces' from the East

In 1959, out of concerns about occult moods that seemed to block the path of the German Federal Republic into the West, the former senior prosecutor Otto Steiner reflected on the lessons of history. Drawing upon Wilhelm Mannhardt, he attempted to shape public opinion through his discussion of *Vampirprozesse in Preußen* (*Vampire Trials in Prussia*), published by the Hamburg Publishing House for Criminal Literature. His primary interest was in the positions adopted by the courts in the trials against grave desecrators held in the early 1870s (see the section entitled 'Demonic Figures in East and East Central Europe' in Chapter 4). According to Steiner, the judges at the time held the preventative decapitation of corpses to be nonsensical superstition and prosecuted them with suitable severity. In this, however, they often had to overturn the decisions of lower courts, in which the criminal conduct was held to have been mitigated by superstitious beliefs. In order to overcome this contradiction, Steiner focused his studies on legal principles, hoping to demonstrate the deficiencies of Prussian legislation and document the progress West Germany had made in contributing to the 'disenchantment of the world' (Max Weber).

In his view, the threat came entirely from the East, and Steiner's standpoint in this respect was entirely unambiguous: one of the chapters in his book is entitled 'The Vampire Pushes over the Eastern Frontier into Prussia'. For Steiner, it was the new 1953 version of the Criminal Code of the Federal Republic of Germany that first offered an instrument against this superstition. The new law provided a comprehensive defence of the corpse, and common sense was raised as a yardstick for criminal responsibility, closing conspicuous loopholes in the law. However, the age of reason that this brought into effect was, from

Steiner's perspective, clearly threatened by the flourishing of 'Magia posthuma' in Eastern Europe.[13] His hope that the Germans would remain preserved from 'vampire maniacs' in the future was, paradoxically, crushed for trivial reasons. When the journal *Der Spiegel* (*The Mirror*) reported in July 1964 on the first vampire case in West German criminal history, it was not 'dark forces' from the East that it held to be responsible, but rather the Anglo-American stagings of Dracula.[14]

Debates over the Origins of Vampirism

In the Federal Republic, the vampire debates of 'Old Europe' not only found resonance in Steiner's treatise on the Prussian vampire cases; alongside this, there was also a protracted research controversy over the origins of the belief in nachzehrers, ignited by a new 1958 edition of the *Atlas der deutschen Volkskunde* (*Atlas of German Ethnology*). Drawing upon the results of a survey conducted in the 1930s, the ethnologist Günter Wiegelmann came to the conclusion in his 1966 paper in the *Zeitschrift für Volkskunde* (*Journal for Folklore*) that nachzehrer conceptions in Germany were based upon Slavic infiltrations. Wiegelmann grounded his thesis on two characteristics, which he held to be constitutive for popular belief in the regions on the other side of the Elbe-Saale line: the presence of dead spirits at the celebration of the funeral banquet on the one hand, and the high intensity of defensive measures against nachzehrers on the other.[15] By contrast, in her 1981 Supplementary Notes to the *Atlas der deutschen Volkskunde*, his colleague Gerda Grober-Glück claimed that the ritual of the funeral banquet ritual, celebrated during the laying-out of the corpse, was based upon the cult of souls, whereas the return of revenants to claim their relatives presupposed the activities of bodies after burial. Therefore, Grober-Glück posited the thesis that the development of a belief in nachzehrers in the German-speaking world emerged from genuine indigenous roots. In doing so, she also relativized the results of the survey from the 1930s by arguing that the belief in nachzehrers had already largely disappeared by this time.[16]

The controversy came to an early conclusion in 1990 in Thomas Schürmann's monograph on *Nachzehrerglauben in Mitteleuropa* (*The Belief in Nachzehrers in Central Europe*) (see the section entitled 'The Nachzehrer of the Early Modern Period' in Chapter 1). Schürmann investigated and depicted the phenomenon in all the diversity of its regional variants, thereby protecting himself against the accusation of ethnically tinged interpretations. At the same time, he also differentiated between moderate West German vampire conceptions and the more brutal expressions in the 'Germania Slavica'. In so doing, he characterized the leaving of the grave as a decidedly Slavic element. Without wanting to belittle the achievement of his sober representation, it is worth pointing to a map here, in which Schürmann differentiated the distribution of nachzehrer conceptions from that of vampire beliefs.[17] The optical impression seems to suggest two things: first, the area of Central Europe covered by the *Atlas der deutschen Volkskunde* suggests that there were only intermittent relicts of superstition in this area. Second, the shading of the nonresearched region of Eastern and Southeastern Europe stylizes these regions as a realm of vampirism. This territory stretches along the Sava and the Danube, via Serbia and Wallachia, from the Adriatic to the Carpathians, and then continues along the Dniester and the Dnieper via Galicia, Belarus and Lithuania, from the Black Sea to the Baltic (see Map 0.2).

Notes

1. Richard Blum and Eva Blum, *The Dangerous Hour: The Lore of Crisis and Mystery in Rural Greece* (London, 1970), 71/72. Cf. Evangelos Avdikos, 'Vampire Stories in Greece and the Reinforcement of Socio-cultural Norms', *Folklore* 124(3) (2013): 307–26.
2. *Nevidimi noshtni gosti*, selection and scientific commentary by Evgeniia Mitseva (Sofia, 1994), 18, 103/104 (no. 59), 104/105 (no. 60).
3. Leposava Spirovska and Tanas Vrazhinovski (eds), *Vampirite vo makedonskite veruvania i predaniia* (Skopje, 1988), 5–21, 80/81 (no. 64); Tanas Vrazhinovski, *Narodna demonologiia na makedontsite* (Skopje, 1995), 93–96, 117 (no. 85). Cf. L'upcho S. Risteski, 'Categories of the "Evil Dead" in Macedonian Folk Religion', in Gábor Klaniczay and Éva Pócs (eds), *Christian Demonology and Popular Mythology* (Budapest, 2006), 202–11.
4. Radoslav Radenković, *Kazivanja o nečastivim silama* (Niš, 1991), no. 40, 45; no. 42, 46.
5. Nikola F. Pavković, *Banatsko selo: Društvene i kulturne promene. Gaj i Dubovac* (Novi Sad, 2009), 597–600.
6. *Štorice od štrig i štriguni*, collected and edited by Drago Orlić (Pula, 1986; 2nd edn Zagreb, 2008), 75. Cf. Luka Šešo, 'O krsniku: od tradicijske pojave u predajama do svarnog iscjelitelja', *Studia ethnologica Croatica* 14/15 (2002/2003): 23–53; Tomo Vinšćak, 'On štrige, štriguni and krsnici on Istrian peninsula', *Studia ethnologica Croatica* 17 (2005): 221–35.
7. Arif Demolli, *Të gjallët dhe të vdekurit e një fëmijërie: Botimi i dytë i plotësuar* (Prishtinë, 2002), 65–74; German translation: Arif Demolli, *Es war ein Dorf in Kosova: Die Lebenden und die Toten meiner Kindheit*, from the Albanian by Basil Schader (Frauenfeld, 2011), 65–74. See also Robert Elsie, *Handbuch zur albanischen Volkskultur: Mythologie, Religion, Volksglaube, Sitten, Gebräuche und kulturelle Besonderheiten* (Wiesbaden, 2002), 47, 131/132, 139.
8. Ioana-Maria Ionescu, 'Rumänische Übergangsriten dargelegt am Beispiel der Lebensbräuche in Oltenien', Ph.D. dissertation (University of Münster, 1986), 510–19.
9. Harry Anthony Senn, *Were-Wolf and Vampire in Romania* (New York, 1982), 108. See also Hedeşan, Otilia, *Şapte eseuri despre strigoi* (Timişoara, 1998). Revised edition under the title *Strigoii*. 2nd revised edn (Cluj-Napoca, 2011).
10. Janusz Bohdanowicz, 'Demonologia ludowa. Relikty wierzeń w strzygonie i zmory', *Literatura ludowa* 2 (1994): 43–62.

11. *Narodnaia demonologiia Poles'ia. Publikatsiia tekstov v zapisiack 80-90-kh godov XX veka*, vol. I: *Liudi so sverkh-estestvennymi svoistvami*, vol. II: *Demonologizatsiia umershikh liudei*, ed. L.N. Vinogradova and E.E. Levkievskaia (Moscow, 2010–12), vol. II, 12, 273–79, 338–46 (Nos. 196–224), 349–54 (Nos. 230–48).
12. See T[atomir] P. Vukanović, 'The Vampire (in the Belief and Customs of the Gypsies in the Province of Kosovo-Metohija, Stari Ras and Novopazarski Sandžak, Yugoslavia)', *Journal of the Gypsy Lore Society* 36 (1957): 125–33; 37 (1958): 21–31, 111–18; 38 (1959): 44–55, reprinted in: Jan L. Perkowski, *Vampires of the Slavs* (Cambridge, MA, 1976), 201–34; E[lwood] B. Trigg, *Gypsy Demons and Divinities: The Magical and Supernatural Practices of the Gypsies* (London, 1973), 136–57.
13. Otto Steiner, *Vampirleichen. Vampirprozesse in Preußen* (Hamburg, 1959), 36–42, 49–57.
14. 'Vampir-Mord aus Aberglauben', *Der Spiegel*, 1 July 1964, 51/52.
15. See Günter Wiegelmann, 'Der "lebende Leichnam" im Volksbrauch', *Zeitschrift für Volkskunde* 62 (1966): 161–83.
16. See Gerda Grober-Glück, 'Der Verstorbene als Nachzehrer', in Mathias Zender (ed.), *Atlas der deutschen Volkskunde. Neue Folge: Auf Grund der von 1929 bis 1935 durchgeführten Sammlungen. Erläuterungen zu den Karten 43–48* (Marburg, 1981), 426–56.
17. Thomas Schürmann, *Nachzehrerglauben in Mitteleuropa* (Marburg, 1990), 120/121, 123 (map), 124, 138.

Conclusion
The Vampire as Local Scapegoat

> I will not attempt to investigate where vampires have their name from, either in the Hungarian or in the Turkish language; rather, I will only state, in jest, that when a German hears this word, he pictures one who has a 'dicke Wampe' (large paunch), i.e. a bloated corpse.
> —*Schlesisches Historisches Labyrinth*
> (*Silesian Historical Labyrinth*), 1737

> Vukodlak is the name given to a person into whom (according to popular saying) some sort of spirit enters forty days after death, reanimating them (vampirising them). Thereafter the vukodlak leaves the grave at night, choking people and drinking their blood.
> —*Srpski rječnik* (*Serbian Dictionary*), 1818

In 1818, a work was published in Vienna bearing the subtitle *Wolf Stephanson's Serbisch-Deutsch-Lateinisches Wörterbuch* (*Wolf Stephanson's Serbian-German-Latin Dictionary*). As the *Srpski rječnik* (*Serbian Dictionary*) of the philologist and ethnologist Vuk Stefanović Karadžić, this book was to become the nucleus of the national reawakening in Serbia. The work contains a remarkable lexical entry on the Serbian vampire, the *vukodlak* ('werewolf', literally 'wolf's skin'), which was republished, along with two additional sentences on the 'Vukodlak or Vampire', in the posthumous *Život i običaji naroda srpskog* (*Life and Customs of the Serbian People*), which appeared in 1867.[1] This entry is remarkable, and not only for the fact that encyclopaedic discussions tend to constitute the exception in the dictionary. It is also striking because this was the only time that the enlightener Karadžić tackled this issue. There is no reference to the vampire in either of his comprehensive collection of ballads, published from 1823 to 1833, or in his 1853 anthology of fairy tales and legends.[2] The 'Serbian Grimm' confined himself to the discussion of the *vila*, a sort of mountain spirit that was a peculiarity of South Slavic legends and, otherwise, the 'Father of

Yugoslavia' appears to have been more concerned with the 'awakening of the Serbian nation' and 'throwing off the Turkish yoke'. In contrast to the Polish national poet Adam Mickiewicz (see the section entitled 'Demonic Figures in East and East Central Europe' in Chapter 4), he did not consider the collective 'rebirth' to be a form of posthumous magic.

In his dictionary, Karadžić preferred the substantive 'vukodlak' as a designation for the Serbian revenant, but he did use the reflexive verb 'to vampirize oneself' (*povampiri se*) when discussing the mysterious animation of a corpse. It is true that, in this, he drew upon popular tales, but, remarkably, he also listed other phenomena, which he seemed to have lifted from German and Polish works of the time (see the section entitled 'Demonic Figures in East and East Central Europe' in Chapter 4). Thus, a demonic spirit would possess the corpse of a dead person forty days after death. As a vukodlak, it would leave his grave at night and visit the houses of the living, in order to choke people and drink their blood. An honest person could only be transformed into a vampire when a bird or another animal had flown or sprung over his body. A vukodlak appears particularly in the winter months, especially between Christmas and Ascension. Should a series of deaths break out in a village community during this period of time, this would inevitably lead to speculation about whether a recently deceased person was on the rampage, or rumoured sightings of a dead person carrying their burial shroud over their shoulder would spread. A black stallion was used to locate the grave, since they were said to shy away from vukodlaks. Should this be the case, the village community would feel themselves emboldened to open the grave and, when the corpse then gave the impression of not being decomposed, it was pierced through with a whitethorn branch and burned on a funeral pyre. However, Karadžić does not make any reference to decapitation.

In passing, Karadžić also lists the following details: a vukodlak lying in the grave has a rosy and bloated complexion, which is generally thought to result from his drinking of blood. At this point, departing from his preference for the term 'vukodlak', Karadžić also mentions the common Polish turn of phrase 'red like a vampire' (Serbian *crven kao vampir*). Among other things, a vukodlak also enjoys sexual relations with his wife, particularly – as Karadžić could clearly not resist commenting – when she is young and beautiful. A child that is result of such relationships is born without bones, a belief that also played a role in the tales of the Roma (see the section entitled 'Lost Souls in the Danube-Balkan Region' in Chapter 4). Finally, in the posthumous edition of the dictionary, there is also the addendum that, in times of famine, the vukodlak prefer mills or granaries as places of assembly. Since a vukodlak could also slip through even the smallest of holes, it was pointless to close the doors.

Two things in this summary of the vampire discourse by the founder of Serbian linguistics and ethnology are surprising. First, Karadžić seems to have been unaware of the classic case from Medveđa in the years 1731 and 1732 (see the section entitled 'The Discovery of the Vampire' in Chapter 3). However, his evidence that vampiric apparitions occurred within the house and at night is also important, since it moves the discourse into the realm of nightmares or horror scenarios. Furthermore, his description also hints at a relationship between the posthumous activities of normal mortals and the life of Jesus, in that these demonic activities are particularly believed to take place in the months between the birth of Christ and his Ascension.

With regard to the vampire, Karadžić focused primarily on the concept of bloodsucking and the measure of burning the corpse. For him, the supposed attacks of a poltergeist were only of secondary importance. In his sexist allusions, he referred back on the one hand to the cult of heroes among the herding communities of the Balkans whilst catering, on the other hand, to the chauvinistic tastes of the educated readership of the time. In light of the fact that everyday life in the mountainous regions of Southeastern Europe was dominated by sheep and goats, the motif of the black stallion, used for the identification of the vampire, seems to be somewhat out of place. More instructive in the South Slavic context is his mention of the boneless vampire child, which had already been described in a more vivid manner in 1732 by an officer in the region of the Austrian Military Frontier (see the section entitled 'Demonic Figures in East and East Central Europe' in Chapter 4). Also new is the departure from the previous interpretation of vampire cases, in that vampirism is no longer traced back to a pestilence among the herding community – an element that is more often to be found in the East Central European region – but rather to a famine threatening the peasants.

The Origins and Significance of Vampirism

In the context of the bewildering array of findings so full of foreign stereotypes and fictive clichés, it can be concluded that there is, in fact, very little to be learned from supposed experts about where vampirism comes from and what the word 'vampire' actually meant in popular conceptions, or about the various forms in which its many shades could be characterized. This is inevitable, since it involves a generalization of the claims of supposed victims or witnesses that are, themselves, subject to terminological misunderstanding.

In view of the variety of manifestations, considerations on the origins of the widespread belief in different forms of vampires are pointless. Nevertheless, there have always been speculation. Through focusing on the migrations of the Vikings in the ninth and tenth centuries on the one hand, and those of the Roma in the thirteenth and fourteenth centuries on the other, such etymologically and culturally geographically diverse regions as Scandinavia and the Indian subcontinent have been posited as the original home of vampirism (see the sections entitled 'The Revenant of the Middle Ages' in Chapter 1 and

'Lost Souls in the Danube-Balkan Region' in Chapter 4). It is important here merely to state that the vampire is not unique. On the contrary, on the one hand, he is only one character within a multifarious world of demons. For the Central Balkans alone, for example, the Macedonian ethnologist Tanas Vražinovski was able to identify the following demons or spirits of the dead: 'water or forest fairies' (*vila, samovila*), 'house snakes' (*zmej*), 'lamia' (*lamiia*), 'monsters' (*karakontsol*), 'birth fairies' (*narechnitsi*), 'child souls' (*navi*) and 'house spirits' (*stopan*).[3] On the other hand, the terminology for the phenomenon known in the West as the undead bloodsucker not only varies from one ethnic group to another, but there are also completely different designations within the individual languages. For the former Yugoslavian region alone, the Serbian ethnologist Tihomir Đorđević compiled the following vocabulary: *vampir, vampirin, vaper, voper, vopir – lampir, lampijer, lipir – vuk, vukodlak, vukozlak, vukozlačina, volkodlak, ukodlak, kodlak, kudlak – vjedogonja, jedogonja, vidogoja – medovina, štrigun, tenac, tenjac, prikosac, kosac, grobnik, gromnik, talasam*.[4] This multitude of words demonstrates that we are dealing with a mysterious phenomenon for which, clearly, no precise designation is possible. Speculation about the etymological significance of the word 'vampire' therefore leads us astray from the outset. Thus, in Poland and Romania, terms such as *strzygoń* and *upiór* or *strigoi* and *moroi* are common, although, in terms of content, these represent something closer to a witch or a sorcerer rather than a bloodsucker in a strict sense.

The fact that the magical or mythological belief-worlds of the peoples of the Danube-Balkan region or the Sarmatian regions of East Central Europe are therefore teeming with various demons and spirits certainly calls one to question and to relativize the exclusivity of the vampire terminology so popular in the Latin West and the anglophone New World. In this respect, the conversation between two Serbian peasants on the meaning of 'vukodlak or vampire', recorded at the beginning of the twentieth century by Salomon Krauss, seems to be particularly striking. According to the Austrian scholar, one peasant represented a conception which had been formulated by Vuk Karadžić: 'this is what we call dead persons, into whom a hellish spirit enters forty days after their death, animating it. At night the vampire leaves his grave and chokes people in their homes and drinks their blood'. According to Krauss, the other peasant, who, whether consciously or unconsciously, evidently realized the discrepancies between this definition and the rules governing their own life-world, contradicted this in the following terms: 'No, you are wrong. The condemned soul is not permitted to enter either heaven or hell. The vampire is much more threatening to animals than it is to baptised souls.'[5] Whereas, in Krauss' depiction, one peasant attempts to identify a characteristic and, focusing on the supposed harmful posthumous magic, takes on the perspective of the victim, the other concentrates on the problems of the everyday, focusing on the well-being of his beloved cattle rather than any direct threat to his nearest relatives.

Incidentally, both interpretations are bound up in Christian thought, which certainly serves to shift the perspective on their actual sensitivities. In any case, the possession of a dead body by a devil is only one of the explanations for alleged posthumous activities. The uncertain destiny of wandering souls constitutes the flipside of this coin.

Also instructive in this context are the fairy tales surrounding the so-called 'Lenore Materials' – derived from Lenore, the bride of the undead soldier in Gottfried August Bürger's ballad of the same name – of the Danube-Balkan region and the Carpathian range, compiled at the end of the nineteenth century. The combination, in particular, of the tale of the encounter of the 'impure' with that of the flower-girl, evident in Serbia, Romania and Ukraine, hints at a cultural transfer or a transnational component (see the sections entitled 'Demonic Figures in East and East Central Europe' and 'Lost Souls in the Danube-Balkan Region' in Chapter 4). The earliest evidence for this subject can be found among the Roma, and it seems to have migrated from the Danube-Balkan region to the Carpathian-Ukraine. The underlying motif is based upon the tabooization of the sacrament of marriage and of female chastity in a patriarchal society. In these texts, young women, often left to the charge of a widow, are expected to enter into the ranks of the married, but are then often led into temptation by demons.[6] These suitors, however, have very little to do with bloodsuckers. Nor, by any stretch of the imagination, are these tales of true love; rather, through these stories, village communities sought to negotiate norms and values. When, in view of the polarization of good and evil, one also takes into consideration bitter old women, who drew the hatred of the neighbours upon themselves through their behaviour and who were accordingly subject to accusations of witchcraft, then one cannot overlook the fact that it was predominantly strangers or outsiders who were characterized as vampires.

The Vampire Belt and the Mora Wedge

On the one hand, this book has sought to establish the relationship between the bloodlust inherent in the Western vampire discourse and those metaphors that had already been shaped in the Latin world before the striking Serbian term of 'vampire' had become at all known. In so doing, it has demonstrated that the Southeast European revenant has had the image of the bloodsucker superimposed on it in order to add content to the attractive terminological shell that the word 'vampire' represented and, at the same time, to underline its supposed uniqueness. On the other hand, it has also contrasted the actual folk traditions surrounding the walking dead in the zone of transition from Catholicism/Protestantism to Orthodoxy with the sensationalist reporting on bloodsuckers in the world of the educated Western readership. In this respect, the epistemic object of interest was the development of the discourse on vampires from their discovery in 1725 up to the publication of Bram Stoker's *Dracula* novel in 1897. Beyond this, in the course of these investigations, it also emerged that the belief in the walking dead among the village communities of Eastern Europe could also still be found, to a surprising extent, in the period between the two world wars of the twentieth century.

In the mirror of the written sources, the issue of vampirism is of particular relevance for two reasons. On the one hand, reports on the vampire disease brought about an investigation on the part of the authorities into an imminent threat of plague. On the other hand, reports on the toleration of grave desecrations by both the secular and church authorities led to a debate that centred on the orientalization and, with this, the exotification of the Latin-Cyrillic zone of contact in the heart of Europe. In the discourse of the Enlightenment, and within the framework of processes of Westernization, a 'vampire belt' was thus constructed in the eighteenth and nineteenth centuries, running between the Romance-Germanic and Slavic peoples and between the Latin and the Greek-Orthodox world. On the cognitive map of Europe, this barrier was dissected by a 'mora wedge', stretching from the Elbe-Saale line to the Carpathian mountain range (see Map 0.1). In popular belief, crossing over cultural boundaries, the *mora* (fem.) in Slavic languages or *moroi* (fem. *moroaică*) in Romanian constitute the Eastern European version of the German *Alp* (nightmare), which make their presence felt through crushing and choking people in their sleep. The painter and writer Johann Heinrich Füssli portrayed this cross-cultural phenomenon in a visionary manner in the two versions of his painting *Der Nachtmahr* (*The Nightmare*) from 1781 and 1790 (see the cover image).

Bloodsucker or Bloated Corpse?

The history of vampirism is a history of impaling, decapitation and the burning of suspect corpses. Through the process of Christianization, the restlessness of dead souls was increasingly traced back to satanic possession. Whereas it was initially nightmares and poltergeists that excited the imagination, these gradually came to be replaced in popular fantasies by messengers of death and the 'impure', that is, the devil. In the sources, whether in protocols of investigations or in scholarly commentaries, the dilettantism of the defensive measures that are carried out should be taken with a healthy dose of irony, and the carnivalesque deception of the authorities was unmasked as a manipulation. Over the course of time, the feeling of threat emanating from the faceless character of the vampire gradually gave way to an increasing personification of the danger. By the end of the nineteenth century, the differentiation between a 'living vampire' (characterized by a red facial colour) and a 'dead vampire' (boneless, and made only of flesh and blood) had begun to proliferate. In this context, the vampire demonstrated a certain schizophrenia. On the one hand, he could appear as a pest, whilst on the other hand, he could be a friend and helper. For example, actual spirit hunters existed, whose ability to destroy vampires was traced back to their being born on a Saturday or being the children of vampires. In the final analysis, the circle of victims increasingly became restricted to marital couples and widows. The popular tales clearly discussed social taboos, such as the violation of sexual morals, which had then been brushed under the carpet, only to become evident through the birth of illegitimate children. Against this backdrop, the arrival of modernity in the twentieth century led to an increasing secularization of the belief in vampires in the sense of the lyrical depiction edifying the enactment of a spectre or the gleeful defamation of a fiend.

Therefore, on the basis of these findings, we can state that, alongside the explanation of plagues and droughts, the belief in vampires in Eastern Europe fulfilled three functions: first, it opened up the possibility of receiving messages from the other side; second, in offering a concrete bogeyman, it provided a possible and consensus-creating explanation for otherwise irrational dangers and a controlled manner of dealing with fears; and finally, and above all, it was instrumentalized in the unmasking of troublemakers and the marginalization or elimination of scapegoats. Basic anthropological constants in the appearance of the deceased in dreams and fantasies were the continued working of guilty consciences or attempts to overcome the guilt arising from social or interpersonal conflicts.

Generally, pre-Christian conceptions intermingled with Orthodox belief, according to which the soul remains on the earth for a period of forty days after death before, based on the generally accepted conviction, finally entering paradise following the decomposition of the corpse. In this sense, from the sixteenth century onwards, the Orthodox Church in the Ottoman Empire introduced a harsher punishment in the form of excommunication, with those thus excluded from the Eucharist also being burdened with the fate of the posthumous incorruptibility of their corpses. In order to fortify the souls of the departed, the seventh and the fortieth days after death were commemorated by those left behind, as were the half-anniversary and anniversary. Afterwards the names of the male departed were inscribed in the list of ancestors. An exhumation was also conducted several years after death, as was a washing and renewed internment of the bones. The aim of this was to ensure that the decomposition had taken place, which signified the passage of the soul of the departed into paradise and, for those left behind, to guarantee the maintenance or re-establishment of the social order.

In this context, it should also be highlighted that the ritual veneration (*slava*, i.e. 'festival') of the house patron in Serbia was normally celebrated during the winter months.[7] The cult of ancestors was therefore particularly marked at a time when cases of vampirism were felt to be rife. Significantly, the closest relatives were always among the first victims. It can be assumed that those families whose bloodline had fallen into disrepute, and in which the patriarchal structures had disintegrated, were particularly affected. Whether or not the sorrow over the postponed decomposing of the dead or the intensity of the cult of the ancestors among the Orthodox population stoked collective fears about revenants to a greater extent than in the Latin world remains an open question. Either way, much to the displeasure of the church and secular authorities, vampirism undoubtedly represented a cross-confessional issue.

In the first instance, the vampire was a product of fantasies and fears, but it was also an expression of guilty consciences or false suspicions. Strikingly, in everyday rural life, it was much less the bloodsucking revenant who posed the real threat and rather the bloated corpse itself. In this respect, the impaling or driving of a stake through the corpse did not necessarily serve primarily to hinder posthumous activities through binding the body to the place of burial, but rather aimed, above all, at the re-establishment of order by letting off steam. Unlike most other authors, the bibliophile collector Christian Stieff identified these components of vampirism in the mid eighteenth century in his *Schlesisches Historisches Labyrinth* (*Silesian Historical Labyrinth*). In considering the Silesian *poltergeist*, the Greek *vrykolakas* and the Serbian *vampire* as various manifestations of the same transnational phenomenon, he shifted the focus from the hypothesis of bloodsucking on to the physiognomy of the corpse. Whilst he may have been mistaken in tracing the vocabulary to Hungarian or Turkish roots, he was completely correct in his observation that the word 'vampire', in German, contained a hidden reference to the 'bloated corpse', or 'dicke Wampe' (large paunch).[8] It is unfortunate that this joke has not been picked up on by other vampirologists, since it does contain a certain portion of truth. In fact, it could be seen as the key to the solution of the mystery of the vampire.

Notes

1. 'Vukodlak ili Vampir', in *Srpski rječnik: Istolkovan njemačkim i latinskim riječima*, collected and edited by Vuk Stefanović (sic) (Vienna, 1818), 88–89; 2nd edn (Vienna, 1852), 79, reprinted in [Vuk Stefanović Karadžić,] *Život i običaji naroda srpskoga* (Vienna, 1867), 213/214.
2. See *Narodne srpske pjesme*, collected and edited by Vuk Stef[anović] Karadžić, 3 vols. (Leipzig, 1822–23), vol. IV (Vienna, 1833); reprint: 4 vols. (Vienna, 1841–1862); *Narodne srpske pripovijetke*, collected and edited by Vuk Stef[anović] Karadžić (Vienna, 1853).
3. Tanas Vrazhinovski, *Narodna mitologiia na makedontsite*, 2 vols. (Skopje, 1998), Vol. I, 161.
4. Tihomir R. Đorđević, 'Vampir i druga bića u našem narodnom verovanju i predanju', Srpski etnografski zbornik, Vol. LXVI. 2nd division. *Život i običaji narodni*, Book 30 (Belgrade, 1953), 147–282, at 150.

5. Salomon F. Krauss, *Slavische Volksforschungen: Abhandlungen über Glauben, Gewohnheitsrechte, Sitten, Bräuche und die Guslarenlieder der Südslaven* (Leipzig, 1908), 127.
6. See W. Wollner, 'Der Lenorenstoff in der slavischen Volkspoesie', *Archiv für slavische Philologie* 6 (1882): 239–69; Ivan D. Schischmanov, 'Der Lenorenstoff in der bulgarischen Volkspoesie', *Indogermanische Forschungen* 4 (1894): 412–48.
7. See Karl Kaser, *Hirten, Kämpfer, Stammeshelden: Ursprünge und Gegenwart des balkanischen Patriarchats* (Vienna, 1992), 272–75; Karl Kaser, 'Ahnenkult und Patriarchalismus auf dem Balkan', *Historische Anthropologie* 1 (1993): 93–122.
8. *Schlesisches Historisches Labyrinth oder Kurzgefaste Sammlung von hundert Historien. Allerhand denckwürdiger Nahmen, Werter, Personen, Gebräuche, Solennitäten und Begebenheiten in Schlesien. Aus den weitläufftigen gedruckten Chronicken und vielen geschriebenen Uhrkunden zum Vergnügen allerhand Liebhaber Schlesischer Geschichte, in einem kürtzern und bessern Zusammenhange mit vielfältigen neuen Beyträgen zu der alten und neuen Schlesischen Historie verfertiget* (Breslau, 1737), 335.

Bibliography

Primary Sources

'Aberglaube'. *Schlesische Provincialblätter* 34 (1801): 186/187.
Aberglaube und Gebräuche aus Böhmen und Mähren. Collected and edited by Joseph Virgil Grohmann. Vol. 1. Prague: Calve, 1864.
Abegg, Johann Friedrich. *Reisetagebuch von 1798*. Edited by Walter and Jolanda Abegg. Frankfurt: Insel-Verlag, 1976; 2nd edn, 1977.
Aelurius, Georgius [Georg Katschker]. *Glaciographia, oder Glätzische Chronica. Das ist: Gründliche historische Beschreibung der berümbten und vornemen Stadt, ja gantzen Graffschafft Glatz, auch des Münsterbergischen Fürstenthumbs in Schlesien*. Leipzig: Ritzsch, 1625.
Afanas'ev, A.N. 'Nechistyi'. In *Narodnye russkie skazki*. Vol. VI, no. 66, 326–31. Moscow: V. Grachev i Komi, 1861. Under the title 'Upyr'. In *Narodnye russkie skazki*. Book III, no. 206, 274–79. 2nd edn. Moscow: K. Soldatenkov, 1873.
Allatius, Leo. *De templis Graecorum recentioribus, Ad Ioannem Morinum; De narthece Ecclesiae veteris, Ad Gasparem de Simeonibus; Necnon De Graecorum hodie quorundam opinationibus, Ad Paullum Zacchiam*. Cologne: Kalcovius, 1645.
Allatius, Leo. *De utriusque ecclesiae occidentalis atque orientalis perpetua in dogmate de Purgatorio consensione*. Rome: Josephus Luna, 1655.
Allom, Thomas/Walsh, Robert. *Constantinople and the Scenery of the Seven Churches of Asia Minor*. 2 vols. London: Peter Jackson, Late Fisher, Son, & Co. [c. 1839].
Antonovich, V.B. *Koldovstvo. Dokumenty – protsessy – issledovanie*. St. Petersburg, 1877.
'Appendice au Vampyrisme'. *Le Glaneur historique, moral, litteraire, galant & calotin* 2, no. 22 (La Haye, 17 March 1732): 4–6.
Banović, Stjepan. 'Vukodlaci'. *Zbornik za narodni život i običaje Južnih Slavena* 26 (1928): 347–57.
Bechstein, Ludwig. *Deutsches Sagenbuch*. Leipzig: Wigand, 1853.
Belius Pannonius, Matthias. *Hungariae antiquae et novae Prodromus*. Nuremberg: Monath, 1723.
Bernaleken, Theodor. *Mythen und Bräuche des Volkes in Österreich: Als Beitrag zur deutschen Mythologie, Volksdichtung und Sittenkunde*. Vienna: Braumüller, 1859.
[Böhm, Martin.] *Die drey grossen Landtplagen Krieg, Teurung, Pestilenz, welche jetzundt vor der Welte Ende in vollem Schwang gehen. Den frommen Kindern Gottes, welchen bey dieser kümmerlichen Zeit herzlich bange ist zu Lehr und Trost: den sichern Weltfindern aber zur*

warnung und schrecken, in XXIII Predigten erkleret durch Martinum Bohemum Laubanensem, Predigern daselbst. Wittenberg: Seuberlich, 1601.

Bohomolec, Jan. *Diabeł w swoiey postaci albo o upiorach, gusłach, wróżkach, losach, czarach, z przydatkiem o ukazywaniu się Duchow y odpowiedzią na zarzuty przeciwko pierwszey Częsci czynione.* Vol. II. Warsaw: Michał Gröll, 1777.

———. *Diabeł w swoiey postaci z okazji pytania, jeśli są Upiory, ukazany.* Vol. I. Warsaw: Michał Gröll, 1772; 2nd edn, Warsaw: Michał Gröll, 1775.

[Böldl, Klaus.] *Die Saga von den Leuten auf Eyr. Eyrbyggja saga.* Edited and translated from the Old Norse by Klaus Böldl. Munich: Diederichs, 1999.

[Boyer, Jean Baptiste de.] 'Lettre Cent-Vint-Cinquieme'. In *Lettres juives ou Correspondance philosophique, historique et critique entre un Juif voyageur à Paris et ses correspondans en divers endroits.* Vol. V, 49–66. The Hague: Pierre Paupier, 1737. English translation: 'Letter CXXXVII'. In *The Jewish Spy: being a philosophical, historical and critical correspondence, by letters which lately pass'd between certain Jews in Turkey, Italy, France, &c. Translated from the originals into French, by the Marquis d'Argens and now done into English*, 2nd edn, vol. IV, 122–32. London: D. Browne, 1744.

Buchner, Eberhard. *Das Neueste von gestern: Kulturgeschichtlich interessante Dokumente aus alten deutschen Zeitungen.* Vol. II: *1700–1750.* Vol. III: *1750–1787.* Munich: Langen, [1912].

Buchner, Eberhard, ed. *Medien, Hexen und Geisterseher. Kulturhistorisch interessante Dokumente aus alten deutschen Zeitungen und Zeitschriften (16.–18. Jahrhundert).* Munich: Langen, 1926.

Calmet, Augustin. *Dissertations sur les Apparitions des anges, des Démons et des Esprits et sur les Revenants et Vampires de Hongrie, de Bohême, de Moravie et de Silésie.* Paris: De Bure l'aîné, 1746. Revised edn: *Dissertations sur les Apparitions des Esprits, et sur les Vampires et Revenans de Hongrie, de Moravie, etc.* New revised and improved edn. 2 vols. Einsiedeln: dans la princiere Abbaie par Jean Everhard Kalin, 1749. English translation: *Dissertations upon the apparitions of angels, daemons, and ghosts and concerning the vampires of Hungary, Bohemia, Moravia, and Silesia. Translated from the French.* London: M. Cooper, 1759.

[Cantemir, Dimitrie.] *Demetrii Kantemirs historisch- geographisch- und politische Beschreibung der Moldau.* Frankfurt/Leipzig: n.p., 1771.

Caraccioli, Louis Antoine. *La vie du pape Benoît XIV, Prosper Lambertini.* Paris: Hôtel Serpente, 1783.

[———.] *Lettres à une illustre mort décédée en Pologne depuis peu de temps : Ouvrage du sentiment, ou l'on trouve des Anecdotes aussi curieuses qu'intéressantes.* Paris: J.F. Bassompierre, 1771.

Cepenkov, Marko K. *Makedonski narodni umotvorbi vo deset knigi. Book 9: Narodni veruvanja. Detski igri*, edited by Kiril Penushliski, Leposava Spirovska. Skopje: Makedonska Kniga, 1972.

Charisius, Christian Ludwig. *Medicinisches Bedenken Von denen Vampyren, oder sogenannten Blutsaugern, Ob selbte vorhanden, und die Krafft haben, denen Menschen das Leben zu rauben?* [Königsberg: n.p., 1739].

Chmielowski, Benedykt. 'O upierach'. In Benedykt Chmielowski. *Nowe Ateny albo akademia wszelkiej sciencyi pełna.* Vol. 3, 247–57. Lwów: Wydawnictwo Literackie, 1754.

The Chronicle of Lanercost. 1272–1346. Translated with notes by Herbert Maxwell. 2 vols. Glasgow: J. Maclehose, 1913. Reprint: Penbryn Lodge: Llanerch, 2001.

Chronicles of the Reigns of Stephen, Henry II., and Richard I. Vol II: *The Fifth Book of the 'Historia rerum anglicarum' of William of Newburgh*, edited from manuscripts by Richard Howlett. London: Longman, 1885. Reprint: Wiesbaden: Kraus Reprint, 1964. Translation: *The History of William of Newburgh*. Translated from the Latin by Joseph Stevenson. London: Seeleys, 1856. Reprint: Felinfach: Llanerch Publishers, 1996.

[Ciszewski, Stanisław Bronisław.] *Lud rolniczo-górniczy z okolic Sławkowa w powiecie Olkuskim. Described by* Stanisław Ciszewski. Kraków: Drukarnia Uniwersytetu Jagiellońskiego, 1887. Reprinted in *Zbiór Wiadomości do Antropologii Krajowej* 10 (1886): 187–336; 11 (1887): 1–129.

Codex Sanitario-Medicinalis Hungariae. Vol. I. Collected by Franciscus Xav. Linzbauer. Buda: Typis Caes.-reg. scient universitatis, 1852–56 [sic].

Comiers, Claude. 'La baguette justifiée, et ses effets démontrez naturels'. *Mercure galant*. (Paris, March 1693): 105–61.

Commercium litterarium ad rei medicae et scientiae naturalis in crementum institutum. Nuremberg: Jo. Ernestus Adelbulnerus, 12 March 1732; 19 March 1732; 30 April 1732; 5 May 1732; 28 May 1732; 11 June 1732; 25 June 1732; 9 July 1732; 23 July 1732; 6 August 1732; 10 September 1732.

'A Confutation of the Stories about Vampires, or Dead Bodies Sucking the Living in Hungary etc'. *The London Magazine: and Monthly Chronologer* 6 (May 1737): 236–38.

Constitutio Criminalis Theresiana oder der römisch-kaiserl. zu Hungarn und Böheim k. k. königl. apost. Majestät Mariä Theresiä Erzherzogin zu Oesterreich k. k. peinliche Gerichtsordnung. Vienna: Johann Thomas Edlen von Trattnern, 1769.

'Copia eines Schreibens aus dem Gradisker District in Ungarn'. *Wienerisches Diarium*, no. 58, 21 July 1725, 11/12.

'Courtes Reflexions Physiques sur le Vampyrisme'. *Le Glaneur historique, critique, politique, moral, littéraire, galant et calotin* 3, no. 18 (The Hague, 23 April 1733).

Crusius, Martin. *Turcograeciae Libri Octo. Quibus Graecorum Status Sub Imperio Turcico, in Politia et Ecclesia, Oeconomia et Scholis, iam inde ab amissa Constantinopoli, ad haec usque tempora, luculenter describitur*. Basel: Sebastian Henricpetrus, 1584.

[D'Anvers, Caleb (= Nicholas Amhurst): 'Political Vampyres'. In] *The Craftsman: Being a Critique of the Times*. London: R. Francklin, 20 May 1732: No. 307, 120–29.

Davanzati, Giuseppe. *Dissertazione sopra i vampiri*. Napoli: Presso i fratelli Raimondi, 1774. 2nd edn. Napoli: Presso Filippo Raimondi, 1789. Revised edn: Giuseppe Davanzati. *Dissertazione sopra i vampiri. A cura di Giacomo Annibaldis*. Bari: Besa, 1998.

Demolli, Arif. *Të gjallët dhe të vdekurit e një fëmijërie: Botimi i dytë i plotësuar*. Prishtinë: Shtëpia Botuese Faik Konica, 2002. German translation: Arif Demolli. *Es war ein Dorf in Kosova: Die Lebenden und die Toten meiner Kindheit*. Translated from the Albanian by Basil Schader. Frauenfeld: Waldgut, 2011.

[Des Noyers, Pierre.] *Lettres de Pierre des Noyers pour servir a l'histoire de Pologne et de Suède de 1655 à 1659*. Berlin: B. Behr, 1859.

Die Nestorchronik. Der altrussische Text der Nestorchronik in der Redaktion des Abtes Sil'vestr aus dem Jahre 1116 und ihrer Fortsetzung bis zum Jahre 1305 in der Handschrift des Mönches Lavrentij aus dem Jahre 1377 sowie die Fortsetzung der Suzdaler Chronik bis zum Jahre 1419 nach der Akademiehandschrift. Reprint of the 2nd edn. Leningrad, 1926–28. Munich: Fink, 1977

Drużbacka, Elzbieta. 'Sprzeczka z rożnymi zakonnikami o upiorach, którym autorka tych wierszow wiary niedaie'. In *Zbior rytmow duchownych, panegirycznych, moralnych y swi-*

atowych W. JMci Pani Elzbiety Druzbackiey z Kowalskich skarbnikowey zydaczewskiey. Vol. I: *Zebranie rytmow przez wierszopisow żyiących lub nászego wieku zeszłych pisanych*, 297–304. Warsaw: Druk. Pijarów, 1752.

'Ein Dokument zur Geschichte der schles. Hexenprozesse'. Prepared by A. Schmidt. *Zeitschrift für Geschichte und Kulturgeschichte Österreichisch-Schlesiens* 2 (1906/1907): 193/194.

Eschker, Wolfgang, ed. *Mazedonische Volksmärchen*. Düsseldorf: Diederichs, 1972.

Eudoxus. 'Bericht von einigen Schriften, so bishero wegen der Vampyren herausgekommen'. In *Auserlesene theologische Bibliothec, oder Gründliche Nachrichten von denen neuesten und besten theologischen Büchern und Schriften*. Vol. 62, 143–52. Leipzig: Joh. Friedrich Brauns sel. Erben, 1732.

———. 'Nachlese von den Schriften wegen der Vampyren'. In: *Auserlesene theologische Bibliothec, oder Gründliche Nachrichten von denen neuesten und besten theologischen Büchern und Schriften*. Vol. 69, 870–81. Leipzig: Joh. Friedrich Brauns sel. Erben, 1732.

'Extract of a Private Letter from Vienna'. *London Journal* 663 (11 March 1732).

'Extractum Litterarum ex Comitatu Liptoviensi in superiori Hungaria 1718, mense Julio'. In *Der Europäische Niemand, Welcher niemanden zu beleidigen, Jedermann aber nützlich zu seyn, beflissen ist; Wie er solches in allerhand vertraulichen Gesprächen von neuen und alten Staats-Angelegenheiten, Hof-Intriguen, Kriegs- und Friedens-Begebenheiten, gelehrten, Sachen, und vielerley andern sonderbaren Materien, zu erkennen gibt*. Part II [Nuremberg,] 1719: 972–80.

Fortis, Alberto. *Viaggio in Dalmazia*. 2 vols. Venice: presso Alvise Milocco, 1774. Reprint: Munich: Sagner, 1974. English translation: *Travels into Dalmatia. Containing General Observations on the Natural History of that Country and the Neighboring Islands; the Natural Productions, Arts, Manners and Customs of the Inhabitants: in a Series of Letters*. London: J. Robson, 1778.

Francisci, Erasmus. *Der Höllische Proteus oder Tausendkünstige Versteller, vermittelst Erzehlung der vielfältigen Bild-Verwechslungen Erscheinender Gespenster, Werffender und polternder Geister, gespenstischer Vorzeichen der Todes-Fälle, Wie auch Andrer abentheurlicher Händel, arglistiger Possen, und seltsamer Aufzüge dieses verdammten Schauspielers, und, Von theils Gelehrten, für den menschlichen Lebens-Geist irrig-angesehenen Betriegers (nebenst vorberichtlichem Grund-Beweis der Gewißheit / daß es würcklich Gespenster gebe)*. Nuremberg: Endter, 1690.

Garmann, Christian Friedrich. *De Miraculis Mortuorum. Über die Wunder[dinge] der Toten. Facsimile der Originalausgabe von 1670 mit Übersetzung und Nachwort*. Edited by Silvio Benetello and Bernd Herrmann. Göttingen: Universitätsverlag Göttingen, 2003.

Geistliche Fama, mitbringend Einige Neuere Nachrichten von Göttlichen Erweckeungen, Wegen, Führungen und Gerichten. No. 8. Sarden: Johann Conrad Dippel, 1733.

Gengell, Georgio. *Eversio atheism, seu pro deo contra atheos libri duo*. Braniewo: Typis Collegij Societatis Jesu, 1716.

Geoffrey of Burton. *Life and Miracles of St. Modwenna*. Edited and translated by Robert Bartlett. Oxford: Clarendon Press, 2002.

[Gerlach, Stephan.] *Stephan Gerlachs deß Aeltern Tage-Buch der von zween glorwürdigsten römischen Kaysern, Maximiliano und Rudolpho, beyderseits den Andern dieses Nahmens höchstseeligster Gedächtniß, an die ottomannische Pforte zu Constantinopel abgefertigten und durch den Wohlgebornen Herrn Hn. David Ungnad, Freiherrn zu Sonnegk und Preyburg u. Römisch-Kayserli. Rath mit würcklicher Erhalt- und Verlängerung des Friedens zwischen dem Ottomannischen und Römischen Kayserthum und demselben angehörigen*

Landen und Köngreichen glücklichst-vollbrachter Gesandtschafft. Herfür gegeben durch seinen Enckel Samuel Gerlach. Frankfurt: Zunner, 1674.
Geyer, Joh[ann] Daniel. *Müßiger Reise-Stunden, Gute Gedancken, Von denen Todten Menschen-Saugern, An die Hochpreißlichen Praesidem und Collegas S. R. I. Academicae Naturae Curiosorum. Neundter Discours.* Dresden: Hilscher, 1735.
Gluziński, Józef. 'Włościanie polscy uważani pod względem charakteru, zwyczajów, obyczajów i przesądów z dołączeniem przysłowiów powszechnie używanych (z rękopismu)'. In *Archiwum domowe do dziejów i literatury krajowej z rękopismów I dzieł najrzadszych*, edited by Kazimierz Władysław Wójcicki, 393–575. Warsaw: Drukarni Rząd. przy Kom. Rząd. Sprawiedliwości, 1856.
Gömöry, David. *Dissertatio inauguralis physico-medica, sistens tentamen de indole aeris Hungarici.* Vienna: Joannes Thomas de Trattnern, 1765.
Grässe, J[ohann] G[eorg] Th[eodor]. *Sagenbuch des Preußischen Staats.* 2 vols. Glogau: Flemming, 1868–71.
Grinchenko, B.D. *Etnograficheskie materialy, sobrannye v Chernigovskoi i sosednikh s nei guberniiakh.* Vol. 1. *Rasskazy, skazki, predaniia, poslovitsy, zagadki i pr.* Chernigov: Tipografiia Gubernskogo zemstva, 1895.
———. *Iz ust naroda. Malorusskie rasskazy, skazki i pr.* Chernigov: Tipografiia Gubernskogo zemstva, 1900.
Groome, Francis Hindus. 'The Vampire: A Roumanian Gypsy Story'. *Journal of the Gypsy Lore Society* 2, no. 3 (1890): 142–48. Reprinted in: Francis Hindes Groome. *Gypsy Folk-Tales*, 14–19. London: Hurst and Blackett, 1899.
Groza, Adriana. *Transylvanian Vampires. Folktales of the Living Dead Retold.* Jefferson, NC: McFarland & Company, Inc. Publishers, 2014.
[Gustawicz, Bronisław.] 'Kilka szczegółów ludonnawczych z powiatu bobreckiego'. Collected by Bronisław Gustawicz. *Lud. Organ Towarzystwa Ludonznawczego w Lwowie* 8, no. 1 (1902): 265–74.
[Hajek z Libočan, Václav (Hayek z Liboczan, Waclaw).] *Kronyka Czeska.* Prague: Seweryn, 1541; *Václava Hájka z Libočan Kronika česká. Podle Originálu z r 1541.* Edited by V. Flajšhans. Vol. I. *Doba Pohanská. R. 644–904.* Vol. II. *Zánik Pohanství. R. 905–1100.* Vol. III. *Cechy vévodké. R. 1101–1253.* Vol. IV. *Čechy královské. R. 1254–1347.* Prague, 1918–33. German version: Wenceslaus Hagecius: *Böhmische Chronica.* Prague: N. Straus for A. Weidlich, 1596.
Hamberger, Klaus, ed. *Mortuus non mordet. Dokumente zum Vampirismus, 1689–1791.* Vienna: Turia & Kant, 1992.
Harmening, Dieter. *Der Anfang von Dracula: Zur Geschichte von Geschichten.* Würzburg: Königshausen & Neumann, 1983.
Harnack, Adolf. *Geschichte der Königlich Preussischen Akademie der Wissenschaften zu Berlin.* Vol. II. *Urkunden und Actenstücke zur Geschichte der Königlich Preussischen Akademie der Wissenschaften.* Berlin: Reichsdruckerei, 1900. Reprint: Hildesheim: Olms, 1970.
Hartkopf, Werner, and Gert Wangemann, eds. *Dokumente zur Geschichte der Berliner Akademie der Wissenschaften von 1700 bis 1990.* Heidelberg: Spektrum Akademischer Verlag, 1991.
Hauber, Eberhard David. *Bibliotheca sive Acta et Scripta Magica.* Lemgovia: Meyer, 1738.
Haupt, Karl. *Sagenbuch der Lausitz.* Vol. I: *Das Geisterreich.* Vol. II: *Die Geschichte.* Leipzig: Engelmann, 1862–63. Photomechanical Reprint: Bautzen: Domowina Verlag, 1991.

Hedeşan, Otilia: *Şapte eseuri despre strigoi*. Timişoara: Marineasa, 1998. *Strigoii*. 2nd revised edn. Cluj-Napoca: Dacia XXI, 2011.

Heineccius, Io[annes] Michael. *Dissertatio theologica inauguralis de absolutione mortuorum excommunicatorum seu tympanicorum in ecclesia Graeca*. Helmstedt: Typis Georgii Wolfgangi Hammii, 1709.

———. *Eigentliche und wahrhafftige Abbildung der alten und neuen Griechischen Kirche, Nach ihrer Historie, Glaubens-Lehren und Kirchen-Gebräuchen in III. Theilen*. Leipzig: Gleditsch, 1711

Henelius, Nicolaus. *Silesiograpia renovata necessariis scholiis: Observationibus et indice aucta*. Breslau/Leipzig: Christoph Bauch, 1704.

Historischer Geschlechtsbericht (Familienchronik) von Georg Buchholtz, dem Älteren, nebst einem Auszuge aus dem Tagebuch seines Sohnes Jakob Buchholtz: Nach den hinterlassenen Handschriften veröffentlicht durch Rudolf Weber. Budapest: Hornyántzky, 1904.

Horst, Georg Conrad. *Zauber-Bibliothek oder von Zauberei, Theurgie und Mantik, Zauberern, Hexen, und Hexenprocessen, Dämonen, Gespenstern, und Geistererscheinungen: Zur Beförderung einer rein-geschichtlichen, von Aberglauben und Unglauben freien Beurtheilung dieser Gegenstände*. 4 vols. Mainz: Kupferberg, 1821–26.

Horton, George. *Home of Nymphs and Vampires: The Isles of Greece*. Indianapolis: Bobbs-Merrill Company, 1929.

Hußty [Huszty von Raszynya], Zacharias Gottlieb, ed. *Diskurs über die medizinische Polizei*. 2 vols. Preßburg/Leipzig: Anton Löwe, 1786.

James, M[ontague] R. 'Twelve Medieval Ghost Stories'. *English Historical Review* 37 (1922): 413–22. English translation from the Latin in: M.R. James. *A Pleasing Terror: The Complete Supernatural Writings of Henry James*, edited by Christopher and Barbara Roden, 457–68. Ashcroft: Ash-Tree Press, 2001.

Javorskii, Jul'ian 'Galitsko-russkie poveriia ob opyriakh'. *Zhivaia starina* 7 (1897): 107–10.

Jósika, Miklós. *Második Rákóczi Ferencz*. 6 vols. Pest: Ráth Mór, 1861. German translation: Nicolaus Jósika. *Franz Rákóczi II*. 6 vols. Pest: Hartleben, 1862.

'Jud Süß'. In *Curieuser Nachrichten aus dem Reich der Beschnittenen: Erste Unterredung. Zwischen Sabathai Sevi, einem in dem vorigen Seculo in den Morgenländern höchst-berüchtigt gewesenen jüdischen Ertzbetrüger, und dem fameusen Württembergischen Avanturier, Jud Joseph Süß Oppenheimer*, 91–94. Frankfurt/Leipzig: n.p., 1738. Reprinted in: *Einhundertundzehn Volks- und Gesellschaftslieder des 16., 17. und 18. Jahrhunderts mit und ohne Singweisen. Nach fliegenden Blättern, handschriftlichen Quellen und dem Volksmunde*, collected and edited by Franz Wilhelm von Ditfurth, 74–78. Stuttgart: Göschen, 1875. Reprinted in: *Die historischen Volkslieder vom Ende des dreißigjährigen Krieges, 1648 bis zum Beginn des siebenjährigen, 1756. Aus fliegenden Blättern, handschriftlichen Quellen und dem Volksmunde*, collected by Franz Wilhelm von Ditfurth, 291–94. Heilbronn: Henninger, 1877.

[Karadžić, Vuk Stefanović] *Narodne srpske pjesme*. Collected and edited by Vuk Stef. Karadžić. 3 vols. Leipzig: Breitkopf und Härtel, 1822–23. Vol. IV. Vienna: Breitkopf & Härtel, 1833. Reprint: 4 vols. Vienna: Štamparija jermenskoga manastira, 1841–62.

———. *Narodne srpske pripovijetke*. Collected and edited by Vuk Stef. Karadžić. Vienna: Štamparija Jermenskoga Manastira, 1853.

———. 'Vukodlak ili Vampir'. In *Srpski rječnik. Istolkovan njemačkim i latinskim riječima*, collected and edited by Vuk Stefanović [Karadzic], 88–89. Vienna: P.P. Armenier, 1818. 2nd edn, Vienna: P. P. Armenier, 1852. Reprint in: *Život i običaji naroda srpskoga,*

described and prepared for publication by Vuk Stefanović Karadžić, 213–14. Vienna: U naklade Ane udove V.S. Karadžića. L. Sommer, 1867.
[Kelemina, Jakob.] *Bajke in pripovedke slovenskega ljudstva*. With a mythological introduction prepared by Jakob Kelemina. Ljubljana: Družba sv. Mohorja, 1930. Reprint: Ljubljana: Založništvo Humar, 1997.
[Klaić, Vjekoslav.] 'Bilješka o vjerovanju u vukodlake na otoku Pašmanu god. 1403'. Collected by Vjekoslav Klaić. *Zbornik za narodni život i običaje južnih slavena* 1 (Zagreb 1896): 223/224.
Klings, Karl. 'Die Seiga'. *Oberschlesien, Zeitschrift zur Pflege und Kenntnis und Vertretung der Interessen Oberschlesiens* 3 (1904): 27–45.
[Knoblauch zu Hatzbach, Carl.] *Taschenbuch für Aufklärer und Nichtaufklärer auf das Jahr 1791*. Edited and with contributions by Carl von Knoblauch zu Hatzbach. Berlin: Joh. Friedrich Unger, 1790.
Knoop, Otto. 'Sagen aus Kujawien'. *Zeitschrift des Vereins für Volkskunde* 15 (1905): 102–5; 16 (1906): 96–100.
———. *Sagen und Erzählungen aus der Provinz Posen*. Collected by Otto Knoop. Posen: Eigenthum der Gesellschaft, 1893.
———. *Volkssagen, Erzählungen, Aberglauben, Gebräuche und Märchen aus dem östlichen Hinterpommern*. Collected by Otto Knoop. Posen: J. Jolowicz, 1885.
Koegler, Joseph. 'Historische Beschreibung der königlichen Stadt Lewin (geschrieben im Jahre 1793)'. In *Chronicken der Grafschaft Glatz*, 415–46. Glatz: Pompejus, 1841/42. Reprint: 'Historische Beschreibung der Königlichen Immediatstadt Lewin'. In Joseph Kögler. *Die Chronicken der Grafschaft Glatz*. Vol. I: *Die Stadt- und Pfarreichroniken von Lewin – Mittelwalde – Wünschelburg – Neurode-Wilhelmstal*. Revised edn by Dieter Pohl, 21–74. Modautal: Dr. Dieter Pohl Verlag, 1992.
Köleséri de Kereseer, Samuel. *Pestis Dacicae anni M.DCC.IX. scrutinium et cura*. Sibiu: Heltzdörffer, 1709.
Koshovik, K. 'Zhivoi upyr' v bor'be s umershimi upyriami'. *Kievskaia starina* 8 (1884): 169–71.
Krauss, Friedrich Salomo. *Sagen und Märchen der Südslaven: Zum Teil aus ungedruckten Quellen*. Vol. I. Leipzig: Friedrich, 1883.
———. *Tausend Sagen und Märchen der Südslaven*. Collected and rendered in German by Friedrich S. Krauss. Vol. 1. Leipzig: Ethnologischer Verlag, 1914. Reprint: Paderborn: Salzwasser Verlag, 2012.
———. *Volkserzählungen der Südslaven. Märchen und Sagen, Schwänke, Schnurren und erbauliche Geschichten*. Edited by Raymond L. Burt and Walter Puchner. Vienna: Böhlau, 2002.
Kühnau, Richard. *Schlesische Sagen*. Vol. I: *Spuk- und Gespenstersagen*. Vol. II: *Elben-, Dämonen- und Teufelssagen*. Vol. III: *Zauber-, Wunder- und Schatzsagen*. Vol. IV: *Register*. Leipzig: Teubner, 1910–13.
Lambertini, Prospero [Benedikt XIV]. *De servorum dei beatificatione et beatorum canonizatione*. 4 vols. Bologna: Longhi, 1734–38. 2nd expanded edn. Passau: Johannes de. Manfrè, 1743, vol. I. 3rd edn: *Benedicto XIV. doctrinam De servorum dei beatificatione et beatorum canonizatione*. Edited with a synopsis by Emmanuel Azevedo. Rome: Typis Generosi Salomoni bibliopolae, 1757. 4th edn: *Benedicti decimiquarti De servorum dei beatificatione et beatorum canonizatione*. 4 vols. *Newest edition, in all parts revised and enlarged*. Venice: Antonius Foglierini, 1764.

[Laukhard, Friedrich Christian.] *Sammlung erbaulicher Gedichte. Mitunter ein Zuchtspiegel für die politischen Vampyrs; wie auch ein Noth- und Hülfsbüchlein für alle die, welche von ihnen widerrechtlich geplagt werden.* Altona: Selbstverlag, 1796.

Leake, William Martin. *Travels in Northern Greece.* 4 vols. London: Rodwell, 1835–41. Reprint: Amsterdam: Hakkert, 1967.

Leposava Spirovska, Tanas Vrazhinovski, eds. *Vampirite vo makedonskite veruvania i predaniia.* Skopje: Institut za folklor 'Marko Cepenkov', 1988.

Leskien, August, ed. *Balkanmärchen. Aus Albanien, Bulgarien, Serbien und Kroatien.* Jena: Diederichs, 1925.

'Lettre écrite de Pologne sur un sujet sort surprenant'. *Mercure historique et politique* 14 (Le Haye, June 1693): 670/671.

Liepopili, Ante: 'Vukodlaci'. *Zbornik za narodni život i običaje južnih slavena* 23 (Zagreb 1918): 277–290. English translation in: Jan L. Perkowski. *The Darkling: A Treatise on Slavic Vampirism,* 85–102. Columbus: Slavica Publishers, 1989.

[Luther, Martin.] *D. Martin Luthers Werke. Kritische Gesamtausgabe. Tischreden.* Vol. 6. Weimar: Böhlau, 1921.

Map, Walter. *De nugis curialium. Courtiers' trifles.* Edited and translated by M.R. James, revised by C.N.L. Brooke and R.A.B. Mynors. Oxford: Clarendon Press, 1994.

[Marigner. 'Creatures des elements'.] *Mercure galant* (Paris, January 1694): 58–166.

———. 'Sur les stryges de Russie'. *Mercure galant* (Paris, February 1694): 13–119.

Martinus, Martini. *Dissertatio inauguralis practico-medica de daemonomania et variis ejus speciebus.* Vienna: Litteris Sonnleithnerianis, 1782.

Matirko jun., Bertalan. 'Die Zipser Volkssage von Kasparek'. *Ethnologische Mitteilungen aus Ungarn* 2 (1890–92): 162–64.

Mayo, Herbert. *On the Truths contained in Popular Superstitions with an Account of Mesmerism.* Edinburgh: Blackwood, 1849.

Mickiewicz, Adam. *Die Ahnenfeier: Ein Poem. Zweisprachige Ausgabe.* Translated, edited und with an epilogue by Walter Schamschula. Cologne: Böhlau, 1991.

———. *Księgi narodu polskiego i pielgrzymstwa polskiego.* Paris: Institut Littéraire, 1982. English translation: *The books and the pilgrimage of the Polish nation.* London: James Ridgway, 1833.

———. *Les slaves. Cours professé au Collége de France (1840–1841).* Vol. I-V. Paris: Au Comptoir des imprimeurs réunis, 1849. German edn: *Vorlesungen über slawische Literatur und Zustände. Gehalten im Collège de France in den Jahren von 1840–1842.* 4 vols. Leipzig/Paris: Brockhaus und Avenarius, 1843–45.

Mikszáth, Koloman. *Kísértet lublon.* Pest: Akad. Kiadó, 1892. German translation: *Das Gespenst von Lublau.* Leipzig: Georg Heinrich Meyer, 1899.

More, Henry. *An Antidote against Atheism, or, An Appeal to the Naturall Faculties of the Minde of Man, wether there be not a God.* London: Printed by James Flesher for William Morden, 1653; 2nd Ededniton corrected and enlarged: London, 1655.

Narodnaia demonologiia Poles'ia: Publikatsiia tekstov v zapisiakh 80-90-kh godov XX veka. Vol. I: *Liudi so sverkh-estestvennymi svoistvami.* Vol. II: *Demonologizatsiia umershikh liudei.* Collected by L.N. Vinogradova and E.E. Levkievskaia. Moscow: Iazyki slavianskikh kultur, 2010–12.

'Neplacha, opata Opatovského, krátká kronika římska a česká'. Prepared for edition by Josef Emler. In *Fontes rerum Bohemicarum.* Vol. III. Prague: Museum Království Českého. 1882. Reprint: Hildesheim: Olms, 2004.

Nevidimi noštni gosti. Selection and scientific commentary by Evgeniia Mitseva. Sofia: Nauka i izkustvo, 1994.
Newton, C. T. *Travels and Discoveries in the Levante*. 2 vols. London: Day, 1865.
[Noyer, Pierre de.'Untitled article'.] *Mercure galant* (Paris, May 1693): 62–70.
Oppenhoff, F[riedrich] C[hristian], ed. *Die Rechtsprechung des königlichen Ober-Tribunals und des königlichen Ober-Appelations-Gerichts in Strafsachen*. Vol. 12. Berlin: Reimer, 1871.
[Orlić, Drago.] *Štorice od štrig i štriguni*. Collected and edited by Drago Orlić. Pula: Istarska Naklada, 1986. 2nd, supplemented and expanded edn. Zagreb: Naklada Zoro, 2008.
[Ossoliński, Józef Maksymilian.] 'Upiór'. In *Wieczory badeńskie czyli powieści o strachach i upiorach Józefa Maksymiliana Hrabi z Tenczyna Osssolińskiego*, 86–89. Kraków: J. Czech, 1852.
Pashley, Robert. *Travels in Crete*. 2 vols. London: Batsford, 1837. Reprint: Athens: Karavias, 1989.
Peter, Anton, ed. *Volksthümliches aus Österreichisch-Schlesien*. Vol. I: *Kinder und Kinderspiele, Volkslieder und Volksschauspiele, Sprichwörter* Vol. II: *Sagen und Märchen, Bräuche und Volksglauben* Vol. III: *Leben der Oppaländer in Vergangenheit und Gegenwart*. Troppau: Selbstverlag, 1865–73.
Piątkowska, Ignaja. 'Jak sobie lud wyobraża istoty świata nadprzyrodzonego'. *Wisła. Miesięcznik gieograficzny i etnograficznej* 15 (1901): 501–4.
[Pico della Mirandola, Giovanni.] *Joh. Francisci Pici Mirandulae Domini Concordiaeque Comitis Strix Sive De Ludificatione Daemonum Dialogi Tres / Nunc primum in Germania eruti ex bibliotheca M. Martini Weinrichii. Cum eiusdem Praefatione luculenta, continente narrationem duorum operum magicorum & iudicii de iis lati, ut veriβimam, ita cognitione digniβimam, itemque Epistola Ad Cl. Medicum Et Philosophum D. Andream Libavium, de quaestione, Utrum in non maritatis & castis mola possit gigni? Et post mortem eius editi Studio & opera, Caroli Weinrichii, F. Argentorati*. Argentoratum [Strasbourg]: Apud Paulum Ledertz, 1612.
Podbereski, Andrzéj.'Materyjały do Demonologii ludu ukraińskiego. Z opowiadań w powiecie Czehryńskim'. *Zbiór wiadomości do antropologii krajowéj* 4 (1880): 3–82.
Pol, Nikolaus. *Jahrbücher der Stadt Breslau*. Edited by Johann Gustav Büsching. 5 vols. Breslau: Graß und Barth, 1813–24.
'Political Vampyres'. *The Gentleman's Magazine: or, Monthly Intelligencer* 2 (May 1732): 750–52.
'Poslanie v Kirillo-Belozerskii monastyr' (1573)'. In *Poslaniia Ivana Groznogo*, edited by V.P. Adrianova-Peretts. Moscow: Akad. Nauk SSSR, 1951, 162–92, 351–69.
[Potocki, Jan.] *Rękopis znaleziony w Saragossie. Romans wydany posmiertnie z dziel Jana Potockiego*. Vol. I. Lipsk: Księgarni Zagranicznej, 1847. French reconstruction in two volumes: *Manuscrit trouvé à Saragosse (version de 1804). Manuscrit trouvé à Saragosse (version de 1810)*. Edited by François Rosset and Dominique Triaire. Paris: GF-Flammarion, 2008.
Pushkin, A. S.'Pesni zapadnykh slavian'. In A.S. Pushkin. *Sochineniia v trekh tomakh*. Vol. I. Moscow: Khudozhestvennaia literatura, 1958.
'Question Physique sur une espéce de Prodige duëment attesté'. *Le Glaneur historique, moral, litteraire, galant & calotin* 2, no. 18 (3 March 1732): 1–4.
Radenković, Radoslav. *Kazivanja o nečastivim silama*. Niš: Prosveta, 1991.
[Raicević, Stefan Ignaz.] *Osservazioni storiche, naturali e politiche intorno la Valachia a la Moldavia*. Napoli: Presso G. Raimondo, 1788.

Ranft, Michael. *De Masticatione mortuorum in tumulus, (Oder von dem Kauen und Schmatzen der Todten in Gräbern,) Liber Singularis: Exhibens Duas Excercitationes, Quarum Prior Historico-critica Posterior Philosophica est.* Lipsiae: Martin. 1728.

―――. *Dissertatio historico-critica de masticatione mortuorum in tumulis: Oder von dem Kauen und Schmatzen der Toten in Gräbern.* Leipzig: Breitkopf, 1725.

―――. *Tractat von dem Kauen und Schmatzen der Todten in Gräbern, Worin die wahre Beschaffenheit derer Hungarischen Vampyrs und Blut-Sauger gezeigt, Auch alle von dieser Materie bißher zum Vorschein gekommene Schrifften recensiret werden.* Leipzig: Teubners' Buchladen, 1734. Revised edn: *Traktat von dem Kauen und Schmatzen der Toten in Gräbern. Michael Ranft in einer Bearbeitung durch Nicolaus Equiamicus.* Diedorf: Ubooks, 2006.

Rękopism X. Bagińskiego, dominikana prowincyi litewskiéj, (1747–1784 r.). Wilno: Eustachego Tyszkiewicza, 1854.

Remarquable Curieuse Brieffe, oder deutliche Beschreibung Alter und Neuer merckwürdiger Begebenheiten, die sich hin und wieder, guten Theils im Churfürstenthum Sachsen und incorporirten Landen zugetragen. Leipzig: n.p., 1732.

Ricaut; Paul. *The Present State of the Greek and Armenian Churches, Anno Christi 1678.* London: John Starkey, 1679.

Richard, François. *Relation de ce qui s'est passé de plus remarquable a Saint-Erini isle de l'Archipel, depuis l'établissement des Peres de la Compagnie de Iesus en icell.* Paris: Cramoisy, 1657.

Rohr, Philippus. *Dissertatio historico-philosophica de masticatione mortuorum.* Leipzig: Vogtius, 1679.

Rzaczynski, Gabrielis. *Historia naturalis curiosa regni Poloniae, magniducatus Litvaniae, annexorumq; provincarium, in tractatus XX divisa.* Sandomierz: Typis Collegii Societatis Jesu, 1721.

S[ain]t Clair, S[tanislas] G [Graham] B[ower]/Brophy, Charles A. *Twelve Years' Study of the Eastern Question in Bulgaria. Being a Revised edition of 'A Residence in Bulgaria'.* London: Chapman and Hall, 1877.

Sammlung aller k. k. Verordnungen vom Jahre 1740 bis 1780, die unter der Regierung des Kaisers Joseph des II. theils noch ganz bestehen, theils zum Theile abgeändert sind, als ein Hilfs- und Ergänzungsbuch zu dem Handbuche aller unter der Regierung des Kaisers Joseph des II. für die k. k. Erbländer ergangenen Verordnungen und Gesetze in einer chronologischen Ordnung. Vol. III. Vienna: J.G. Mössle, 1786.

Saxonia, Hercules. *De plica quam Poloni gwoździec, Roxolani kołtunum vocant.* Padua: Pasquato Lorenzo, 1600.

Schott, Arthur, and Albert Schott eds. *Walachische Mährchen. Mit einer Einleitung über das Volk der Walachen und einem Anhang zur Erklärung der Mährchen.* Stuttgart: Cotta, 1845.

[Schmidt, Bernhard.] *Griechische Märchen, Sagen und Volkslieder.* Collected, translated and explained by Bernhard Schmidt. Leipzig: Teubner, 1877.

[Scrofani, Saverio.] *Viaggio in Grecia di Saverio Scrofani siciliano fatto nell'anno 1794, 1795.* 2 vols. London: n.p., 1799.

Siewinski, Antoni. 'Opowiadania ludu w powiecie sokalskim i buczackim'. *Lud. Organ Towarzystwa Ludoznawczego w Lwowie* 12, no. 1 (1906): 250–63.

'Slovo sv Grigoriia, izobreteno v toltsekh, o tom kako pervoe pogani sushche iazysti klanialisia idolom i treby im klali'. In N.M. Gal'kovskii. *Bor'ba khristianstva s ostatkami iazychestva v drevnei Rusi*. Vol. II, 17–35. 2 vols. Khar'kov: Eparkhialnaia tipografiia, 1913–16.

Stebler, Franciscus Antonius Ferdinandus. 'Sub vampyri, aut sanguisugae larva a verae philosophiae et rationalis medicinae placitis detectum ac dejectum depravatae imaginationis spectrum'. In *Acta physico-medica Academiae caesarae Leopoldino-Carolinae naturae curiosorum*. Vol. IV, 89–112. Nuremberg: Wolfgang Schwarzkopf, 1737.

Sterne, Carus. 'Der Vampyr-Schrecken im neunzehnten Jahrhundert'. *Die Gartenlaube. Illustrirtes Familienblatt* (1873) no. 34: 555–58; no. 35: 569–71; no. 37: 598–600.

[Stieff, Christian.] *Schlesisches Historisches Labyrinth oder Kurzgefaste Sammlung von hundert Historien. Allerhand denckwürdiger Nahmen, Werter, Personen, Gebräuche, Solennitäten und Begebenheiten in Schlesien: Aus den weitläufftigen gedruckten Chronicken und vielen geschriebenen Uhrkunden zum Vergnügen allerhand Liebhaber Schlesischer Geschichte, in einem kürtzern und bessern Zusammenhange mit vielfältigen neuen Beyträgen zu der alten und neuen Schlesischen Historie verfertiget*. Breslau: Hubert, 1737.

Stoianov, Zakhari. *Zapiski po bŭlgarskite vŭstaniia*. Vol. I–II. *Razkaz na ochevidtsi. 1870–1876*. Vol. III. *Zatvorite*. Plovdiv: Nauka i Iskustvo, 1884–92.

[Swieten, Gerhard van.] 'Vampyrismus von Herrn Baron Gerhard van Swieten verfasset, aus dem Französischen ins Deutsche übersetzet, und als ein Anhang der Abhandlung des Daseyns der Gespenster beigerücket'. In [A. Mayer.] *Abhandlung des Daseins der Gespenster, nebst einem Anhange vom Vampyrismus*. Augsburg: [n.p.], 1768. Reprint: 'Vampyrismus von Herrn Baron Gerhard van-Swieten verfasset, aus dem Französischen ins Deutsche übersetzet'. In *100 Jahre Dracula*, edited by Rainer M. Köppl, 37–46. Vienna: Böhlau, 1998.

Sybel, Heinrich von. *Geschichte der Revolutionszeit von 1789 bis 1795*. Vol. 3. Düsseldorf: Buddeus, 1860. Reprint: *Geschichte der Revolutionszeit 1789–1800. Wohlfeile Ausgabe*. Vol. 5. Stuttgart: J. G. Cotta, 1898.

[Tallar, Georg.] *Visum repertum anatomico-chirurgicum oder Gründlicher Bericht von den sogenannten Blutsäugern, Vampier, oder in der wallachischen Sprache Moroi, in der Wallachey, Siebenbürgen, und Banat, welchen eine eigends dahin abgeordnete Untersuchungskommission der löbl. k. k. Administration im Jahre 1756 erstattet hat, Durch Georg Tallar, Wundarzten*. Vienna/Leipzig: Johann Georg Mössle, 1784.

Tettau, W.J.A. von, and J.D.H. Temme. *Die Volkssagen Ostpreußens, Litthauens und Westpreußens*. Berlin: Nicolai, 1837. Revised edn: Berlin: Nicolai, 1865. Reprint: Hildesheim: Olms, 1994.

Teutsch, Joseph. „Nachlese zu den kurzgefassten Jahrgeschichten von Ungarn und Siebenbürgen". In *Quellen zur Geschichte der Stadt Brassó*. Vol. IV: *Chroniken und Tagebücher*. Part 1: (*1143–1867*), 403–89. Braşov: Zeidner, 1903.

[Thévenot, Jean.] *Relation d'un voyage fait au Levant dans laquelle i lest curieusemet traite des Estats sujets au Grand Seigneur, des Moeurs, Religions, Forces, Gouuernemens, Politiques, Langues, & coustumes des Habitans de ce grand Empire. Par Monsieur Thevenot*. Paris: L. Bilaine, 1664. English translation: *The Travels of Monsieur de Thevenot into the Levant*. London: Printed by H. Clark, for H. Faithorne, J. Adamson, C. Skegnes, and T. Newborough, 1687.

Topographia Bohemiae, Moraviae et Silesiae, das ist Beschreibung und eigentliche Abbildung der Vornehmsten und bekandtisten Stätte und Plätze in dem Königreich Boheim und einverleibten Ländern Mähren und Schlesien. Frankfurt: Merian, 1650.

Tournefort, Joseph Pitton. *Relation d'un voyage du Levant, fait par ordre du roy*. 3 vols. Paris:

Imprimerie Royale, 1717. English translation: *A Voyage into the Levant perform'd by command of the late French King*. 2 vols. London: Midwinter, 1741.
'Travels of Three English Gentlemen, from Venice to Hamburgh, Being the grand Tour of Germany, in the year 1734'. *The Harleian Miscellany; or, A collection of scarce, curious, and entertaining Pamphlets and Tracts, as well in Manuscript as in Print, found in the Earl of Oxford's Library* 11 (1810): 218–355.
'Upior osobliwszy'. *Pamiętnik polityczny y historyczny* 2 (1783): 74–77.
Valvasor, Johann Weichard. *Die Ehre des Herzogthums Crain*. 15 books in 4 volumes. Nuremberg: Endter, 1689. New edn: Novo Mesto: Krajec, 1877–79. Facsimile: Munich: R. Trofenik, 1970–74.
[Veckenstedt, Edmund.] *Wendische Sagen, Märchen und abergläubische Gebräuche*. Collected and retold by Edmund Veckenstedt. Graz: Leuschner und Lubensky, 1880.
'Von dem Königreich Servien in Ober-Hungarn'. In *Neu-eröffnetes Welt- und Staats-Theatrum, welches die in allen Theilen der Welt, sonderlich aber in Europa vorfallende Staats-[,] Kriegs- und Friedens-Affairen, wie auch andere merckwürdige Begebenheiten in einem deutlichen Auszuge vorstellet. Vierdte Eröffnung*, 224–36. Erfurt: Jungnicol, 1732.
'Von dem Polnischen Upiertz oder sich selbst fressenden Todten, und der daraus entstandenen Furcht vor Pest- und Vieh-Sterben'. In *Sammlung von Natur- und Medicin- Wie auch hierzu gehörigen Kunst- und Literatur-Geschichten. 19. Versuch*, 82–88. Leipzig: David Richter, 1722.
Voltaire: 'Vampires'. In: *Œuvres complètes de Voltaire. Nouvelle édition.* [Vol. 42:] *Dictionnaire philosophique*, Vol. VII, 406–13. Paris: Baudouin, 1827.
Vrazhinovski, Tanas. *Narodna demonologiia na makedontsite*. Skopje: Matitsa makedonska, 1995.
———. *Narodna mitologiia na Makedontsite*. 2 vols. Skopje: Matitsa makedonska, 1998.
Vujić, Joakim. *Putešestvije po Serbiji*. Buda: Pečatnja Kraljevskog sveučilišta Peštanskoga, 1828.
Walsh, R[obert]. *A Residence at Constantinople During a Period Including the Commencement, Progress, and termination of the Greek and Turkish Revolutions*. 2 vols. London: Frederick Westley and A. H. Davis, 1836.
'Wampirs, fait singulier et de plus extraordinaires, s'il est vrai'. *Mercure de France* (May 1732): 890–98.
Wilkinson, William. *An Account of the Principalities of Wallachia and Moldavia: with various Political Observations relating to them*. London: Longman, 1820. Reprint: New York: Arno Print, 1971.
[Wlislocki, Heinrich von.] *Volksdichtungen der siebenbürgischen und südungarischen Zigeuner*. Collected and from unedited original texts translated by Heinrich von Wlislocki. Vienna: C. Graeser, 1890.
[Wójcicki, Kazimierz Władysław.] *Klechdy, starożytne podania i powieści ludu Polskiego i Rusi*. Collected and inscribed by Kazimierz Władysław Wójcicki. 2 vols. Warsaw: P. Bobrycki, 1837. Extended version: *Wybór i opracowanie Ryszarda Wochciechowskiego, słowo wstępne Juliana Krzyżanowskiego*. Warsaw: Państwowy Instytut Wydawniczy, 1972.
———. 'Czerwony iak Upior'. In *Przysłowia narodowe*. 143–63. Vol. I. Warsaw: Hugues et Kermen, 1830.
Zakonik Stefana Dušana Cara Srpskog 1349 i 1354. Anew edited and described by Stojan Novaković. Beograd: Državna Štamp, 1898.

Secondary Sources

Abbott, G.F. *Macedonian Folklore*. Cambridge: Cambridge University Press, 1903. Reprint: Chicago: Argonaut, 1969.
Achim, Viorel. *The Roma in Romanian History*. Budapest: Central European Universita Press, 2004.
Adanır, Fikret. *Die Makedonische Frage. Ihre Entstehung und Entwicklung bis 1908*. Wiesbaden: Steiner, 1979.
———. 'Heiduckentum und osmanische Herrschaft: Sozialgeschichtliche Aspekte der Diskussion um das frühneuzeitliche Räuberwesen in Südosteuropa'. *Südost-Forschungen* 41 (1982): 43–116.
Afanas'ev, A.N. *Poeticheskie vozzreniia slavian na prirodu. Opyt sravnitel'nogo izucheniia slavianskikh predanii i verovanii v sviazi s mificheskimi skazaniiami drugikh rodstvennykh narodov*. 3 vols. Moscow: K. Soldatenkov, 1865–1869. Reprint: Moscow: Sovremenyi pisatel, 1995.
Antonljak, Stjepan. 'Sultan Jahja' u Makedoniji'. *Godišen zbornik na Univerzitet vo Skopje* 13 (1962): 109–66.
Arata, Stephen D. 'The Occidental Tourist: Dracula and the Anxiety of Reverse Colonization'. *Victorian Studies* 33 (1990): 627–34. Reprint in: *Dracula. Bram Stoker*, edited by Glennis Byron, 119–44. New York: St Martin's Press, 1999.
Ariès, Philippe. *The Hour of Our Death: The Classic History of Western Attitudes Toward Death Over the Last One Thousand Years*, translated by Helen Weaver. New York: Alfred A. Knopf, Inc., 1981.
Arlaud, Daniel. 'Vampire, Aufklärung und Staat: Eine militärmedizinische Mission in Ungarn, 1755–1756'. In *Gespenster und Politik. 16. bis 21. Jahrhundert*, edited by Claire Gantet and Fabrice d'Almeida, 127–41. Munich: Fink, 2007.
Augustynowicz, Christoph, and Ursula Reber, eds. *Vampirglaube und magia posthuma im Diskurs der Habsburgermonarchie*. Vienna: Lit, 2011.
Avdikos, Evangelos. 'Vampire Stories in Greece and the Reinforcement of Socio-cultural Norms'. *Folklore* 124, no. 3 (2013): 307–26.
Aycibin, Zeynep. 'Osmanlı Devleti'nde Cadılar Üzerine Bir Değerlendirme'. *OTAM (Ankara Üniversitesi Osmanlı Tarihi Araştırma ve Uygulama Merkezi Dergisi)* 24 (2008): 55–70.
Balassa, Iván and Gyula Ortutay. *Ungarische Volkskunde*. Munich: C.H. Beck, 1982.
Bandić, Dušan. 'Vampir u religijskim shvatanjima jugoslovenskih naroda'. *Kultura* 50 (Beograd, 1980): 81–103. Reprint in: Dušan Bandić. *Carstvo zemaljsko i carstvo nebesko. Ogledi o narodnoj religiji*, 85–115. 3rd edn. Beograd: Čolović, 2008.
Baranowski, Bohdan. *W kręgu upiorów i wilkołaków*. Łódź: Wydawnictwo Łódzkie, 1981.
Barber, Paul. *Vampires, Burial and Death: Folklore and Reality*. New Haven: Yale University Press, 1988. With a new introduction. New Haven: Yale University Press, 2010.
Bartlett, Robert. *England under the Norman and Angevin Kings*. Oxford: Clarendon Press, 2000.
———. 'The Miracles of Saint Mordwenna of Burton'. *Staffordshire Studies* 8 (1996): 24–35.
Baroti, L[udwig/Lajós]. 'Beiträge zur Geschichte des Vampyrismus in Südungarn'. *Ethnologische Mitteilungen aus Ungarn* 3, no. 1–2 (1893–94): col. 219–21.
Bazala, V. 'Kroatisch-slawonische Militärgrenze als Gesundheitsfaktor mit besonderer Berücksichtigung des sog: Pestkordons'. In *Acta Congressus Internationalis XXIV His-*

toriae Artis Medicinae: 25–31 Augusti, Budapestin. Vol. I, edited by J. Antall and G. Buzinkay, 527–41. Budapest: Museum, Bibliotheca et Archivum Historiae Artis Medicinae, 1976.

Behringer, Wolfgang. *Hexen. Glaube, Verfolgung, Vermarktung*. 5th edn. Munich: C.H. Beck, 2009.

Benzing, Johannes: *Islamische Rechtsgutachten als volkskundliche Quelle*. Wiesbaden: Verlag der Akademie, der Wissenschaften und der Literatur 1977.

Beresford, Matthew. *From Demons to Dracula: The Creation of the Modern Vampire Myth*. London: Reaktion Books, 2008.

Berger, Karl. 'Zum Hexen- und Vampirglauben in Nordmähren'. *Zeitschrift des deutschen Vereins für die Geschichte Mährens und Schlesiens* 8 (1904): 201–24.

Bertschik, Julia, and Christa Agnes Tuczay, eds. *Poetische Wiedergänger. Deutschsprachige Vampirismus-Diskurse vom Mittelalter bis zur Gegenwart*. Tübingen: Francke, 2005.

Beza, Marcu. *Paganism in Roumanian Folklore*. London: J.M. Dent & Sons Ltd., 1928.

Biale, David. *Blood and Belief. The Circulation of a Symbol between Jews and Christians*. Berkeley: University of California Press, 2007.

Birkhan, Helmut. *Magie im Mittelalter*. Munich: C.H. Beck, 2010.

Blum, Richard and Eva: *The Dangerous Hour: The Lore of Crisis and Mystery in Rural Greece*. London: Charles Scribner's Sons, 1970.

Boehlich, E. 'Die Hexe von Lewin (1345): Ein Beitrag zur Geschichte des Vampirismus'. *Glatzer Heimatblätter* 14, no. 1 (1928): 1–16.

Bohdanowicz, Janusz. 'Demonologia ludowa: Relikty wierzeń w strzygonie i zmory'. *Literatura ludowa*, no. 2 (1994): 43–62.

Bogatyrev, Petr. *Vampires in the Carpathians: Magical Acts, Rites, and Beliefs in Subcarpathian Rus'*. New York: Columbia University Press, 1998.

Bohn, Thomas M. 'Das Gespenst von Lublau: Michael Kaspereks/Kaspareks Verwandlung vom Wiedergänger zum Blutsauger'. *Kakanien Revisited*, 28 October 2009. Retrieved 2 November 2018 from http://www.kakanien.ac.at/beitr/vamp/TBohn2.pdf. Reprint in: *Vampirglaube und magia posthuma im Diskurs der Habsburgermonarchie*, edited by Christoph Augustynowicz and Ursula Reber, 147–61.Vienna: Lit, 2011.

———. 'Der Dracula-Mythos: Osteuropäischer Volksglaube und westeuropäische Klischees'. *Historische Anthropologie* 14 (2006): 390–409.

———. 'Schlesien als Eldorado für Vampirjäger'. In *Mythos Vampir – Bissige Lektüren*, edited by Thomas M. Bohn and Kirsten von Hagen, 45–56. Bonn: Romanistischer Verlag, 2018.

———. 'Vampirismus in Österreich und Preußen: Von der Entdeckung einer Seuche zum Narrativ der Gegenkolonisation'. *Jahrbücher für Geschichte Osteuropas* NF 56 no. 2 (2008): 161–77. Reprint: *Kakanien Revisited*, 20 January 2009. Retrieved 2 November 2018 from http://www.kakanien.ac.at/beitr/vamp/TBohn1.pdf.

Bohn, Thomas M., and Kirsten von Hagen, eds. *Mythos Vampir – Bissige Lektüren*. Bonn: Romanistischer Verlag, 2018.

Bologa, Valeriu L. 'Raportul din 1756 al unui chirurg german despre credițele românilor asupra moroilor'. *Anuarul arhivei de folklor* 3 (1935): 159–68.

Bošković-Stulli, Maja. 'Kresnik – Krsnik, ein Wesen aus der kroatischen und slovenischen Volksüberlieferung'. *Fabula. Zeitschrift für Erzählforschung* 3 (1960): 275–98.

Boulay, Juliette du. 'The Greek Vampire: A Study of Cyclic Symbolism in Marriage and Death'. *Man* 17 (1982): 219–38. Reprint in: *The Vampire. A Casebook*, edited by Alan Dundes, 85–108. Madison, WI: University of Wisconsin Press, 1998.

Braccini, Tommaso. *Prima di Dracula: Archeologia del vampiro.* Bologna: Saggi, 2011.
Bräunlein, Peter. 'Die Rückkehr der "lebenden Leichen": Das Problem der Untoten und die Grenzen des ethnologischen Erkennens'. *kea. Zeitschrift für Kulturwissenschaften* 9, (1996): 97–126.
———. 'The Frightening Borderlands of Enlightenment: The Vampire Problem'. *Studies in History and Philosophy of Biological and Biomedical Sciences* 43, no. 3 (2012): 710–19.
Briese, Olaf. *Angst in Zeiten der Cholera.* Vol. I: *Über kulturelle Ursprünge des Bakteriums: Seuchen-Cordon I.* Vol. II: *Panik-Kurve. Berlins Cholerajahr 1831/32: Seuchen-Cordon II.* Vol. III: *Auf Leben und Tod. Briefwelt als Gegenwelt: Seuchen-Cordon III.* Vol. IV: *Das schlechte Gedicht: Strategien literarischer Immunisierung. Seuchen-Cordon IV.* Berlin: Akademie-Verlag, 2003.
Burkhart, Dagmar. 'Vampirglaube und Vampirsage auf dem Balkan'. In *Beiträge zur Südosteuropaforschung: Anläßlich des I. Internationalen Balkanologenkongresses in Sofia. 26.VIII.–1.IX.1966,* 211–52. Munich: Rudolf Trofenik, 1966. Reprint in: Dagmar Burkart. *Kulturraum Balkan: Studien zur Volkskunde und Literatur Südosteuropas,* 65–108. Berlin: Reimer, 1989.
Butler, Erik. *Metamorphoses of the Vampire in Literature and Film: Cultural Transformations in Europe, 1732–1933.* Rochester, NY: Camden House, 2010.
Caciola, Nancy Mandeville. *Afterlives: The Return of the Dead in the Middle Ages.* Ithaca: Cornell University Press, 2016.
Cain, Jimmie E. Jr. *Bram Stoker and Russophobia. Evidence of the British Fear of Russia in Dracula and the Lady of the Shroud.* Jefferson, NC: McFarland, 2006.
Čajkanović, Veselin. 'Ubijanje vampira'. *Srpski književni glasnik* NS 9 (1923): 268–84. Reprinted in: Veselin Čajkanović. *Sabrana dela iz srpske religije i mitologije.* Book I: *Studije iz srpske religije i folklore,* 221–239. Beograd: Srpska Književna Zadruga, 1994. English translation: 'The Killing of a Vampire'. *Folklore – Forum* 7 (1974): 260–71. Reprint in: *The Vampire: A Casebook,* edited by Alan Dundes, 72–84. Madison, WI: University of Wisconsin Press, 1998.
Cazacu, Matei. *Dracula. Suivi du Capitaine Vampire: Une nouvelle roumaine par Marie Nizet (1879).* Paris: Tallandier, 2004.
Ceglia, Francesco Paolo. 'The Archbishop's Vampires: Giuseppe Davanzati's Dissertation and the Reaction of "Scientific" Italian Catholicism to the "Moravian Events"'. *Archives internationales d'histoire des sciences* 61 (2011): 487–510.
Chalupecký, Ivan: 'Die Zipser Deutschen im 18. Jahrhundert'. *Südostdeutsches Archiv* 54/55 (2001/2002): 21–30.
Copper, Basil. *The Vampire in Legend, Fact and Art.* London: Hale, 1973.
Coundouriotis, Eleni. 'Dracula and the Idea of Europe'. *Connotations. A Journal of Critical Debate* 9, no. 2 (1999/2000): 143–60.
Cremene, Adrien. *La Mythologie du Vampire en Roumanie.* Monaco: Éditions du Rocher, 1981.
Danneberg, Stéphanie. '"Vampire sind äußerst unordentliche Untertanen": Überlegungen zur Funktion und Instrumentalisierung des Vampirphänomens'. *Zeitschrift für Siebenbürgische Landeskunde* 33, no. 2 (2010): 177–92.
Day, Peter, ed. *Vampires: Myths and Metaphors of Enduring Evil.* Amsterdam: Editions Rodopi, 2006.
Demetracopoulou Lee, B. 'Greek Accounts of the Vrykolakas'. *Journal of American Folklore* 55, no. 217 (1942): 126–32.

Demidovich, P. P. 'Iz oblasti verovanii i skazanii belorussov'. *Etnograficheskoe obozrenie* 8, no. 1 (Moscow, 1896): 91–120.
Dettke, Barbara. *Die asiatische Hydra. Die Cholera von 1830/31 in Berlin und den preußischen Provinzen Posen, Preußen und Schlesien*. Berlin: De Gruyter, 1995.
Dimić, Milan V. 'Vampiromania in the Eighteenth Century: The Other Side of Enlightenment'. *Man and Nature. Proceedings of the Canadian Society for Eighteenth-Century Studies* 3 (1984): 1–22.
Dinzelbacher, Peter. *Die letzten Dinge: Himmel, Hölle, Fegefeuer im Mittelalter*. Freiburg im Breisgau: Herder, 1999.
Dömötör, Tekla. *Volksglaube und Aberglaube in Ungarn*. Budapest: Corvina Kiadó, 1981.
[Đorđević] Gjorgjević, Tihomir R. 'Die Zigeuner in Serbien. Ethnologische Forschungen'. Vol. I. Ph.D. dissertation, Ludwig Maximilian University of Munich, 1902. Budapest: Buchdruckerei Thalia, 1903.
Đorđević, Tihomir R. 'Gradja za srpske narodne običaje iz vremena prve vlade kneza Miloša. (Druga zbirka)'. *Srpski etnografski zbornik* 19 (1913): 443–67.
———. 'Vampir i druga bića u našem narodnom verovanju i predanju'. In *Srpski etnografski zbornik*. Vol. LXVI. 2nd division. *Život i običaji narodni*. Book 30, 147–282. Belgrade: Srpska Kraljevska Akademija, 1953.
Drechsler, Paul. *Sitte, Brauch und Volksglaube in Schlesien*. 2 vols. Leipzig: B.G. Teubner, 1903–6.
Drettas, Georges. 'Questions de vamprisme'. *Études rurales* 97–98 (1985): 201–18.
Dundes, Alan, ed. *The Vampire: A Casebook*. Madison, WI: University of Wisconsin Press, 1998.
Dürbeck, Gabriele. *Einbildungskraft und Aufklärung: Perspektiven der Philosophie, Anthropologie und Ästhetik um 1750*. Tübingen: Niemeyer, 1998.
Durham, Mary E[dith]. 'Of Magic, Witches and Vampires in the Balkans'. *Man. The Journal of the Royal Anthropological Institute* 23 (1923): 189–92.
Durst, Benjamin. '". . . da sie in den närrischen Wahn gestanden, daß es Vampyren gebe." Dimensionen des Aberglaubensbegriffs und Strategien der Aberglaubenskritik in gelehrten Beiträgen zur Vampirdebatte der 1730er Jahre'. *Mitteilungen des Instituts für Europäische Kulturgeschichte* 19 (2010): 32–104.
Eckert, Edward A. 'The Retreat of Plague from Central Europe, 1640–1720: A Geomedical Approach'. *Bulletin of the History of Medicine* 74 (2000): 1–28.
———. *The Structure of Plagues and Pestilences in Early Modern Europe: Central Europe, 1560–1640*. Basel: Karger, 1996.
Eckert, Georg, and P. E. Formozis: *Geister- und Dämonenglaube im Pontos*. Thessaloniki: [n.p.], 1943.
———. *Mazedonischer Volksglaube. Magie, Aberglaube und religiöse Vorstellungen in Saloniki und der West-Chalkidike*. Thessaloniki: [n.p.], 1943.
Efimenko, P.S. 'Upyri. (Iz istorii narodnikh verovanii)'. *Kievskaia starina* 6 (1883): 371–379.
Elsie, Robert. *Handbuch zur albanischen Volkskultur. Mythologie, Religion, Volksglaube, Sitten, Gebräuche und kulturelle Besonderheiten*. Wiesbaden: Harrassowitz, 2002.
Elvert, Christian d'. 'Das Zauber- und Hexenwesen, dann der Glauben an Vampyre in Mähren und Oesterr. Schlesien'. *Schriften der historisch-statistischen Section der k. k. mährisch-schlesischen Gesellschaft des Ackerbaues, der Natur- und Landeskunde* 12 (1859): 319–79. Reprint in: Ferdinand Bischof and Christian d'Elvert. *Zur Geschichte des Glaubens an Zauberer, Hexen und Vampyre in Mähren und Oesterr. Schlesien*, 62–122. Brünn: Rud. Erben, 1859.

———. 'Die Vampyre in Mähren'. *Schriften der historisch-statistischen Section der k. k. mährisch-schlesischen Gesellschaft des Ackerbaues, der Natur- und Landeskunde* 12 (1859): 410–21.

Erb, Rainer. 'Die Ritualmordlegende: Von den Anfängen bis ins 20. Jahrhundert'. In *Ritualmord: Legenden in der europäischen Geschichte*, edited by Susanna Buttaroni and Stanisław Musiał, 12–20. Vienna: Böhlau, 2003.

Faivre, Antoine. 'Du vampire villageois aux discours des clercs. (Genèse d'un imaginaire à l'aube des Lumières.)' In *Les Vampires. Colloque de Cerisy*, 45–74. Paris: Dervy, 1993.

Faivre, Tony. *Les vampires : Essai historique, critique et littéraire*. Paris: Eric Losfeld, 1962.

Farin, Michael, ed. *Heroine des Grauens: Wirken und Leben der Elisabeth Báthory in Briefen, Zeugenaussagen und Phantasiespielen*. 3rd, corrected and extended edn. Munich: Kirchheim, 2003.

Faroqhi, Suraiya. *Geschichte des Osmanischen Reiches*. Munich: C.H. Beck, 2000.

Filipovič, Milenko S. 'Die Leichenverbrennung bei den Südslawen'. *Wiener völkerkundliche Mitteilungen* 10/New Series 5, no. 1–4 (1962): 61–71.

Fine, John V.A. Jr. 'In Defense of Vampires: Church/State Efforts to Stop Vigilante Actions Against Vampires in Serbia during the First Reign of Miloš Obrenović'. *East European Quarterly* 21 (1987): 15–23. Reprinted in: *The Vampire: A Casebook*. Edited by Alan Dundes, 57–66. Madison, WI: University of Wisconsin Press, 1998.

Finucane, R[onald] C. *Appearances of the Dead: A Cultural History of Ghosts*. Buffalo, NY: Prometheus Books, 1984.

Fischer, Wilhelm. *Aberglaube aller Zeiten*. Vol. 3: *Dämonische Mittelwesen, Vampir und Werwolf in Geschichte und Sage*. Stuttgart: Strecker & Schröder, n.d. [about 1910].

Frenschkowski, Marco. 'Die Unverweslichkeit der Heiligen und der Vampire: Eine Studie über kulturelle Ambivalenz'. In *Vampirglaube und magia posthuma im Diskurs der Habsburgermonarchie*, edited by Christoph Augustynowicz and Ursula Reber, 53–68. Vienna: Lit, 2011.

———. 'Keine spitzen Zähne. Von der interkulturellen Vergleichbarkeit mythologischer Konzepte: das Beispiel des Vampirs'. In *Poetische Wiedergänger: Deutschsprachige Vampirismus-Diskurse vom Mittelalter bis zur Gegenwart*, edited by Julia Bertschik and Christa Agnes Tuczay, 43–59. Tübingen: Francke, 2005.

———. 'Vampire in Mythologie und Folklore'. In *Draculas Wiederkehr: Tagungsband 1997*, edited by Thomas Le Blanc, Clemens Ruthner and Bettina Twrsnick, 28–58. Wetzlar: Förderkreis Phantastik, 2003.

García Marín, Álvaro. 'Colonialismo metafórico y angustia de la influencia: el discurso fantástico en e filo de la disemia griega'. In *Mediterráneos: An Interdisciplinary Approach to the Cultures of the Mediterranean Seas*, edited by Sergio Carro Martin, Arturo Echavarren, Esther Fernández et al., 149–65. Newcastle: Cambridge Scholars Publishing, 2013.

———. 'Cuestiones preliminares para un studio de la literatura fantástica griega: un caso de repression en el canon literario nacional'. *Erytheia. Revista de Estudios Bizantinos y Neogriegos* 30 (2009): 285–303.

———. 'Haunted Communities: The Greek Vampire, or Uncanny at the Core of Nation Construction'. In *Monstrosity from the Inside out*, edited by Teresa Cutler-Boyes and Marko Teodorski, 109–42. Oxford: Inter-Disciplinary Press, 2014.

———. *Historias del vampiro griego*. Madrid: Consejo Superior de Investigaciones Cientificas, 2017.

———. 'Our Vampires, (Not) Ourselves: The Greek Undead in the Age of Racialization'. In *Race in the Vampire Narrative*, edited by U. Melissa Anyiwo, 7–22. Rotterdam: Sense Publishers, 2015.

———. '"The Son of the Vampire": Greek Gothic, or Gothic Greece?' In *Dracula and the Gothic in Literature, Pop Culture and the Arts*, edited by Isabel Ermida, 21–43. Leiden/Boston: Brill Rodopi, 2016.

Georgieva, Ivanichka. *Bŭlgarska narodna mifologiia*. Third, revised and enlarged edn. Sofia: Izdatelstvo na BAN 'Prof Marin Drinov', 2018.

Gerard, Emily. *The Land beyond the Forest: Facts, Figures, and Fancies from Transylvania*. 2 vols. Edinburgh: W. Blackwood and Sons, 1888.

———. 'Transylvanian Superstitions'. *The Nineteenth Century* 18 (July 1885): 130–50.

Gerrits, Andre, and Nanci Adler, eds. *Vampires Unstaked: National Images, Stereotypes and Myths in East Central Europe*. Amsterdam: North-Holland, 1995.

Gerschke, Leo. 'Vom Vampirglauben im alten Westpreußen'. *Westpreußen-Jahrbuch* 12 (1962): 89–94.

Gibson, Matthew. *Dracula and the Eastern Question: British and French Vampire Narratives of the Nineteenth-Century Near East*. Basingstoke: Palgrave Macmillan, 2006.

Gieysztor, Aleksander. *Mitologia Słowian: Warszawa 1982*. 3rd, revised and enlarged edn. Warsaw: Wydawnictwo Uniwersytetu Warszawskiego, 2006.

Goldsworthy, Vesna. *Inventing Ruritania: The Imperialism of the Imagination*. New Haven: Yale University Press, 1998.

Görres, Joseph von. 'Magischer Bezug der untersten Vitalkräfte im Todtenreiche; Vampyrism'. In *Die christliche Mystik*. Vol. 3, edited by Joseph von Görres, 275–88. Regensburg: Manz, 1840.

Gordon, Joan, and Veronica Hollinger, eds. *Blood Read: The Vampire as Metaphor in Contemporary Culture*. Philadelphia, PA: University of Pennsylvania Press, 1997.

Grenz, Rudolf. 'Archäologische Vampirbefunde aus dem westslawischen Siedlungsgebiet'. *Zeitschrift für Ostforschung* 16 (1967): 255–65.

Grober-Glück, Gerda. 'Der Verstorbene als Nachzehrer'. In *Atlas der deutschen Volkskunde. Neue Folge. Auf Grund der von 1929 bis 1935 durchgeführten Sammlungen. Erläuterungen zu den Karten 43–48*, edited by Matthias Zender, 426–56. Marburg: N. G. Elwert, 1981.

———. 'Volksglaubenvorstellungen über die scheidende Seele: Erscheinungsformen in Deutschland und Österreich um 1930'. *Jahrbuch für Volkskunde* New Series 6 (1983): 149–81.

Groom, Nick. *The Vampire: A New History*. New Haven: Yale University Press, 2018.

Győry, Tiberius von. *Morbus Hungaricus: Eine medico-historische Quellenstudie, zugleich ein Beitrag zur Geschichte der Türkenherrschaft in Ungarn*. Jena: Fischer, 1901.

Haase, Felix. *Volksglaube und Brauchtum der Ostslaven*. Reprint: Beslau: Märtin, 1939. Reprint: Hildesheim: Georg Olms Verlag, 1980.

Hamberger, Klaus. *Über Vampirismus: Krankengeschichten und Deutungsmuster 1801–1899*. Vienna: Turia & Kant, 1992.

Hammer, Anton v. *Geschichte der Pest, die von 1738 bis 1740 im Temeswarer Banate herrschte: Ein aus glaubwürdigen Quellen geschöpfter Beitrag zur Geschichte dieses Landes*. Temeswar: Joseph Reichel, 1839.

Harnack, Adolf. *Geschichte der Königlich Preussischen Akademie der Wissenschaften zu Berlin*. Vol. I. Part 1. *Von der Gründung bis zum Tode Friedrich's des Großen*. Part 2. *Vom*

Tode Friedrich's des Großen bis zur Gegenwart. Berlin: Reichsdruckerei, 1900. Reprint: Hildesheim: Olms, 1970.
Härtel, Hans-Joachim, and Schönfeld, Roland. *Bulgarien: Vom Mittelalter bis zur Gegenwart*. Regensburg: Pustet, 1998.
Harris, Robin: *Dubrovnik: A History*. London: Saqi Books, 2003.
Hartnup, Karen. '*On the Belief of the Greeks': Leo Allatios and Popular Orthodoxy*. Leiden: Brill, 2004.
Hasenfratz, Hans-Peter. *Leben mit den Toten: Eine Kultur- und Religionsgeschichte der anderen Art*. Freiburg im Breisgau: Herder, 1998.
Havekost, Ernst.'Die Vampirsage in England'. Ph.D. dissertation, Halle/Saale: Buchdruckerei Hohmann, 1914.
Heiden, Anne von der. *Der Jude als Medium: 'Jud Süß'*. Zürich: Diaphanes, 2005.
———.'Der Zerstörer allen Lebens:'Jud Süß' als politischer Vampir'. In *Jud Süß': Hofjude, literarische Figur, antisemitisches Zerrbild*, edited by Alexandra Przyrembel and Jörg Schönert, 325–36. Frankfurt: Campus Verlag, 2006.
Hellwig, Albert. 'Deutscher Volksglaube vor Gericht'. *Archiv für Religionswissenschaft* 18 (1915): 287–300.
———. *Verbrechen und Aberglaube: Skizzen aus der volkskundlichen Kriminalistik*. Leipzig: Teubner, 1908.
Hempler, Franz. *Psychologie des Volksglaubens, insbesondere der volkstümlichen Natur- und Heilkunde des Weichsellandes*. Königsberg: Gräfe und Unzer, 1930.
Hennigsen, Gustav.'Das Ende der Hexenprozesse und die Fortsetzung der populären Hexenverfolgung'. In *Das Ende der Hexenverfolgung*, edited by Sönke Lorenz and Dieter R. Bauer, 315–28. Stuttgart: Steiner, 1995.
Hepp, Oliver. *Der bekannte Fremde: Der Vampir in der Literatur des 19. Jahrhunderts*. Frankfurt: Peter Lang, 2017.
Hepp, Oliver.'Vom Aberglauben hin zur "magischen Würckung" der Einbildung. Michael Ranffts Tractat von dem Kauen und Schmatzen der Todten in Gräbern'. In *Vampirglaube und magia posthuma im Diskurs der Habsburgermonarchie*, edited by Christoph Augustynowicz and Ursula Reber, 105–23. Vienna: Lit, 2011.
Heppner, Harald, and Damiela Schanes:'The Impact on the Treaty of Passarowitz on the Habsburg Monarchy'. In *The Peace of Passarowitz, 1718*, edited by Charles Ingrao, Nikola Samardžić and Jovan Pešalj, 53–62. West Lafayette, IN: Purdue University Press, 2011.
Hering, Gunnar.'Das Jahr 1683 und die orthodoxen Völker Südosteuropas'. *Römische Historische Mitteilungen* 26 (1984): 361–85. Reprint in: Gunnar Hering. *Nostos. Gesammelte Schriften zur südosteuropäischen Geschichte*, edited by Maria A. Stassinopoulou, 149–76. Frankfurt: Lang, 1995.
Himstedt-Vaid, Petra.'Der Vampir in der südslawischen und rumänischen Volksdichtung'. In *Romanica et Balcanica: Wolfgang Dahmen zum 65. Geburtstag*, edited by Thede Kahl et al., 559–88. Munich: Akademische Verlagsgemeinschaft, 2015.
Hochedlinger, Michael. *Austria's Wars of Emergence: War, State and Society in the Habsburg Monarchy, 1683–1797*. London: Longman, 2003.
Hock, Stefan. *Die Vampyrsagen und ihre Verwertung in der deutschen Literatur*. Berlin: A. Duncker, 1900. Reprint: Hildesheim: Gerstenberg Verlag, 1977.
Höfert, Almut. *Den Feind beschreiben: 'Türkengefahr' und europäisches Wissen über das Osmanische Reich 1450–1600*. Frankfurt: Campus Verlag, 2003.

Hösch, Edgar. *Geschichte des Balkans*. Munich: C.H. Beck, 2004.
Hösler, Joachim. *Slowenien: Von den Anfängen bis zur Gegenwart*. Regensburg: Pustet, 2006.
Huet, Marie-Hélène. 'Deadly Fears: Dom Augustin Calmet's Vampires and the Rule over Death'. *Eighteenth-Century Life* 21 (1997): 222–32.
Hughes, William. 'A Singular Invasion: Revisiting the Postcoloniality of Bram Stoker's Dracula'. In *Empire and the Gothic: The Politics of Genre*, edited by Andrew Smith and William Hughes, 88–102. Basingstoke: Palgrave Macmillan, 2003.
Ionescu, Ioana-Maria. 'Rumänische Übergangsriten dargelegt am Beispiel der Lebensbräuche in Oltenien'. Ph.D. dissertation, University of Münster, 1986.
Irgang, Winfried. 'Die Stellung des Deutschen Ordens zum Aberglauben am Beispiel der Herrschaften Freudenthal und Eulenburg'. In *Von Akkon bis Wien. Studien zur Deutschordensgeschichte vom 13. bis zum 20. Jahrhundert. Festschrift zum 90. Geburtstag von Althochmeister P. Dr. Marian Tumler O. T. am 21. Oktober 1977*, edited by Udo Arnold, 261–71. Marburg: N.G. Elwert, 1978.
Jagić, V. 'Vukòdlak – Kodlàk vor Gericht'. *Archiv für slawische Philologie* 6 (1882): 618–20.
Jakobsson, Ármann. 'The Fearless Vampire Killers: A Note about the Icelandic Draugr and Demonic Contamination in Grettis Saga'. *Folklore* 120 (2009): 307–16.
———. 'Vampires and Watchmen: Categorizing the Mediaeval Icelandic Undead'. *Journal of English and Germanic Philology* 110, no. 3 (2011): 281–300.
Janion, Maria. *Wampir. Biografia symboliczna*. Gdańsk: Słowo/Obraz terytoria, 2004.
Jellinek, Arthur L. 'Zur Vampyrsage'. *Zeitschrift des Vereins für Volkskunde* 14 (1904): 322–28.
Jireček, Constantin. *Das Fürstentum Bulgarien: Seine Bodengestaltung, Natur, Bevölkerung, Wirthschaftliche Zustände, geistige Cultur, Staatsverwaltung und neueste Geschichte*. Prague: Tempksy, 1891.
Jung, Martin H. *Reformation und Konfessionelles Zeitalter (1517–1648)*. Göttingen: Vandenhoeck & Ruprecht, 2012.
Kaser, Karl. 'Ahnenkult und Patriarchalismus auf dem Balkan'. *Historische Anthropologie* 1 (1993): 93–122.
———. *Familie und Verwandtschaft auf dem Balkan: Analyse einer untergehenden Kultur*. Vienna: Böhlau, 1995.
———. *Freier Bauer und Soldat: Die Militarisierung der agrarischen Gesellschaft an der kroatisch-slawonischen Militärgrenze (1535–1881)*. Vienna: Böhlau, 1997.
———. *Hirten, Kämpfer, Stammeshelden: Ursprünge und Gegenwart des balkanischen Patriarchats*. Vienna: Böhlau, 1992.
———. *Macht und Erbe. Männerherrschaft, Besitz und Familie im östlichen Europa (1500–1900)*. Vienna: Böhlau, 2000.
Kättlitz, Christian. "'... Man braucht also nicht nur auf dem Balkan zu suchen." Oder: Wie slawisch darf Dracula sein?' *Bohemia* 50 (2010): 333–50.
Keyworth, David. 'The Aetiology of Vampires and Revenants: Theological Debate and Popular Belief'. *Journal of Religious History* 34, no. 2 (2010): 158–73.
———. *Troublesome Corpses: Vampires and Revenants from Antiquity to the Present*. Southend-on-Sea: Desert Island Books, 2007.
———. 'Was the Vampire of the Eighteenth Century a Unique Type of Undead-Corpse?' *Folklore* 117, no. 3 (2006): 241–60.
Kırgı, Salim Fikret. *Osmanlı Vampirleri: Söylenceler, Etkiler, Tepkiler*. Istanbul: İletişim Yayınları, 2018.

Klaniczay, Gábor. 'Decline of Witches and Rise of Vampires in 18th Century Habsburg Monarchy'. *Ethnologia Europea* 17 (1987): 165–80.
Klapper, Josef. 'Die schlesischen Geschichten von den schädigenden Toten'. *Mitteilungen der schlesischen Gesellschaft für Volkskunde* 11 (1909): 58–93.
Klare, Hans Joachim. 'Die Toten in der altnordischen Literatur'. *Acta Philologica Scandinavica* 8 (1933/1934): 1–56.
Kleinpaul, Rudolf. *Die Lebendigen und die Toten in Volksglauben, Religion und Sage*. Leipzig: Göschen, 1898.
Klingmann, Gail. *The Wedding of the Dead: Ritual, Poetics and Popular Culture in Transylvania*. Berkeley: University of California Press, 1988.
Köhbach, Markus. 'Ein Fall von Vampirismus bei den Osmanen'. *Balkan Studies* 20 (1979): 83–90.
Kolberg, Oskar. *Lud. Jego zwyczaje, sposób życia, mowa, podania, przysłowia, obrzędy, gusła, zabawy, pieśni, muzyka i tańce*. Series VII. *Krakowskie*. Vol. 3. Kraków: Drukarnia Uniwersiteta Jagiellońskiego, 1874; Vol. 7. Kraków: Drukarnia Universiteta Jagiellońskiego, 1882. Reprint: 1962. Series XV. *W. Ks. Pozańskie*. Vol. 7. Kraków: Drukarnia Uniwersiteta Jagiellońskiego, 1882. Reprint: 1962. Series XVII. *Lubelskie*. Vol. 2. Kraków: Drukarnia Uniwersiteta Jagiellońskiego, 1884. Reprint: 1962.
Konstantinos. *Vampires: The Occult Truth*. St Paul, MN: Llewellyn Publications, 1996.
Köpeczi, Béla. 'Un Scandale des Lumiéres. Les Vampires'. In *Thèmes et figures du siècle des Lumières. Mélanges offerts à Roland Mortier*, edited by Raymond Trousson, 123–35. Genève: Librairie Droz, 1980. Reprint: 'Les vampires de Hongrie : un scandale des Lumières'. *Artes populares. A Folklore Tanszék Évkönyve* 7 (1981): 87–105.
Köppl, Rainer M. *Der Vampir sind wir: Der unsterbliche Mythos von Dracula bis Twilight*. Vienna: Residenz, 2010.
Kormina, Zh. V., and S. A. Shtyrkov. 'Mir zhivykh i mir mertvykh: sposoby kontaktov (dva varianta severnorusskoi traditsii)'. In *Vostochnoslaviansko-etnolingvisticheskii sbornik. Issledovaniia i materialy*, 206–31. Moscow: Indrik, 2001.
Kosior, Wojciech. 'Kompleks upiora-wampira i jego realizacja we współczesności. Duchowość wampiryczna'. *Ex Nihilo. Periodyk młodych religioznawców* 1 (2009): 64–81.
Kostić, Zvonimir. 'Vampir u našem narodnom verovanju, zapisima i pričima'. In *Srpska fantastika: Natprirodno i nestvarno u srpskoj književnosti. Urednik: Predrag Palavestra*, 245–59. Beograd: Sprska akad. nauka i umetnosti, 1989.
Krauss, Friedrich S. 'Der Tod in Sitte, Brauch und Glauben der Südslaven: Vorwiegend nach eigenen Ermittlungen'. *Zeitschrift des Vereins für Volkskunde* 1 (1891): 148–63.
———. *Sitte und Brauch der Südslaven: Nach heimischen gedruckten und ungedruckten Quellen*. Vienna: Hölder, 1985.
———. *Slavische Volksforschungen: Abhandlungen über Glauben, Gewohnheitsrechte, Sitten, Bräuche und die Guslarenlieder der Südslaven*. Leipzig: Heims, 1908.
———. 'Vampirglaube in Serbien und Lithauen'. *Mittheilungen der Anthropologischen Gesellschaft in Wien* 17 (1887): 67/68.
Kremer, Peter. *Draculas Vettern: Totenglaube und Wiedergängerfurcht im vorindustriellen Deutschland*. Düren: PeKa.De-Verlag, 2009.
Kreuter, Peter Mario. *Der Vampirglaube in Südosteuropa: Studien zur Genese, Bedeutung und Funktion. Rumänien und der Balkanraum*. Berlin: Weidler Buchverlag, 2001.
———. 'Krankheit und Vampirglaube: Ein Beitrag zur Phänomenologie des blutsaugenden Wiedergängers in Südosteuropa'. *Quo vadis, Romania? Zeitschrift für eine aktuelle Romanistik* 18/19 (2001/2002): 59–72.

———. 'The Name of the Vampire: Some Reflections on Current Linguistic Theories on the Etymology of the Word Vampire'. In *Vampires: Myths and Metaphors of Enduring Evil*, edited by Peter Day, 57–80. Amsterdam: Editions Rodopi, 2006.

———. 'The Role of Women in Southeast European Vampire Belief'. In *Women in the Ottoman Balkans: Gender, Culture and History*, edited by Amila Buturović and İrvin Cemil Schıck, 231–41. London: I.B. Tauris, 2007.

———. 'Vom "üblen Geist" zum "Vampyr": Die Darstellung des Vampirs und seines kulturellen Hintergrunds in den Berichten österreichischer Militärärzte zwischen 1725 und 1756'. In *Poetische Wiedergänger: Deutschsprachige Vampirismus-Diskurse vom Mittelalter bis zur Gegenwart*, edited by Julia Bertschik and Christa Agnes Tuczay, 113–27. Tübingen: Francke, 2005.

Krieglieder, Wynfried, Andrea Seidler, and Jozef Tanzer, eds. *Deutsche Sprache und Kultur in der Zips*. Bremen: Edition Lumière, 2007.

Kührer, Florian. *Vampire. Monster – Mythos – Medienstar*. Kevelaer: Butzon & Bercker, 2010.

Lambrecht, Karen. *Obrigkeiten und Hexenverfolgungen: Zaubereiprozesse in den schlesischen Territorien*. Vienna: Böhlau, 1995.

———. 'Wiedergänger und Vampire in Ostmitteleuropa – Postume Verbrennung statt Hexenverfolgung?' *Jahrbuch für deutsche und osteuropäische Volkskunde* 37 (1994): 49–77.

Landgrebe, Alix. *'Wenn es Polen nicht gäbe, dann müßte es erfunden werden': Die Entwicklung des polnischen Nationalbewußtseins im europäischen Kontext von 1830 bis in die 1880er Jahre*. Wiesbaden: Harrassowitz, 2003.

Lange, Erwin Rudolf. *Sterben und Begräbnis im Volksglauben zwischen Weichsel und Memel*. Würzburg: Holzner, 1955.

Langer, Official. 'Serbien unter der kaiserlichen Regierung 1717–1739'. *Mitteilungen des k. k. Kriegsarchivs* 3 (1889): 155–247.

Lauper, Anja. 'Das Blut der Vampire'. In *Blood in History and Blood Histories*, edited by Mariacarla Gadebusch Bondio, 255–71. Florence: Sismel, 2005.

———. *Die phantastische Seuche: Episoden des Vampirismus im 18. Jahrhundert*. Zürich: Diaphanes, 2011.

———. 'Die "phantastische Seuche": Johann Christoph Harenbergs Theoretisierung der vampiristischen Einbildungskraft'. In *Dracula unbound: Kulturwissenschaftliche Lektüren des Vampirs*, edited by Christian Begemann Britta Herrmann and Harald Neumeyer, 51–73. Freiburg im Breisgau: Rombach, 2008.

Lawson, John Cuthbert. *Modern Greek Folklore and Ancient Greek Religion: A Study in Survivals*. Cambridge: Cambridge University Press, 1910. Reprint: New York: University Books, 1964.

Lecouteux, Claude. *The Return of the Dead: Ghosts, Ancestors and the Transparent Veil of the Pagan Mind*. Translated by Jon E. Graham. Rochester, VT: Inner Traditions, 2009.

———. *The Secret History of Vampires: Their Multiple Forms and Hidden Purposes*. Translated by Jon E. Graham. Rochester. Vermont: Inner Traditions, 2010.

———. *Witches, Werewolves and Fairies: Shapeshifters and Astral Doubles in the Middle Ages*. Translated by Clare Frock. Rochester, VT: Inner Traditions, 2003

Leithner, Andreas, and Christian Reiter. 'Vampirismus aus medizinischer Sicht'. In *100 Jahre Dracula*, edited by Rainer M. Köppl, 147–53. Vienna: Böhlau, 1998.

Leschber, Corinna. 'Vampirismus in Bulgarien und seine globalen Parallelen'. In *Deutsch-Bulgarischer Kultur- und Wissenschaftstransfer*, edited by Helmut Schaller and Rumjana Zlatanova, 187–96. Berlin: Frank & Timme, 2013.

Lesky, Erna. 'Die österreichische Pestfront an der k. k. Militärgrenze'. *Saeculum* 8 (1957): 82–106.
Lettenbauer, Wilhelm. 'Über Krankheitsdämonen im Volksglauben der Balkanslaven'. In *Serta Monacensia: Franz Babinger zum 15. Januar 1951 als Festgruß dargebracht*, edited by Hans Joachim Kissling and Alois Schmaus, 120–35. Leiden: Brill, 1952.
Levenstim, A. *Sueverie i ugolovnoe pravo*. St Petersburg, [1897].
Light, Duncan. *The Dracula Dilemma: Tourism, Identity and the State in Romania*. Farnham: Ashgate, 2012.
Lilek, Emilijan. 'Etnološki pabirci po Bosni i Hercegovini'. *Glasnik Zemaljskog muzeja u Bosni i Hercegovini* 11 (1899): 700–21.
———. 'Familien- und Volksleben in Bosnien und in der Herzegowina'. *Zeitschrift für österreichische Volkskunde* 6 (1900): 23–30, 53–72, 164–72, 202–25.
Lompa, Joseph. 'Schlesien in slavisch-mythologischer Hinsicht'. *Schlesische Provinzialblätter* 1 (1862): 393–96.
Longinović, Tomislav Z. *Vampire Nation: Violence as Cultural Imaginary*. Durham, NC: Duke University Press, 2011.
Lotter, Friedrich. 'Innocens virgo et martyr: Thomas von Monmouth und die Verbreitung der Ritualmordlegende im Hochmittelalter'. In *Die Legende vom Ritualmord: Zur Geschichte der Blutbeschuldigung gegen Juden*, edited by Rainer Erb, 25–72. Berlin: Metropol Verlag, 1993.
Lübeck, K.L. 'Die Krankheitsdämonen der Balkanvölker'. *Zeitschrift des Vereins für Volkskunde* 8 (1898): 241–49, 379–89.
Lübke, Christian, ed. *Struktur und Wandel im Früh- und Hochmittelalter: Eine Bestandsaufnahme aktueller Forschungen zur Germania Slavica*. Stuttgart: Stuttgart 1998.
Lugt, Maaike van der. 'The Incubus in Scholastic Debate: Medicine, Theology and Popular Belief'. In *Religion and Medicine in the Middle Ages*, edited by Peter Biller and Josef Ziegler, 175–200. York: York Medieval Press, 2001.
Łysiak, Wojciech. *W kręgu wielkopolskich demonów i przekonań niedemonicznych*. Międzychód: Eco, 1993.
Mackenzie, Andrew. *Dracula Country: Travels and Folk Beliefs in Romania*. London: Barker, 1977.
Mader, Wilhelm. *Chronik der Stadt Lewin*. Habelschwerdt: G. Göbel, 1868; 2nd supplemented edn, Lewin: G. Göbel, 1903.
Magyar, László András. 'Die siebenbürgische "Vampir-Krankheit"'. *Communicationes de historia artis medicinae* 186–87 (2004): 49–62.
———. 'Über die siebenbürgische Vampir-Krankheit: Ein Bericht des deutschen Chirurgen Georg Tallar aus dem Jahre 1755'. *Zeitschrift für siebenbürgische Landeskunde* 25 (2002): 161–64.
Maiello, Giuseppe. *Vampyrismus a Magia posthuma: Vampyrismus v kulturních dějinách Evropy a Magia posthuma Karla Ferdinanda Schertze (první novodobé vydání)*. 2nd enlarged edn. Prague: Epocha, 2014.
Malinka A.N. [Cover: Malinka A.N. Tschernigow]: *Ukrainische Dämonologie: Überlieferte Ursprünge und kultisches Brauchtum der Hexen und Hexer über das Leben der Toten, der Geister, Werwölfe und Vampire*. 2nd edn. Leipzig: Bohmeier Verlag, 2005.
Mannhardt, Wilhelm. *Die praktischen Folgen des Aberglaubens, mit besonderer Berücksichtigung der Provinz Preußen*. Berlin: C. Habel, 1878.
———. 'Über Vampyrismus'. *Zeitschrift für deutsche Mythologie und Sittenkunde* 4 (1859): 259–82.

Marinov, D. *Narodna viara i religiozni narodni obichai*. Sofia: Izdatelstvo na Bŭlgarskata Akademiia na naukite, 1914.

McClelland, Bruce A. *Slayers and their Vampires: A Cultural History of Killing the Dead*. Ann Arbor: University of Michigan Press, 2006.

McNally, Raymond T. *A Clutch of Vampires: These Being among the Best from History and Literature*. Greenwich, CT: New York Graphic Society, 1975.

Medek, Vaclav. 'Vom Satanismus auf dem nordmährischen Herrschaftsbesitz des Deutschen Ordens'. In *Acht Jahrhunderte Deutscher Orden in Einzeldarstellungen*, edited by Klemens Wieser, 387–93. Bad Godesberg: Verlag wissenschaftliches Archiv, 1967.

Meyer, Hans B. *Das Danziger Volksleben*. Würzburg: Holzner, 1956.

Mézes, Ádám. 'Visum Repertum: Georg Tallar és az 1753-as Vámpírvadászat'. In *Boszorkányok, varázslók és démonok Közép-Kelet-Európában*, edited by Gábor Klaniczay and Éva Pócs, 109–54. Budapest: Balassi Kiadó, 2014.

Milićević, M.Đ. *Kraljevina Srbija. Novi krajevi*. Beograd: Kr.- Srp. Državne Štamparije, 1884.

Mischke, Marianne. *Der Umgang mit dem Tod: Vom Wandel in der abendländischen Geschichte*. Berlin: Dietrich Reimer, 1996.

Moszyński, Kazimierz. *Kultura ludowa słowian: Kultura materialna*. Vol. II: *Kultura duchowa*. 2 vols. Kraków: Polska Akademia Umiejętności, 1929–34; 2nd edn, Warsaw: Książka i Wiedza, 1967.

Mücke, Marion. 'Wissenschaft im Netz: Die Deutsche Akademie der Naturforscher (Leopoldina) und ihre Verbindungen nach Wien um 1750'. In *Wiener Gespräche zur Sozialgeschichte der Medizin: Wissensaustausch in der Medizin des 18. Jahrhunderts*, edited by Sonia Horn, Gabriele Dorfner and Rosemarie Eichinger, 25–44. Vienna: Verlagshaus der Ärzte, 2007.

Mücke, Marion, and Thomas Schnalke, eds. *Briefnetz Leopoldina*. Berlin: De Gruyter, 2009.

Müller, Friedrich. 'Beiträge zur Kenntniss der Rom-Sprache'. *Sitzungsberichte der Kaiserlichen Akademie der Wissenschaften. Philosophisch-Historische Classe* 61, no. 1 (1869): 149–206.

Murgoci, Agnes. 'The Vampire in Roumania'. *Folklore. A Quarterly Review of Myth, Tradition, Institution and Custom* 37 (1926): 320–49. Reprint in: *The Vampire: A Casebook*, edited by Alan Dundes, 12–34. Madison, WI: University of Wisconsin Press, 1998.

Nadmorski [= Józef Łegowski]. *Kaszuby i kociewie: Język, zwyczaje, przesądy, podania, zagadki i pieśni ludowe v pólnocnej części Prus zachodnich*. Poznań: Czcionkami drukarni Dziennika Poznańskiego, 1892. Reprint: Gdańsk: Zrzeszenie Kaszubsko-Pomorkie, 1991.

Negelein, Julius. 'Die Reise der Seele in Jenseits'. *Zeitschrift des Vereins für Volkskunde* 11 (1901): 16–28, 149–58, 263–71.

———. 'Macedonischer Seelenglaube und Totenkultus'. *Zeitschrift des Vereins für Volkskunde* 14 (1904): 19–35.

Niendorf, Mathias. *Das Großfürstentum Litauen: Studien zur Nationsbildung in der Frühen Neuzeit (1569–1795)*. Wiesbaden: Harrassowitz, 2006

Niederle, Lubor. *Život starých Slovanů: Zaklady kulturnich starožitnosti slovanských*. Vol. II. Part 1. 2nd edn. Prague: Bursíka & Kohouta, 1924.

Nowosadtko, Jutta. 'Der Vampir als abergläubisches Wunderwerk: Konfessionell geprägte Auseinandersetzungen mit dem südosteuropäischen Vampirglauben'. In *Anfechtungen der Vernunft: Wunder und Wunderglaube in der Neuzeit*, edited by Ute Küppers-Braun, Jutta Nowosadtko and Rainer Walz, 175–89. Essen: Klartext, 2006.

———. 'Der "Vampyrus Serviensis" und sein Habitat: Impressionen von der österreichischen Militärgrenze'. *Militär und Gesellschaft in der Frühen Neuzeit* 8 (2004): 153–70.
Oinas, Felix. 'East European Vampires & Dracula'. *Journal of Popular Culture* 16, no. 1 (1982): 108–16. Reprint in: *The Vampire. A Casebook*, edited by Alan Dundes, 47–56. Madison, WI: University of Wisconsin Press, 1998. Reprint in: Felix Oinas. *Essays on Russian Folklore and Mythology*, 111–20. Columbus, OH: Slavica Publishers, 1985.
———. 'Heretics as Vampires and Demons in Russia'. *Slavic and East European Journal* 22 (1978): 433–41. Reprint in: Felix Oinas. *Essays on Russian Folklore and Mythology*, 121–30. Columbus, OH: Slavica Publishers, 1985-
Oldrige, Darren. '"Dead Man Walking": The Historical Context of Vampire Beliefs'. In *Vampires: Myths and Metaphors of Enduring Evil*, edited by Peter Day, 57–80. Amsterdam: Editions Rodopi, 2006.
———. *Strange Histories: The Trial of a Pig, the Walking Dead, and Other Matters of Fact from the Medieval and Renaissance Worlds*. London: Routledge, 2005.
Olivares Merino, Eugenio. 'El Vampiro en la Europa medieval: el caso inglés'. *Cuadernos del Cemyr* 14, no. 12 (2006): 205–32.
———. 'The Old English Poem "A Vampire of the Fens": A Bibliographical Ghost'. *Miscelánea. A Journal of English and American Studies* 32 (2005): 87–102.
Palladino, Irmgard. *Johann Weichard von Valvasor (1641–1693): Protagonist der Wissenschaftsrevolution der Frühen Neuzeit. Leben, Werk und Nachlass*. Vienna: Böhlau, 2008.
Panzac, Daniel. *La peste dans l'Empire ottoman. 1700–1850*. Leuven: Peeters, 1985.
Pavković, Nikola F. *Banatsko selo: Društvene i kulturne promene. Gaj i Dubovac*. Novi Sad: Matica srpska, Odeljenje za društvene nauke, 2009.
Pełka, Leonard. *Polska demonologia ludowa*. Warsaw: Wydawnictwo Naukowe PWN, 1987.
Perkowski, Jan L. *The Darkling: A Treatise on Slavic Vampirism*. Columbus, OH: Slavica Publishers, 1989.
———. 'The Romanian Folkloric Vampire'. *East European Quarterly* 16 (1982): 311–22.
———. 'The Vampires of Bulgaria and Macedonia: An Update'. *Balkanistica* 12 (1999): 83–94.
———. *Vampires of the Slavs*. Cambridge, MA: Slavica Publishers, 1976.
Petoia, Erberto. *Vampiri e lupi mannari: Le origini, la storia, le leggende di due tra le più inquietanti figure demoniache, dall'antichità classica ai nostri giorni*. Rome: Newton Compton, 1991.
Petri, Anton Peter. *Beiträge zur Geschichte des Heilwesens im Banat*. Marquartstein: Breit, 1988
———. *Heimatbuch der Marktgemeinde Neuarad im Banat*. Marquartstein: Breit, 1985.
———. 'Zur Volkskunde der Banater Rumänen und Serben. "Blutsauger" (Vampire) in den Aktenauszügen der Temeschburger Landesadministration 1725–1753'. *Südostdeutsches Archiv* 4 (1961): 140–143.
Petzold, Ruth. 'The Comeback of the Vampires: The History of the Motif from Medieval Legends to Contemporary Literature'. In *Demons: Mediators between This World and the Other. Essays on Demonic Beings from the Middle Ages to the Present*, edited by Ruth Petzold and Paul Neubauer, 153–64. Frankfurt: Peter Lang, 1998.
Pletzing, Christian. *Vom Völkerfrühling zum nationalen Konflikt: Deutscher und polnischer Nationalismus in Ost- und Westpreußen 1830–1871*. Wiesbaden: Harrassowitz, 2003.
Pócs, Eva. *Between the Living and the Dead: A Perspective on Witches and Seers in the Early Modern Age*. Budapest: Central European University Press, 1999.

———. *Fairies and Witches at the Boundary of South-Eastern and Central Europe*. Helsinki: Suomalainen Tiedeakatemia, 1989.

Podskalsky, Gerhard. *Griechische Theologie in der Zeit der Türkenherrschaft (1453–1821): Die Orthodoxie im Spannungsfeld der nachreformatorischen Konfessionen des Westens*. Munich: C.H. Beck, 1988.

Popov, Rachko. 'Vampirŭt v bŭlgarskite narodni viarvaniia.' *Vekove* 12, no. 1 (1983): 36–43.

Porset, Charles. 'Vampires et Lumières.' *Studies on Voltaire and the Eighteenth Century* 266 (1989): 125–50.

Radulović, Lidija. 'Vampir: osujećeni mitski predak i symbol osujećenog muškog seksualnog potencijala.' *Etnoantropološki problemi* 1, no. 1 (2006): 181–202.

Radin, Ana. *Motiv vampira u mitu i književnosti*. Belgrade: Prosveta, 1996.

Ragagnin, Elisabetta. 'Is "Vampire" a Turkic Word?' In *Tra quattro paradisi. esperienze, ideologie e riti relativi alla morte tra Oriente e Occidente*, edited by Antonio Fabris, 60–70. Venice: Edizioni Ca' Foscari, 2013.

Ralston, W.R.S. *Russian Folk-Tales*. London: Smith, Elder & Co., 1873.

———. *The Songs of the Russian People, as illustrative of Slavonic Mythology and Russian Social Life*. London: Ellis & Green, 1872.

Ranke, Friedrich. 'Der Huckup.' In Friedrich Ranke. *Volkssagenforschung: Vorträge und Aufsätze*, 39–69. Breslau: Maruschke & Berendt, 1935.

Ranke, Lepold. *Die serbische Revolution: Aus serbischen Papieren und Mittheilungen*. Hamburg: Friedrich Perthes, 1829; 2nd edn, Berlin: Duncker and Humblot, 1844.

Rau, Tilman. *Das Commercium Litterarium: Die erste medizinische Wochenschrift in Deutschland und die Anfänge des medizinischen Journalismus*. Bremen: Edition Lumière, 2009.

Rauer, Constantin. 'Von der Aufklärung des Vampirismus zum Vampirismus der Aufklärung: Eine west-östliche Debatte zwischen einst und heute.' *ethic@ – Revista internacional de Filosofia da moral* 7, no. 1 (2008): 87–107.

Reiter, Christian. 'Der Vampyr-Aberglaube und die Militärärzte.' *Kakanien revisited*, 17 August 2009. Retrieved 2 November 2018 from http://www.kakanien.ac.at/beitr/vamp/CReiter1.pdf. Reprinted in: *Vampirglaube und magia posthuma im Diskurs der Habsburgermonarchie*, edited by Christoph Augustynowicz and Ursula Reber, 125–46. Vienna: Lit, 2011.

Reiter, Norbert. *Das Glaubensgut der Slawen im europäischen Verbund*. Wiesbaden: Harrassowitz, 2009.

Rieger, Miriam. *Der Teufel im Pfarrhaus. Gespenster, Geisterglaube und Besessenheit im Luthertum der Frühen Neuzeit*. Stuttgart: Steiner, 2011.

Risteski, L'upcho S. 'Categories of the "Evil Dead" in Macedonian Folk Religion.' In *Christian Demonology and Popular Mythology*, edited by Gábor Klaniczay and Éva Pócs, 202–11. Budapest: Central European University Press, 2006.

Robinson, Sara Libby. *Blood Will Tell. Vampires as Political Metaphors before World War I*. Boston: Academic Studies Press, 2011.

Rock, Stella. *Popular Religion in Russia: 'Double Belief' and the Making of an Academic Myth*. London: Routledge, 2007.

Rößler, Helmut. *Die freie Bergstadt Bennisch. Ein Rückblick auf Schicksal und Lebensart einer sudetendeutschen Kleinstadt*. Munich: Selbstverlag Heimatkreisrat Freudenthal, 1962.

Roth, Harald. *Kleine Geschichte Siebenbürgens*. 4th ed. Cologne: Böhlau, 2012.

Rothenberg, Gunther E. 'The Austrian Sanitary Cordon and the Control of the Bubonic Plague: 1710–1871.' *Journal of the History of Medicine and Allied Sciences* XXVIII, no. 1 (1973): 15–23.

———. *Die österreichische Militärgrenze in Kroatien 1522 bis 1881.* Vienna: Herold, 1970.

Ruickbie, Leo. 'Evidence for the Undead: The Role of Medical Investigation in the 18th-Century Vampire Epidemic'. In *The Universal Vampire: Origins and Evolution of a Legend*, edited by Barbara Brodman and James O. Doan, 75–90. Plymouth: Fairleigh Dickinson University Press, 2013.

———. 'Memento (non)mori: Memory, Discourse and Transmission during the Eighteenth-Century Vampire Epidemic and after'. In *Undead Memory: Vampires and Human Memory in Popular Culture*, edited by Simon Bacon and Katarzyna Bronk, 21–58. Oxford: Peter Lang, 2014.

Runciman, Steven. *The Great Church in Captivity: A Study of the Patriarchate of Constantinople from the Eve of the Turkish Conquest to the Greek War of Independence.* Cambridge: University Press, 1968.

Ruthner, Clemens. *Am Rande: Kanon, Kulturökonomie und die Intertextualität des Marginalen am Beispiel der (österreichischen) Phantastik im 20. Jahrhundert.* Tübingen: Francke, 2004.

———. 'Undead Feedback: Adaptions and Echoes of Johann Flückinger's Report, Visum et Repertum (1732), until the Millennium'. In *The Universal Vampire: Origins and Evolution of a Legend*, edited by Barbara Brodman and James O. Doan, 91–108. Plymouth: Fairleigh Dickinson University Press, 2013.

———. 'Untote Verzahnungen: Prolegomena zu einer Literaturgeschichte des Vampirismus'. In *Poetische Wiedergänger: Deutschsprachige Vampirismus-Diskurse vom Mittelalter bis zur Gegenwart*, edited by Julia Bertschik and Christa Agnes Tuczay, 11–41. Tübingen: Francke, 2005.

Ryan, W[illiam] F. *The Bathhouse at Midnight: An Historical Survey of Magic and Divination in Russia.* University Park, PA: Pennsylvania State University Press, 1999.

———. 'The Witchcraft Hysteria in Early Modern Europe: Was Russia an Exception?' *Slavonic and East European Review* 76 (1998): 49–84.

Rybakov, B. A. *Iazychestvo drevnei Rusi.* Moscow: Sofiia – Gelios, 2001.

———. *Iazychestvo drevnikh slavian.* Moscow: Nauka, 1981; 2nd edn, Moscow: Sofiia – Gelios, 2002.

Sariyannis, Marinos. 'Of Ottoman Ghosts, Vampires and Sorcerers: An Old Discussion Disinterred'. *Archivum Ottomanicum* 30 (2013): 191–216; *Turkish Historical Review* 4 (2013): 83–117.

Sauer, Paul. *Ein kaiserlicher General auf dem württembergischen Herzogsthron: Herzog Carl Alexander von Württemberg 1684–1737.* Filderstadt: Markstein Verlag, 2006.

Scharfe, Martin. 'Wiedergänger: Die Lebenden sterben, die Toten leben – Anmerkungen zu einer flüssigen Kulturgrenze'. In *'Hexen, Wiedergänger, Sans-Papiers...' Kulturtheoretische Reflexionen zu den Rändern des sozialen Raumes*, edited by Johanna Rolshoven, 66–90. Marburg: Jonas-Verlag, 2003.

Schaub, Hagen. *Blutspuren: Die Geschichte der Vampire.* Graz: Leykam, 2008. Approved and updated licensed edn: *Vampire: Dem Mythos auf der Spur.* Wiesbaden: Marix Verlag, 2011.

Schischmanov, Ivan D. 'Der Lenorenstoff in der bulgarischen Volkspoesie'. *Indogermanische Forschungen* 4 (1894): 412–48.

Schmidt, Bernhard. *Das Volksleben der Neugriechen und das hellenische Altertum.* Vol. I. Leipzig: Teubner, 1871.

Schmitt, Jean-Claude. *Ghosts in the Middle Ages: The Living and the Dead in Medieval Society.* Translated by Teresa Lavender Fagan. Chicago: University of Chicago Press, 1998.

Schneeweis, E[dmund]. *Serbokroatische Volkskunde.* Vol. I: *Volksglaube und Volksbrauch.* Berlin: De Gruyter, 1961.
Schröder, Aribert. *Vampirismus: Seine Entwicklung vom Thema zum Motiv.* Frankfurt: Akademische Verlagsgesellschaft, 1973.
Schürmann, Thomas. *Nachzehrerglauben in Mitteleuropa.* Marburg: N.G. Elwert, 1990.
Senn, Harry Anthony. *Were-Wolf and Vampire in Romania.* New York: Boulder, 1982.
Serrier, Thomas. *Provinz Posen, Ostmark, Wielkopolska: Eine Grenzregion zwischen Deutschen und Polen 1848–1914.* Marburg: Herder-Institut, 2005.
Šešo, Luka, 'O krsniku: od tradicijske pojave u predajama do svarnog iscjelitelja,' *Studia ethnologica Croatica* 14/15 (2002/2003): 23–53.
Sh., Ja (anonymously). 'Ubiistvo upyria v Kievshchine vo vremia chumy 1770 goda'. *Kievskaia starina* 28 (1890): 338–341.
Simon, Friedrich Alexander. *Der Vampirismus im neunzehnten Jahrhundert oder über wahre und falsche Indikation zur Blutentziehung.* Hamburg: Hoffmann und Campe, 1830.
Simonides, Dorota. *Śląski horror o diabłach, skarbnikach, utopcach i innych strachach.* Katowice: Śląski Instytut Naukowy, 1984.
Simpson, Jacqueline. 'Repentant Soul or Walking Corpse? Debatable Apparitions in Mediaeval England'. *Folklore* 114, no. 3 (2003): 389–402.
Sjöberg, Anders. 'Pop Upir' Lichoj and the Swedish Rune-carver Ofeigr Upir'. *Scando-Slavica* 28 (1982): 109–24.
Šmitek, Zmago. 'Kresnik. An Attempt at a Mythological Reconstruction'. *Studia Mythologica Slavica* 1 (1998): 93–118.
Smoleński, Władysław. *Przewrót umysłowy w Polsce wieku XVIII. Studya historyczne.* Vol. 1. Kraków: G. Gebethner i Spółka, 1891. Vol. 2: Warsaw: Wydawnictwo Komitetu Obchodu, 1923. Vol. 3: Warsaw: Państwowy Instytut Wydawniczy, 1949.
Spencer Wilson, Dennell. 'The Gypsies' Belief in Vampires: A Historical Perspective'. *Roma. Half-Yearly Journal on the Life, Language and Culture of Roma* 3, no. 2 (1977): 8–13.
Stachowski, Kamil/Stachowski, Olaf. 'Possibly Oriental Elements in Slavonic Folklore: Upiór ~ Wampir*'. In *Essays in the History of Languages and Linguistics: Dedicated to Marek Stachowski on the Occasion of His 60th Birthday*, edited by Michał Németh et al., 643–93. Kraków: Księgarnia Akademicka, 2017.
Steindorff, Ludwig. *Kroatien: Vom Mittelalter bis zur Gegenwart.* Regensburg: Pustet, 2001.
Steiner, Otto. *Vampirleichen: Vampirprozesse in Preußen.* Hamburg: Kriminalistik-Verlag, 1959.
Steinhauer, Eric W. *Vampyrologie für Bibliothekare: Eine kulturwissenschaftliche Lektüre des Vampirs.* Hagen-Berchum: Eisenhut, 2011.
Stewart, Charles. *Demons and the Devil: Moral Imagination in Modern Greek Culture.* Princeton: Princeton University Press, 1991.
Stitzl, Josef. 'Der Morbus Hungaricus im Banat'. *Medizinische Zeitschrift. Fachblatt der deutschen Ärzte in Rumänien* 11 (1937): 96–106, 147–56.
Stone, Daniel. *The Polish-Lithuanian State, 1386–1795.* Seattle, WA: University of Washington Press, 2001.
Strausz, Adolf. *Die Bulgaren. Ethnographische Studien.* Leipzig: Grieben, 1898.
Stülzebach, Annett. 'Vampir- und Wiedergängererscheinungen aus volkskundlicher und archäologischer Sicht'. *Concilium medii aevi* 1 (1998): 97–121.
Summers, Montague. *The Vampire: His Kith and Kin.* London: Kegan Paul, Trench, Trubner & Co., 1928.

———. *The Vampire in Europe*. London: Kegan Paul, Trench, Trubner & Co., 1929.
Sundhaussen, Holm. *Geschichte Serbiens. 19.–21. Jahrhundert*. Vienna: Böhlau, 2007.
Svobodová, Kamila. 'Dva příklady vampyrismu v Neplachově kronice'. In *Ad vitam et honorem Jaroslao Mezník. Profesoru Jaroslavu Mezníkovi přátelé a zaci k pětasedem desátým narozeninám*, edited by Tomás Borovský Jan Libor and Martin Wikuda, 571–77. Brno: Moravianuss, 2003.
Szyjkowski, Maryan. *Dzieje polskiego upiora przed wystąpieniem Mickiewicza*. Kraków: Gebethnet i Wolff, 1917.
Teichert, Matthias. '"Draugula": The Draugr in Old Norse-Icelandic Saga Literature and His Relationship to the Post-medieval Vampire Myth'. In *The Universal Vampire: Origins and Evolution of a Legend*, edited by Barbara Brodman and James O. Doan, 3–16. Plymouth: Fairleigh Dickinson University Press, 2013.
———. 'Nosferatus nordische Verwandtschaft: Die Erzählungen von vampirartigen Untoten in den Isländersagas und ihr gesamtgermanisch-europäischer Kontext'. *Zeitschrift für deutsches Altertum und deutsche Literatur* 141 (2012): 2–36.
Ther, Philipp. 'Deutsche Geschichte als imperiale Geschichte: Polen, slawophone Minderheiten und das Kaiserreich als kontinentales Empire'. In *Das Kaiserreich transnational. Deutschland und die Welt 1871–1914*, edited by Sebastian Conrad and Jürgen Osterhammel, 129–48. Göttingen: Vandenhoeck & Ruprecht, 2004.
Tiutiundzhiev, Ivan, and Pavlin Chaushev. *Vampirete v bŭlgarskite zemi*. Veliko Tŭrnovo: M-Pres, 2017.
Tommasini, Giacomo Filippo. 'De Commentari storici-geografici della Provincia dell' Istria'. *Archeografo triestino. Raccolta di opusculi e notizie per Trieste e per l'Istria* 4 (1837): 1–554.
Trigg, E[lwood] B. *Gypsy Demons and Divinities: The Magical and Supernatural Practices of the Gypsies*. London: Sheldon Press, 1973.
Todorova, Maria. *Imagining the Balkans*. Updated edn. Oxford: Oxford University Press, 2009.
Tuczay, Christa. *Geister, Dämonen, Phantasmen: Eine Kulturgeschichte*. Wiesbaden: Marixverlag, 2015.
———. 'Interactions with Apparitions, Ghosts, and Revenants in Ancient and Medieval Sources'. In *From Shaman to Scientist: Essays on Humanity's Search for Spirits*, edited by James Hournan, 97–126. Lanham, MD: Scarecrow Press, 2004.
———. '". . . swem er den tôt getuot, dem sûgents ûz daz warme bluot": Wiedergänger, Blutsauger und Dracula in deutschen Texten des Mittelalters'. In *Poetische Wiedergänger: Deutschsprachige Vampirismus-Diskurse vom Mittelalter bis zur Gegenwart*, edited by Julia Bertschik and Christa Agnes Tuczay, 61–82. Tübingen: Francke, 2005.
Unterholzner, Bernhard. 'Vampire im Habsburgerreich, Schlagzeilen in Preußen: Wie Mythen zu politischen Druckmitteln werden'. In *Vampirglaube und magia posthuma im Diskurs der Habsburgermonarchie*, edited by Christoph Augustynowicz and Ursula Reber, 89–103. Vienna: Lit, 2011.
Ursinus, Michael. 'Osmanische Lokalbehörden der frühen Tanzimat im Kampf gegen Vampire? Amtsrechnungen (masārıf defterleri) aus Makedonien im Lichte der Aufzeichnungen Marko Cepenkovs (1829–1920)'. *Wiener Zeitschrift für die Kunde des Morgenlandes* 82 (1992): 359–74.
Vakarelski, Christo. *Bulgarische Volkskunde*. Berlin: De Gruyter, 1969.
'Vampir-Mord aus Aberglauben'. *Der Spiegel*, 1 July 1964: 51/52.

Vax, Louis. 'Dom Calmet et les Vampires'. In *Aspects du Classicisme et de la Spiritualité. Mélanges en l'honneur de Jacques Hennequin*, edited by Alain Cullière, 423–36. Paris: Klincksieck, 1996.
Vermeir, Koen. 'Vampirisme, corps mastiquants et force de l'imagination : Analyse de premiers traites sur les vampires (1659–1755)'. *Camenae* 8 (2010). Retrieved 2 November 2018 from http://lettres.sorbonne-universite.fr/IMG/pdf/6-_Veirmeir.pdf. Reprint: 'Vampires as Creatures of the Imagination: Theories of Body, Soul, and Imagination in Early Modern Vampire Tracts (1659–1755)'. In *Diseases of the Imagination and Imaginary Disease in the Early Modern Period*, edited by Yasmin Haskell, 341–73. Turnhout: Brepols, 2011.
Vidal, Fernando. 'Ghosts, the Economy of Religion, and the Laws of Princes: Dom Calmet's Treatise on the Apparitions of Spirits'. In *Gespenster und Politik. 16. bis 21. Jahrhundert*, edited by Claire Gantet and Fabrice d'Almeida, 103–26. Munich: Fink, 2007.
Vinogradova, L.N. *Narodnaia demonologiia i mifo-ritualnaia traditsiia slavian*. Moscow: Indrik, 2000.
Vinšćak, Tomo. 'On štrige, štriguni and krsnici on Istrian peninsula'. *Studia ethnologica Croatica* 17 (2005): 221–35.
Vlačić, Vlado. 'Militärberichte und Vampirmythos'. In *Vampirglaube und magia posthuma im Diskurs der Habsburgermonarchie*, edited by Christoph Augustynowicz and Ursula Reber, 69–87. Vienna: Lit, 2011.
Völkl, Ekkehard. *Rumänien. Vom 19. Jahrhundert bis in die Gegenwart*. Regensburg: Pustet, 1995.
Vrabie, Gheorghe. *Zur Volkskultur der Rumänen: Volksdichtung und Brauchtum im europäischen Kontext*. Bucharest: Editura Ştiinţifică şi Enciclopedică, 1989.
Vukanović, T[atomir] P. 'The Vampire (in the Belief and Customs of the Gypsies in the Province of Kosovo-Metohija, Stari Ras and Novopazarski Sandžak, Yugoslavia)'. *Journal of the Gypsy Lore Society* 36 (1957): 125–33; 37 (1958): 21–31, 111–18; 38 (1959): 44–55. Reprinted in: Jan L. Perkowski. *Vampires of the Slavs*, 201–34. Cambridge, MA: Slavica Publishers, 1976.
Walser Smith, Helmut. 'An Preußens Rändern oder: Die Welt, die dem Nationalismus verloren ging'. In *Das Kaiserreich transnational. Deutschland und die Welt 1871–1914*, edited by Sebastian Conrad and Jürgen Osterhammel, 149–69. Göttingen: Vandenhoeck & Ruprecht, 2004.
Wasylewski, Stanisław. 'W sprawie wampiryzmu'. *Lud. Organ Towarzystwa Ludonznawczego w Lwowie* 12 (1907): 291–98.
Weslowski, Elias. 'Die Vampirsage im rumänischen Volksglauben'. *Zeitschrift für österreichische Volkskunde* 16 (1910): 209–16; 17 (1911): 67–78.
Wessely, Kurt. 'Neuordnung der ungarischen Grenze nach dem großen Türkenkrieg'. In *Die k. k. Militärgrenze. Beiträge zur ihrer Geschichte*, 29–93. Vienna: Österreichischer Bundesverlag für Unterricht, Wissenschaft und Kunst, 1973.
Wiegelmann, Günter. 'Der 'lebende Leichnam' im Volksbrauch'. *Zeitschrift für Volkskunde* 62 (1966): 161–83.
Wilson, Katharina M. 'The History of the Word "Vampire"'. *Journal of the History of Ideas* 46 (1985): 577–83. Reprinted in: *The Vampire. A Casebook*, edited by Alan Dundes, 3–11. Madison, WI: University of Wisconsin Press, 1998.
Winkel, Jaqueline. 'Vampire zum Anfassen: Jure Grando und Michał Gašpareks Metamorphosen von gefürchteten Wiedergängern zu touristischen Stadtlegenden'. In *Mythos*

Vampir – Bissige Lektüren, edited by Thomas M. Bohn and Kirsten von Hagen, 45–56. Bonn: Romanistischer Verlag, 2018.

Wittwer, Héctor, Daniel Schäfer, and Andreas Frewer et al., eds. *Sterben und Tod: Geschichte – Theorie – Ethik. Ein interdisziplinäres Handbuch*. Stuttgart: Metzler, 2010.

Wlislocki, Heinrich von. *Aus dem inneren Leben der Zigeuner: Ethnologische Mitteilungen*. Berlin: Felber, 1892.

———. 'Gebräuche der transsilvanischen Zeltzigeuner bei Geburt, Taufe und Leichenbestattung'. *Globus* 51, no. 16/17 (1887): 249–51 and 267–70. Reprinted in: Heinrich von Wlislocki. *Zur Ethnographie der Zigeuner in Südosteuropa: Tsiganologische Aufsätze und Briefe aus dem Zeitraum 1880–1905*, edited by Joachim S. Hohmann, 245–59. Frankfurt: Lang, 1994.

———. 'Quälgeister im Volksglauben der Rumänen'. *Am Ur-quell. Monatsschrift für Volkkunde* 6 (1896): 17–19, 60–62, 90–92, 108–10, 142–44.

———. *Volksglaube und religiöser Brauch der Zigeuner vorwiegend nach eigenen Ermittlungen*. Münster: Aschendorff, 1891.

———. *Vom wandernden Zigeunervolke: Bilder aus dem Leben der Siebenbürger Zigeuner. Geschichtliches, Ethnologisches, Sprache und Poesie*. Hamburg: Verlagsanstalt und Druckerei Actien-Gesellschaft, 1890.

Wojtucki, Daniel. 'Elementy wiary w szkodliwą, pośmiertną aktywność zmarłyh na Śląsku i Morawach w świetle relacji i dokumentów z XVI-XVIII wieku'. In *Oblicza wampiryzmu*, edited by Anna Depta et. al., 13–34. Wrocław: Trickster, 2018.

———. 'Przypadek Poltergeista z Rybnicy Leśnej z 1709 r. Przyczynek do wierzeń w magia posthuma na Śląsku'. In *Staropolski ogląd świata. Nulla dies sine linea. Księga jubileuszowa dedykowana Profesorowi Bogdanowi Rokowi w 70. Rocznicę urodzin*, edited by Elżbieta Kościk, Filip Wolański and Rościsław Żerelik, 229–43. Toruń: Wydawnictwo Adam Marszałek, 2017.

———. '"Żywe trupy": wiara w powracających zmarłych w jednym ze śląskich miast w latach 1591–1592'. In *W kręgu myśli Władysława Czaplińskiego*, edited by Filip Wolański and Leszek Ziątkowski, 151–62. Wrocław: Wydawnictwo Chronicon, 2016.

Wolff, Larry. *Inventing Eastern Europe: The Map of Civilization on the Mind of the Enlightenment*. Stanford: Stanford University Press, 1994.

Wollman, František. 'Vampyrické pověsti v oblasti středoevropské'. *Národopisný věstník českoslovanský* 14, no. 1 (1921): 1–16; 14, no. 2 (1921): 1–57; 15, no. 1 (1922): 1–58; 16 no. 1–2 (1923): 80–96, 133–49; 18 no. 1–4 (1925): 133–61.

Wollner, W. 'Der Lenorenstoff in der slavischen Volkspoesie'. *Archiv für slavische Philologie* 6 (1882): 239–69.

Würgler, Andreas. *Medien in der frühen Neuzeit*. Munich: Oldenbourg, 2009.

Wuttke, Adolf. *Der deutsche Volksaberglaube der Gegenwart*. Hamburg: Agentur des Rauhen Hauses, 1860. 2nd completely revised edn, Berlin: Wiegand & Griben, 1869. 3rd edn by Elard Hugo Meyer. Berlin: Wiegandt & Grieben, 1900. 4th edn, Leipzig: Ruhl, 1925.

Zander, Helmut. *Geschichte der Seelenwanderung in Europa: Alternative religiöse Traditionen von der Antike bis heute*. Darmstadt: Wissenschaftliche Buchgesellschaft, 1999.

Zečević, Slobodan. *Kult mrtvih kod Srba*. Belgrade: Vuk Karadžić, 1982.

———. *Mitska bića srpskih predanja*. Belgrade: Vuk Karadžić, 1981.

Zelenin, D.K. *Ocherki russkoi mifologii. Vol. I: Umershie neestestvennoiu smert'iu i rusalki*. Petrograd: A.V. Orlov, 1916. Reprinted in: D.K. Zelenin. *Izbrannye trudy. Ocherki russkoi mifologii: Umershie neestestvennoi smert'iu i rusalki*. Moscow: Indrik, 1995.

Zelenin, Dmitrij. *Russische (Ostslavische) Volkskunde*. Berlin: De Gruyter, 1927.
Zelepos, Ioannis. *Kleine Geschichte Griechenlands: Von der Staatsgründung bis heute*. Munich: C.H. Beck, 2014.
———. 'Vampirglaube und orthodoxe Kirche im osmanischen Südosteuropa: Ein Fallbeispiel für die Ambivalenzen vorsäkularer Rationalisierungsprozesse'. In *Das osmanische Europa: Methoden und Perspektiven der Frühneuzeitforschung zu Südosteuropa*, edited by Andreas Helmedach et al., 363–79. Leipzig: Eudora-Verlag, 2014.
Zielonka, Bonifacy. 'Stanowsko wielkokulturowe w Adolfinie w pow. Aleksandrowskim'. *Przegląd archeologizny* 13 (1960): 197–204.
Zukal, Josef. 'Magia posthuma auf der Herrschaft Groß-Herlitz im 18. Jahrhundert'. *Zeitschrift für Geschichte und Kulturgeschichte Österreichisch-Schlesiens* 3 (1907/1908): 171/172.

Index of Persons

A

Abegg, Johann Friedrich (1765–1840), 98
Aelurius, Georgius (Katschker, Georg; 1596–1627), 30
Afanasyev, Alexander (Afanas'ev, Aleksandr; 1826–71), 149–50
Agioreitis, Nikodimos (1749–1809), 161
Allatius, Leo (1586–1669), 38, 68–69, 70, 71, 73, 74
Anna Tonnerin, 140
Argens, Marquis de (1703–71). *See* Boyer, Jean-Baptiste de, Marquis d'Argens
Ariès, Philippe (1914–1984), 14, 15
Aristotle (384–322 BC), 96
Arnkel, 18–19
Arnond Paole (Arnold Paul), 83, 87–89, 93
Audoin-Rouzeau, Frédérique (*1957; pseudonym: Fred Vargas), xi, 9
Azevedo, Emmanuel de (1713–96), 102

B

Bagiński, Wojciech Wincenty (1726–1784), 129–30
Baier, Johann Jakob (1677–1735), 92
Banović, Stjepan (1884–1961), 174
Barberini, Francesco (1597–1679), 68
Baróti, Lajos (till 1884 [called] Grünn, Ludwig; 1856–1933), 194
Basarab, Matei (1580–1654), 73–74
Báthory, Elisabeth (1560–1614), 146
Bechstein, Ludwig (1801–1860), 140–41
Belius, Matthias (Bel, Matej; 1684–1749), 113–14

Benedict XIV (Lambertini, Prosper; 1675–1758), 101–2, 103, 128
Blagojević, Petar, 78–79, 87
Boehlich, Ernst, 31
Böhm, Martin (1557–1622), 35–36
Bohomolec, Jan (1724–1795), 129
Borovinčić, Marin, 170, 171, 173
Bouillard, Ismael (1605–94), 59
Boyer, Jean-Baptiste de, Marquis d'Argens (1703–71), 108
Brâncoveanu, Constantin (1674–1714), 74
Brodka, 27, 29–31
Buchholz, Georg, 113
Bürger, Gottfried August (1747–94), 6, 131, 138, 234

C

Čajkanović, Veselin (1881–1946), 177–78
Calmet, Augustin (1672–1757), 30, 59–60, 90, 101–04, 127–128, 129
Cantemir, Dimitrie (1673–1723), 73
Caraccioli, Louis Antoine (1719–1803), 128–29
Casimir III, the Great (Kazimierz III Wielki), King of Poland (1310–70), 31
Catherine II, the Great (Ekaterina Alekseevna), Empress of Russia (1729–96), 3
Celefa, Pero, 169
Cepenkov, Marko (1829–1920), 184
Charles VI (Karl VI.), Holy Roman Emperor (1685–1740), 92

Charles Alexander of Württemberg (Carl Alexander von Württemberg; 1684–1737), 81, 92, 97
Chmielowski, Benedykt (1700–63), 128
Cinânî, Mustafa (†1595), 66
Ciszewski, Stanisław (1865–1930), 137
Comiers, Claude (†1693), 60
Crusius, Martin (1526–1607), 64
Cuza, Alexandru Ioan (1820–1873), 190
Czerniczky, Michael, 115–16

D
Davanzati, Giuseppe (1665–1755), 101
Dede, Piri, 67
Demidovich, Pavel (1871–1931), 155
Demolli, Arif (*1949), 222–23
Đorđević, Tihomir (1868–1944), 233
Dracula (Vlad the Impaler, Prince of Wallachia), 6, 9, 196. 197, 206
Drużbacka, Elżbieta (1695/1698–1765), 128
Ducháč, 29
Duncan Delisle, 25
Dundović, Luka, 170
Dzigcielski, Johann, 144

E
Eckert, Georg (1912–74), 166–67
Eichner, Georg, 44–45
Endter, Johann Andreas (1653–90), 46
Engelbrecht, Martin (1684–1756), 88
Englisch, Christoph, 99
Ettmüller, Johann Friedrich (1697–1748), 89

F
Foliot, Gilbert, 24
Formozis, P.E., 166
Fortis, Alberto (1741–1803), 173
Franchi, Andjel, 168–69
Francis (Ferencz) II Rákóczi, Prince of Transylvania (1676–1735), 115
Francisci, Erasmus (Finx, Erasmus; 1627–94), 46–47
Frederick II, the Great (Friedrich II, der Große), King of Prussia (1712–1786), 108–09

Frederick Louis of Württemberg (Friedrich Ludwig von Württemberg; 1698–1731), 92
Frederick William I (Friedrich Wilhelm I.), King of Prussia (1688–1740), 92, 93, 108
Fritsche, Johann Christoph, 95
Frombald, 78–80
Fulmis, Lovro, 170
Fulmis, Luka, 172
Füssli, Johan Heinrich (1741–1825), 235

G
Garmann, Christian Friedrich (1640–1708), 36
Gehrke, 143
Gengell, Jerzy (1657–1727), 61–62
Geoffrey of Burton (†1150), 21–23
Georgio, 48–49
Gerard, Emily (1849–1905), 7, 196–98
Gerasim, 175
Gerhard, Wilhelm (1780–1858), 2–3, 133
Gerlach, Stephan (1546–1612), 65
Gerschke, Leo, 142–43
Giamos, Aleksandr, 220
Giorgiiova, Stoina, 220
Gluziński, Józef (1799–1866), 134
Goethe, Johann Wolfgang von (1749–1832), 6, 134, 138
Gogol, Nikolai (1809–52), 6
Gorća, 4, 5
Goser, Johannes, 106
Gostovski, Robert von, 145
Graben zum Stein, Otto von (1690–1756), 93
Grando, Giure (slow. Jure; †1672), 45–49
Grässe, Johann (1814–85), 31
Gregory of Nazianzus (c. 329–90), 58
Grohmann, Joseph Virgil (1831–1919), 31
Groome, Francis Hindes (1851–1902), 206–07
Grundling, Jakob Paul von (1673–1731), 93
Gustawicz, Bronisław (1852–1916), 154

H

Hajek of Libočan, Wenceslaus (Václav Hájek z Libočan †1553), 27–31
Hakonsson, Hakon, 18
Hammer, Anton von (1809–89), 194
Hannibal, Wolfgang (1660–1738), 103
Harenberg, Johann Christoph (1696–1774), 95, 96, 121
Hartnup, Karen, 63
Hauber, Eberhard David (1647–1729), 114–15
Haupt, Carl (1829–82), 146
Heineccius, Johann Michael (1674–1722), 73
Heitz, Markus (*1971), xi, 9
Hellwig, Albert (1880–1950), 145, 148
Helwing, Georg Andreas (1666–1748), 62
Hennefeld, Nicolaus Henel von (1582–1656), 38
Hercules Saxonia (Ercole Sassiones; 1551–1607), 59
Hock, Stefan (1877–1947), 142
Horst, Georg Conrad (1767–1832), 114–15
Horton, George (1860–1942), 164
Houmanidou, Angelika, 166
Hrinchenko, Borys (1863–1910), 152–53

I

Ianettis, 70
Ivan the Terrible (Ivan IV Vasilyevich Groznyi), Tsar of Russia (1530–84), 58

J

Jablonovski, Johannes, 104
Jagić, Vatroslav (1838–1923), 173
Jakubović, Konstantin, 2, 5
Jaworskij, Juljan (1873–1937), 153
Jireček, Konstantin (1854–1918), 188, 190
John of Bohemia (Johann von Böhmen), King of Bohemia, Count of Luxembourg (1296–1346), 31
Jósika, Miklós (1794–1865), 115

K

Káláritt, Marinko, 194–95
Kalenichenka, Semyon, 150
Kant, Immanuel (1724–1804), 98
Karadžić, Vuk (1787–1864), 178, 230–32, 233
Kasparek, Michael (Polish Michał Kasperek; †1718), 45–46, 110–17
Klaić, Vjekoslav (1849–1928), 63
Klings, Karl (1867–1940), 148
Knoop, Otto (1853–1931), 135–36, 147
Kögler, Joseph (1765–1817), 30
Kokot, Marin Nika, 170
Kołbasiuk (Kovbasiuk), Lesko, 123
Kolberg, Oskar (1814–90), 135
Köleseri, Samuel (1663–1732), 192
Konstantinos, 165
Kornmann, Heinrich (1580–1640), 63
Kostova, Elizabeth (*1964), xi, 9
Kottwitz, Alexander von, 89
Kozić, Marin Kolendić, 170
Krause, Ernst, 143
Krauss, Friedrich Salomon (1859–1938), 158, 178–80, 181–82, 233
Kühnau, Richard (1858–1930), 31, 38, 142
Kunze, Johannes, 38, 39–44

L

Lambertini, Posper. *See* Benedict XIV
Laudun, William, 24
Lawson, John Cutbert (*1874), 163, 164
Le Fanu, Joseph Sheridan (1814–73), 6, 138
Leake, William Martin (1777–1860), 162
Lee, Christopher (1922–2015), 3
Levkievskaia, Elena, 225
Lilek, Emilijan (1851–1940), 159–69
Lompa, Józef (1797–1863), 134
Louis XIV, or Louis the Great, King of France (1638–1714), 72
Lucenta, Lovro, 169
Luther, Martin (1483–1546), 34, 35–36, 42

M

Maglanovich, Hyacinthe, 1
Malaxos, Manuel, 64–65, 68, 73
Malinka, Oleksandr (1865–1941), 150

Mannhardt, Wilhelm (1831–1880), 141, 197–98, 226
Map, Walter (*c. 1140; †between 1208 and 1210), 21–22, 24
Maria Theresa (Maria Theresia), Holy Roman Empress (1717–80), 46, 100, 104, 106–09, 129, 195, 204
Marianna Saligerin, 106, 108
Marie Louise Gonzaga (Ludwika Maria Gonzaga de Nevers), Queen of Poland (1611–67), 59
Marigner, 61
Marin (Bulgarian), 187
Marin (Croatian), 169
Marschner, Heinrich (1795–1861), 138
Martinus, Martin, 193
Matirko, Bertalan, 114
Matkowski, Michał (Matkov'skyi, Mychailo), 126–27
Maximos III (†1482), 64–65
Mayo, Herbert (1796–1852), 89
Mehmed II the Conquerer (Mehmed II Fatih), Ottoman Sultan (1432–1481), 63, 64, 65, 68, 196
Mehmed Ebussuud Efendi (1490–1574), 66, 67
Merian, Matthäus (1593–1650), 30, 39
Mérimée, Prosper (1803–70), 1–4, 133
Meyer, Hans B., 147
Meyer, Stephenie (*1973), x, 8–9
Mickiewicz, Adam (1798–1855), 6, 130, 131–33, 140, 231
Mikszáth, Kalman (1847–1910), 115–16
Mikuš, Antun, 169
Miliza (Milica), 84
Miloe (Miloje), 86
Miloš Obrenović (1780–1860), 169, 174, 177
Mirandola, Giovanni Pico della (1470–1533), 37
Mitseva, Evgeniia, 219
More, Henry (1614–87), 37
Moțoc, Varlaam (†1657), 73
Murad III, Ottoman Sultan (1546–1595), 66
Murgoci, Agnes (1875–1929), 198, 202
Myslata (Mislata), 27–28, 29, 30, 111

N
Neplach, Jan (c. 1322–71), 27–29, 30
Nesheva, Zdravka Dimitrovna, 219
Newton, Charles Thomas (1816–94), 162
Notaras, Chrysanthos (1669–1707), 74
Noyers, Pierre des (†1693), 59, 60

O
Oppenheimer, Joseph Süß (1698–1738), 97
Oppenhoff, Friedrich (1811–75), 143
Orlić, Drago (*1948), 222
Ossenfelder, Heinrich August (1725–1801), 4
Ossolinski, Joseph Maximilian (Ossoliński, Józef Maksymilian; 1748–1826), 130, 131

P
Pamfile, Tudor (1883–1923), 202
Paracelsus (c. 1493–1541), 96
Pashley, Robert (1805–95), 162
Patino, 70
Pavković, Nikola, 222
Pavlović, Antun, 170
Pavlović, Marin, 170
Pavlović, Pavel, 63
Pavlović, Pavo (called Pizin), 170
Perić, Boris (*1966), 46
Pero, 182
Peter, Anton, 44
Petrovici, Emil (1899–1968), 203
Pihsin, Dorothea, 104
Plogojowitz, Peter. See Blagojević, Petar
Poblocki, Franz von, 144
Poblocki, Josef von, 144
Poblocki, Josephine von, 144
Podbereski, Andrzéj, 152
Pohl, Johann Christoph (1706–80), 95
Pol, Nikolaus (1564–1632), 32
Polidori, John William (1795–1821), 4, 131, 138
Potocki, Jan (1761–1815), 130–31
Pushkin, Alexander (1799–1837), 2–5

R
Raab, Johann Christoph, 44
Raicević, Stefan, 196

Ranft, Michael (1700–74), v, 36, 80, 86, 91, 93, 97, 98
Rešić, Ivan Antun, 170
Ricaut (Rycau), Paul (1628–1700), 71–72
Rice, Anne (*1943), x, 8
Richard, François, 69–70, 72
Roger the Poitevin (c. 1065–1140), 22
Rohr, Philip, 36
Rosa(lia) Polakin, 105–07
Rubtsov, 155
Ruthner, Clemens, 10
Rzączyński, Gabriel (1664–1737), 61, 62

S
Šagor, Antun, 169
Saiakov, Stoian Dimitrov, 219
Saint-Urbain, Ferdinand de (1654–1738), 90
Schertz, Carl Ferdinand von (†1724), 30, 99–100
Schmidt, Bernhard (1837–1917), 163
Scholario, Gennadios II. (c. 1405–73), 64
Schott, Albert (1809–1847), 197–98
Schott, Arthur (1814–1875), 197–98
Scrofani, Saverio (1756–1835), 161
Senn, Harry Anthony, 224
Shedden-Ralston, William Ralston (William Shedden; 1828–89), 150
Shepherd of Blow. *See* Myslata (Mislata)
Siewiński, Antoni, 154
Sinold, Philipp Balthasar (1657–1742), 114
Sjöberg, Anders, 57
Śliwicki, Piotr Hiacynt (1705–74), 128
Snorri Thorgrimsson (963–1031), 18, 21
Sofronio, 71
Sori, Petar, 168
Śroka, 136
St Modwen, 21
Stanno (Stana), 84
Stanoicka (Stanojka), 86
Stebler, Franz Anton (1705–89), 92
Stefan Duschan (Stefan Uroš IV Dušan; 1308–55), 63
Steiner, Otto, 226–27
Sterne, Carus (Krause, Ernst; 1839–1903), 143

Stewart, Charles, 66
Stieff, Christian (1665–1751), 38, 39, 40, 43, 237
Stock, Johannes Christian, 95
Stoker, Bram (1847–1912), x, 5, 6–7, 8, 9, 27, 117, 160, 191, 196–98, 235
Stoyanov, Zahariy (1850–1889), 187–88
Strauss, Friedrich Salomon (1859–1938), 144
Strausz, Adolf (1853–1944), 188, 189–90
Swieten, Gerard van (1700–72), 106–08
Sybel, Heinrich von (1817–95), 140
Szembek, Michal, 110
Szulczewski, 136
Szymanek, 136

T
Tallar, Georg, 104, 105, 195
Tanski, Anton, 150–51
Temme, Jodocus (1798–1881), 140
Tettau, Wilhelm, 140, 142
Thévenot, Jean de (1633–1667), 70–71
Thomas of Monmouth (c. 1149–72), 25
Thorgunna, 19–21
Thorodd, 19–20
Thorolf Baegifot, 18–20
Timon, 189–90
Tökölyi, Imre (1657–1705), 115
Tolstoy, Aleksey (1817–75), 4–5
Tolstoy, Leo (1828–1910), 4
Tommasini, Giacomo Filippo (1595–1655), 47
Tournefort, Joseph Pitton (1656–1708), 72
Trigg, Elwood B. (1940–2007), 226
Turgenev, Ivan (1818–1883), 5

U
Upir' Likhoi (Ofeigr Upir), 57

V
Vabst, Christian, 106
Valvasor, Johann Weichard (Valvasor, Janez Vajkard; 1641–93), 46–48
Vargas, Fred. *See* Audoin-Rouzeau, Frédérique
Veckenstedt, Edmund (1840–1903), 146

Verlien, Giovanni, 173
Vinogradova, Liudmila, 225
Vlad the Impaler (Vlad III Țepeș),
  Voivode of Wallachia (1431–1476). See
  Dracula
Vladimir the Great (Vladimir
  Sviatoslavich, c. 960–1015), 56
Vogt, Gottlob Heinrich, 95
Vogt, Johann, 40
Voltaire (1694–1778), 103, 117
Voss, Christian Friedrich (1724–95),
  109
Vražinovski, Tanas, 233
Vseslav the Sorcerer (Vseslav
  Briachislavich, c. 1039–1101), 56
Vujić, Joakim (1772–1847), 175–177
Vukanović, Tatomir (1907–97), 226
Vukotić, Vule, 117

W
Warlin, Marynna, 130
Wasylewski, Stanisław (1885–1953), 137
Weinrich, Karl, 37
Weinrich, Martin (1548–1609), 37, 38,
  39, 40, 43
Weslowski, Elias (1867–1944), 199
Wiegelmann, Günter (1928–2008), 227
William of Newburgh (c. 1136–98), 21,
  23–24, 25
William of Norwich (1132–44), 25
Witch of Levin. See Brodka
Wlislocki, Heinrich von (1856–1907),
  198–99, 200, 204–06, 226
Wójcicki, Kazimierz Władysław (1807–
  79), 130, 133, 134
Wollschläger, 142
Wollschläger, Joseph von, 142–43
Wuttke, Adolf (1819–70), 141

Y
Yefymenko (Efymenko), Petro (1835–
  1908), 150

Z
Zdenka, 5
Zopf, Johann Heinrich, 95

Index of Places

A

Abbazia (Croatian Opatija), 173
Adrianople (Turkish Edirne), 67, 160
Albania, 222–23
Altdorf, 89, 92
Amărăşti, 202
Anantis, 23
Anatolia, 66, 70
Angerburg (Polish Węgorzewo), 62
Arachova, 163
Arad, 194
Arcadia, 165
Armenia, 72
Athens (Greek Athina), 128, 131, 166
Athos, 65
Attica, 166

B

Babscha (Romanian Babşa), 194
Baja (German Frankenstadt), 177
Balkan, xi, xiii, 1, 2, 4–7, 13, 47, 62–63, 65, 66, 80–81, 96, 99, 105, 156–57, 178, 182, 183, 186, 187, 189, 190, 204, 220, 231, 232, 233, 234
Banat, 80–81, 105, 191–92, 194–95, 197, 204, 221
Belarus' 56, 125, 129, 148, 150, 155, 225, 228
Belgrade (Serbian Beograd), 81, 83, 89, 92, 177
Bendschin. *See* Bennisch
Bennisch (Czech Horní Benešov), 39, 40, 42, 43, 44, 105, 110
Berdychiv (Ukrainian Berdyčiv), 151
Berlin, 6, 91, 92, 93, 109, 148, 156, 157, 167, 183, 191
Berwick, 23
Biskupitz (Polish Biskupice), 136
Blagoevgrad, 219
Blow or Vlow, 27, 29, 30, 111
Bóbrka (Ukrainian Bibrka), 153
Bohemia, 13, 27, 29, 30, 31, 36, 39
Bosnia, 5, 78, 81, 83, 167, 177, 178, 182, 189, 193
Botoşani, 202
Breslau (Polish Wrocław), 32, 35, 37, 38
Brudzyn (Polish Brudzyń), 136
Buckingham, 23
Buczacz (Ukrainian Buchach), 154
Bukowno, 137
Bulgaria, 157, 182, 183, 186, 187, 188, 189, 219
Burton upon Trent, 22, 23
Byland Abby, 26

C

Carniola, 46, 47, 48
Čengić, 182
Chernigov (Ukrainian Chernihiv), 152
Chios, 68, 71
Chyhyryn, 152
Clydesdale, 25
Constantinople (Turkish Istanbul), xii, 6, 63, 65, 67, 71, 72, 73, 160, 161, 174, 182, 183, 190, 196
Crete, 72, 162, 165
Crişana (Hungarian Körösvidék), 192
Croatia, 48, 80, 83, 167, 181, 222

D

Dalmatia, 2, 167, 168, 173, 174, 178
Danzig (Polish Gdańsk), 144–146, 147
Dečani, 175
Deva, 195
Dıraç (Albanian Durrës), 66
Dubovac, 222
Dubrovnik, 167, 168–72, 196
Dźwinogród (Ukrainian Zvenihorod), 154

E

Edirne. *See* Adrianople
Engelsberg (Czech Andělská Hora), 99
England, 13, 21, 23, 25, 160

F

Facsád (Romanian Făget), 194
Fehérvar (Romanian Alba Iulia), 192
Felsőbánya (Romanian Baia Sprie), 103–4
France, 4, 59, 99, 131, 140, 156, 160
Frankfurt, 94
Frei-Hermersdorf. *See* Hermersdorf
Freudenthal (Czech Bruntál), 99, 105
Friedland (Czech Břidličná), 99
Froda, 19, 20

G

Gaj, 222
Galicia, 125, 153, 197, 228
Georgia, 72
Glatz (Polish Kłodzko), 30–31, 109
Gllogovicë (Serbian Glogovica), 222
Gniezno, 136
Greece, 10, 64, 92, 160–61, 164, 183, 218–19
Groß Mochbern (Polish Muchobór Wielki), 32
Großgorschütz (Polish Gorzyce), 130

H

Hanoverian Wendland, 32
Hebrides, 19
Hereford, 24
Herinbiesch (or Herendesch; Romanian Herendeşti; Hungarian Herendjest), 194
Hermannstadt (Romanian Sibiu), 7, 192, 197
Hermersdorf (Czech Svobodné Heřmanice), 105, 106, 108
Hesse (German Hessen), 32
Hrubieszów, 134
Humińce (Ukrainian Humentsy), 126
Hungary, 5, 11, 34, 45, 78, 81, 95, 101, 105, 110, 111, 115, 125, 127, 167, 177, 191, 192, 195, 204
Hvamm, 18, 18, 21

I

Iceland, 13, 17–19, 56
Istanbul. *See* Constantinople
Istria, 47, 48, 167, 173, 180, 222
Ivanić, 83
Iviron Monastery, 65

J

Jägerndorf (Czech Krnov), 39, 40, 109
Jakobsdorf (Polish Zamarte), 142, 143
Janów (Ukrainian Ianiv; today: Ivano-Frankove), 154

K

Kadaň, 27, 29
Kalikráti, 162
Kallatsa (Romanian Călacea), 195
Kalugerovo, 189
Kamianets-Podilskyi (Polish Kamieniec Podolski), 126
Kantrzyno (or Kantrschin; Polish Kętrzyno), 143
Kapnik (Hungarian Kapnikbánya; Romanian Cavnik), 103–4
Karansebesch (Romanian Caransebeş; Hungarian Karánsebes), 194
Karthaus (Polish Kartuzy), 147
Katowice, 137
Kesmark (Hungarian Késmárk; Slovak Kežmarok), 113
Kimpolung (Romanian Câmpulung), 199, 200
Kirillo-Belozersky Monastery, 57
Kis-Kerék (German Kradendorf; Romanian Broşteni), 192
Kisolova (Serbian Kisiljevo), 78
Klausenburg (Romanian Cluj-Napoca), 204

Klein Dikva (Romanian Ticvaniu Mic), 195
Klisura, 175–76
Kodnya, 127
Konitz (Polish Chojnice), 142
Köprülü (Macedonian Veles), 183
Kosovo, 87, 89, 167, 175, 226
Kotel, 187
Kovin (German Kubin; Hungarian Kevevára; Romanian Cuvin), 194
Kraków, 131, 133, 135, 137, 152
Kringa, 45, 48, 49
Kronstadt (Romanian Brașov), 7, 193, 197
Kucklina (Serbian Kuklina), 89
Küçük Kaynarca, 156

L
Lanercost, 25
Larissa, 162
Lastovo (Italian Lagosta), 168–72
Lauban (Polish Lubań), 35
Lauenburg (Polish Lębork), 144
Lausanne, 156
Leipzig, 2, 36, 80, 86, 91
Lemberg (Polish Lwów; Ukrainian L'viv), 154
Lesbos, 162
Lewin (Czech Levín), 27–31
Libotschan (Czech Libočany), 27
Lichten (Czech Lichnov), 40
Lichtewerden (Czech Světlá Hora), 99
Lincoln, 22
Lithuania, 55, 58, 61, 125, 126, 129, 144, 148, 228
Litoměřice, 27, 31
Łódź, 137
London, 91, 218
Lorraine, 90, 101, 194
Lublau (Hungarian Lubló; Slovak Stará Ľubovňa), 45, 110–11, 113–16
Lublin, 58, 125, 128, 135
Lugoj (Hungarian Lugos), 194
Lusatia (German Lausitz), 33, 35, 146

M
Macedonia, 183–84, 189, 220
Manastir (Macedonian Bitola), 183
Maramureș, 192

Marásia, 67
Marča, 83
Medveđa, 80, 83, 86–87, 89, 92, 97, 108, 110, 115
Merul, 192, 193
Milos, 71
Mitterburg (Croatian Pazin), 48
Moldova, 4, 5, 73, 202
Moravia, 11, 36, 39, 99, 101, 127
Muntenia, 203
Mureș (Hungarian Maros), 194
Mykonos, 72

N
Nagybánia (Romanian Baia Mare), 103, 104
Navahrudak, 155
Neretva, 174
Neu-Arad (Romanian Aradul Nou; Hungarian Újarad), 194
Neustadt (Polish Wejherowo), 143
Niedersommerkau (Polish Ząbrsko Dolne), 147
Niš, 177
Norway, 18
Nucșoara, 203
Nuremberg (German Nürnberg), 91, 92, 111
Nussbach (Romanian Măieruș), 193

O
Oburschta (Romanian Obârșia), 195
Ohabă, 203
Olmütz (Czech Olomouc), 30, 99, 100, 103, 105, 106
Oltenia, 202, 203
Opatovice, 27
Oxford, 22

P
Paraćin, 83
Pasadur, 168
Pašman, 63
Passarowitz (Serbian Požarevac), 81, 110, 191
Patmos, 70
Pazin. See Mitterburg
Peloponnes, 67, 71, 160, 165, 166

Pirgovo, 187
Pleternica, 181
Płock, 129
Podolia, 62, 131, 148
Podosy, 151
Pókafalva (German Törnen; Romanian Păuca), 192
Polchau (Polish Połchowo), 145
Polesia, 225
Polotsk (Belarusian Polatsk), 56
Pomerania (German Pommern), 32, 33, 141, 144, 145
Posen (Polish Poznań), 135, 136, 138
Požega (German Poschegg; Hungarian Pozsega), 89, 175
Prilep (Turkish Perlepe), 184, 189, 220
Provadia, 188
Przewrocie (Ukrainian Privorottia), 126
Putzig (Polish Puck), 145
Pyrgos, 70, 165
Paris, 2, 9, 91, 125
Prussia, x, 4, 32, 33, 37, 55, 97, 99, 108–10, 113, 125, 138, 140, 141, 144, 156, 226
Poland, 11, 39, 58, 60, 61, 110, 114, 125–26, 127, 129, 134, 136, 138, 140, 141, 147, 148, 161, 224–25, 233

R
Ratibor (Polish Racibórz), 130, 147, 148
Reimswaldau (Polish Rybnica Leśna), 44, 45
Rogoźno, 136
Romania, 156, 187, 190–91, 192, 193, 196, 198, 199, 200, 202, 203, 223–24, 233, 234
Rome, 67, 68, 93
Roslasin (Polish Rozłazino), 144
Ruse (Turkish Rusçuk), 187
Russia, 3, 5, 55, 56, 58, 60, 61, 101, 125, 135, 140, 156, 160

S
Saloniki. *See* Thessaloniki
Santorini, 69
Šarbanovac, 174
Satu Mare (Hungarian Szatmár), 192

Scandinavia, 57, 232
Schaplitz (Polish Czapielsk), 147
Schebell (Romanian Jebel), 195
Schildberg (Polish Ostrzeszów), 136
Schlesien. *See* Silesia
Selanik. *See* Thesasaloniki
Sénones, 101
Serbia, 11, 39, 62, 80, 81, 85, 94, 115, 144, 156, 167, 174–75, 178, 181, 183, 191, 194, 207, 221, 222, 226, 228, 230, 234, 236
Sereth (Romanian Siret), 200
Sergiyev Posad, 57
Siebenbürgen. *See* Transylvania
Sieradz, 137
Silesia (German Schlesien), 11, 30, 31, 36–37, 39–40, 44, 92, 99, 101, 108–09, 127, 130, 142, 148
Skálaholt (today Skálholt), 19, 20
Skole, 154
Skrivena Luka, 168
Slavonia, 80, 88, 167
Slovakia, 110, 112, 146
Slovenia, 46, 48
Smyrna (Turkish Izmir), 71, 164
Snæfellsnes, 17
Spiš (German Zips), 110, 111, 112, 115
St. Helena, 71
Staffordshire, 22
Stepanok (Ukrainian Stepok), 151
Svilengrad, 219

T
Temeswar (Romanian Timișoara; Hungarian Temesvár), 191, 195
Terebovlia (Polish Trembowlja), 131
Thessaloniki (Saloniki; Turkish Selanik), 66, 166
Tikveš, 183
Toruń, 59, 129, 133
Trabzon, 166
Transylvania (German Siebenbürgen), x, 6, 7, 8, 9, 10, 13, 80, 191–92, 196, 197, 198, 204
Trnava, 220
Troppau (Czech Opava), 44, 108, 109
Trzeszawa, 59
Tupanari, 177

U
Ub, 174
Ubli, 168
Ukraine, xiii, 11, 58, 59, 62, 103, 127, 131, 134, 135, 199, 201, 202, 225, 234
Uppland, 57

V
Veliko Tarnovo (Bulgarian Veliko Tărnovo; Turkish Tırnova), 186
Vienna, 1, 34, 79, 81, 82, 84, 86, 92, 109, 110, 131, 156, 188, 189, 191, 192, 207, 230
Vilia, 166
Vojvodina, 194, 221

W
Wallachia, 6, 73, 74, 92, 156, 190, 196, 204, 223, 228
Warsaw (Polish Warszawa), 62, 113, 114, 115, 116, 125, 128, 129, 130
West Prussia (German Westpreußen), 32, 140, 142
Winnental, 92
Wirsitz (Polish Wyrzysk), 136
Worcester, 24
Wresznia (Polish Września), 136
Wujtowce (Ukrainian Vijtivci), 127

Z
Zadar, 63
Zagreb, 83, 174
Zakopatica, 168
Zamość, 134
Zips. *See* Spiš
Zvornik, 182

Index of Subjects

A

academy, 57, 89, 92, 93, 108, 125, 207. *See also* science
afterlife, xxi, 13, 14, 15, 34, 64, 72, 155–56, 157, 174, 199, 202, 204, 220, 225
Albanians, 18, 87
Alp (Alpdruck), 37, 43, 134, 146, 235
animal, 19, 22, 26, 29, 42, 47, 73, 159, 165, 185–86, 189, 197, 199, 200, 204, 208, 219, 220, 223, 231, 233
apparitions, xii, xiii, 15, 17, 18, 19, 20, 23, 27, 30, 34, 42, 45, 56, 57, 70, 71, 72, 101, 102, 106, 129, 136, 143, 146, 153, 155, 166, 180, 181, 225, 232
Aufhocker, 28, 37, 146
Austria-Hungary. *See* Habsburg Empire
authorities, xiii, 11, 22, 30, 33, 37, 39, 43, 45, 48, 58, 66, 67, 72, 80–84, 87, 89, 92, 96, 99, 101, 102, 104, 106–8, 109, 115, 117, 130, 151, 161, 171, 172, 182, 184, 186, 190, 194, 195, 235, 237. *See also* Church authorities; military administration
autopsy, 86, 104

B

Belarusians, 55, 57, 60, 150, 155, 225–26
belief, x–xv, 10, 14, 15, 17, 20, 22, 28, 29, 34, 35, 39, 45, 48, 59, 62, 64, 65, 68, 69, 73, 100, 101, 102, 103, 104, 135, 136, 138, 140, 143, 161, 162, 165, 169, 170, 173, 187, 189, 192, 196, 197, 205, 207, 208, 222, 225, 226, 227, 228, 231, 232, 233, 235
    belief in nachzehrers, xvi, 32, 59, 228
    belief in vampires, x–xiv, 32, 37, 55, 58, 74, 103, 109, 128, 129, 132, 134, 141–42, 144, 159, 163, 165, 174–75, 177, 184, 187, 188, 218, 220, 221, 226, 236
    See also popular belief
bite (biting), 2, 7, 89, 90, 98, 111, 133, 135, 137, 141, 154, 186, 197
Black Death, 63. *See also* pest, plague
blasphemy, 6, 103
blood, x, xi, 1, 8, 10, 19, 22, 24, 27, 28–29, 35, 42, 43, 44, 61, 67, 84, 87, 89, 98, 116, 136, 138, 153, 161, 162, 163, 169, 174, 180, 181, 189, 190, 195, 207, 220, 221, 223, 234, 235, 237
    flowing of (fresh) blood, 48, 59, 71, 72, 79, 90, 97, 99, 102, 104, 106, 113, 140, 142, 144, 145, 147, 152, 194
bloodsucker (bloodsucking), x–xv, 1, 5, 6, 9, 13, 23–25, 27, 29, 31, 32, 37, 47, 48, 57, 60, 61, 66, 74, 80, 83–86, 90, 91, 93, 94–95, 96, 97, 98–99, 103, 104, 106, 108–10, 114–15, 131–33, 134, 137–38, 140, 141, 142, 146–47, 150, 152, 153, 159, 163, 165, 169, 171, 172, 173, 175, 179, 180, 181, 185, 190, 191–94, 197–99, 202–3, 205, 219, 221, 222, 224, 225, 230, 231–32, 233–34, 237
bogeyman, 9, 182, 236
border region, 4, 10, 11, 30, 81, 82, 103, 133
Bram Stoker's Dracula. *See* Count Dracula
Bulgarians, 2, 188–199, 219

burial, xi, 2, 3, 8, 14, 15, 17, 18–19, 22, 24, 29, 33, 38, 41, 43, 45, 48, 56, 58, 59, 67, 69, 70, 71, 72, 87, 105, 106, 109, 111, 128, 130, 137, 140, 142, 143, 144, 145, 147, 158, 165, 166, 168, 170, 172, 175, 189, 197, 200, 201, 205, 206, 222, 227, 231, 237
burning, xiv, 7, 11, 19, 27, 28, 31, 37, 63, 65, 72, 100, 104, 106, 107, 111, 127, 128, 150, 165, 178, 186, 190, 197, 232, 235

C

Catholicism, 37, 57, 68, 234
    Catholic Church, xi, 58, 67, 69, 70, 82, 171
    Catholic cemetery, 2, 109, 145
caul, 56, 136, 141, 147, 223
child, 17, 42, 68, 89, 136, 145, 147, 149, 155, 164, 166, 173, 199, 205, 206, 207, 231, 232, 233
choking, 27, 78, 100, 110, 111, 174, 225, 230, 235
Christ, xi, 21, 25, 26, 58, 140, 174, 177, 232
Christianity, 18, 19, 20, 56, 65
Christianization, 15, 17, 55, 235
Christians, 2, 7, 62, 66, 67, 72, 157, 161, 187
chronicles, 27, 44, 142
Church, xi, xii, xiii, xv, 15, 20, 22, 27, 29, 34, 35, 40–44, 56, 58, 63–65, 68, 69, 70, 72, 73, 74, 83, 100, 102, 103, 107, 111, 135, 145, 149, 154, 160, 161, 163, 165, 169–72, 179, 180, 182, 183, 185, 180, 194, 195, 196, 201, 202, 203, 207, 223, 236, 237
Church authorities, 11, 22, 33, 99, 102, 130, 172, 235
cemetery, 2, 29, 99, 105, 108, 109, 127, 129, 145, 147, 154, 155, 161, 162, 166, 184, 188, 189, 190, 192, 201, 202
cinema, 2, 116
civilization, 4
colonization, 6, 10, 17, 32, 140, 142
coffin, 7, 8, 20, 22, 56, 108, 137, 138, 142, 143, 144, 145, 146, 147, 149, 155, 180, 184, 191, 224

corpse, xi, xiii, xiv, xv, 1, 13, 3, 7, 11, 13, 14, 17–21, 22, 23, 24, 26, 27–29, 32, 33, 35, 36, 37, 38–39, 41–44, 45, 48, 49, 56, 59, 60, 61, 62, 65, 66, 67, 68–70, 71, 72, 73, 74, 78, 79, 84–87, 90, 93, 99, 100, 101, 102, 104, 106–08, 111, 113, 114, 116, 128, 129, 131, 132, 133, 135, 136, 137, 138, 139, 140, 141, 143, 144, 145, 146, 147, 148, 151, 152, 154, 155, 157, 158, 159, 161, 164, 165, 166, 169, 170, 171, 172, 173, 174, 175, 177, 180, 182, 184, 186, 189, 190, 192, 193, 194–95, 198, 200, 202, 203, 205, 219, 220, 222, 223, 225, 226, 227, 231, 232, 235, 236, 237
    bloated corpse, 18, 19, 24, 44, 60, 68, 69, 74, 104, 159, 180, 182, 188, 190, 203, 230, 235–37
    See also living corpses; harmful corpses
Count Dracula, x, xiii, 3, 4, 6–8, 9, 13, 117, 160, 191, 196, 197, 218, 227, 235
crime, xi, 9, 25, 115, 117, 126, 129–30, 145, 148, 163, 164, 168, 201, 224
Croatians, 167

D

damnation, xv, 7, 10, 14, 64, 70, 74, 187
death, xi–xii, xv, 6, 10, 13–15, 17, 18–20, 22, 23, 24, 25, 26, 28, 29, 31, 32, 34, 35, 36, 40–41, 42, 43, 44, 45, 46, 48, 56, 57, 59, 60, 61, 62, 64, 65, 69, 70, 71, 72, 78, 83, 84, 86–89, 92, 95, 96, 99, 100, 102, 104, 105, 106, 109, 111, 112, 113, 114, 116, 117, 127, 128, 130, 134–35, 136–37, 141, 143, 145, 146–48, 149, 151, 152, 153, 154, 155, 157–59, 163, 167, 170, 172, 173, 179, 180, 181, 182, 185, 188, 192, 193, 194, 197, 200, 201, 202, 204, 205, 206, 207, 208, 218, 219, 220, 221, 223, 225, 230, 231, 233, 235, 236
    series of death, 32, 35, 66, 109, 136, 148, 154, 182, 221, 231
decapitation, xiv, 7, 22, 35, 45, 59, 60, 61, 62, 66, 86, 90, 113–14, 129, 136, 138, 140, 144, 145, 147, 148, 192–93, 199, 205, 225, 226, 231, 235

deceased, xi, xii, 3, 7, 15, 17, 18, 26, 41, 49, 56, 63, 64, 66, 72, 73, 78, 86, 136, 154, 157, 161, 166, 187, 219, 223, 231, 236
decomposition, xv, 14, 22, 33, 39, 43, 45, 61, 64–65, 68–69, 70–71, 84, 86, 96, 97, 104, 106, 145, 158, 173, 194, 197, 205, 207, 236
nondecomposition, xiii, xiv, 39, 64, 65, 66, 68–69, 70, 78, 84, 91, 93, 96, 97, 106, 108, 137, 150, 159, 163, 175, 186, 192, 193, 196, 223, 224
defensive measures, 7, 28, 33, 35, 39, 66, 102, 129, 134, 140, 169, 221, 225, 227, 235
demon, 8, 61, 68, 106, 127, 133, 138, 148, 164, 179, 190, 193, 197, 202, 222
demonology, 47, 101, 102, 130, 150, 152, 220, 225
desecration of bodies, 25, 67, 101, 106, 141, 145, 148, 151, 155, 170–73, 186, 192, 194–95, 203. *See also* desecration of graves
devil, xv, 7, 29, 30, 34, 35, 40–41, 44, 46, 60, 65, 66, 69, 70, 71, 100, 103, 107, 113, 114, 126, 128, 129, 155, 159, 163, 165, 175, 179, 181, 192, 196, 199, 200, 234, 235
dhampir, 223, 226
Dracula. *See* Count Dracula; Bram Stoker's Dracula; Vlad the Impaler
draugr, 13, 17

E

Eastern Question, 1, 6, 156
Enlightenment, 1, 3, 10, 15, 27, 30, 36, 37, 45, 58, 65, 80, 85, 90–96, 116, 130, 177, 193, 195, 235
epidemic, xii, 5, 7, 21, 59, 61, 69, 114, 148, 151, 154, 155, 169, 171, 172, 192
Eros and Thanatos, 6, 46, 117
evil eye, 18, 153, 223
examination, xii, xiv, 2, 67, 94, 106, 108
excommunication, xiii, xv, 21, 26, 63–65, 66, 67–69, 71, 73–74, 151, 159, 160, 161, 165, 171, 194, 196, 197, 236
exhumation, xiv, 24, 27, 29, 38, 45, 63, 70, 72, 79, 86–87, 99, 100, 111, 154, 158, 170–71, 174, 175, 184, 186, 189, 192, 193, 195, 200, 202, 224, 236
exorcism, 7, 62, 66, 69, 70, 100, 111, 114–15, 128, 129, 190, 196, 198

F

family, 2, 3, 4, 5, 10, 18, 19, 29, 31, 41, 43, 47, 70, 78, 81, 82, 87, 90, 113, 137, 140–45, 147, 158, 161, 162, 165, 181, 182, 185, 198, 199, 205, 207, 219, 224, 225. *See also* relatives
fairy tales, 66, 116, 133, 146–47, 149–50, 168, 174, 178, 180, 197, 230, 234
fantasy, xi, 5, 6, 9, 97, 103, 112, 129, 192, 203
fear, xii, xiii, 14, 15, 17, 19, 21, 24, 33, 34, 41, 45, 56, 62, 67, 69, 73, 78, 84, 86, 103, 127, 131, 134, 144, 148, 153, 157, 160, 164, 165, 174, 175, 181, 218, 224, 236, 237
folklore, 2, 5, 44, 56, 163, 165, 197–98, 202, 219, 220, 227
funeral, xi, xii, 17, 20, 23, 32, 33, 41, 45, 48–49, 66, 69, 71, 72, 115, 144, 154, 157–58, 161, 170, 177–78, 181, 182, 187, 192, 200, 201, 223, 227, 231

G

garlic, 7, 8, 82, 198, 199, 221, 223
Germans, 31–32, 36–37, 91, 110, 138, 140–42, 191, 194, 227
ghost, 18, 26, 34, 38–39, 41–42, 66, 73, 110, 115–16, 142, 168, 180, 190
God, xv, 14, 17, 22, 24, 25, 34, 41, 64, 66, 96, 101, 103, 111, 113, 128, 139, 169, 170, 171, 174, 179, 184, 201, 203, 206, 207
grave, xii, xiii, 1, 2–3, 10, 13, 18–19, 21, 22, 23–25, 28–29, 32, 33, 35, 36, 39, 42–44, 45, 48, 59, 60–61, 62–63, 64, 66, 67, 68–69, 71, 73, 74, 78, 80, 84, 86, 87, 90, 97, 98, 99–100, 101, 104, 106, 109, 114, 127, 128, 129, 131, 132, 133, 135, 136–137, 138–139, 141, 143–45, 146–47, 149, 150, 151, 152, 153, 154, 155, 157, 158, 159–60, 162, 164, 165, 166, 167, 168, 169–73, 174, 175, 178, 179, 182, 186–88, 189, 190,

192, 193, 194, 197–99, 201, 202, 205, 206–7, 208, 219, 222, 223–24, 225, 226, 227, 230, 231, 233, 235
  desecration of graves, 22, 33, 48, 60, 62, 66, 67, 69, 73, 80, 99, 101, 106, 141, 143, 144, 145, 148, 151, 155, 168, 170–73, 174, 186, 192, 194, 203, 226, 235 (*see also* desecration of bodies)
  leaving the grave, 23, 29, 32, 39, 45, 48, 59, 71, 100, 135, 141, 147, 150, 151, 152, 159, 162, 164, 165, 173, 178, 179, 187, 197, 208, 224, 227, 230, 231, 233
  opening of graves, 2, 18, 23–24, 29, 32, 35, 38, 42, 45, 49, 59, 60, 61, 63, 64, 68, 71–72, 78, 90, 114, 136–37, 139, 143, 147, 154, 155, 158, 164, 169–71, 178, 182, 192, 194, 197, 198, 201, 202, 231
gravedigger, 28, 45, 62, 99, 144–45, 201, 207
Great Powers, 2, 4, 7, 125, 156, 190
Greeks, 1, 2, 62, 64–65, 67–68, 70–73, 159, 160, 163, 166, 167, 186, 198
growth of hair and nails, 78, 97, 102, 136, 151
guilt, xii, 15, 35, 63, 133, 143, 145, 149, 170, 171, 236, 237

H

Habsburg Empire, x, xiii, 81, 99, 101, 109, 167, 191, 196, 204
Hajduk, 80–82, 86–87, 88, 97
harmful corpses, 18, 21, 30, 44, 60, 63, 64–65, 78, 133–35, 150, 153, 172, 173, 180, 184, 190, 218, 220, 233
heart, 7, 22, 24, 39, 60, 61, 63, 69, 72, 80, 90, 111, 113, 128–29, 133, 136, 147, 150, 153, 155, 164, 165, 169, 172, 175, 195, 197, 198, 199, 202, 207, 223, 224
heaven, xi, xii, 15, 61, 69, 113, 114, 174, 187, 197, 233
hell, xi, xii, 14, 15, 23, 65, 69, 113, 174, 187, 197, 199, 233
hunter, 151, 164, 186, 187, 188–90, 222, 236
hysteria, 67, 72, 101, 171

I

imagination, x, xi, xii, xiv, xv, 15, 17, 44, 46, 66, 80, 89, 103, 107, 108, 131, 168, 196, 234, 235
immortality, x, xi, 6, 8, 9, 96, 197
impalement, xiv, 3, 7, 11, 28, 29, 65, 66, 87, 93, 132, 139, 151, 169, 170, 171, 72, 174, 178, 179, 186, 193, 235, 237
impure, 7, 131, 149, 150, 157, 159, 175, 187, 203, 234, 235
incineration, 40, 66, 108, 114
incubus, 28, 39, 41, 43
Islam, 65, 166, 181, 187
Islandic Sagas, 17–21

J

Jews, 25, 62, 98, 127, 131, 154
journal, 62, 63, 65, 89, 91, 92, 94, 97, 108, 112, 130, 133, 136 137, 138, 141, 148, 150–54, 155, 165, 168, 174, 177, 184, 188, 192, 197, 198, 199, 202, 203, 206
jurisdiction, 11, 81, 108

K

kodlak, 47, 173, 233

L

Latin, x, xiv, 3, 21, 36, 38, 43, 47, 55, 63, 64, 73, 92, 98, 105, 111, 126, 161, 223, 230, 234–35, 237
Latin Christendom, xi–xiii, 5, 9, 10, 13, 32, 70, 233
legend, xiv, 3, 6, 16, 24, 25, 30–31, 36, 38, 44, 64, 83, 93, 114, 116, 133, 135, 146, 147, 153, 160, 162, 163, 168, 178, 184, 230
literature, 2–3, 5–6, 9, 13, 15, 25, 27, 55, 62, 68, 93, 117, 130–31, 142, 173, 198, 204, 207, 226
living corpses, xi, 10, 17, 86

M

Macedonians, 220
Magia posthuma, 27, 30, 45, 55, 99, 100, 103, 105–09, 195, 227
magic, 6, 9, 17, 32, 39, 67, 70, 91, 100, 102, 106, 108, 111, 114, 149, 152–53, 162, 199, 231, 233

black magic, 25, 28–30, 48, 59, 61, 65, 73, 100–1, 153, 159
   harmful magic, 175, 192, 199, 218–19, 221, 223
   posthumous magic, 231, 233
medicine, 138, 140, 144, 149
mental maps, 10, 91
Middle Ages, x, xii, 7, 13–15, 17, 31, 34, 36–37, 56, 101, 140, 146, 190, 192, 232
military, xii, 2, 3, 9, 11, 56, 79–81, 83–84, 86–89, 97, 110, 125, 127, 150, 157, 183, 194
   military administration, 11, 80–81, 83–84, 87, 96, 194
Military Frontier, xiii, xvi, 4, 9, 38–39, 43, 78, 80–81, 83, 88, 91, 92, 103, 126, 181, 191, 194, 232
mora, 31, 134, 159, 179, 234, 235
moroi (moroaică), 7, 105, 195, 197, 223, 233, 235
monastery, 5, 27, 57, 58, 65, 66, 101, 129, 142, 143, 151, 175, 176
monster, 4, 6, 8, 9, 13, 21, 23, 24, 28, 143, 147, 174, 181, 185, 186, 233
moon, 20, 129, 199, 205
Morbus hungaricus, 82, 105, 191, 195
murderer, 60, 163, 164, 185, 204
Muslims, 65–67, 70, 72, 160, 181, 187
mythos, xv, 10, 17, 38, 47, 138, 141, 142, 163, 197, 233

N

Nachzehrer, xii, xiii, 10, 24, 29, 31–33, 34, 36–37, 46–47, 59, 61–62, 68, 83, 97, 99, 100, 110, 128, 138, 146, 153, 174, 180, 192, 193, 222, 225, 227
newspaper, 7, 62, 78, 80, 91, 94, 97, 106, 109, 148, 173, 177, 186
nightmare, xii, 3, 37, 42–44, 84, 86, 97, 104, 106, 117, 135, 138, 146, 175, 192, 232, 235
nobility, 24, 32, 34, 46, 80, 125, 143, 179, 191, 196, 198
nonbelievers, 62, 66
nosferatu, 7, 196–98
novel, x, xi, 4–9, 46, 115, 130–32, 138, 140, 196, 222, 235
nymph, 6, 164, 184

O

omen, 19, 20, 41, 47, 141, 223
Orthodoxy, xi, xiii, xv, 2, 3, 5, 10, 32, 55, 56, 62, 63–64, 67–70, 82–83, 97, 101, 103, 125, 127, 128, 129, 132, 157–58, 161, 176, 179, 182–83, 190, 191, 194–96, 207, 234, 235, 236, 237
   Orthodox Patriarchate, 63, 67, 182–83
Ottoman Empire, x–xiii, 4, 6, 38, 62–63, 65, 68–69, 80–84, 97, 156, 157, 159–60, 167, 168, 183, 186, 191, 198, 204, 236

P

pagan, 15, 19, 20, 25, 63, 126, 132
paradise, xi, 14, 15, 17, 28, 64–66, 72, 105, 140, 187, 223, 236
peasants, 22, 71, 80, 81, 84, 97, 137, 151, 155, 160, 182, 197, 232, 233
   German Peasants' War, 34
people-eater, 154, 172
pest, plague, xiii, 10, 14, 19, 22–24, 33–35, 57, 59, 61–62, 78, 82–84, 97, 126–27, 132, 133, 134, 136, 141, 145, 152, 154, 171, 184, 189–90, 192–94, 221, 232, 235, 236
philosophy, 163
physician, 9, 36, 59, 79, 83–86, 89, 81, 92, 95, 97, 103–4, 106, 108, 138, 144, 192, 193
poetry, 2, 6, 66, 128, 130, 132, 138, 148, 204, 231
Poles, 2, 36, 55, 60, 126, 140, 190
Polish-Lithuanian Commonwealth, xii, xiii, 32, 125–26, 129, 150
Poltergeist, 34, 36–39, 43, 44–45, 46, 99, 110, 113, 137, 142, 150, 151, 181, 222, 225, 232, 235, 237
popular belief, 10, 23, 33, 36, 38, 47, 64, 68, 69, 73, 115, 125, 128, 132, 133, 134, 135, 141, 147, 150, 155, 159, 162, 163, 166, 177, 199, 227, 235
popular culture, 15, 37, 47, 56, 115, 130–31, 195, 197–98, 220
possession, xii, 20, 61, 65, 68–69, 128, 134, 136–37, 163, 170, 172, 182, 223, 234–35

posthumous activities, 23, 30, 33, 37, 46, 48, 59, 61, 65, 70–72, 111, 128, 133, 141, 173, 175, 194, 208, 220, 223, 232, 234, 237
prayer, 3, 22, 23, 35, 66, 151, 153, 165, 174, 184, 186, 188
priest, 21, 24, 27, 31, 45, 49, 57, 59, 60, 63, 64, 65, 66, 69, 71, 79, 111, 113, 127, 128, 129130, 132, 135, 137, 139, 144, 146, 149, 155, 162, 164, 165, 169, 170–71, 175, 178–80, 182, 187–88, 194, 196, 197, 202, 219, 224
prosecution, 15, 108, 143, 226
Protestantism, 30, 34–35, 37, 39, 68, 80, 97, 111, 115, 116, 138, 145, 234

R
reanimation, 66, 135, 163, 175, 202
Reformation, xii, xiv, 17, 30, 34, 37, 46, 110, 191, 193
relatives, xii, xiii, 17, 33, 36, 38, 45, 59, 60, 66, 83, 86, 90, 108, 111, 135, 136, 137, 142, 143, 145, 149, 154, 157, 159, 173, 188, 197, 202, 205, 227, 233, 236. *See also* family
resurrection, xi, 102, 103, 132, 140
revenant, xii–xiv, 3, 7, 10, 13, 15, 17, 18–21, 22–25, 27, 28, 29, 35, 37, 39, 40–44, 45, 47–49, 56, 58, 60, 62, 63–68, 70, 71–72, 73, 78, 92, 99, 102, 103, 104, 105, 107, 110, 112–17, 126, 129–30, 131, 133, 134, 135, 137, 138, 140, 143, 144, 146, 149, 150–51, 152, 153, 154, 155, 157, 162, 163–64, 165, 166–67, 168–73, 174, 180, 182, 184, 185, 193, 195, 200–3, 205, 207–8, 218, 220, 221, 223–24, 225, 227, 231, 234, 237
ritual, xi, 2, 9, 14, 25, 29, 72, 135, 157, 205, 227, 236
    Christian, 153, 190
    pre-Christian, 29, 126
Roma, 86, 181, 190. 198, 203–8, 226, 231, 232, 234
Romanians, 191–92, 197, 202–3, 206
rumour, 23, 28, 29, 33, 35, 38–39, 40, 41, 43, 45, 46, 72, 90, 92, 104, 111, 116, 127, 129, 130, 131, 150, 160, 168, 171, 184, 231

Russians, 55, 125, 153
Ruthenians, 55, 116, 125, 128, 150

S
salvation, xi, xiii, 13–14, 17, 18, 45, 64, 70, 71, 86, 128, 164, 174, 186, 220, 224
scandal, 49, 86, 106, 117
scapegoat, xii, xiii, 10, 37, 63, 86, 101, 104, 117, 127, 137, 149, 168, 190, 224, 230, 236
scholar, 6, 10, 47, 55, 57, 66, 73, 82, 92–94, 97, 100, 114, 134, 141, 156, 163, 173, 177, 197, 221, 233
science, 15, 92, 96, 108, 173, 184, 207
Serbs, 1, 2, 63, 81, 87, 92, 157, 167, 177, 178–79, 191, 194–95, 207–8, 221, 233
sexuality, xiii, 42, 44, 46, 48, 78, 89, 110, 114, 137, 172, 175, 178, 199, 203, 207, 219, 220, 231, 236
    sexual taboos, 175, 198
shroud, xii, 20, 24, 29, 32–33, 59, 104, 154, 158, 160, 182, 192, 231
    devouring or eating of the funeral shroud, xii, 29, 32, 35, 36, 59, 60, 61, 128, 192
sin, x, 7, 14, 17, 27, 29, 39, 60, 65, 69, 102
soil, 3, 21, 82, 96, 130, 144, 160, 205, 223
soul, xi–xiii, xv, 7, 14, 15–16, 26, 28, 33, 44, 56, 58, 60–61, 64, 65, 66, 69, 86, 91, 96, 105, 114, 127, 128, 131, 132, 134–35, 136–37, 155, 156–59, 161, 163, 172, 174, 187, 196, 198, 204, 206–7, 219–20, 223, 225, 226, 227, 231, 233, 234, 235–36
    damned souls, 61, 159, 163, 235
    dualism of body and soul, xi, 15, 28, 64, 91, 96, 127, 207
    immortality of the soul, xi, 96
    poor soul, 15, 26, 179
spirit, xii, xv, 2, 6, 20–21, 26, 29–31, 34, 35, 41, 47, 58, 60, 67, 71, 73, 91, 93, 96–97, 100, 101, 114, 116, 128, 131–32, 136, 142, 159, 161, 164, 170, 177, 178, 179, 183, 189, 190, 198, 220, 230, 231, 233, 236
    dead spirit, xii, 34, 136, 159, 227
    evil spirit, 6, 47, 56, 58, 67, 70, 71, 111, 114, 146, 149, 159–60, 162,

165, 166, 172, 174, 185, 187, 189–90, 196, 197–98, 225, 226, 233
water spirit, 73, 115, 204
stake, 9, 18, 19, 27, 28, 29, 37, 42, 48, 49, 60, 63, 67, 69, 71, 80, 90, 127, 128, 129, 147, 151 153, 155, 162, 164, 182, 188, 197, 198, 200, 205, 237
strigoi/strigoică, 7, 73–74, 197, 199–200, 203, 223–24, 233
strix, 37, 47, 173
strzygoń/strzyga, 58–59, 60, 130, 133–35, 137, 142, 147, 224, 233
suicide, 17, 38–39, 43, 55, 131, 132, 140, 150, 165, 225
superstition, v, 4, 10, 22, 31, 32, 35–36, 63, 69, 91, 96, 87, 109, 114, 117, 129, 134, 138–41, 145, 149, 152, 166, 168, 171, 173, 175, 177, 181, 188, 195, 196–97, 225, 226, 228
suspicion, 2, 32, 35, 44, 65, 69, 104, 172, 193, 201, 237
swollen corpse, 24, 27, 79

T

theology, 15, 25, 28, 55, 58, 59, 73, 94, 100, 101, 171, 196, 198
transgressions, xii, 34, 218, 222
travelling, 11, 37, 65, 67, 101, 136, 161–62, 173, 175, 178, 189, 204–5
travel writers, xiv, 70–72, 130, 161–62, 173, 175, 196
Tsarist Empire, x, 3, 4, 125–26, 135, 148–50, 190
tympaniaios, 68, 70, 73, 74

U

Ukrainians, 55, 60, 126, 128, 150–54
undead, xii, 6, 8, 23, 28, 71, 109, 138, 153, 178–79, 195, 203, 224, 233–34
Unhier, 147
university, xv, 59, 92, 98, 188, 189, 191, 204
upir, xiv, 55, 57–58, 60, 103
upiór, xii, 55, 59, 103, 128–29, 130–33, 134–36, 138, 152, 154, 224, 233
upyr, xii, 3, 5, 55, 59, 126–27, 148–53

V

victim, 8, 18, 20, 22, 23, 24, 27, 29, 32, 33, 60–61, 79, 84, 87, 89, 104, 105, 106, 132, 133, 141, 144, 147, 148, 150, 151, 152, 155, 163, 164, 165, 172, 179, 180, 197, 199, 201, 206, 222, 232–33, 236
village, xiv, 4, 6, 7, 22, 24, 27, 28, 29, 30, 32, 35, 44, 59, 63, 66, 67, 68, 70–72, 78, 79, 81–82, 83–84, 86–89, 99, 106, 109, 126, 127, 131, 136, 144, 145, 146–47, 151, 152–54, 155, 162, 164, 165–66, 174, 175, 177, 178, 180, 182, 183, 184, 187, 188, 189, 192, 193, 195, 200, 201, 202–3, 219–22, 231, 234, 235
villagers, 9, 22, 27, 28, 69, 72, 78, 79, 83, 86, 87, 126, 127, 136, 154, 177, 192, 193, 220, 221, 222, 235
vukodlak, xiv, 9, 47, 63, 163, 169, 173–74, 230–31, 233
vrykolakas, xiii, 10, 38, 62, 64, 66, 67, 69, 70, 72–74, 159, 161–67, 186, 198, 218, 237

W

walking dead, 17, 20, 225–26, 23–35
Wallachians (Vlachs), 9, 74, 190–91, 193, 197
werewolf, 9, 73, 230
widow, 18, 23, 38, 41, 42, 45, 48, 49, 64, 70, 78, 89, 113, 116, 135, 137, 148, 154, 155, 164, 165, 169, 172, 177, 178, 181, 185, 219, 225, 234, 236
witch, 5, 6, 11, 27, 29–31, 34, 47, 59, 73, 74, 91, 99–101, 109, 115–16, 128, 129, 130, 137, 141, 150, 152, 159, 177, 187, 192, 198–200, 202, 206, 222, 223–24, 225, 233
    witch hunt, 11, 30, 37, 99–101, 142
    witch sabbath, 29, 133
    witch trial, 97, 99–101, 104
    witchcraft, 13, 29, 37, 39, 43, 104–07, 109, 117, 150, 234

Z

zmora, 133–35, 137, 225

www.ingramcontent.com/pod-product-compliance
Lightning Source LLC
Chambersburg PA
CBHW072145100526
44589CB00015B/2106